ST. MARY'S CITY, MARYLAND 20686

ASPECT IN ENGLISH

Studies in Linguistics and Philosophy

Volume 75

Managing Editors

GENNARO CHIERCHIA, *University of Milan*
PAULINE JACOBSON, *Brown University*
FRANCIS J. PELLETIER, *University of Alberta*

Editorial Board

JOHAN VAN BENTHEM, *University of Amsterdam*
GREGORY N. CARLSON, *University of Rochester*
DAVID DOWTY, *Ohio State University, Columbus*
GERALD GAZDAR, *University of Sussex, Brighton*
IRENE HEIM, *M.I.T., Cambridge*
EWAN KLEIN, *University of Edinburgh*
BILL LADUSAW, *University of California at Santa Cruz*
TERRENCE PARSONS, *University of California, Irvine*

The titles published in this series are listed at the end of this volume.

ASPECT IN ENGLISH

A "Common-Sense" View of the Interplay
between Verbal and Nominal Referents

by

Krasimir Kabakčiev

*Institute for the Bulgarian Language,
Bulgarian Academy of Sciences,
Sofia, Bulgaria*

KLUWER ACADEMIC PUBLISHERS
DORDRECHT / BOSTON / LONDON

A C.I.P. Catalogue record for this book is available from the Library of Congress.

ISBN 0-7923-6538-0

Published by Kluwer Academic Publishers,
P.O. Box 17, 3300 AA Dordrecht, The Netherlands.

Sold and distributed in North, Central and South America
by Kluwer Academic Publishers,
101 Philip Drive, Norwell, MA 02061, U.S.A.

In all other countries, sold and distributed
by Kluwer Academic Publishers,
P.O. Box 322, 3300 AH Dordrecht, The Netherlands.

Printed on acid-free paper

All Rights Reserved
© 2000 Kluwer Academic Publishers
No part of the material protected by this copyright notice may be reproduced or
utilized in any form or by any means, electronic or mechanical,
including photocopying, recording or by any information storage and
retrieval system, without written permission from the copyright owner.

Printed in the Netherlands.

To my wife Valentina and my son Alexander

TABLE OF CONTENTS

Preface	ix
Acknowledgements	xi
Introduction	xiii
Chapter 1. On the essence of aspect	1
Chapter 2. Vendler's classification of situations, and the problem of its interpretation	31
Chapter 3. Verkuyl's theory of compositional aspect	55
Chapter 4. The article and the related markers of quantity in the expression of aspect in English	69
Chapter 5. Extension in time of subjects and objects from a "common-sense" point of view	91
Chapter 6. The mechanism for mapping the temporal values of subjects and objects	123
Chapter 7. The interdependence between markers of boundedness in verbs and in nouns	153
Chapter 8. The Progressive in English	163
Chapter 9. Lexical meanings of verbs, and aspect in English	181
Chapter 10. Meanings of nouns and noun phrases, and aspect in English	211
Chapter 11. The impact of adverbials in the sentence, and aspect in English	241
Chapter 12. On negativity and the explication of perfectivity	263
Chapter 13. On aspectual classes in English	279
Chapter 14. On 'knowledge of the world' in the explication of aspect in English	309
Conclusion	327
Appendix. The major characteristics of the Bulgarian tense-aspect system	329
References	333
Index of terms	339
Index of authors	347

PREFACE

This book is based on a monograph published in Bulgarian, *Vidăt v anglijskija ezik. Za bălgarite, razbirašti (i običasti) tozi ezik* [Aspect in English. For Bulgarians who understand (and love) this language], Sofia, 1992: Albo, ISBN 954-8141-01-9. It offers, however, a fairly enlarged and updated version of the original publication as well as analyses or results of analyses reported elsewhere (e.g. in Kabakčiev 1989; 1993a; 1993b; 1993c; 1996). Recent years have seen an explosion of investigations on aspect both as a cross-linguistic category and as a structural or semantic fact of the English language. This book represents, among other things, an attempt to overview some of the development of aspectology based mainly on data from Modern Standard English. Naturally, apart from the translation, updating and revising that had to be done, this edition also differs from the original in other ways – to suit the specificity of a new audience. However, it purposefully follows the original in the attempt to employ an explanatory style rid of bizarre phraseology or cumbersome formalism. Special phraseology and different formal analyses, as will become clear later on in the book, may be nice tools for the study of language but often raise obstacles to acquiring a better understanding of certain phenomena.

Another difference from the previous edition results in a reduction of some of the specific comparisons between English and Bulgarian that were essential for the original audience. However, not all of the comparisons between these two languages (or, more generally, between languages of the Germanic and the Slavic type) have been removed, and some have even been dealt with in greater detail. Although translation from one language into another is often snubbed at as a poor tool for analysing the semantics of sentences, it will be seen that in some cases, contrasting translation equivalents can serve as a good expedient for uncovering certain readings of sentences in a given language that otherwise remain hidden for the investigator. In an account of English that is not strictly formalised it is usually the English language itself that serves as the metalanguage of the semantic description. But in this case Bulgarian, being a Slavic language, will often prove to be a better metalanguage for the study of aspect, and for a long time in linguistics Slavic languages were considered the aspectual languages *par excellence*. Furthermore, it will be shown that an adequate conception of aspect in English is, in fact, difficult to obtain without a prior understanding of the way the two major aspectual systems, the compositional one (as, e.g., in English) and the verbal one (as, e.g., in Bulgarian), transverse natural languages. Other changes in this English version of the book include a number of detailed analyses of some recent advances in aspectology, and the addition of two new chapters, entitled *On negativity and the explication of perfectivity* and *On aspectual classes in English*.

Preface

GENERAL CONTENTS OF THE BOOK, GUIDELINES TO READING

Leaving aside the cognitive basis of aspect and the dependence of the explication of aspectual values on knowledge of the world, from the point of view of mainstream linguistics it can be argued that this book offers a comprehensive grammatical and semantic description of the phenomenon studied. Or, perhaps, that it offers an amalgamation of ideas belonging to separate linguistic spheres, identified as, for example, lexicology, morphology, and syntax, into a unified grammatical and semantic framework. This statement is valid also in the sense that the separate chapters of the book can hardly be viewed as a possible reference guide to check the aspectual or other similar values of particular words, of sentences or of other structural language entities. The outlines of the overall system of aspect in English, seen mainly as a complex and subtle interplay between verbal and nominal referents, are progressively revealed and the phenomena belonging to the system are surveyed in terms of their interrelationships. The indices at the end of the book offer guidelines with respect to problems that can arise and are meant to facilitate their solution. However, it seems reasonable to advise that if the potential reader is to get an adequate understanding of the complex nature of aspect, it is recommended to read the book from the beginning to the end – possibly omitting passages containing familiar information. It may be also helpful to remember that many of the examples introduced initially are then repeatedly used elsewhere with their original numbering.

The idea of putting together a monograph of this kind dates back a long time. Several articles on the problems dealt with in this edition have been published in either Bulgarian or English (publications in English are Kabakčiev 1984a; 1984b; 1989; 1993a; 1993b; 1993c; 1996). The book is primarily designed for researchers of aspect and related problems (tense, temporality, verbal and nominal reference) but it can also be useful for a broader audience, including students of English at an advanced level of prior acquisition. Thus, while generally the aim of the present work is to offer a theory of aspect in English (and hence in similar languages) oriented towards specialists (aspectologists, theoretical and applied linguists, grammarians, semanticists, psycholinguists, logicians, philosophers of language), other readers to whom the specificity of the English language is appealing from a larger scientific or cultural perspective could also find it worth investigating.

ACKNOWLEDGEMENTS

I would like to thank Gerald Mayer from Fordham University, New York, Jim Miller and Sheila Glasbey from the University of Edinburgh who kindly gave me their native speakers' interpretations of many English examples construed or modified by me. I thank all the colleagues from the universities of Uppsala, Stockholm, Lund, Gothenburg, Helsinki and Oslo who attended my lectures and expressed interest in the general theory of aspect presented in this book. Among them it was Sven Gustavsson who initiated the idea for my lecture tours in the Scandinavian countries (in 1987 and 1990), and Östen Dahl, Thore Pettersson, Arne Hult, Jouko Lindstedt, Kjetil Rå Hauge, Roger Jullin, Gunilla and Ivan Fredriksson, Jordan Zlatkov, Birgitta and Minko Dimitrov turned them into a pleasant and fruitful experience. But most of all I am indebted to Boris Ivanov from Uppsala University, now a respected novelist and poet both in Sweden and in Bulgaria, who was tragically deprived of his country, his family and friends for three decades: for his perpetual hospitality during my stay in Scandinavia, for his remarkable literary and poetic insights, and for an example of how one can survive under fierce political and moral oppression. A research stay at the Max Planck Institute for Psycholinguistics in Nijmegen in 1990 organised by Wolfgang Klein is also gratefully appreciated.

I would like to thank Henk Verkuyl: for the discussions we had on aspect and on social issues in the wake of the dramatic changes in Eastern Europe; and, more importantly, on behalf of the aspectological community, for his contribution – the writing of the book *On the Compositional Nature of the Aspects*. Viewed as a cornerstone in the development of aspectology, it takes (along with its 1993 sequel) a very prominent place in the present work.

The completion of the English version of the book was financially made possible by the Royal Society of Edinburgh whose 1996 Caledonian Research Foundation European Visiting Research Fellowship I gratefully acknowledge. The Department of Linguistics at the University of Edinburgh, Scotland, headed by Ronnie Cann, provided an advanced technological medium and a friendly academic atmosphere that facilitated the process of updating the original publication. In Edinburgh I also took part in the Centre for Cognitive Science *Tense and Aspect* seminar and had interesting discussions with Sheila Glasbey, Diego Mollá-Aliod and Frank Schilder. It was Jim Miller from the Department of Linguistics at the University of Edinburgh, who nominated me for the Royal Society Fellowship and who offered permanent professional, practical and moral support. To him I am most indebted for the completion of the work. Back in Sofia, John Muirhead, formerly of the Free University in Berlin, gave me valuable advice on the interpretation of some of the most difficult examples and polished the text of the manuscript. My thanks go again to the Royal Society of Edinburgh and to RSE member Ron Asher for enabling me to travel to Edinburgh to prepare the final draft of the book.

Acknowledgements

My family's contribution was also significant. Valentina, my wife, took up my home obligations during my stay in Edinburgh, and Alexander, my son, prepared the diagrams. I dedicate this book to them.

Finally, since the motivation for doing research is inseparable from the social conditions underlying it, gratitude is once again expressed, as in the original edition, to those without whom this book would have, in all probability, remained unwritten: to those people in Bulgaria who banished an epoch of disgrace to the history books and enabled the free expression of will and thought.

INTRODUCTION

The problem of aspect in English has been treated through a large variety of approaches within the framework of grammar and semantics or, in comparatively more recent times, formal semantics. In spite of this, in the different linguistic descriptions of the English language made nowadays all over the world – in linguistic, logical and philosophical studies, in grammars, textbooks and dictionaries – aspect usually occupies very little space, if regarded at all (cf. a similar view in Tobin 1993: 15). In any case, and this will soon become clear, the way the phenomenon of aspect is handled in the present work differs substantially in many respects from most other approaches.

The study is based on an investigation of most of the areas that are considered relevant to the specific problems of aspect – broadly, grammar, formal (mainly logical, Montague-type) grammar, psycholinguistics, pragmatics. The sources are abundant, so attention is drawn mainly to those works that are felt to be more relevant to the present model. In a way, the book is an attempt to reconcile the seeming incompatibility of many conceptual frameworks. For example, it tries to eliminate or minimize the existing substantial discrepancy between the way aspect is handled in some of the advanced research in the area on the one hand, and in the grammars of English, theoretical or practical, on the other. And by outlining the major structural and semantic devices for the explication of aspect in English, it also strives to fill in the existing gaps in textbooks, grammars and dictionaries with respect to the ways through which aspectual distinctions are expressed.

But a purely syntactico-semantic approach is insufficient for determining the various parameters of the phenomenon of aspect. Therefore, the mechanism of its ultimate expression is also linked to, and can be explained by, certain processes that have to do with concept formation and the handling of (mainly) short-term concepts in memory. Of course, since the nature of these psychological and neurophysiological processes is extremely complex, the description of the way they are relevant to aspect is, inevitably, far from exhaustive. It could be argued, however, that what the development of an interdisciplinary area sometimes requires is just a small contribution outlining the scope of the necessary research. And, apart from the domain of psycholinguistics, and of concept formation in particular, another specific area relevant to aspect has lately been recognised by most aspectologists. Not only context but also, broadly speaking, knowledge of the world plays a very important role in determining the aspectual interpretation of sentences that lack overt, grammatical, aspectual markers[1] (cf. in this respect, e.g., Comrie 1985: 38; Moens 1987: 111, 135; Caenepeel 1989: 46; Verkuyl 1993: 133-135; Glasbey 1994). In spite of the fact that this area has usually been neglected, it can be argued that any attempt at

---

[1] An overt, grammatical, marker of aspect in English is the Progressive.

INTRODUCTION

a description of the overall aspect mechanism in English would need a pragmatic component. One such possible component, organized along the lines of certain rules underlying linguistic communication, is proposed in the final chapter of this book.

It is to be emphasized that proper knowledge of the formal (structural) and lexical devices in English and their interplay for the explication of aspectual distinctions is of special importance not only for learners of English that are native speakers of "aspect languages" (like, e.g., the Slavic languages). What has often been referred to as "aspect languages" are languages that strictly distinguish between completed and non-completed actions, i.e., between perfectivity and imperfectivity, in the verb system. The distinction between completion and non-completion of an action (or an attempt at an action), between the achievement and non-achievement of something, and, more generally, between success and failure, forms part and parcel of both collective and individual mentality – that is, of mankind and the human being. What is more, an even stronger case can be made. Human thinking is **preoccupied** by success and failure – in both the broadest conceptual and the most practical, everyday terms. Therefore, here is another reason to maintain that it should not be surprising if the contrast between perfectivity and imperfectivity – in general semantic or in purely grammatical terms – is found to be captured systematically by **all** natural languages. Hence, anyone investigating the subtleties of the grammar and semantics of what is traditionally called an "aspectless language" would have to be able to pinpoint the devices (semantic or grammatical) marking the distinction.

Aspectual problems viewed along the lines of the perfective/imperfective distinction, not in terms of the Progressive/Non-Progressive or the allegedly aspectual (according to some authors) Perfect/Non-Perfect opposition, are, indeed, occasionally given some treatment in certain English grammars and textbooks. But, unfortunately, even in the best of them, the description of aspect is usually based on an underlying theoretical model which is either poorly developed, or misleading, or simply inadequate. This book contains, to the relief of the potential reader, no incomprehensible descriptions of complex grammatical or semantic phenomena, nor does it use any specific formal machinery accessible only to a relatively small circle of semanticists and logicians. A strong attempt is made to avoid the confusion reigning in the sphere of aspectology: and where special terminology cannot be omitted, it is explained in detail. Of course, adequate command of modern sophisticated language (or metalanguage), be it based on one's own mother tongue or on a foreign one, is impossible without the prior acquisition of some basic rules of grammar. Hence, naturally, at least a minimum of grammatical knowledge is presupposed for the proper understanding of the linguistic phenomena, regularities and interrelationships discussed in this book.

A NOTE FOR THE NON-LINGUIST

Perhaps a large number of people with no linguistically-oriented training (i.e., the large majority of people) adhere to the view that the grammar of a language at a particular stage of its development is something given once and for ever, and there is

INTRODUCTION

nothing in it that must be or could be corrected. This view is, of course, wrong. Any particular grammar, however adequate it may seem today, is not so much language reality as a theory for modelling language reality. As a matter of fact, many aspects of various linguistic phenomena, including grammatical ones, have so far remained unexplained, even in a language like English that has been studied in depth, and will obviously continue to challenge and trouble linguists far into the future. This study of aspect in English offers proof of the thesis that even some of the most fundamental tenets of mainstream grammar can be found to be simply wrong.

It is true that grammars of languages today contain a large number of entities or constructs that are regarded as indisputable, as entities or constructs that need no re-estimation and the interpretation of which seems generally consistent and uncontradictory. It would be vacuous, for example, to dispute the existence in English of verb forms of the *be* + *-ing* type, called progressive or (sometimes) continuous. No doubt, these verb forms largely express non-completed actions being carried out at a particular moment or period of time. No doubt, there are verbs (viewed as lexical entries) that are usually not used in the Progressive. Facts of this kind have generally been recognised and adequately described in English grammars (albeit not in all of them). And at the same time, there can hardly be found an existing grammar of English today giving a satisfactory answer to the fundamental question whether these forms are true aspectual forms. And, hence, why they **are** or why they are **not** aspectual forms. The reason is that until only recently (about a decade ago) studies in this linguistic sphere were astonishingly underdeveloped. Now that aspectology, the discipline dealing with aspect and belonging to general linguistic theory, has reached a certain degree of maturity, it is high time for its achievements to be reflected in the grammars, theoretical or practical, of many languages that were thought to be aspectless languages, in textbooks and in dictionaries. Whether, on the other hand, descriptions of the Progressive in purely linguistic terms and most analyses of the Progressive in logico-linguistic frameworks live up to the challenge of 'the mystery of language' is another question. The problem will be dealt with later on in the book.

THEORETICAL FRAMEWORK

To say that the literature on aspect and related problems is rich would be a massive understatement. Hosts of approaches have been put forward, and many of these have proved legitimate and fruitful. A major assumption for the present study, which is in consistence with the views and findings in a large number of publications, is that it is the perfective/imperfective (or bounded/non-bounded) distinction that is the basic aspectual opposition in language – whether expressed formally, e.g., periphrastically, through affixation, through complex semantico-syntactic schemata, or in general semantic terms, e.g., through lexical, phraseological, sentential or contextual means. Among the publications mentioned are Verkuyl (1971/1972; 1993), Comrie (1976), Dahl (1985), Bybee (1985: 141), Bybee et al (1994: 148-149). English will be shown to display almost all of the aspectual tools described above, with the exception of the strictly morphological (affixal) ones, that are typical of, for example, the

INTRODUCTION

Slavic languages. It is to be noted, however, that while both the perfective/imperfective and the bounded/non-bounded distinctions are valid at the level of the sentence and are often synonymously used as terms, it is the latter and not the former that can be said to apply also at the level of separate words (verbs and nouns) and of separate phrases in English.

In a recent comprehensive study of the history of research into tense and aspect from Aristotelian times to the late 80s of the 20th century, Binnick wrote:

> "No complete aspectual description of any language exists. Nor does current aspectological theory provide an adequate theoretical base for such description"

Binnick (1991: 213). The present work will demonstrate that, if the first of these two statements is largely correct, for it is a very difficult task to provide a full description of all aspectual exponents and aspect-related parameters in a language, the second statement is wrong. Firstly, some large studies of representative samples of languages around the world (Dahl 1985; Bybee 1985; Bybee et al 1994) have convincingly shown that it is precisely the perfective/imperfective distinction that cuts across languages (albeit in various grammatical disguises) as a basic aspectual opposition. Secondly, this book will establish aspect along the lines of a compositional mechanism similar to the one proposed by Verkuyl (1971/1972; 1993) to explicate perfectivity and imperfectivity, the two major universal aspectual values. It will then draw on a long-established theory (outlined in Kabakčiev 1984a; 1984b) presenting verbal aspect in Slavic (and hence aspect in other sometimes so-called aspect languages) as a mirror image of compositional aspect. Thirdly, when these two facets of a general aspectual theory are combined, it will be seen that there remain no theoretical restrictions to hinder the gradual comprehensive aspectual description of many and even all natural languages.

This general theory of aspect will emerge by viewing the language phenomenon in question as a reflection of certain cognitive abilities and mental preoccupations some of which have already been mentioned above. And the grammatical overt (verbal) marking of aspect, usually regarded as the starting point for any investigation, is, consequently, viewed not as a necessity *per se*, but as a **compensatory phenomenon**. Overt markers of aspect, wherever they exist, will be shown to function just to make up for the lack of other overt (grammatical) markers in a particular language (cf. Kabakčiev 1984b). Furthermore, among the major claims in this book will be the following. Firstly, the outlines of the aspectual system of English offered are definitive. Secondly, they provide a solid basis for future in-depth studies. Thirdly, investigations along the lines provided could grow into a fairly exhaustive all-round description of the system.

As already mentioned, apart from viewing Vendler's well-known classification of verbs and verb phrases and Verkuyl's (1972) original aspectual theory as a starting point for describing the mechanism of explicating aspect in languages like English[2],

---

[2] Verkuyl's extended aspectual theory (Verkuyl 1993) represents a departure from the original one in that NPs in the extended theory are viewed as purely atemporal. It will be argued later in this book (see Chapter Ten, *Meanings of nouns and noun phrases, and aspect in English*) that the step towards atemporality is a step in the wrong direction.

xvi

INTRODUCTION

the approach in the present work differs from most of the other descriptions of aspect in English available today. There are at least four major assumptions in the present study that set it apart from most approaches. Firstly, aspect is a complex language device reflecting the conceptualisation of reality. Secondly, grammatical marking of aspect should be seen not so much as a device to explicate the properties of situations designated by verbs but as a compensatory internal language phenomenon. Thirdly, it is the contribution of nouns and NPs (or their referents – depending on the level of analysis) that is crucial for the explication of aspect compositionally, i.e., outside the verb within the sentence. Fourthly, there is a universal mechanism for mapping properties of referents of NPs onto referents of verbs – or, vice versa, from referents of verbs onto referents of NPs. Studies that bear resemblance to the present one in at least some of these basic assumptions are comparatively few. Apart from Vendler's (1957) classic *Verbs and Times* and the early important contributions of Mittwoch (1971), Heinämäki (1978) and Dowty (1979) in modern aspectology, among them are mostly G.N.Carlson's (1977/1980) work, which established the concepts of the so-called stages, individuals and kinds, Cooper's (1985), Hinrichs's (1985) and Krifka's (1989), which deal with the stages of individuals relevant to the aspectual properties of the sentence, Langacker's (1987/1991), which draws some important parallels between the general semantics of verbs and nouns, and, above all, Verkuyl's (1972) groundbreaking work on compositional aspect which will be considered in detail throughout the book.

Some comparatively recent descriptions of aspect in English (and similar languages) that this book differs considerably from in its approach are, for example, Quirk et al (1985), Tobin (1993), Smith (1991), Tenny (1994), Bartsch (1995) – and, generally, some of these descriptions are mutually incompatible anyway. If these works are taken to present an adequate picture of the state of the art in aspectology, then aspectology has failed to establish at least a set of basic common assumptions, and ought to be regarded as far from settled as an independent discipline. But whether one can identify some consensus on certain issues or not, another assumption in this book is that there are good grounds for arguing that the history of aspectology can be divided into pre-Verkuylian and post-Verkuylian. Some of the typical ideas and representatives of pre-Verkuylian aspectology are covered in the first chapter of the book. Post-Verkuylian aspectology – though no general overview of it is provided, due to its dynamic and complex current development – is analysed in the course of the investigation of particular problems concerning the explication of aspect at the level of the sentence.

BASIC THESES OF THE APPROACH

Among the basic theses of this work are the following. Aspect can be regarded both as a grammatical category and as a conceptual category universally represented in all languages. The opposition between perfectivity and imperfectivity can be seen as the **major** aspectual distinction in language, and grammatical categories like the corresponding contrast in Slavic or the Progressive in English are just some concrete manifestations of the general distinction. Or, in other words, there is a "pure" distinction between perfectivity and imperfectivity which goes beyond the semantic description of grammatical categories like the perfective/imperfective contrast in Slavic (Russian *soveršennyj/nesoveršennyj vid*). Furthermore, it will be shown that the grammatical distinction between perfective and imperfective in Slavic does not cover entirely the "pure", universal distinction between perfectivity and imperfectivity.

Viewed from a different angle, usually outside the grammatical domain, aspect can be found in situations *per se*. A 'situation' is a general term for a wide variety of states of affairs, occurrences, eventualities, etc. (see the discussion of terminology three paragraphs below), and there can be several types of strictly identified situations, depending on the criteria for establishing a particular classification. For example, Vendler's (1957) classification based on English (which will be considered in detail) contains four situational types. However, regardless of the number of possibly identifiable situations, a situation is either perfective or imperfective, whatever its outward, superficial linguistic expression (grammatical, or complex, semantico-syntactic) in a particular language.

The semantico-syntactic expression of aspect is also called compositional, after Verkuyl's (1972) pioneering work. This book takes Verkuyl's (1972) theory as a point of departure but, unlike Verkuyl (1993), lays a special emphasis on the importance of the temporal status of participants – that is, of the referents of mostly nouns and NPs (and also more complex structures) in the sentence. It will be shown that all participants in situations, even entities of a 'physical nature', can be regarded as having their own temporal values that are covert for the ordinary speaker of the language. And, after the establishment of this covert temporal status of all participants, a "common-sense" explanation of the phenomenon will be offered. As far as aspect in its traditional sense is concerned (as a device for expressing the way an event or a state is realised on the time axis), it will be seen that, in the long run, the recognition of an aspectual value by an addressee relates to the type of situation intended by the speaker, whereby the temporal status of the participants in it is a consequence of the intention. It will also be demonstrated that states or events can be interpreted by the addressee in different ways, which may or may not be aspectually different and may or may not be conceived of as common in terms of people's experiences. Hence, a distinction will be made between states or events that are perfectly natural and states or events that are atypical, and this distinction will be held to be relevant to the explication of the aspectual values.

Aspect can also be regarded as part of a complex human psycho-physiological mechanism to perceive, store and process data from reality – with the ultimate objective of modelling reality according to human needs. The covert nature of the temporal status of participants in situations is a consequence of the need to conceptualize **stable** entities instead of their separate occurrences. Finally, although a complete semantico-syntactic mechanism of explicating aspect at the level of the sentence will manifest itself in a fairly exhaustive manner, it will eventually turn out that this aspect mechanism can be overridden by pragmatic constraints on the

INTRODUCTION

interpretation of many sentences within discourse, or even outside it. In other words, it will be seen that an adequate investigation of the phenomena analysed cannot afford to ignore 'knowledge of the world' as a factor for the explication of aspect.

MAJOR OBJECTIVE OF THE BOOK

In spite of the abundance of world-wide aspectological studies employing different methodologies and analysing various language data, no consensus in linguistics has so far been reached about what exactly aspect is and which exactly its exponents in many languages are (cf. Binnick 1991). According to the approach assumed in this book, aspect covers the contrast between perfectivity and imperfectivity, which is taken to be the major aspectual distinction across languages. The major objective of this work is to give a definitive overall description of the mechanism of expressing aspect in English in terms of a universal theory in which compositional aspect is a mirror image of verbal aspect. Aspect is expressed in English in both verbal and compositional terms: it can be expressed directly, through a formal device in the verb system, the Progressive, or can be explicated compositionally through a very subtle and complex interplay between verbal and nominal referents. Naturally, since it is non-verbal aspect that presents most difficulties, the main focus will be on compositional aspect, with its several closely intertwined domains: purely linguistic (morphological, lexical, semantic, semantico-syntactic), psycholinguistic (cognitive) and pragmatic (knowledge of the world). But the role of formal (verbal) expression of aspect and its links with compositional explication has never been clearly defined, although both have been the object of a lot of research. This books claims to offer a model unifying the two types of aspect, verbal and compositional, with a theoretical significance and a heuristic potential that go far beyond the concrete language data analysed.

NOTES ABOUT THE TERMINOLOGY EMPLOYED

Throughout the book, the term *explication* and, even more often, the verb *to explicate* are used. *Explication*, roughly speaking, stands for something in between 'implication' and 'expression'. Later on, it will be shown in detail why this word can suit very well the analysis of aspect in many languages, including English. This is because aspect is, as a linguistic phenomenon, not always expressed (or signified, or denoted, or designated) in such an overt manner as it is for example in the Slavic languages, or in the English Progressive for that matter. And since aspect in English (outside the use of the Progressive) is usually neither **expressed**, nor is it exactly only **implied**, it is – when its meaning is conveyed through an identifiable combination, however complex, of grammatical devices, lexical features and even pragmatic implicatures – **explicated**. Here are some examples to, partly, in advance, clarify this specific point. Native speakers of English will agree, first, that, while a sentence like (1a), describes a completed, that is bounded, perfective, action, the sentences (1b) and (1c) describe non-completed, that is non-bounded, imperfective, actions:

Introduction

(1) a. John drank the beer
    b. John was drinking the beer
    c. John drank beer

Second, native speakers of English will also generally agree that both (1a) and (1b) imply a single occasion of drinking whereas sentence (1c), conversely, more naturally implies more than one occasion of drinking. It is in the very essence of implication that a certain piece of meaning is not obligatory or necessary (unlike *explication*, which has a terminological status, the word *implication* is used in the book in its wider sense, not necessarily in consistence with current linguistic thought). However, if the imperfectivity of sentence (1b) is expressed – through the use of the progressive form of the verb – a major thesis for this book is that the perfectivity of (1a) and the imperfectivity of (1c) are neither expressed through the verb form (it being the same), nor just implied. The aspectual values of perfectivity and imperfectivity are explicated – which still means that they are necessary for the sentence to be understood correctly.

Finally, as far as the term 'explication' itself is concerned, by some happy coincidence, it also has the flavour of the word *explanation* – and this is exactly what is intended to be given in this book on the phenomenon of aspect. The explanation will be provided in a straightforward fashion and it will, furthermore, take into account not only current aspectological thought but also, a point which is often ignored, the common-sense intuitions of the ordinary language speaker – that is, the one non-versed in the intricacies of the language system.

The notions of perfectivity and imperfectivity in the sense roughly revealed and illustrated in the sentences in (1) above have already been well established in the study of aspect not only in the Slavic languages but also in languages like English, although some linguists express reservations as to the appropriateness of the use of the terms perfectivity and imperfectivity for non-Slavic languages and, generally, for languages in which aspect is not directly marked on the verb. Pairs of terms like 'bounded'/'non-bounded' and 'telic'/'atelic', along with many others, have also been used as equivalent in meaning to 'perfective'/'imperfective'. Here, all of these terms will be made use of: 'perfective'/'imperfective' and 'bounded'/'non-bounded' will very often be applied in an identical fashion, but it is to be noted that the latter ('bounded'/'non-bounded') will be applied more universally – for example, to verbs and nouns, to verbal and nominal referents, to aspectual readings isolated at the level of verb phrases and sentences. The notions 'telic' and 'atelic' ('telicity' and 'atelicity') will be employed in the domain of lexical semantics to signify the potential of verbs to imply or explicate the aspectual values of perfectivity/imperfectivity (boundedness/non-boundedness) in English and in similar languages without overt grammatical marking of aspect on verbs. In Germanic and Slavic grammars at least (and in studies of these languages), a distinction is also made between 'aspect', which is held to cover the expression of aspect generally, be it at the level of the verb or at the level of the sentence, and 'Aktionsart' (German, meaning 'mode of action'), which is employed as a term describing aspectual properties of verbs as lexical items, or sometimes, as in Hinrichs (1985), describing aspectual properties of verbs and verb phrases usually called 'situations' or 'schemata'. The term 'Aktionsart' will not be used in this study, unless reference to other publications is made, and the lexical aspectual potential of verbs will be described as 'telic' and 'atelic'.

Another terminological problem for a study of aspect is how in English (and also in other languages) to refer to what a verb generally denotes. Not that words are in short supply, cf. 'situation', 'state of affairs', 'occurrence', 'eventuality', 'event', 'happening', 'state', 'process', 'act', 'action', 'activity', and others. But terms like 'situation' and 'state of affairs' generally cover (or at least strongly imply) the participants and the setting of what happened or is happening or will happen, not just what **the verb** generally refers to. 'Eventuality', 'happening' and 'occurrence' somehow lack the important element of agentivity present in many sentences. 'Event' and 'act' are often employed in the literature to refer to a completed action, and 'activity', 'state' and 'process' are imperfective situations anyway, so the simultaneous use of these five would prove inconvenient. Thus 'action' seemed to be the most appropriate word, capable of denoting both perfectivity (largely, completedness) and imperfectivity (largely, non-completedness), and it was chosen to cover, as well as to distinguish between, the two fundamental aspectological notions despite the fact that it leaves 'states' out of consideration. 'States' can be assumed under actions – and although this is not the most felicitous way to employ 'action' as a term, it is made use of in precisely this way in grammars and studies of many languages. Alternatively, actions can be taken to reflect the major and the prototypical, and not all possible situations denoted by verbs. Hence, the use throughout this book, of phrases like a bounded/perfective/completed action, on the one hand, and a non-bounded/imperfective/non-completed action, on the other. When states are to be specifically taken into account along with actions, the term 'situation' will be used – regarded as the most general one.

Another terminological problem is reference in English to nouns that are accompanied by an article and nouns that are not accompanied by an article. The adjectival term 'bare' is only partly useful for nouns that have no article, because it also implies the lack of other determiners and quantifiers. What is worse, its counterpart 'non-bare' does not at all signal that it is specifically an article that is present. 'Non-bare' signals that a noun has either an article, a determiner or a quantifier, and this is not quite the same thing as not having an article. A good way to resolve the problem would be to use terms like 'articled noun' and 'non-articled noun', but they seem to sound unacceptable for the English ear. Hence the long and awkward 'noun accompanied/unaccompanied by an article' in this book. The problem is, however, further aggravated by the lack of consensus in linguistics as to exactly which (and what kind of) language entities are determiners, which and what kind of entities are quantifiers. Why it is so important that reference should be made to nouns that are accompanied by an article will become clearer later on.

CHAPTER 1

ON THE ESSENCE OF ASPECT

WHAT IS ASPECT?

In his review of Thore Pettersson's book *On Russian Predicates. A Theory of Case and Aspect*, almost three decades ago Issatschenko wrote:

> "Russian aspects are often considered to be awe-inspiring and mystical categories to be treated only by the initiated, i.e. by the native speaker"

(Issatschenko 1974: 141). This famous quotation applies to Slavic aspect. But the same thesis has been taken to be valid with respect to other languages, including English, and today it can still be generalised that aspect remains a mysterious phenomenon. What aspect in Modern English is from a contemporary point of view can vary greatly from study to study and from linguist to linguist. To the authors of the largest grammar of English, for example (Quirk et al 1985), aspect is represented by the distinctions between progressive and non-progressive and perfect and non-perfect forms of the verb. A large number of other authors subscribe to the same view, or at least a similar one (see Saurer 1984; Brinton 1988; Binnick 1991; Tobin 1993; Hatav 1993; Mellor 1995). To Bartsch (1995), not only the Perfect, the Future is also an aspect! As we shall see later, however, this approach can hardly be said to be prevalent in aspectology and, furthermore, investigations of aspect on a large cross-language scale do not support it at all. Aspect in the model to be advanced in this book, to put it simply at the beginning, has to do first and foremost with completion and non-completion of situations and should by no means be regarded as a morphological (periphrastic) phenomenon restricted to the verb.

To come back to the beer-drinking example, suppose John is in a pub. Somebody (henceforward to be called an observer or a speaker[1]) enters the pub and the first thing he sees is John holding a glass of beer in his hand and drinking it down. A little later, however, John is seen drinking the last drops of the beer and leaving the glass on the table. Now if the observer is to report about John's actions and whether John accomplished the drinking act or not, he will probably use a sentence like (2a) in the first case, and a sentence like (2b) in the second:

---

[1] A person observing a certain situation with the intention of encoding it linguistically will be called an observer. If an utterance describing the situation is made, then the observer becomes a speaker. The receiver of an utterance is a hearer or an addressee.

(2) a. John was drinking the/his beer
    b. John drank the/his beer

The difference is that in the first case (2a) the speaker reports John's drinking as an unfinished act, as an activity in which no definite beginning and no definite end are expressed or implied. This is because the observer is in the middle of the drinking and, hence, cannot see it as finished. In the second case (2b) the speaker reports an action which is carried out to its completion: it has a definite end to which, hence, a definite beginning can be presumed. Note that this kind of difference in meaning does not necessarily arise from the difference in the tense/aspect forms of the verb (Past Progressive in the first instance, Simple Past in the second), for non-completed could also be an action described in a sentence with a Simple Past Tense form of the verb, cf. sentence (1c), already used above:

(1) c. John drank beer

Since, as already mentioned, a completed action has a definite end (be it directly observed or inferred or imagined etc.) and, hence, it can be presumed to have a definite beginning too, the notions of completed/completion and non-completed/non-completion can be referred to as bounded/boundedness and non-bounded/non-boundedness, respectively. That is, an action may have time bounds or may not have time bounds (cf. Klein's 1995 discussion of how aspect could be defined through the concept of time). Other terms covering the same notions are perfective/perfectivity and imperfective/imperfectivity. These have been employed in the literature more often because of the tradition stemming from the study of aspect in the Slavic languages – that were once considered to be the aspect languages *par excellence*. Perfective (perfectivity) and imperfective (imperfectivity) usually describe the completion and non-completion of actions through separate verbs, as in the Slavic languages (or in languages with similar aspectual systems), and it is usually forgotten that in the grammars of Slavic languages perfective and imperfective verbs are actually called completed and non-completed verbs: Russian *soveršennyj glagol* 'completed verb', *nesoveršennyj glagol* 'non-completed verb'; Bulgarian *svăršen glagol* 'completed verb', *nesvăršen glagol* 'non-completed verb'. This terminological issue is not a debatable one: the notions of completion and non-completion, as will be shown later, have a strong intuitive base which is often ignored in aspectological studies of both Slavic and Western-European languages.

If we take it that aspect covers precisely the notion of boundedness vs. non-boundedness of actions or, largely, of situations arising mainly through the use of a verb, anyone who has seriously taken up the task of studying the English language – be it, say, a curious university student, a teacher of English recognising the necessity to explain the subtleties of the English verbal system, or a researcher striving to disclose (and marvelling at) the profound regularities in the functioning of language – is invariably going to face the problem of the expression of aspect distinctions. Indeed, this is especially valid for native speakers of languages with a strongly developed verbal aspectual system, such as the Slavic languages. But although certain close correspondences between the mechanisms of expressing aspect in languages like English and languages like Russian have often been pointed out (see, e.g. Lindstedt 1985; Smith 1991; Mellor 1995), it will be seen later that there is much more to aspect in the two groups of languages (the Slavic languages and the Germanic languages) than a mere visible correspondence between the semantics of certain types of sentences in English and the perfectivity and imperfectivity of verbs in Slavic.

Within the Slavic group of languages it is the Bulgarian language that has features distinguishing it considerably from the rest of the group (e.g. from Russian, Czech or Polish). Bulgarian is a very convenient tool for linguistic comparison and it will be used here in two ways: first, as a structural model for contrasting the two languages, English and Bulgarian (and the two groups of languages, the Germanic and the Slavic ones), at a systemic level, that is, as languages featuring certain grammatical entities; and, second, as a metalanguage for the description of the way the distinction between boundedness and non-boundedness is expressed or explicated in English.

It is intuitively clear that the explication of aspect in English (that is, not its **expression** through the Progressive) is mainly, though not solely, carried out at the level of entire (simple) sentences, and not through the grammatical or semantic properties of the verb only. To draw a useful comparison between the expression of verbal aspect, as in the Slavic languages, and non-verbal aspect, as in English, consider the denotation of perfective actions. In Bulgarian, the completion of a simple action like eating (up) one's sandwich is denoted by a verb which is said to be a perfective one, in this case $izjam_{pfv}$ 'eat', see (3) below (perfectivity will henceforward be abbreviated as pfv, usually as a subscript after the verb):

(3) Iskam   da izjam$_{pfv}$ sandvič-a si
     Want-I   to eat-I   sandwich-the mine
     'I want to eat my sandwich'

Non-completion of the action is denoted by a different, imperfective, verb, in this case jam_{impfv} 'eat', see (4) below (imperfectivity will henceforward be abbreviated as impfv, again usually as a subscript after the verb):

(4) Iskam   da jam$_{impfv}$ sandvič-a si
     Want-I   to eat-I   sandwich-the mine
     'I want to eat my sandwich'

Note, however, that the proper equivalent of the Bulgarian sentence (3) above might be said to be a sentence like (5a) in English (see below) while the English sentence (5b) below might be said to cover **both** the perfective Bulgarian sentence (3) above and the imperfective Bulgarian sentence (4) above:

(5) a. I want to eat up my sandwich
b. I want to eat my sandwich

This is a very important point to be remembered from the very beginning of the discussion. Almost any simple English sentence with, for example, a verb in the infinitive or in the Simple Past Tense (also in the Future Indefinite, in the non-progressive perfect tenses, etc.) can, broadly speaking, be interpreted as either denoting a bounded or a non-bounded action – although, of course, there are different kinds of boundedness and non-boundedness as well. The major problem, however – and this has to do with the fundamental problem of aspect – is that there are other various factors in the sentence that are to be taken into account if the aspectual reading of a particular sentence is to be determined.

It hardly needs any special proof that the English verb *eat* is not a perfective one anyway. Clearly, it can be used to denote completed (that is, perfective) as well as non-completed (that is, imperfective) actions. The use of *up* in (5a) helps the explication of perfectivity – cf. Brinton's (1988) study of post-verbal particles – but it is by no means as widespread as the Slavic aspectual phenomenon (consisting of specialised verbs for the expression of boundedness) which practically spans the whole verb system of any Slavic language[2]. In that case, won't the aspectologist be forced to assume that, first,

in English the aspect of an action (its completion or non-completion) simply finds no expression whatsoever?

Or that, second,

maybe, the aspect of an action does find some expression outside the verb, but this happens in various roundabout ways and only when it is strictly necessary?

This kind of reasoning, rejecting the very heart of the idea that aspect in a language like English can be identified at some structural level was (cf. Zandvoort 1962) and is to a certain extent still common among authors dealing with aspect in, e.g. Slavic-Germanic (cf., e.g., Dušková 1983), or general comparative terms (see Binnick 1991 – who at least only doubts the existence of universal aspectual parameters). For some linguists, the attractive part of this line of reasoning may be that it is conclusive: there is nothing to seek, so why bother to delve into the problem? But the negative side is also that it is conclusive – for it may baffle other, more inquisitive researchers. What if there **is** something worth seeking?

Hence, should an alternative way of reasoning be followed, namely, that completion of an action is a notion that is too important to remain unexpressed in a language, then any learner, researcher or teacher of English (and, in the long run, any

---

[2] In every Slavic language, apart from the large bulk of perfective and imperfective verbs, there is a group of so-called biaspectual verbs that may be said to fall outside the system of aspect. However, they can be regarded as an exception. More on (Slavic) biaspectuality later on.

learner, researcher or teacher of **any** language) will invariably face a fundamental question: what is, in fact, aspect?

This question will henceforward be explored on a level that goes far beyond the observation that aspect concerns the completion and non-completion of actions, and it can be divided into two basic subquestions:

1) What is the essence of aspect (i.e., its meaning, its functions, the possible devices of its expression) for all languages in general or, in other words, for language in general?

2) What is the essence of aspect (i.e., its meaning, its functions, the concrete devices of its expression, the rules governing the use of these devices) in a given language, like for example English?

Until only recently, approximately two decades ago, linguists had no possible answer to the first question. What is more, few dared even to ask it. Unfortunately, in spite of the great progress made in the last two decades, a hefty confusion still reigns in aspectology and, generally, the first question still remains unanswered. Hence, the answer, or, rather, the different possible answers to the second question – concerning particular languages – is still seriously hampered. For how can one define the essence of aspect, say, in English and in Bulgarian respectively, when aspect phenomena observed in these two languages, despite certain roughly identifiable similarities, differ considerably in their expression, in their meaning, in their use? And, of course, the answer to the second question is rendered even more difficult and confused by the fact that aspect does not exist as an independent verb category in a large number of languages. For example, if Bulgarian verbs, with some exceptions, are lexically identified as being perfective and imperfective (both in terms of sentential analysis and as dictionary entries), and English verbs could also be said to possess aspect within the verb system (the Progressive), in the rest of the Germanic languages there are no aspect verb forms at all, although there are certain syntactic constructions (similar to the perfective *eat up* in English or the imperfective *used to* in English) that are used to signal aspectual values. Compare imperfective German expressions like *am Schreiben sein* 'be writing [(literally) be in the writing]'. There is no aspect (understood in this fashion) in most other European non-Slavic languages as well, although, for example, the Romance languages feature past tenses that distinguish actions with respect to termination and lack of termination of states or actions but not with respect to completion and non-completion proper. Bulgarian also features this kind of tenses – which will be considered later on. It is also common knowledge that although Finnish has no aspect verb forms, perfective and imperfective actions **can** be explicated there – through the use of special case affixes in the subject and in the object of the sentence (see, e.g., Markkanen 1979, Lindstedt 1985).

Is it possible, then, to speak of a category of aspect, related, broadly, to the way situations (designated by verbs, their arguments – objects, subjects – and other sentential or contextual entities) are presented as either perfective or imperfective? Is it possible to speak of a basic aspectual category, e.g. perfectivity or imperfectivity, that could be found in any language or (at least) in most languages? The answer to such a question seems positive, provided the category is regarded not as a grammatical one (expressed through certain formal markers, mainly in verbs) but as a conceptual category. Should such an answer be found acceptable, then it would generally be possible for perfectivity and imperfectivity to be expressed in one way or another in any (traditionally so-called) "aspectless" language: through the meaning and use of words, through the meaning and use of whole phrases and sentences. Indeed, an idea of this kind is not at all new (cf., e.g., Sapir 1921: 108; Jespersen 1924: 286-289), but it would thus even appear possible for aspect to have some other type of formal, outward expression in languages without verbal (or similarly marked) aspect. Of course, this outward expression would be expected to be a fairly complex one.

As already mentioned in the preface of this book, the discussion of aspect in it was originally designed for Bulgarian learners and researchers of English – and Bulgarians are capable of grasping the essence of aspect more easily than native speakers of languages without verbal aspect. But even in this version of the book, oriented mainly towards native speakers of English, it is worth exploiting the Bulgarian point of view: because the Bulgarian language gives its speakers the rare opportunity to be able to present all past, present or future events, all actions, activities and other kinds of happenings (observed in reality, planned or imagined) always, or almost always, in two different ways, as completed or as non-completed. Therefore, a brief discussion of the Bulgarian verb system is in place here (a more detailed description can be found in the Appendix).

The great majority of Bulgarian verbs are either perfective or imperfective, like *izjam*$_{pfv}$ 'to eat (up)' and *jam*$_{impfv}$ 'to eat', already used above. But, as far as their use in a Simple (Non-Perfect) Past Tense is concerned, yet another distinction comes into play – a contrast between the (so-called) Past Completed Tense (the Aorist) and the (so-called) Past Non-Completed Tense (the Imperfect). Hence, four different verb forms in Bulgarian can be derived (in this case, in the 1st pers. sing.):

(i) a perfective Aorist, *izjadoh* 'ate';
(ii) an imperfective Imperfect, *jadjah* 'ate [repeatedly or habitually]/was eating';
(iii) an imperfective Aorist, *jadoh* 'ate';
(iv) a perfective Imperfect, *izjadjah* 'ate' (Aorist and Imperfect will henceforward be abbreviated Aor and Imp, usually as subscripts after the verb).

And since Bulgarian is to serve as a tool for comparing aspectual values in English, consider now these four possible Bulgarian verb forms in the description of four possible situations related to the consumption in the past of an apple by a child. The translation equivalents, being sentences of standard English, would be expected to reveal certain characteristics of possible meanings – that might be expressed in one way or another in English. In the four sentences below, two 'objects' (an agent and a patient) take part in the action of eating: one animate, one inanimate. One can say in Bulgarian:

(6) a. Dete-to   jade_impfvAor   jabălka-ta
       Child-the ate   apple-the
       'The child ate the apple [as if continued with adverbials like *for three minutes*]'

   b. Dete-to   jadeše_impfvImp jabălka-ta
      Child-the ate   apple-the
      'The child was eating the apple/ate the apple [repeatedly/habitually]'

   c. Dete-to   izjade_pfvAor   jabălka-ta
      Child-the ate   apple-the
      'The child ate the apple'

   d. Izjadeše_pfvImp li   jabălka-ta,   dete-to   izlizaše_impfvImp   ot staja-ta
      Ate   prt. apple-the,   child-the   came-out   from room-the
      'Whenever the child ate the apple, it left the room'

From the point of view of the native speaker of Bulgarian, as well as from the point of view of the meanings of these four sentences as conveyed into English, the following question arises:

> Are the sentences in (6) to be considered as representations of four different actions or as representations of the same action viewed in four different ways?

It may seem a little trivial. However, as will be seen later, there is, as yet, no general agreement about the precise characteristics of a particular 'situation' already identified by aspectologists. A 'situation', as already stated, is what is generally referred to by a verb in conjunction with its arguments (subject, objects) and other sentential or contextual entities. Nor is there a consensus among linguists as to exactly how many possible (aspectually identifiable) 'situations' there are.

To try to obtain an answer to the question above, let us consider what exactly the sentences in (6) above describe. As already mentioned in the introduction, situations, in contrast to actions, can be said to cover also the participants and the setting of what happened or is happening, not just what happened or was happening. At first sight it may seem perfectly clear that the participants in the four situations are identical: *deteto* 'the child' and *jabălkata* 'the apple'. Different are only the verb forms describing the action: *jade*_impfvAor, *jadeše*_impfvImp, *izjade*_pfvAor, *izjadeše*_pfvImp. Obviously, these represent different ways of carrying out the action of eating. However, not only the actions are different, the situations are different too. Because the fashion in which the action takes place seems to influence the participants.

For example, in the first case, sentence (6a), the action of eating is terminated but is not taken to its natural endpoint – to the consumption of the whole of the apple. This leads to the inference that the apple has in all probability been left partly uneaten. Note that this is just an inference, not a meaning incorporated into a sentence of this kind. In the progressive-like reading of sentence (6b), there is eating at a particular moment or, so to say, the sentence presents a picture (still or moving) of the process of eating an apple. Hence, the apple is not yet eaten to the end. Again, this is an inference, not a strictly identifiable meaning present in the sentence, just as it is in the English translation of the sentence when using the progressive form of the verb. In the third case, sentence (6c), eating is brought to its natural end. Therefore, the apple referred to in (6c) is no longer in existence or is at least in a condition inappropriate for further eating (i.e. only the core is left). Note that this time we can speak not of an inference but of a true component of the overall meaning of the sentence. In the fourth case, sentence (6d), there is again eating brought to its natural end. But here, unlike in (6c), the eating takes place not on a single occasion. It happens repeatedly and, going deeper into the essence of a repeated accomplishment of an action, different possibilities can be found to be involved. Thus if a sentence like (6c), repeated below, sounds fine and denotes a single non-repetitive action, it generally sounds strange or incorrect to say something like (7) below – because there is normally no way for an apple to be restored every time. Compare sentence (6c) and sentence (7), including the English translations:

(6)   c.   Dete-to   izjade$_{pfvAor}$ jabălka-ta
                Child-the   ate   apple-the
                'The child ate the apple [completely]'
(7)   Dete-to   tri   păti   izjade$_{pfvAor}$ jabălka-ta
                Child-the   three   times   ate   apple-the
                'The child ate the apple [completely] three times'

Note, however, first, that in dreams, in certain feature films, computer games, etc. sentence (7) might not sound strange at all. Second, more importantly, with the same type of verb form (the perfective Aorist), a non-repetitive, as well as a repetitive action can still, in principle, be denoted in Bulgarian. Cf. sentences (8a) and (8b):

(8)   a.   Dete-to   izpi$_{pfvAor}$ lekarstvo-to
                Child-the   drank   medicine-the
                'The child took the medicine [implied: once]'
       b.   Dete-to   tri   păti   izpi$_{pfvAor}$ lekarstvo-to
                Child-the   three   times   drank   medicine-the
                'The child took the medicine three times [either one "whole" repetitive action, or three actions]'

Thus a very interesting and revealing aspect of the aspect problem comes to the fore. If in (8a) above *lekarstvoto* 'the medicine' is, so to say, a single material object, in (8b) *lekarstvoto* 'the medicine' is already to be understood either as three separate material objects, or as a token, a nomenclature item (e.g. quinine) that can be reproduced in a multitude of concrete exemplars. The fact that this phenomenon is discussed using Bulgarian data here should not bother the reader, for, clearly, it can be, and will later be, exemplified using English data – furthermore, the English glosses and translations here provide some exemplification, too.

But isn't the situation in (6d) above, where, no doubt, there is a repetition of the action, a similar one? The child could not possibly restore the apple every time (again, leaving aside dreams, feature films, computer games, etc.) to be able to eat it over and over again (cf. 8b). Then, it is not merely the action of eating that can be different according to the way it is carried out in (6a), (6b), (6c), and (6d). Even the apple, at least in (6a) and (6c), is rather different. What is more, it is different in different ways. Because, looked at from another angle, even after the completion of the action in (6a), the apple (not entirely eaten, as mentioned earlier), is physically different from the apple after the accomplishment of the action in a sentence like (6c). Note once again that all these different nuances of meaning, implied or explicated by the Bulgarian sentences, could also be perceived in the English translation equivalents.

Furthermore, if we continue discussing the meanings and implications of sentences like (6a), (6b), (6c) and (6d) in Bulgarian, it will inevitably turn out that not only the objects of the actions differ. The agents in the situations could also be said to differ in certain ways, in spite of the fact that at first sight they are, so to say, the same person: *deteto* 'the child'. We could, for example, ask if *deteto* 'the child' in (6d) represents **one** child taking part in different acts of eating an (the) apple. Consider (6d) again, including its English equivalent:

(6) d. Izjadeše$_{pfvImp}$ li jabălka-ta, dete-to izlizaše$_{impfvImp}$ ot staja-ta
       Ate   *prt.* apple-the, child-the came-out   from room-the
       'Whenever the child ate the apple, it left the room'

If we pause to think, we will see that it could be the same child but it could also **not** be the same child. But even if it is the same child, could we, given these circumstances, say that there is no difference between what is expressed by *deteto* 'the child' in (6d) and, say, *deteto* 'the child' in (6a)? Compare again these two sentences, (6d) above and (6a) below, and their English translations.

(6) a. Dete-to jade$_{impfvAor}$ jabălka-ta
       Child-the ate   apple-the
       'The child ate the apple [as if continued with adverbials like *for three minutes*]'

It is becoming obvious that an adequate answer to questions of this kind concerning the status of referents of subjects and objects of perfective and imperfective sentences could not be given straight away. It will be provided gradually throughout this book and, of course, primarily using English data.³

But after what has been discussed so far, one is inevitably led to the conclusion that the four (at least) different situations in the four Bulgarian sentences in (6) above would bring any serious investigator of aspect in English, really keen on the subtleties of its expression, to the formulation of (at least) the following two questions:

1) Is it not possible for a language like English, and, in the long run, for any other language, to be able to express all or at least part of the meanings of the action (actions) in sentences like those in (6) above?

2) If we accept that the languages spoken by a large part of the modern world cannot be so poor as to be incapable of explicating the various meanings and nuances of meanings present in (6), how could this explication be effected systematically?

The answers to these two questions are far from easy and will also be developed gradually in the course of the discussion in the present book. It is becoming more and more apparent, however, that in English there ought to be certain devices for the denotation of the different types of situations: from the point of view of their completion or non-completion; from the point of view of their repetition or non-repetition; from the point of view of the type of the repetition involved (limited/bounded, as in (8b), or unlimited/non-bounded, as in (6d)); from the point of view of other possible ways of their occurrence; from the point of view of the status of their participants – in space and time.

And so, to continue asking questions, what could be, generally speaking, the essence of aspect? And, in spite of the many views to the contrary, doesn't it have to do precisely with what the perfective/imperfective opposition in the Slavic languages is all about? Doesn't a language like Bulgarian give us a much better opportunity to understand what underlies this phenomenon? How is it possible that an important notion concerning the temporal properties of events that is granted to a particular language should be absent in a large number of other languages, including English?

From the point of view of the Slavic phenomenon, it is not difficult at all to understand why English speakers rarely pay any attention to the aspectual contrast discussed so far. While very often the distinction can be intuited in the context of a spoken or written text, in the standard English dictionaries verbs are never marked with respect to the aspectual characteristics they have or might have⁴. It would, therefore, be instructive to see how verbs are represented from an aspectual point of view in bilingual dictionaries covering English and a (traditionally so-called) "aspect language".

---

³ It will be seen that the referents of subjects and objects (participants in the situation) in sentences of this kind can also be regarded as temporal entities.

⁴ English verbs do have important aspectual characteristics that play a decisive role in the composition of the aspect of a sentence. This is a complex issue which is to be gradually clarified and resolved within the theoretical framework assumed.

ON THE LEXICOGRAPHIC REPRESENTATION OF ASPECT

In a Bulgarian-English dictionary, there are different possible ways to cover aspectual differences. Let us have a look at how actual dictionaries present them. First, if a perfective Bulgarian verb is to be checked on, the reader is usually referred to its imperfective correspondence:

dam *vž.* **davam**
give(pfv) see give (impfv)

For example, look at this solution in Atanassova et al (1988a: 148). In other words, if the meaning of a perfective Bulgarian verb is to be checked on, for some reason one has to find its imperfective partner at its alphabetical place. There, the imperfective verb and the perfective verb are given as forming an aspectual pair, and their semantics is rendered into English as **a single unified** meaning. Cf.:

davam, dam 1. give (**njakomu nešto** s.o. s.th.,
  s.th. to s.o.); (*podavam*) hand, pass...

This representation is employed in Atanassova et al (1988a: 145).

In the second possible case, a perfective verb (for example, *napravja* 'make, do') may come together with two imperfective verbs (*napravjam, pravja* 'make, do') in the same lexical entry, the three verbs forming an aspectual triple and represented as having, supposedly, identical meanings:

napravjam, napravja *vž.* **pravja; vednaga šte**
  go naprawja I'll get it done in no time...

See this solution in Atanassova et al (1988b: 477).

An explanation concerning the aspectual triple is due here. Bulgarian verbs like *napravjam*$_{Imfvp}$ 'make, do' or *napisvam*$_{impfv}$ 'write' belong to the group of so-called secondary imperfective verbs which denote a bounded action – the same as the one denoted by the perfective verb (*napravja*$_{pfv}$ 'make, do [to the end]' or *napiša*$_{pfv}$ 'write [to the end]') but which is repeated an indefinite number of times. Henceforward, for these verbs the abbreviation impfv2 (in subscript) will be used, and their specific nuance of meaning may be given in square brackets, for instance: *napravjam*$_{Imfvp2}$ 'make, do [to the end repeatedly]', *napisvam*$_{impfv2}$ 'write [to the end repeatedly]'. These verbs are regularly formed in Bulgarian (in contrast to other Slavic languages where the phenomenon, called secondary imperfectivisation, is less widespread) by adding the suffix -*vam* to the perfective verb – certain minor additional morphophonetic changes may also occur. Some of these secondary imperfectives, for example *napravjam*$_{impfv2}$ 'do/make [to the end repeatedly]', are in fact used less often, because the primary imperfective (*pravja*$_{Imfvp}$ 'make, do' or *piša*$_{impfv}$ 'write') is usually found to be also capable of expressing the boundedness of the individual action – which can be presented as indefinitely serialised.

However, although for the meanings of *napravjam*_{impfv2} and *napravja*_{pfv} 'make, do' there is a cross-reference to *pravja*_{impfv} 'make, do' in the dictionary discussed above, the entry for *pravja*_{impfv} 'make, do' does not at all list *napravjam*_{impfv2} and *napravja*_{pfv} 'make, do':

pravja 1. *(izrabotvam, proizveždam)* make; *(izvǎršvam, izpǎlnjavam, ureždam)* do...

See Atanassova et al (1988b: 700).

In the third possible lexicographic version, in which again there is an aspectual triple, an imperfective verb and a perfective verb are listed together in a single entry (*napisvam*_{impfv2}, *napiša*_{pfv} 'write') but there is no cross-reference for the other imperfective verb (*piša*_{impfv} 'write'). Cf.

napisvam, napiša write, write down, take down...

See Atanassova et al (1988a: 476). Again, the true aspectual correspondence of perfective *napiša* 'write' is usually not *napisvam*_{impfv2}, which conveys a special bounded meaning that is indefinitely serialised, but *piša*_{impfv} 'write'. However, although the real partner of perfective *napiša* 'write' is *piša*_{impfv} 'write', the entry for *piša*_{impfv} 'write' lists *piša* only, and neither *napiša*_{pfv} 'write', nor the secondary imperfective *napisvam*_{impfv2} 'write':

piša 1. write (**njakomu** to s.o., **za** about)...

See Atanassova et al (1988b: 634). There are also other possible variants of presenting aspectual data in Bulgarian-English dictionaries – all of them equally inappropriate, which will not be discussed here.

To sum up the way of presenting aspect in Bulgarian-English dictionaries, the two-volume dictionary cited above (Atanassova et al 1988a; 1988b) does not at all constitute some specific instance. The lexicographic solution in it is the standard one found in the overwhelming majority of dictionaries – and the brief analysis above shows that aspect remains almost totally neglected in bilingual (Slavic-English) lexicography. Whatever aspects of aspectual data dictionaries cover, they do it in an entirely unjustifiable and unsystematic way. It is sufficient to conclude that, as can be seen from the dictionary quotations given above, as a rule, even the aspectual values (perfective and imperfective) of verbs are not at all given, and this makes the non-native speaker's task to determine the meaning of a Slavic verb and its possible English equivalents extremely complicated.

In English-Bulgarian dictionaries, perfective verbs are not even listed as correspondences to English verbs that are capable of expressing or implying a perfective meaning. Perfective verbs are omitted because, according to the prevailing view in lexicography, they are to be subsumed under imperfective ones. Compare the following dictionary excerpt from the lexical entry of *write* in which the first meaning contains only the primary imperfective *piša* 'write', the secondary meaning contains only the secondary imperfectives *napisvam* 'write [repeatedly]' and *izpisvam* 'write the whole of [repeatedly]' and at the same time the perfective *izpiša* (in its particular tense-aspect form *izpisah*$_{pfvAor}$) is given in the translation of the example *I wrote two sheets*:

write ... **1** piša; ... **2** napisvam, izpisvam; **I wrote two sheets** izpisah dva lista...

See Rankova et al (1987: 506).

Could these lexicographic solutions for the representation of aspect in English-Bulgarian and Bulgarian-English dictionaries be adequate and acceptable?

Yes – if, firstly, aspect is to be considered a strange Slavic phenomenon that has no equivalent or near-equivalent in English, and if, secondly, we take it that the users of the dictionaries in question are only native speakers of Bulgarian capable of grasping the differences of meaning involved in the separate verbs or in the aspectual pairs or triples. (It is worth noting, however, that the rules for forming aspectual pairs or triples in Bulgarian represent an extremely complex grammatical issue: they are many, and ordinary native speakers do not know them; they learn the differences only by intuition.)

No – if, firstly we take it that Bulgarian aspect **is** to be expressed in English in *some* way. No if, secondly, we take into account the fact that the users of the dictionaries will not always be native Bulgarian speakers and will not always be able to identify the perfective members of the aspectual pairs or triples (and, generally, find their way through the dictionary). Not at all if, thirdly (and last but by far not least), a bilingual dictionary is to properly exercise its functions by giving a fairly exhaustive and representative account of the semantic and grammatical data of the languages described.

However, if English-Bulgarian and Bulgarian-English dictionaries do not give perfective verbs at all or do not present them in the most appropriate way, they certainly bring the user to the conclusion that equivalents of the Bulgarian perfective verbs *izjam, izpija, napravja, dam, vzema* are the English verbs *eat, drink, make, give, take*, respectively. And correspondences of the Bulgarian imperfective verbs *izjaždam*$_{impfv2}$/*izjadam*$_{impfv2}$, *izpivam*$_{impfv2}$, *napravjam*$_{impfv2}$/*pravja*$_{impfv}$, *davam*$_{impfv}$, *vzemam*$_{impfv}$ again are the English verbs given above. A conclusion like this may seem either not entirely justified or wholly trivial. But would a conclusion of this kind not be essential for the understanding of the devices for the expression of perfective and imperfective actions in English – provided such devices exist?

Therefore, let us explore in further detail the problem of whether a distinction between perfectivity and imperfectivity should be made in both Bulgarian and English – this time not on the basis of isolated dictionary entries but on the basis of an authentic text.[5]

---

[5] It will be shown later, that although certain correspondences between Slavic and Germanic aspect have been pointed out and discussed at length in the enormous literature dealing with the problem, as a

TRANSLATING A TEXT FROM AN "ASPECTLESS" LANGUAGE INTO AN "ASPECT" LANGUAGE

Take any novel or any short story written in English and translated into Bulgarian. In its Bulgarian version almost every sentence will contain a verb which, in the prevailing majority of cases, will necessarily be either a perfective or an imperfective one and will denote either a perfective or an imperfective action – later it will be seen that there is no permanent equivalence between a perfective verb and the expression of a perfective action and an imperfective verb and the expression of an imperfective action. Can we take it then that the choice of a perfective or an imperfective verb in the Bulgarian translation is a sole consequence of the **internal language rules** of Bulgarian and that this choice has nothing to do with the original situation described in the English (original) version of the text?

To try to answer this question, let us compare the following: an original passage extracted from Joseph Heller's novel *Catch 22* (Heller 1962), the authentic passage of its Bulgarian translation (Heller 1990), and a manipulated version of the translation passage. In the manipulated passage, the aspects of the separate verbs (perfective and imperfective) and, where relevant, their tense-aspect forms (Aorist and Imperfect), have been changed. It is true that the actual comparisons concerning the aspectual meanings conveyed in these passages can properly be made by Bulgarianists, Slavists or at least by linguists with a strong aspectological background. For non-Slavists and non-specialists in aspectology, an approximation of the manipulated Bulgarian text is given in English.[6] In any case, both Slavists and non-Slavists will be able to see that superficial differences of the distribution of language elements in the two separate languages do not at all stand for different meanings. That is, the outward absence of aspect markers in English does not necessarily lead to the conclusion that aspectual distinctions in English identical to the Slavic ones cannot be explicated. Now compare the three passages, plus the translation into English of the manipulated Bulgarian passage:

THE ORIGINAL PASSAGE

"Men," Colonel Cargill began in Yossarian's squadron, measuring his pauses carefully. "You're American officers. The officers of no other army in the world can make that statement. Think about it."

Sergeant Knight thought about it and then politely informed Colonel Cargill that he was addressing the enlisted men and that the officers were to be found waiting for him on the other side of the squadron. Colonel Cargill thanked him crisply and glowed with self-satisfaction as he strode across the area. It made him proud to observe that twenty-nine months in the service had not blunted his genius for ineptitude.

(Heller 1962: 27)

---

rule, authors have failed to identify one-to-one structural correspondences of aspectual meanings in Slavic and in Germanic (but see Kabakčiev 1984a; 1984b).

[6] On the other hand, note that what is at issue here is a highly specialised matter: any fluent speaker of Bulgarian as a foreign language without a linguistic training or any native Bulgarian speaker without a linguistic training would have serious difficulty grasping the differences.

THE AUTHENTIC TRANSLATED PASSAGE

"– Vojnici – započna_pfvAor polkovnik Kargil pred eskadrilata na Josarjan, kato otmervaše_impfvImp grižlivo pauzite si, – vie ste amerikanski oficeri. Oficerite ot nikoja druga armija na sveta ne mogat da kažat_pfv tova za sebe si. Pomislete_pfv vărhu tova!
Seržant Nait pomisli_pfvAor vărhu tova i posle učtivo uvedomi_pfvAor polkovnik Kargil, če toj govori_impfv na vojnicite i če oficerite go čakat_impfv na drugata strana na lagera. Polkovnik Kargil mu blagodari_biaspAor otrivisto i sijaejki ot samodovolstvo trăgna_pfvAor prez zonata. Čuvstvaše se_impfvImp gord, poneže zabeljaza_pfvAor, če dvadeset i devette meseca voenna služba ne bjaha prităpili_pfv negovija genij za nekadărnost."

(Heller 1990: 29).

A MANIPULATED BULGARIAN PASSAGE: WITH REPLACED ASPECT FORMS OF VERBS

– Vojnici – započvaše_impfvImp polkovnik Kargil pred eskadrilata na Josarjan, kato ?otmeri_pfvAor grižlivo pauzite si, – vie ste amerikanski oficeri. Oficerite ot nikoja druga armija na sveta ne mogat da kazvat_impfv tova za sebe si. Mislete_impfv vărhu tova!
Seržant Nait misleše_impfvImp vărhu tova i posle učtivo uvedomjavaše_impfvImp polkovnik Kargil, če toj *pogovori_pfv na vojnicite i če oficerite go *počakat_pfv na drugata strana na lagera. Polkovnik Kargil mu blagodareše_impfvImp otrivisto i sijaejki ot samodovolstvo trăgvaše_impfvImp prez zonata. Počuvstva se_pfvAor gord, poneže zabeljazvaše_impfvImp, če dvadeset i devette meseca voenna služba ne bjaha prităpjavali_impfv negovija genij za nekadărnost.

A MANIPULATED ENGLISH PASSAGE: TRANSLATION OF THE BULGARIAN PASSAGE WITH THE REPLACED ASPECT FORMS OF VERBS

"Men," Colonel Cargill was beginning in Yossarian's squadron, and then measured up his pauses carefully. "You're American officers. The officers of no other army in the world can keep making that statement. Keep thinking about it."
Sergeant Knight was thinking about it and then was politely informing Colonel Cargill that he addressed the enlisted men and that the officers were to be found to wait for him for some time on the other side of the squadron. Colonel Cargill was thanking him crisply and glowed with self-satisfaction as he was striding across the area. It made him proud to be observing that twenty-nine months in the service had not been blunting his genius for ineptitude.

It can easily be seen, at least by any speaker of Bulgarian, that in the manipulated Bulgarian passage the substitution of aspect forms is in many cases impossible. It either leads to ungrammaticality (there and henceforward ungrammaticality is marked with an asterisk) or to an obvious narrative inconsistency (marked with a question mark) in the use of particular verbs, verb phrases or whole sentences. For the reader who cannot cope with the Bulgarian text, the English translation of the manipulated Bulgarian text also gives an idea of the way the manipulated text distorts the initial message, though, indeed, the inadequacy of the manipulated Bulgarian text cannot be perfectly rendered in English. And in those cases in which the Bulgarian phrases or sentences are even grammatical and correct, there is partial or (most often) total confusion in the narrative. The order and the interrelationships of the actions contained in the original passage are entirely or almost entirely destroyed. Singular acts are turned into actions that are indefinitely serialised, events are thus unnaturally stretched over time. Activities or non-completed repetitive actions are, vice versa, arbitrarily compressed into singular (completed) acts. The information about which events move the narrative forward and which states or actions/activities serve as a background for them is lost. Indeed, in several cases the alternative use of aspect forms in Bulgarian does not change the overall meaning (cf. Colonel Cargill's words to the officers). And in one case the change of aspect is impossible, because the verb (*blagodarja* 'thank') is biaspectual – but the overall picture of the situation is nevertheless corrupted again through the use of an Imperfect instead of an Aorist verb form.[7]

It is apparent, however, that the chronological order of the actions, their perfectivity and imperfectivity and the other nuances of their occurrence could not be but perfectly described in the English original of the extract from the novel. We could also suppose that in most cases they would be rendered by strict equivalents in the other language. Is it possible then for perfectivity and imperfectivity in the Bulgarian version to be a purely Slavic "invention", a requirement imposed by "exotic language phenomena" typical of certain languages only? Or are perfectivity and imperfectivity conditioned by the narration itself – no doubt, correctly described in the original? Is it possible for the narrative in the original not to be based on certain regularities inherent in the English language itself? Accounts of the relationship between aspect at the level of sentences and the discourse which they form have already been made, along with the way the reader incorporates the sentences (and clauses) "into a model of the discourse in which they occur" (see, e.g., Caenepeel 1989). But most of the questions above, to which the most general answer appears almost self-evident, have hardly ever been raised by linguists, and a fact of this kind calls for an explanation.

To sum up the discussion in the last two sections of this chapter, a comparison has been made of the way the perfective/imperfective distinction is represented lexicographically and textually – in English, a language in which perfectivity is expressed, generally, outside the verb system, and in Bulgarian, a language in which perfectivity is expressed within the verb system. The comparison led to the assumption that in English there must be devices similar to the Slavic ones for the expression of perfectivity and imperfectivity of situations – that is, of events, happenings, actions, activities, processes, states and other similar abstract entities. But grammars of English do not take into account the way aspect should be handled, although, as will be shown later, the last two decades in linguistics saw a large number of publications correctly describing the basic aspectual system of English. Some of these publications deal with the way aspect is explicated in narrative or at the suprasentential level (e.g., Caenepeel 1989; Danchev 1992; Glasbey 1994). What

---

[7] There are several hundred biaspectual verbs in Bulgarian. It is worth noting that they function in a way similar to the functioning of verbs in English. They are defined, traditionally and generally, as verbs whose meanings are expressed within context. That is, they are defined in the same manner as English aspect (viz., the distinction between boundedness and non-boundedness of an action) is described in traditional terms as being expressed within context.

the means for the expression of perfectivity and imperfectivity are, is still not known, but the comparison has revealed a number of significant facts in and across the two languages:

– verbs in English do not possess the grammatical category of aspect such as is possessed by most Bulgarian verbs;
– equivalents of verbal aspect (perfective/imperfective) pairs in Bulgarian like *izjam*$_{pfv}$/*jam*$_{impfv}$ 'to eat', *izpija*$_{pfv}$/*pija*$_{impfv}$ 'to drink', *napravja*$_{pfv}$/*pravja*$_{impfv}$ 'to make, to do', *dam*$_{pfv}$/*davam*$_{impfv}$ 'to give', *vzema*$_{pfv}$/*vzemam*$_{impfv}$ 'to take', etc. are single English verbs: *to eat, to drink, to make, to do, to give, to take*;[8]
– English features an aspect verb form, the Progressive, which in its simple (non-perfect) form denotes imperfective actions in progress at a definite point or period of time and is incapable of expressing perfective situations; it is also incapable of denoting situations that are imperfective but are habitual or repetitive over some longer stretch of time extended beyond the definite point or period subsumed under it;
– both types of general situations described above (one which is in progress at a definite point or period of time, and one which is habitual or repetitive over some longer stretch of time) can be expressed through imperfective verbs and the Imperfect (Tense) verb form in Bulgarian.

As far as the question about what aspect is is concerned, and its two subquestions formulated later, the reasons why they have remained without an adequate answer in linguistics are gradually becoming clear. Whenever asked, these questions are capable of raising a host of other related issues. But doesn't the answer to questions of a certain kind partly depend on the preliminary formulation of the questions? In a book revealing the development in the understanding of tense and aspect from Aristotelian to modern times, Binnick reviews the confusion in the literature on aspect and asks:

> "But are formal, functional, or semantic categories the ones that link language-specific phenomena to universal categories? And can specific categories be linked without concern for the overall systems of languages? Is the Greek imperfect aspect, for example, the same as the Slavic imperfective? How do we know, and what do we mean by saying this? Here there are widely differing opinions"

(Binnick 1991: 147). Later on it will be shown that while opinions may, indeed differ, a model for viewing aspect in cross-language terms as a unified and universal language phenomenon has already been proposed (Kabakčiev 1984b). And in the following passages it will be seen that the lack of a satisfactory answer to the question whether there is aspect in English has probably also been caused by the lack of an appropriately formulated question. Therefore, it even seems better if the question about what aspect is remains unanswered for the time being – even

---

[8] Here the old problem of Slavic grammar whether some of these verb pairs should be regarded as "true" aspect pairs or not is ignored.

provided it is a legitimate one. And it **is** a legitimate one: if somebody observing aspect in Bulgarian would like to discover the way it is expressed in English, it would be better firstly to ask not what aspect in Bulgarian is but what aspect in general is. In the course of the discussion in this book, not only an answer to the question about English aspect will gradually arise; but also an answer to the question about the very essence of aspect in general will be proposed.

IS THERE ASPECT IN ENGLISH? AN EXCURSION INTO SOME OF THE HISTORY OF ASPECTOLOGY

Whether there is aspect in English is a question that has been asked over and over again by many linguists, grammarians and teachers of English. For many decades the development of modern linguistics was dominated by the idea that in English a distinction similar to the perfective/imperfective verb opposition in the Slavic languages does not exist, or, if it exists, it does not find any grammatical realisation:

> "Aspect is expressed in English by all kinds of idiomatic turns rather than by a consistently worked out set of grammatical forms"

(Sapir 1921: 108). This idea persisted totally unchallenged until as late as the beginning of the 1970s. The majority of researchers, knowingly or unknowingly, followed a widespread dogma that was most strongly worded by Zandvoort (1962). According to it, devices for the expression of perfectivity and imperfectivity in English should, its adherents insisted, simply not be sought – because aspect in English, understood as the Progressive/Non-Progressive opposition, denoted something which is entirely different from Slavic aspect. Several decades earlier Jespersen (1924: 288) had also insisted that "it would be better to do without the terms perfective and imperfective except in dealing with the Slavic verb", although he admitted that aspect in English could be associated with the meaning of the separate verb, with verbal expressions, the expanded (i.e. the progressive) tenses, the context, etc (see Jespersen 1924: 286-289). And even today, after the breakthrough that occurred during the last two decades in the study of aspect in English and in the framework of a general theory of language, many linguists still either find it hard to accept the idea that the English language features such devices or follow the mainstream of grammarians who ascribe aspect solely to what is visible in the verb – that is, to both the progressive (*be* + *ing*) and the perfect (*have* + *-ed*) verb forms (cf., e.g., Bartsch 1995; Binnick 1991; Hatav 1993; Mellor 1995; Quirk et al 1985; Tobin 1993).

Therefore, at least some of the history of research into the aspect problem would be in place prior to the presentation of contemporary ideas in the field. This history is particularly interesting from a general scientific and especially a methodological point of view. It is useful and instructive from the standpoint of the present to reveal the achievements, as well as the meanderings of thought on the way to scientific truth, to analyse the reasons why so many erudite scholars and even whole linguistic schools followed a wrong direction in the efforts of their research. After all, many lessons can be learned from history – however obvious certain truths may seem today. Following some of the development of the research into English aspects is to assume that this can promote a better understanding of the phenomenon and help disperse prevailing or remaining dogmas.

As already mentioned, many linguists would not hesitate to give a positive answer to the question about whether there is aspect in English and would point to the Progressive as an exponent of an aspectual meaning, whatever its precise definition. From today's point of view, this is a correct statement, although there are other linguists who would reject the idea of viewing the Progressive as an aspect form. The (Non-Perfect) Progressive denotes imperfectivity at a particular moment or period, the moment or period being explicitly or implicitly given. But if the Progressive does express imperfectivity, it is a subtype of the general category of imperfectivity, excluding repetitive actions or states and state-like situations holding or occurring over a (comparatively) extended period of time. Another important point to make is that the imperfective Progressive does not enter into any formal opposition with some perfective verb form or forms. Perfectivity is not marked in any way in the English verb. Adverbial elements (like *up* in *to eat up*) help in the explication of perfectivity but they are of small significance, given their infrequent use. It is precisely this feature that distinguishes English from "aspect" languages like the Slavic ones. Hence the long-time predominant idea in linguistics that English is an "aspectless" language; and that perfectivity, and also to a certain extent imperfectivity, simply cannot be expressed in it.

Slavic linguists were among the first to try to find equivalent or related devices in English for the expression of Slavic aspect. Voroncova (1948), a Russian anglicist, modified the traditional attempts to reveal aspect parameters in the meanings of English verbs as lexical entries. She put forward a classification in which English verbs are divided into three groups: telic verbs (Russian *predel'nye glagoly*), atelic verbs (Russian *nepredel'nye glagoly*) and verbs with a mixed character. Voroncova's intention was to make a close parallel between the aspect of Russian verbs and certain aspectual characteristics of English verbs. Her classification was based on a differentiation earlier made by Vinogradov (1947) between telicity and atelicity in the meanings of Russian verbs outside their aspectual meanings of perfectivity and imperfectivity. But what are telicity and atelicity?

Telic (Greek *telos*) means 'directed towards a goal', and hence although sometimes this term is employed as an equivalent of 'bounded' or 'perfective', it is usually **not** taken to mean the actual attainment of the goal. According to the prevailing assumption in Russian linguistics, either telic or atelic can only be imperfective verbs, not perfective ones. On the one hand, telic imperfective verbs are taken to be able to yield perfective verb forms because the action denoted by them is considered capable of attaining some goal – reaching some kind of completion/endpoint which is, so to say, in view. Perfective verbs, on the other hand, can only be telic and they **always** denote the attainment of a goal. Thus imperfective Russian verbs like *belit'* 'bleach, whitewash', *delat'* 'make, do', *tajat'* 'melt', etc. are said to be telic, whereas other imperfective verbs, like, for example, *kričat'* 'shout', *ležat'* 'lie', *spat'* 'sleep', etc. are said to be atelic. The difference is held to depend on the nature of the situation denoted, on the presence or absence of certain types of objects to the verbs or eventually on context in general. Hence, e.g. *sdelat'*$_{pfv}$/*delat'*$_{impfv}$ 'make, do' is a regular aspect pair, whereas *prospat'*$_{pfv}$/*spat'*$_{impfv}$ 'sleep' is not.

Although this thesis is incorporated into the largest Russian grammar published (Russian Grammar 1982), it is a rather unconvincing one. For what can be the logical or common-sense motivation to insist that the endpoint of actions like *belit'*$_{impfv}$ 'bleach, whitewash', *delat'*$_{impfv}$ 'make, do' and *tajat'*$_{impfv}$ 'melt' is "in view" and the endpoint of actions like *kričat'*$_{impfv}$ 'shout', *ležat'*$_{impfv}$ 'lie' and *spat'*$_{Imp}$ 'sleep' is not in view? On the contrary, it even seems reasonable to maintain that one can make, e.g. chairs or blunders most of one's life, i.e., without any endpoint of the action in view, and that, normally, one does not or cannot lie, sleep or shout for a long time. It is true that the endpoint of some situations is more 'in sight' than the endpoint of other situations (cf. the discussion in Leinonen 1982: 22-34). The point made in the Russian Grammar (1982: 583) is that if a sleep-situation is to be represented as telic, not *spat'*$_{impfv}$ 'to sleep', but a totally different verb, *prospat'*$_{pfv}$ 'to sleep', is to be used. This would mean, however, that the verb *spat'*$_{impfv}$ 'to sleep' ought to be represented as two separate lexical items in the dictionaries[9] – as two verbs, *spat'*$^{1}_{impfv}$, *spat'*$^{2}_{impfv}$, a solution that can hardly be justified, for, intuitively, *spat'*$_{impfv}$ 'to sleep' is a unitary lexical notion.

The standard explanation simply takes the easy, morphological, way out. It assigns telicity to those verbs that happen to form aspectual pairs and assigns atelicity to verbs that do not happen to form aspectual pairs. Thus it totally fails to explain why certain verbs have to be viewed as telic and others as atelic from a semantic point of view. If, alternatively, an ontological point of view is explored, all actions, activities and the like, at least those in what is referred to as the "real world", are bound to be over at one or another point in time, as it is inevitable that their agents stop to exist at one or another point – with the possible exception of categories like 'matter' with its eternal movement (and, of course, "matter" in this sense is a not a physical, "real-world" concept but a metaphysical one).

Apparently, the problem of the meaning of aspect in language is to be discussed on a higher level of abstraction. It does not seem to be related to the magnitude of the duration of events, processes or states. Thus, to signify a state with an absolute minimum of duration, an imperfective verb can be used in Bulgarian, *traja*$_{impfv}$ 'last', as in (9a), and to refer to an extremely generalised event as the one in (9b) a perfective verb (*prebăda*$_{pfv}$ 'be') can, and in this case must, be used. Compare sentences (9a), (9b) and the non-grammatical (9c):

(9) a. Učudvane-to   mu   traja$_{impfvAor}$ samo   mig
       Astonishment-the his   lasted   only   moment
       'His astonishment lasted only a moment'

---

[9] This was pointed out to me by Jim Miller (personal communication).

b. Čoveška-ta civilizacija šte prebăde$_{pfv}$/prosăštestvuva$_{pfv}$ văv vekove-te
Human-the civilisation will be/exist in centuries-the
'Human civilisation will be preserved for centuries'

c. *Čoveška-ta civilizacija šte băde$_{impfv}$/săštestvuva$_{impfv}$ văv vekove-te
Human-the civilisation will be in centuries-the
'Human civilisation will be preserved for centuries'

Voroncova's classification of English verbs was later developed by Ivanova, whose basic contribution can be seen in rendering the idea that English verbs feature aspectual characteristics more explicit. Ivanova substituted Voronvcova's term 'mixed lexical character' of the verb for 'aspectual character' (Ivanova 1961: 64) and grouped English verbs into telic, atelic, and verbs of a dual aspectual nature (Ivanova 1961: 65-70). According to one of her theses, certain atelic verbs cannot become telic (ibid.). However, in a somewhat non-typical use probably all atelic verbs will be able to attain a clearly perfective, hence telic, meaning. Compare, for example, the Bulgarian translation equivalent (10b) of the English sentence (10a), quoted by Danchev and Alexieva (1974: 308):

(10) a. He suddenly hated that man
b. Toj izvednăž namrazi$_{pfvAor}$ tozi čovek
He suddenly hated this man

The introduction of adverbials like *suddenly* in sentences like (10a) makes English verbs like *love, detest* and their synonyms expressing similar feelings behave like telic verbs. This change of states (imperfectives) into perfective inchoatives (that is, verbs, phrases, etc. denoting the ingression of a situation) is an important phenomenon that remained unnoticed by Ivanova. It can be argued, however, that if the semantic representation of a verb like *spat'*$_{impfv}$ 'sleep' in Russian can hardly be divided into two separate meanings, telic and atelic, there are strong intuitive grounds for maintaining that in a comprehensive lexicographic representation of English the lexical entries for verbs like *hate* ought to contain a separate perfective inchoative meaning.

Ivanova's analysis was influenced by the aspectological thinking of the 60s. While she correctly insisted that, for example, a direct object to the verb is capable of delimiting the action, this argument is refuted by one of her own examples:

(11) At times he wrote stories unworthy of him

(Ivanova 1961: 69). Should the action in (11) be considered a telic one? First, there is no pragmatically identifiable goal "in sight". Secondly, even if we ignore the presence of a type of object in the sentence (*stories*) which will later turn out to play an essential role in the expression of imperfectivity (because it is unaccompanied by an article or other markers of quantity), the sentence also contains an adverbial (*at times*) which clearly denotes a non-bounded repetition of the action and, hence, could by no means be associated with the expression of (or the arrival at) a goal. The problem also concerns the exact definition of telic. The action in this sentence (11), viewed in its totality, ought to be regarded as atelic and imperfective, denoting non-bounded repetition if the lack of markers of boundedness on both sides of the time axis is taken into account. Whether the separate acts contained in the overall action (*wrote stories*) should, however, be regarded as bounded, completed, and hence telic, is another question – which will receive a separate treatment in this book, in Chapter Six, *The mechanism for mapping the temporal values of subjects and objects*.

Thus while classifying English verbs into telic, atelic and of a dual aspectual nature appears justified, a description of this kind should apparently by no means ignore a large number of other factors within the sentence influencing its aspectual interpretation. Some other publications of that time (Ryle 1949, Garey 1957; Vendler 1957; Kenny 1963) had already established, first, that what is here defined as perfectivity and imperfectivity can be implied by English verbs and, second, that the implication of perfectivity and imperfectivity may depend on whether the particular verb is used transitively or intransitively. Compare, for example, sentences like (12a) and (12b) below, in the first of which the action is perfective (hence, telic), and in the second imperfective (and atelic):

(12) a. Peter sang a song
b. Peter sang in the church choir

But, as later research into the problem in the 1970s and 1980s (to be discussed and quoted in the forthcoming chapters) would show, telicity and atelicity depend not only on whether the verb is used transitively or intransitively. They also depend on the type of the object to the verb. Consider sentence (12a) above, in which the action is perfective (hence telic), and sentence (13a), in which the action is imperfective and atelic:

(13) a. Peter sang songs
b. Peter sang a song from time to time

Furthermore, telicity and atelicity depend on the lack or presence of certain adverbials in the sentence. Compare (12a) and (13b) above. While the first sentence explicates perfectivity of the action, a certain type of adverbial complementation (in this case *from time to time*) can render it imperfective and atelic.

Thus the grounds for a strict division of verbs in English into telic and atelic appear to be rather unstable – unless separate telic and atelic meanings could be identified for every single verb. The examples above also show that the distinction between telic and atelic meanings resembles to a certain degree the contrast between transitivity and intransitivity. But while the transitive/intransitive distinction is almost always reflected in dictionaries, the telic/atelic opposition remains ignored – despite its obvious significance for the interpretation of many sentences and the fact that it has already been recognised and discussed in the literature for a long time.

The attempts to characterise verbs as reflecting aspectual distinctions projected well into the 1990s but displayed an almost total lack of consensus in linguistics with respect to the problem of verbal aspectual characteristics. To give just one example, in an extremely idiosyncratic study of the semantics of several English verbs (incompatible with the present approach) Tobin (1993) attempted to characterise verb pairs like *make/do, listen/hear, say/tell, close/shut* etc. in terms of a process/result contrast broadly equivalent to the perfective/imperfective (bounded/non-bounded) distinction, as defined in this work. Strangely enough, although the author quoted most of the relevant modern aspectological literature dealing with these issues, he failed to incorporate into his study the observations made above (and in the literature mentioned) concerning the changeability of aspectual values in English verbs, including verb pairs like *make/do, listen/hear, say/tell, close/shut*.

SOME NATIVE SPEAKERS' POINTS OF VIEW

Although in the 1960s and 1970s aspect often attracted the attention of non-English-speaking investigators of English, some native speakers' judgements at that time came closer to today's understanding of aspect. For example, Leech (1971: 4) made a distinction between 'events' and 'states' equivalent to the distinction between perfectivity and imperfectivity of situations. He made an analogy between the event/state distinction and the count/non-count opposition in nouns reminding that while the latter is of a grammatical nature (it has to do with the rules of using the article and some other formal rules), the former is of a semantic nature and concerns lexical meanings of verbs only. Two sentences adduced by Leech exemplify the interrelationship between his categories 'event' and 'state' and the perfective/imperfective opposition. The verb *remember* in (14a) below is an 'event' verb while in (14b) it is a 'state' verb:

(14) a. Suddenly I remembered the letter
     b. I shall remember that moment until I die

Earlier, M.Joos (1964) had used the terms 'process' verbs and 'status' verbs to refer to more or less the same notions. Of course, the term 'process' turned out inappropriate, for it was later employed to refer to imperfective situations: either to an activity carried out at a particular point or period (as with the English Progressive) or to an activity or state developing over a more extended and indefinite, non-bounded stretch of time (cf., e.g., Bach 1981; Bybee et al 1994: 55; Bartsch

1995: 7, 13, 31, ff.; Moens 1987: 42-43, to quote but a few).[10] Bounded situations denoted by 'process' verbs in the Simple Past Tense did not, however, escape Joos' attention who identified them as an expedient for advancing the plot, for pushing the narrative forward. Later Forsyth (1970: 10) argued in a similar vein with respect to Russian perfective verbs. As Joos put it, while the grammar of the English verb has "afforded no devices at all for doing the same job" (Joos 1964: 129), *be + -ing* forms, conversely, serve as the background for actions carrying the narrative forward (Joos 1964: 126-137).

Similar views, rejecting the availability of means for the explication of perfectivity in English, were held by F.Palmer (1965). According to him, there is only a certain **tendency** for the action in sentences like (15a) below, in contrast to (15b), to be perceived as completed (Palmer 1965: 79):

(15)   a. I painted the table this morning
        b. I was painting the table this morning

Or, in other words, both Joos and Palmer insisted that the Simple Past Tense in English (they used different terms to refer to it) is incapable of expressing the perfectivity of a situation by itself. This, according to the approach assumed in this book, is a correct statement. As noted by Dušková (1983: 20), it is clear, for example, that sentences like (16a) and (16b) below both refer to perfective actions. Combined in (16c), however, they become imperfective, and broadly equivalent or similar in meaning to a sentence like (16d) with a verb in the Progressive:

(16)   a. He wrote the letter
        b. I checked the addresses
        c. While he wrote the letters, I checked the addresses
        d. While he was writing the letters, I was checking the addresses

But it should be noted also that the opposite view, namely, that the Simple Past Tense in English is an exponent of perfectivity, is not without advocates – cf. Smith (1991) whose theses will be discussed later in the book.

Let us consider this point in some more detail. Aspectologists in the 1960s either ignored or exaggerated the influence of tense on the explication of the aspectual value in a given sentence in English. Recall that verbs that often refer to a state can be put in a sentence expressing an event (14a), and verbs that seem to be marked members of the group of 'state' verbs, can refer to perfective situations in certain sentences or contexts like (10a):

(14)   a. Suddenly I remembered the letter
(10)   a. He suddenly hated that man

---

[10] As often noted (see, e.g., Danchev 1976; Dahl 1981; Brinton 1988: 4-5; Binnick 1991: 179), terminological confusion and even chaos have always been characteristic of aspectological studies.

Tense can here be found to promote the explication of perfectivity because if these two sentences are changed into (14a') and (10a'), i.e., with verbs in the Simple Present, they tend to explicate imperfectivity, at least in the normal, repetitive (non-past) interpretation of the sentence:

(14) a'. Suddenly I remember the letter
(10) a'. He suddenly hates that man

Conversely, verbs that seem to be strongly telic and 'event'-denoting can also signify imperfective actions/situations. This ought to be regarded as a general rule of English grammar valid in most cases when a Simple Present Tense form of a verb of this type is used, for the following reason. Typically, the Present is incompatible with the expression of perfective actions, unless the event described is repetitive, conditional or related to the future. Compare the sentence (17a) below, where the event is non-bounded, with the sentences in (17b) and (17c), where the prototypical non-bounded interpretation of the Simple Present Tense verb form is cancelled and a conditional or futurate perfective meaning obtains in the subordinate clause:

(17) a. John gets up late
      b. If John gets up early, wake me up
      c Wake me up when John gets up

The unbounding feature of the Present Tense could even be raised to the status of a universal or near-universal regularity. In Bulgarian, certain types of clauses and simple sentences preclude the use of a perfective verb. Thus sentence (18a) with a perfective verb below is not just "non-grammatical to a large degree" which is the usual case of non-grammaticality; it is an absolutely impossible sentence. Compare, however, sentences of type (18b), (18c) and (18d), in which the perfective verb implies repetition, conditional modality and a future action, respectively, and which are fully grammatical, normal and even common:

(18) a. *Ivan   stane$_{pfv}$
          Ivan   stands up
      b. Ivan   e   nerven   –   tu   stane$_{pfv}$,   tu   sedne$_{pfv}$
          Ivan   is   nervous   –   once   stands up,   once   sits down
          'Ivan is nervous – keeps standing up and sitting down'
      c. Ako   staneš$_{pfv}$ rano,   obadi   se$_{pfv}$
          If   rise-you   early,   call   *prt.*
          'If you get up early, call'
      d. Kogato   staneš$_{pfv}$,   obadi   se$_{pfv}$
          When   rise-you,   call   *prt.*
          'When you get up, call'

Note that the Bulgarian perfective Present is only allowed in special syntactic environments – for example, there must be two conjoined perfective verbs, as in (18b), or a verb in a subordinate clause of a conditional or futurate meaning, as in (18c) and (18d). In any case, the English translation equivalents of (18c) and (18d) above again show that the general rule of English grammar precluding the explication of perfectivity in the Simple Present Tense does not hold in cases involving conditional or futurate meaning in a subordinate clause.

To conclude this section of the chapter, let us review the point of view of some other native speakers studying English aspect. Although some of the ideas of Allen (1966) are hardly acceptable from a contemporary aspectological standpoint, his observations on the meanings of nouns without quantifiers, articles or other markers of nominal determination are worth taking into account. According to him, separate nouns in English, as well as whole verb-noun phrases are analysable in both spatial and temporal terms (Allen 1966: 195-197). Following a thesis in an often quoted article revealing important characteristics of aspect in French (Garey 1957), Allen noted that the introduction of a verb-complementing element (object, adverbial) into the sentence may be crucial to the explication of the perfective/imperfective distinction. Thus if a phrase like *play bridge* signifies non-boundedness, phrases like *play a rubber of bridge* and *play a card* denote 'extended' and 'momentary' boundedness, respectively. Unfortunately, these valuable observations did not develop into generalisations. For example, there could hardly be an essential difference between phrases denoting extended and momentary types of boundedness. Both *play a rubber of bridge* and *play a card* constitute events taking a definite stretch of time and the 'extended' nature of *play a rubber of bridge* with respect to *play a card* may be meaningful from a general semantic or a pragmatic point of view, but not grammatically (compare the discussion of the Bulgarian sentences (9a) and (9b) above). However, despite some inconsistencies, Allen's contribution to aspectual theory is to be recognised as essential with the explanation of certain space-time relationships rendered through the meanings of verbs and nouns. Also, it is Allen who is considered to have introduced the term 'bounded', widely used today in the description of aspectological mechanisms.

SOME MORE SLAVIC INVESTIGATIONS OF ENGLISH ASPECT

Aspect distinctions in English continued to draw the interest of Slavic linguists in the 1970s. Recognising the role of the verb's environment for the expression of various situations, Danchev (1974) asserted the presence of aspectual characteristics in a specific, morphologically defined, class of English verbs, with Bulgarian serving as the background for his analysis. He assigned perfectivity to the group of so-called de-adjectival *-en* verbs (*to darken*, etc.), thus establishing a connection between the formal (word-formation) structure of these verbs and aspect distinctions. But if a connection of this kind really existed, a problem would arise concerning the identification of the formal correspondences in English of many other perfective verbs in Bulgarian or in any other Slavic language. It is clear that the translation equivalents in Bulgarian of the so-called de-adjectival -*en* verbs in English constitute a fairy restricted group of lexemes, as the author himself admitted:

> "Naturally, in Modern English there are many verbs with a perfective meaning which are not marked in any formal way, e.g. *hit, take, bring* and many others"

(Danchev 1974: 24). But if this thesis is correct, would it not suggest that for the expression of perfectivity and imperfectivity in English, and in any other language like English, systemic, not peripheral devices ought to be sought?

Danchev made some valuable observations on context-dependency in the explication of aspect in English. Certain sentences, like (19) below, can receive a dual interpretation according to the way the addressee conceives of a situation described (i.e., depending on the viewpoint of the observer/speaker).

(19) a. The river deepened
     b. The lake widened
     c. The forest thickened

This point is worth noting. Modern aspectological studies tend to ignore the fact that, as already seen in many of the examples above, practically all simple sentences in English of the type considered here can have more than one aspectual reading in terms of the perfective/imperfective distinction. But as far as Danchev's thesis is concerned, the author focused on another aspect of the aspect mechanism in English that is also often ignored: the necessity to isolate an aspectually neutral context to determine correctly the aspectual reading of an English sentence. This necessity was later discussed by Moens (1987: 94) who realised the need for a null context to define the aspectual characteristics of verbs and specified conditions for the assignment of a basic aspectual value to verbs or verb phrases. However, as pointed out by Glasbey (1994: 238-239), the procedure of assigning basic aspectual values to verbs can be seen as arbitrary in a large number of cases. What Danchev especially emphasised concerning the need to isolate a neutral aspectual context is that, on the one hand, adverbials determining the manner of the action and its duration should be eliminated. On the other hand, many properties of the referents of the subject, and in many cases of the object, ought to be taken into account.

In a larger study of aspect in English, Danchev and Alexieva (1974) proposed so-called correlation models of the translation of the English Simple Past Tense into Bulgarian. Their analysis revealed certain regularities in the translation of the English Simple Past Tense through the Aorist or the Imperfect in Bulgarian. Their conclusion was that a number of factors have to do with the expression of aspect. For example, the formal structure and the lexical meaning of the subject and the object in the sentence, the use of personal and non-personal pronouns, certain semantic features like, e.g., 'animate' and 'inanimate', sometimes the article or the distinction between definite and indefinite plurality may influence the aspectual reading of a particular sentence. The results of the study were later quoted in an article by Danchev (1976) who proposed three important generalisations:

a) the adverbial is the strongest aspect marker in English;
b) aspect markers in English occupy a large stretch of the discourse;
c) aspect can be analysed as a unified conceptual category which finds various formal expression in the different languages.

In the past it was common for investigators of English to base their ideas about English aspectual contrasts on the notion of aspect in Slavic languages where, in contrast to languages like English, aspect is expressed entirely through the verb in the sentence. But the approach to aspect in which it is regarded as a category located solely or mainly in the verb not only in the Slavic languages but even in English reveals itself to be an entirely wrong one and linguists proved unable to overcome it until as late as the end of the 1960s. One of its last followers was M.Ridjanović, who made a comparative analysis of aspect distinctions in English and Serbo-Croatian in his 1969 dissertation, published later in 1976 (Ridjanović 1969/1976). Verbs, according to him, possess what he calls intrinsic aspect both in English and in Serbo-Croatian, but in Serbo-Croatian aspect is formally marked. Albeit in a rather fragmentary way, Ridjanović actually managed to describe an important part of the mechanism for the expression of perfectivity and imperfectivity in English. He showed how non-count nouns and nouns unaccompanied by an article, as well as count nouns unaccompanied by an article in the plural, functioning as objects in the sentence, are capable of changing the aspect of the sentence (Ridjanović 1976: 55-56). This can be seen when comparing the ungrammaticality of a sentence like (20b) below with the grammaticality of (20b):

(20) a. *He drank up milk for breakfast
b. He drank milk for breakfast

The difference between his sentences in (21) below also reveals aspectual nuances. If (21a) could refer to both a perfective or an imperfective action, compared to (21b) it much more easily allows an imperfective interpretation:

(21) a. He gave orders
b. He gave an order

It turns out then that, first, there is incompatibility between the completion/perfectivity of an action denoted by an expression like *drank up* and the quantitative indefiniteness/non-boundedness of the substance denoted by the object *milk* in (20a) which is represented by a noun unaccompanied by an article and other determiners or quantifiers. Second, there exists an interdependency: on the one hand, between a plural, unquantified object-NP without an article and the imperfectivity of an action/situation, and, on the other hand, between an object-NP with an article and the perfectivity of an action/situation.

Furthermore, Ridjanović noticed a similar interdependency in the subject. If a sentence like *Noise entered*, constructed by the author, is slightly changed, so that sentences like (22a) and (22b) below can be contrasted, it can easily be seen that, for example, while the sentence with the subject with no article tends to explicate imperfectivity, the sentence with the subject containing an article tends to explicate perfectivity.

(22) a. Noise was heard
b. A noise was heard

And if the metalanguage test is employed, (22a) will definitely be the translation equivalent of Bulgarian (23a), where an imperfective verb in the Imperfect is used, whereas (22b) will definitely be the translation equivalent of Bulgarian (23b), where a perfective verb in the Aorist is used:

(23) a. Čuvaše se$_{impfvImp}$ šum
Heard *prt.pass.* noise
'Noise was heard'
b. Ču se$_{pfvAor}$ šum
Heard *prt.pass.* noise
'A noise was heard'

With the observations described above, Ridjanović touched upon the very essence of the mechanism of denoting perfectivity and imperfectivity in English but failed to reach the appropriate generalisations. None of the scholars discussed so far and no other linguist working in the field of aspectology until the beginning of the 1970s managed to suggest an adequate solution of the problem of aspect in English. In spite of a large number of correct observations and conclusions made, aspect had until then remained a major mystery in linguistics. And the lack of an adequate approach towards aspect distinctions in "aspectless" languages like English hampered the investigations of "aspect" languages, due to the impossibility of making an appropriate parallel between the expression of aspect at the level of the isolated verb and at the level of the sentence.

It was in 1971 that Henk Verkuyl, a Dutch linguist, managed to give a correct solution to the aspect problem in languages like Dutch and English in his dissertation, published a year later (Verkuyl 1971/1972). But even after the appearance of his work, the connection between aspect in Slavic and aspect in non-Slavic languages was to remain unclear for a long time in linguistics. Verkuyl's theory is to be discussed in detail in the forthcoming chapters of this book. But in order to follow the chronology in the development of research on English aspect properly, it will now be necessary to pay due attention to an earlier short philosophical composition that made the strongest impact in the history of aspectology.

CHAPTER 2

VENDLER'S CLASSIFICATION OF SITUATIONS, AND THE PROBLEM OF ITS INTERPRETATION

Studies on aspect in English and many other languages in the last two decades have drawn heavily upon a classification of verbs and phrases which sprang up between the 1940s and 1960s in the writings of three scholars (Ryle 1949; Vendler 1957; Kenny 1963). In his article on verbal aspect in French, Garey (1957) also addressed many of the issues associated with the classification – which dealt mainly with the meanings of verbs and verb phrases in conjunction with their behaviour towards adverbials of time and the Progressive. As already seen in the discussion of Voroncova's and Ivanova's works, the idea of grouping verbs in English according to their aspectual characteristics had been hanging in the air for a long time, and was also tackled by non-native linguists. The origin of the idea could even be dated much further back, to the Old Greeks. Aristotle noticed that some verbs contained in their meaning a goal or result of the action denoted while other verbs did not. Today it is usually Vendler's classification that is considered to be the best one, and, in studies of aspect and similar problems, it is his name that is most often associated with classifying verbs and verb phrases according to their aspectual properties. The curious thing is that the three scholars, Ryle, Vendler and Kenny, were primarily interested in the philosophical implications of the language data they explored, and the importance of their work for linguistics and aspectology in particular came to be properly understood many years later. On the other hand, as Mourelatos put it:

> "the distinctions they [Kenny and Vendler] sought to articulate had long been studied by linguists under the heading of verb aspect"

(Mourelatos 1981: 194). But this is not to say that an equivalence or a close link between **verbal** aspect and Vendler's classification was later taken for granted in aspectology, or that it is usually taken for granted today.

AN OVERVIEW OF VENDLER'S CLASSIFICATION

Vendler's classification consists of four groups, also called schemata.

Group One. Most verbs and phrases in this group express feelings, mental attitudes or things like possession, presence of a particular property or properties in a subject or object, activities characteristic of a subject for an extended period of time, more or less permanent relationships between the referents of subjects and objects in the sentence. Vendler named these entities 'states'. Below is a list of Vendler's examples of 'states' which are given along with their Bulgarian counterparts. The reasons why the Bulgarian counterparts are given are explained below, after the description of the four schemata.

Here is the list of 'states' and their Bulgarian counterparts:

English	Bulgarian
know	znaja$_{impfv}$
believe	vjarvam$_{impfv}$
think	mislja$_{impfv}$
love/hate	običam$_{impfv}$/mrazja$_{impfv}$
dominate/rule	dominiram$_{impfv}$/upravljavam$_{impfv}$
have/possess	imam$_{impfv}$/pritežavam$_{impfv}$
desire/want	želaja$_{impfv}$/iskam$_{impfv}$
like/dislike	haresvam$_{impfv}$/ne haresvam$_{impfv}$
be married/healthy/ill	ženen/zdrav/bolen săm$_{impfv}$
be present/absent	prisăstvam$_{impfv}$/otsăstvam$_{impfv}$
be hard/yellow	tvărd/žălt săm$_{impfv}$
work for a company	rabotja$_{impfv}$ văv firma
play chess	igraja$_{impfv}$ šah
smoke	puša$_{impfv}$
paint	risuvam$_{impfv}$/bojadisvam$_{impfv}$
write books	piša$_{impfv}$ knigi
catch dogs	lovja$_{impfv}$ kučeta
drive a cab	karam$_{impfv}$ taksi

Note that verbs or phrases like *think*, *play chess*, *paint*, etc. are viewed as states not generally but in one of their possible meanings: for example, when the action denoted is valid for a longer non-bounded period of time and/or constitutes a characteristic feature of the referent of a subject.

Group Two. Vendler named these verbs and phrases 'activities'. According to him:

"the concept of activities calls for periods of time that are not unique or definite"

However, since uniqueness and definiteness apparently stand for boundedness (see also Group Three below), the lack of this feature unites activities and states into imperfectives. Below is the list of all or most of the examples of activities that Vendler used:

English	Bulgarian
pull/push a cart	teglja$_{impfv}$/tikam$_{impfv}$ količka
draw	risuvam$_{impfv}$ s moliv
swim/walk/run	pluvam$_{impfv}$/vărvja$_{impfv}$/bjagam$_{impfv}$
work	rabotja$_{impfv}$

play chess	igraja$_{impfv}$ šah
smoke	puša$_{impfv}$
write	piša$_{impfv}$
drive a cab	karam$_{impfv}$ taksi
think	mislja$_{impfv}$
paint	risuvam$_{impfv}$/bojadisvam$_{impfv}$

It is clear from the lists of states and activities that the same verb or verb phrase very often can be a state as well as an activity. This is hardly surprising, for one may drive a taxi, i.e. be a taxi driver, but one may also drive a taxi on a particular occasion even without being a taxi driver. One may smoke, i.e. be a smoker, but one may also smoke on a particular occasion without being a smoker. This holds for most other activities like playing chess, thinking or swimming. Hence, in many cases verbs and verb phrases can be used in a paradoxical manner. As Vendler pointed out,

> "*He thinks that Jones is a rascal* might be said truthfully of someone who is sound asleep"

Vendler (1957). Compare the English sentence (24a) and its Bulgarian equivalent (24b):

(24) a. Smith, who is now sleeping, thinks that Jones is a rascal
 b. Smit, kojto sega spi$_{impfv}$, misli$_{impfv}$, če Džouns e mošenik
 Smith who now sleeps thinks that Jones is rascal

However, the use of identical tense-aspect verb forms (*spi*$_{impfv}$ 'sleeps' and *misli*$_{impfv}$ 'thinks' are Present Tense forms of imperfective verbs) in the Bulgarian translation (24b) shows that it is not the Progressive that makes such a statement possible in English. The distinction between a state and an activity in the meanings of verbs and verb phrases plays a significant role in language communication and can be identified in any language. Furthermore, these two aspectual values can be changed depending on the use of verbs and verb phrases in particular contexts. Hence, the distinction in question could be said to be only partly reflected in grammar, viz. in sentence structure. Compare the two simultaneous activities in the example (17c), already given. The meaning observed in (17c) is equivalent, at least in one of the possible interpretations of the sentence, to the meaning observed in sentence (17d):

(17) c. While he wrote the letters, I checked the addresses
 d. While he was writing the letters, I was checking the addresses

That is, activities are not necessarily always expressed through the Progressive in English.

Group Three. Below is the list of the verbs and verb phrases that Vendler named accomplishments:

English	Bulgarian
give/attend a class	iznesa$_{pfv}$/posetja$_{pfv}$ urok
deliver a sermon	iznesa$_{pfv}$ propoved
build a house	postroja$_{pfv}$ kăšta
make a chair	napravja$_{pfv}$ stol
write a letter/a novel	napiša$_{pfv}$ pismo/roman
read a novel	pročeta$_{pfv}$ roman
catch a dog	ulovja$_{pfv}$ kuče
draw a circle	narisuvam$_{pfv}$ krăg
paint a picture	narisuvam$_{pfv}$ kartina [s boi]
push a cart	pritikam$_{pfv}$ količka
run a mile	probjagam$_{pfv}$ edna milja
play a game of chess	izigraja$_{pfv}$ partija šah
grow up	porasna$_{pfv}$
recover from illness	văzstanovja se$_{pfv}$ ot bolest
get ready (for something)	prigotvja se$_{pfv}$ za nešto

Accomplishments, according to Vendler,

> "imply the notion of unique and definite time periods"

In other words, in contrast to states and activities, whose time stretches are non-bounded, accomplishments are situated on bounded intervals of time. The beginning of the interval is definite but remains in many cases implicit. The action of an accomplishment is terminated after the attainment of a goal implicitly or explicitly given in the lexical meaning of the verb and/or in the overall meaning of the phrase. (It would be useful to compare the notion of telicity discussed above).

Group Four. Vendler named the following English verbs and phrases (listed together with their Bulgarian counterparts) achievements:

English	Bulgarian
know (suddenly)	razbera$_{pfv}$
realise	osăznaja$_{pfv}$
recognise	poznaja$_{pfv}$
spot	zabeleža$_{pfv}$
reach the summit	dostigna$_{pfv}$ vărha
win the race	spečelja$_{pfv}$ nadbjagvaneto
lose/find	izgubja$_{pfv}$/namerja$_{pfv}$
cross the border	preseka$_{pfv}$ granicata
start/resume/stop	započna$_{pfv}$/văzstanovja$_{pfv}$/spra$_{pfv}$
be born/die	rodja se$_{pfv}$/umra$_{pfv}$
get married	oženja se$_{pfv}$

Achievements, according to Vendler,

> "involve unique and definite instants"

These situations denote transitions from one state into another at a particular moment and, hence, create problems for the analysis of the sentences they are used in. Unlike accomplishments, they refer to moments, not to periods (intervals), and as such they are necessarily bounded.

VENDLER'S CLASSIFICATION AND THE SLAVIC POINT OF VIEW

The reason why Slavic counterparts are given in the present discussion of Vendler's classification is at least two-fold. Vendler's classification has had very little, if any, influence on studies of aspect in Slavic languages on the part of native investigators. This is because, as a rule, native speakers of a Slavic language, including linguists, think of a particular verb expression as one that is strictly perfective or strictly imperfective, and not, as in Vendler's classification, where generally a particular expression, being a state or an activity, on the one hand, or an accomplishment or an achievement, on the other, **tends** to denote either perfectivity or imperfectivity but generally has different aspectual readings. And if verbs and verb phrases in Vendler's classification can always express more than one of the four possible situations, they are not overtly, grammatically, marked for aspect like the verbs in the Slavic languages. Hence, a question arises about how the idea of Vendler's schemata should be conveyed in Slavic. If one is to try to find a parallel phenomenon in Slavic, where a verb or a verb phrase has a particular situational meaning not marked in the verb, one seems to have two options: to point either to a biaspectual verb, i.e., a verb not marked for aspect,[1] or to an aspectual pair. Since the first option is available with a relatively restricted number of verbs, the second option has been felt to be the natural one by most Slavic linguists. It has turned out to be the wrong one, however, as will become clear below.

The first two groups (or schemata, in Vendler's terms) represent non-bounded situations and the second two groups represent bounded situations. This is easily manifested here by the Bulgarian equivalents which contain imperfective verbs in the former two cases and perfective verbs in the latter two cases. Of course, the four schemata are types of realisations of verb meanings, not merely lists of verbs and verb phrases. This is the reason why occasionally the same verb or phrase is listed in different groups: *know* can be a state ('hold in memory') and also an achievement ('suddenly understand'); *work, think, drive* and many other verbs of similar meaning typically denote or imply states and activities; *write, smoke, paint* etc. can be

---

[1] These verbs, present in all Slavic languages, usually have a couple of most typical endings (*-iram* or *-iziram* and *-vam* in Bulgarian, *-irovat'* in Russian). And the prevailing majority of these verbs, not surprisingly, represents borrowings from the three major Western languages, English, German and French, or, more generally speaking, from the international, mostly Latin-based, lexicon. Here belong hundreds of verbs of intellectual or technical activities like *organise* (Bulg. *organiziram*, Russian *organizirovat'*), *plan* (Bulg. *planiram* and *planuvam*, Russ. *planirovat'*), *electrify* (Bulg. *elektrificiram*, Russ. *elektrificirovat'*), etc.

associated with the expression of states, activities and, given an appropriate complement, accomplishments. Certain lexical entities could even partake of the characteristics of all four schemata, e.g. *push a cart* could be a state, an activity, an accomplishment or an achievement depending on the circumstances to be denoted by the phrase. The possibility for one of the four schemata to be activated in a particular verb or phrase used in a particular utterance is contained in the lexical meaning of the verb or the meaning of the whole phrase. The meaning of a whole verb phrase is composed as a combination of the lexical meanings of the words taking part in it but it is not necessarily a simple sum of the lexical meanings of the words. In most cases a particular verb or phrase has one basic, representative situational meaning – which sends the verb or phrase in question into one of the four schemata. For instance, most verbs expressing feelings basically denote states – consider the usual normal way verbs like *love* or *hate* are used. But in certain types of sentences or in a larger specific context these verbs are capable of expressing achievements, i.e., they may refer to a change of the emotional attitude – from a neutral state into the one denoted, as in the sentence (10a) already used earlier:

(10) a. He suddenly hated that man

In contrast, other verbs, like for example *lose* or *find*, have a basic 'achievement' meaning. But in a habitual context they acquire a 'state' reading:

(25) a. Kate always lost her pencils
 b. John often found Peter in the pub

It can be, and has already been, argued that "basic meanings" of verbs and verb phrases manifest themselves in certain conditions that are to be regarded as typical and neutral. For example if *die* and *cross the border* are predominantly achievements, used in the Progressive, they turn into processes (or, in Vendler's terms, 'activities'):

(26) a. The old man was dying
 b. When we were crossing the border, it started to rain

It is not only the Progressive that can change the type of realisation of the meaning of a verb or verb phrase. This can also be effected by the Simple Present Tense in which accomplishment and achievement verbs and verb phrases (viewed as such when isolated) are typically unable in most simple sentences to express their basic situational meaning. The reason for this is the general semantics and the rules governing the use of the Simple Present Tense itself which typically denotes situations that are habitual or habitual-like, or at least consist of indefinitely repeated states or actions. A similar phenomenon has already been noted for the Bulgarian Present Tense. Perfective verbs in it cannot be used with a non-repetitive meaning, as in the non-grammatical sentence (18a), in contrast to the grammatical sentence (18b) which denotes indefinite repetition:

(18) a. *Ivan stane_pfv
       Ivan stands up
    b. Ivan e   nerven – tu   stane_pfv, tu   sedne_pfv
       Ivan is nervous – once stands up, once sits down
       'Ivan is nervous – keeps standing up and sitting down'

Therefore, neither the Progressive, nor the Simple Present Tense in English can serve to indicate properly to which schema a particular verb or a verb phrase belongs.

Let us at this point consider again the reasons why Vendler's schemata are not popular in Slavic linguistics. The problem for the Slavic linguist is that, even if they are familiar with Vendler's classification, they fail to transfer the regularities into his mother tongue. And he fails to transfer them because he finds that, for example, any of the verbs or verb phrases that are classified as accomplishments or achievements, can be translated with either a perfective or an imperfective verb. This presents itself as the natural solution and as sufficient evidence that, if Vendler's classes are valid (presumably they are valid if they have drawn the attention of so many aspectologists), then Slavic aspect is a phenomenon that cannot be described in terms of a classification like Vendler's. What the Slavic linguist should actually do to understand the implications of Vendler's schemata for Slavic aspect seems easy at first sight. It is to assign imperfectivity to Vendler's states and activities and perfectivity to Vendler's accomplishments and achievements. This is what has already been done here, but it is also precisely what Slavic linguists have been reluctant to do! The underlying assumption probably runs like this: if perfectivity is assigned to a phrase like *read a novel*, it ought to translate into a Slavic language **always** through a perfective verb. If *read* (in isolation, not complemented with an object) is taken to express imperfectivity, it ought to translate **always** through an imperfective verb – which, of course, is not the case. And the assumption appears otherwise perfectly reasonable – because if English lacks verbal aspect and if Vendler's schemata represent aspectual distinctions, then there would be a one-to-one correspondence between states/activities and imperfectivity and accomplishments/achievements and perfectivity. But there isn't – is the argument of the Slavic aspectologist. Because, for instance, English *read a novel* translates into both perfective (Bulgarian) *da pročeta roman* and the imperfective *četa roman*, while *read* often translates as not only the perfective *da pročeta* (which is strictly transitive, and this seems to corroborate Vendler's thesis) but also as another, delimitative, perfective (*da početa* 'read for some time')[2]. The conclusion follows that all this either strongly undermines Vendler's enterprise or shows that it is just a semantic one having little to do with aspect proper, overtly and elegantly represented in Slavic.

---

[2] More on the delimitative later on, see Chapter Thirteen, *On aspectual classes in English*.

The failure on the part of Slavic linguists to see the significance of Vendler's schemata is actually the Slavic counterpart of the dogma that whatever aspect is, it is to be directly observed, unequivocally expressed and marked by its own exponents. Dogmas have to do with allegiance to authority and obstinacy in the face of facts. Authority, in this case, is personified by the linguists who have failed to overcome their obstinacy and see what was a very easy thing to see – if one looked at it from a slightly different angle. And the facts are that Vendler's first two schemata do, indeed, equal imperfectivity, and the second two schemata do equal perfectivity, if viewed as prototypes, not as exemplars. The easy thing that the Slavic linguist has failed to do was take Vendler's four schemata for granted, unite them into two groups, perfectives (accomplishments and achievements) and imperfectives (states and activities), and then equate these two groups with the two basic Slavic aspectual schemata, perfectivity and imperfectivity. Although the procedure below repeats what has already been done, it is carried out again for methodological reasons: to show that, first, **the schemata are to be equalled**, as in Table 1 below, not verbs and verb phrases divorced from the schemata.

Table 1

Vendler's aspectual schemata		Slavic aspectual schemata	
perfective	**imperfective**	**perfective**	**imperfective**
accomplishments	states		
achievements	activities		

And, second, only after the schemata have been equalled, does it remain for the language instances of the schemata to be equalled, as is done in Table 2 below. Provisionally, the Bulgarian aspectually adequate equivalents of the English states, activities, accomplishments, and achievements can be assigned the same situational values.

Table 2

Language instances of Vendler's aspectual schemata	Language instances of Slavic aspectual schemata
Perfective	**Perfective**
accomplishments	accomplishments
write a letter/read a novel	napiša pismo/pročeta roman
catch a dog/draw a circle	ulovja kuče/narisuvam krăg
achievements	achievements
spot	zabeleža
reach the summit	dostigna vărha
win the race	spečelja nadbjagvaneto
lose/find	izgubja/namerja
Imperfective	**Imperfective**
states	states
believe/love/hate	vjarvam/običam/mrazja
have/possess	imam/pritežavam
like/dislike	haresvam/ne haresvam
be married/healthy/ill	ženen/zdrav/bolen săm
work for a company	rabotja văv firma
smoke/work/write	puša/rabotja/piša
write books	piša knigi
activities	activities
play chess	igraja šah
smoke/write/work	puša/piša/rabotja

Such a solution has not been reached in Slavic linguistics. Or at least in so far as there have been attempts to apply Vendler's schemata to Slavic languages (see, e.g., Hoepelman 1981; Smith 1991; Mellor 1995), the correspondences do not follow a pattern similar to the one given here. For example, in his study of the Russian verbal aspect Hoepelman wrote:

> "I started from the same assumption [...]: there are aspects like in the Slavic ones somewhere hidden in languages like Dutch, English and German and if we have a precise explanation of whatever it is that makes the verbs behave as they do, we will be able to give a unified system for the Slavic as well as for at least some non-Slavic verb systems [...]. It remains to be seen, however, whether this hypothesis can be retained upon closer inspection of the data of Russian"

(Hoepelman (1981: 18). Later on in his book, however, although Hoepelman took Vendler's schemata to be a fairly universal phenomenon that could be reflected in

any language, he did not establish a close correspondence between Vendler's schemata and Russian aspect. For him, Russian verbs can be, for example, accomplishments whether they are perfective (e.g. *opravit's'a*$_{pfv}$ 'recover', *zakryt'*$_{pfv}$ 'close') or imperfective (e.g. *opravl'at's'a*$_{impfv}$ 'recover', *zakryvat'*$_{impfv}$ 'close'). For detail, see Hoepelman (1981: 125-126); cf. the similar theses in Smith (1991) and Mellor (1995).

Lastly, and unfortunately, dogma is something many stick to without any reason, and to the detriment of the community. Dogmas often take ages, literally or metaphorically, and enormous efforts to dispel. This book represents one such effort and the community in question is the linguistic one.[3]

SMITH'S MODEL OF ASPECT

Furthermore, even if there has been a relative consensus in linguistics about the perfective/imperfective (or bounded/non-bounded) distinction as a basic one, the study of English aspect has been carried out in different, often idiosyncratic, ways. One instance of a specific understanding of aspect along the lines of Vendler's classification can be found in Smith (1991). According to Smith's model, aspect, first, is not so much a feature of situations presented in language, as a choice speakers can or must make. Second, a basis for positing a universal perfective/imperfective aspectual distinction is not boundedness and non-boundedness of situations but the English Progressive/Non-Progressive contrast. Smith simply equates what she calls the perfective view, a basic aspectual value, with non-progressive verb forms in English and the imperfective viewpoint, the opposite basic aspectual value, with the Progressive. Such a model could be seen as an attempt for a rather outdated kind of view maintained a long time ago by, e.g., Hirtle (1967), to be revived. Vendler's four classes, plus another class, semelfactives (momentary non-achievement events like *tap* or *knock*), proposed by Smith herself, are 'situation types' that constitute the second component in a so-called two-component theory of aspect. Viewpoint (perfective or imperfective), the first component, is imposed on

---

[3] An anonymous reviewer of this work was unhappy with the stress laid on the several-decades-long misunderstanding of aspectual phenomena by the linguistic community (defined here as dogmatism). But if today a large number of linguists do regard aspect as a distinction between perfectivity and imperfectivity (boundedness and non-boundedness) and view it as a phenomenon present in all languages, in the 1970s the conjecture that the structure of English features a perfective/imperfective distinction largely identical to that in the Slavic languages sounded like a heresy in most linguistic circles. It is a well-known fact today that Vendler's and similar classifications, some published as early as the late 1940s, were not properly understood (in aspectological terms) until the 1980s. Verkuyl's (1971) work, regarded today as a major contribution in the field (to be dealt with later), remained grossly misunderstood and underestimated throughout the 1970s and even in the 1980s, and, as will be shown in this book, many of its major theses remain misunderstood to the present day. On the other hand, many aspectologists still disagree dramatically on a large number of issues. The history of misunderstanding is probably worth investigating (elsewhere) in more detail. Is the reason behind the current advances in aspectology that progress in theoretical linguistics in the recent decades allowed a much better understanding of certain language phenomena? Or is it because gradually more and more scholars somehow came to be convinced that, after all, "there is aspect in English"?

the situation type – the situation type being of a primarily lexical nature, and viewpoint marked grammatically.

Though more peripherally, a similar (and similarly idiosyncratic) view can be found in other works as well, for example, Langacker's (1987/1991). Though in Langacker's work, aspect is by far not the basic object of interest, for him not only achievements and accomplishments, activities, too, are 'perfective'. Hence, firstly, imperfectives occur in the Simple Present Tense, but not in the Progressive (Langacker 1991: 86), and secondly:

> "a perfective process portrays a situation as changing through time, while an imperfective process describes the extension through time of a stable situation"

(Langacker 1991: 86). These definitions, the author admits, have nothing to do with the identically termed Slavic phenomena. Still, at the lexical level, the author distinguishes between 'canonical perfectives' like *jump, kick, learn, explode, arrive, cook, ask* and imperfectives like *resemble, have, know, want, like*, a description largely compatible with Vendler's classes (see Langacker 1991: 86).

At first sight, it makes sense to have, as in Smith's model, states, activities, semelfactives, accomplishments and achievements subjected to the progressive or the simple (non-progressive) forms of the verb that impose a grammatical meaning, whatever it is, on the primarily lexical information. Because, as is often considered to be the case, and as the author herself argues in her own specific terms, not only does the Progressive change an inherently bounded situation (e.g. an accomplishment) into a non-bounded situation – cf. below the bounded (27a) and the non-bounded (27b) – but, for example, the Simple Present, too, is able to impose its prototypical (grammatically expressed) meaning on accomplishments transforming them into non-bounded (habitual) situations, cf. (27a) and (27c).

(27) a. John read the newspaper
b. John was reading the newspaper
c. John reads the newspaper

However, certain uses of the Simple Present, as in all the sentences in (28) below, seem to have escaped Smith's attention, and, in fact, this use of the Simple Present is usually ignored in studies of the interrelationship between aspect and the present tense.

(28) a. If John reads the newspaper, call me
b. Provided John reads the newspaper, call me
c. In case John reads the newspaper, call me
d. When John reads the newspaper, call me

In each of these sentences with the Simple Present both verbs undoubtedly refer to typically bounded situations (accomplishments). One way to avoid the inconsistency in a description in which the Simple Present is defined as inherently imperfective is to state that sentences like those in (28) should be considered to represent grammatical forms homonymous with the present, e.g. a 'conditional mood', cf. the sentences in (28a), (28b), and (28c), or a special, e.g. 'futurate', use of the Simple Present, cf. the sentence in (28d).

Still, even if the specificity of these cases and their relatively restricted use are disregarded, there remains a serious problem for Smith's thesis. Are there real grounds for the Non-Progressive in general to be viewed as a category with a definite aspectual value that is imposed onto the meaning of each situation type in a specific way? According to the approach in this study, the Present Simple Tense in English and especially the abstraction called Non-Progressive should, rather, be regarded as a category with a zero or near-zero aspectual value that allows all or most sentences to acquire default aspectual meanings according to the situation type explicated in the sentence.[4] But Smith claims a universal validity for her model in which the perfective and the imperfective viewpoints are categories with definite values imposed on situation types, and draws extensive grammatical data and examples from several languages to substantiate her theses.

Smith's aspectual theory is especially interesting in so far as she discusses Russian, one of the several languages she tried to describe from an aspectual point of view. But Russian apparently also presents a serious problem, and it ties in exactly with the problem of how Vendler's classification is to be interpreted. Smith defines Russian as a language with perfective and imperfective viewpoints coinciding with the grammatically expressed perfective/imperfective distinction in verbs. But if the author could be said to have partly succeeded in equalling (albeit rather artificially) the Progressive/Non-Progressive distinction in English with the perfective/imperfective distinction through a complex semantic analytical enterprise (in which the perfective viewpoint in English is taken to somehow include endpoints of situations in non-stative expressions), she handles situation-types in Russian in a rather unconvincing way. At first she states that "the five situation types [Vendler's classes plus her own semelfactives] are covert categories in Russian" (Smith 1991: 298). In other words, it is not the case that, for example, accomplishments are perfective and activities are imperfective, but, somehow, the so-called perfective or imperfective view is imposed onto whatever is just a **preliminary** achievement, accomplishment, activity, etc.

Since perfectivity and imperfectivity (whatever their exact content) are 'viewpoints' imposed on verbs, Smith rarely ascribes situational meanings to separate verbs in Russian. In certain cases, however, verbs do get situational meanings. For example, perfective verbs like *dopisat'* 'add in writing', *nadpisat'* 'write above',

---

[4] As can be seen from some of Vendler's examples, aspect can be explicated through the interchange between an object with or without an article. For instance, *write a book* basically denotes a completed action, that is, it explicates perfectivity and is an accomplishment in Vendler's terms. Conversely, *write books* basically denotes a non-completed action, that is, it explicates imperfectivity and is either a state or an activity in Vendler's terms. Or, as we shall see later, aspect is explicated compositionally in the sentence and the 'article'/'zero article' interchange is one of the major aspects of the compositional explication of aspect. Smith (1991: 7-8) recognises the compositional mechanism of aspect but only at the level of the 'situation-type', not at the level of the 'viewpoint' (see the following chapter in this book dealing with compositional aspect theory).

opisat' 'prepare an inventory' are assigned the property of accomplishment, and a verb lie *popisat'* 'write for a while' is assigned the property of activity (Smith 1991: 316).

On the one hand, it is hardly a viable idea to consider a verb like *popisat'* as designating an activity in Vendler's terms, for *popisat'* is a verb representing a bounded action and activities are non-bounded actions – the problem of this type of verbs and the corresponding English phenomenon will be dealt with later on, in Chapter Thirteen, *On aspectual classes in English*. On the other hand, as shown peripherally by some of Smith's own argumentation and examples, if perfective verbs in Russian, **can** in fact denote accomplishments, it is but easy to find their accomplishment equivalents in English. For instance, in the case of *dopisat'*$_{pfv}$, the true equivalent is not just *add in writing* but *add something in writing*; in the case of *nadpisat'*$_{pfv}$ it is not just *write above*, but *write something above something* (or *sign something*). And, as far as the verb *opisat'*$_{pfv}$ is concerned, clearly *prepare an inventory/a catalogue* is a good equivalent, and, furthermore, having in mind that *opisat'* is a verb that can only be transitive, the true equivalence relation ought to be represented not as *opisat'* = *prepare an inventory/a catalogue* but, rather, as *opisat' čto-to* = *prepare an inventory/a catalogue of something*. And, of course, here Russian *čto-to* and its English equivalent *something* are to be taken to stand for count nouns and not for non-count or mass nouns or, in other words, are to be taken to represent specific entities linguistically encoded through a noun accompanied by an article, a determiner or a quantifier. As the review of the aspectological literature has shown so far, the presence of an object with an article to the verb in such cases tends to support the explication of perfectivity.

Hence, if a perfective transitive verb like *opisat'*$_{pfv}$ 'prepare an inventory/a catalogue' denotes an accomplishment, then clearly what its imperfective (transitive or intransitive) partner *opisyvat'*$_{impfv}$ 'catalogue' will typically denote is an activity or a state – depending on whether it is carried out at a particular place and time, as in (29a) below, or whether it obtains as a characteristic behaviour of somebody, as in (29b). Compare (29a) and (29b):

(29) a. Kogda ja uvidel$_{pfv}$ ee v biblioteke,   Vera opisyvala$_{impfv}$ knigi
   When I   saw   her in library,   Vera catalogued   books
   'When I saw her in the library, Vera was preparing a catalogue of (some) books'
   b. Vera rabotala$_{impfv}$ v biblioteke,   ona opisyvala$_{impfv}$ knigi
   Vera worked   in library,   she catalogued   books
   'Vera worked in a library, she prepared catalogues of books'

It is true that Russian aspect, and Slavic aspect in general, present serious theoretical difficulties with respect to the potential of the two aspects to express meanings in certain more or less peripheral semantico-syntactic patterns that fall outside the basic meanings of the aspects. For instance, although it should be primarily viewed as an activity or a state, the verb *opisyvat'*$_{impfv}$ 'catalogue' could be used, just like most other imperfective verbs in Russian, to refer to an accomplishment in certain cases. But can this be surprising – in view of, for example, the trivial fact that most of Vendler's verbs and verb phrases can, as already shown above, change their class according to the sentence they occur in or in the context of their use? Therefore, it can be argued that Smith's model in which aspect is treated as a result of the interaction between two major components, of which one ('viewpoint') is imposed onto another ('situational class'), is an unnecessarily complicated enterprise which cannot handle adequately the overall aspect mechanism – neither in language-specific, nor in universal terms.[5]

Furthermore, since perfective and imperfective are regarded as 'viewpoints' in Smith's work, not as values inherent in the particular verb phrase or in the sentence as a whole, the stress is (necessarily) laid on aspectual choice. Here are the three opening sentences of Chapter 10, *The Aspectual system of Russian*, written in collaboration with G.C.Rappoport, in Smith (1991):

> "Aspectual choice is salient perceptually and morphologically in Russian. The formal contrast of perfective and imperfective viewpoints appears in every finite verb form and in many non-finite verb forms as well (the imperative, infinitive, and certain participial forms). Speakers are keenly aware of aspectual choices and of their pragmatic and rhetorical effects"

(Smith 1991: 297). But native speakers of Russian, and also of the rest of the Slavic languages, whatever their education, can hardly be said to be aware of the use of aspectually different verb forms. (Which is not the case with non-native speakers of Russian who **have to** learn the subtleties of aspectual usage and are often capable of formulating them.) Slavic aspect forms are used spontaneously by the native speaker, and people with no special linguistic education, for example, are not always able to determine the aspect of a verb form, be it considered within context or out of context. Uneducated native speakers, on their part, do not have the slightest idea of what aspect is (and even educated Slavs know about aspect little more than that "it has something to do with the verb"), but this does not at all prevent them from employing in a perfectly correct manner aspectual verb forms, with their enormous complexity. It can easily be generalised that both educated and non-educated native speakers of Slavic languages practically make no mistakes with respect to aspect, unless a particular form represents a specific case of morphological complexity or irregularity. But then the mistake committed counts only in terms of the requirements of standard word-formation or grammar, not in terms of the specific encoding of aspect distinctions by a particular individual.

All this represents sufficient reason to take it that aspect is inherent in situations *per se*. Situations are either perfective or imperfective, but there can be further

---

[5] Smith's approach is followed by Mellor (1995) who goes even much further, suggesting that

> "while the English simple aspect only allows a completed event reading, the Russian perfective can have either this reading or the result state reading"

(Mellor 1995: 61). It has already been made clear that a model of this kind, assigning perfectivity to non-progressive verb forms in English and confusing aspect with the totally different category of perfect, is entirely incompatible with the approach in this book.

subdivisions from a more pragmatically-oriented point of view within the two general categories. The subdivisions, as in Vendler's classification (states and activities, on the one hand, accomplishments and achievements, on the other), are made according to whether a non-bounded situation is realised as taking place at a particular moment or period in time or whether it holds as a property of the subject, whether a bounded action is conceived of as taking time or as taking place momentaneously, etc. According to the thesis in this work, which will be developed further on in the forthcoming chapters, aspect cannot be a viewpoint imposed on situations that are regarded as states, activities, accomplishments and achievements **in advance**, as in Smith's model. Rather, states and activities are, simply, imperfective; accomplishments and achievements are, simply, perfective.[6]

ON THE SIGNIFICANCE AND THE MISUNDERSTANDING OF VENDLER'S CLASSIFICATION

But let us now return to the discussion of Vendler's own schemata. An appropriate medium for the explication of meanings of verbs and verb phrases as belonging to one or another of the schemata is the Simple Past Tense. The Simple Past Tense allows the denotation of various events, actions, states: bounded and non-bounded, repetitive and non-repetitive, with a definite or indefinite repetition. Verbs in the

---

[6] A handful of examples will suffice to show Smith's rather idiosyncratic account of Russian aspect. The author describes the Russian sentence *On napisal$_{pfv}$ pis'mo* 'He wrote a letter' as an accomplishment by saying that a perfective viewpoint is imposed on an accomplishment sentence (Smith 1991: 301). But if 'situation type' is a covert category in Russian, as the author maintained earlier (Smith 1991: 298), where does the accomplishment here arise from? Is it inherent in the perfective expression *napisat' pismo* 'write a letter', or is it somehow extracted from the imperfective expression *pisat' pis'mo* 'write a letter'? Smith does not give an answer to this question, but one could guess, because, in spite of her own contention that situation type is covert in Russian, Smith does assign situation types to verbs from time to time (as mentioned earlier) – without motivating the choice of the situation type. For example, the perfective verb *pomoč'* 'help' is for some reason held to be an activity (Smith 1991: 307), the imperfective *čitat'* 'read' is defined as an accomplishment, and the perfective *dat'* 'give' as an achievement. Indeed, different authors assign situation types to Slavic verbs differently: Klein (1995: 677), for example, assigns both the perfective *dat'* 'give' and the imperfective *davat'* 'give' an accomplishment value. More importantly, however, it can be argued that excluding the contribution of nominal complements from the analysis is to ultimately render any explanation of aspect (be it verbal or compositional aspect) insufficient. Note that assigning an accomplishment value to *čitat'* 'read' is much more implausible than assigning an accomplishment value to English *read* – for *čitat'* is an imperfective verb, while English *read* could be regarded as collocable with NPs like *a/the/this book, some/three books*, etc. that are capable of imputing an accomplishment value to the whole phrase.

Furthermore, an important issue for Russian aspect is why perfective verbs do not always signify bounded situations, and why imperfective verbs do not always signify non-bounded situations. Apparently aware of it, Smith (1991: 306) affords it no explanation. If her theory of imposing perfective and imperfective viewpoints on situation types is to be followed in an attempt at solving the issue, a third component would have to be posited, consisting of, say, a bounded and a non-bounded viewpoint, to be imposed onto a perfective or imperfective viewpoint. This issue has in fact already found a sufficiently elegant solution in Lindstedt's so-called nested aspects, in a publication quoted in Smith's book – Lindstedt (1985).

In a recent article Smith (1999: 503) made a certain correction of her 1991 system but preserved it as a whole. More on this in Chapter 13, *On Aspectual Classes in English*.

Simple Past can even refer to imperfective actions being carried out at a particular period or moment, that is, to actions typically denoted in English through the Progressive, as in the already adduced examples (17c) and (17d):

(17) c. While he wrote the letters, I checked the addresses
d. While he was writing the letters, I was checking the addresses

The semantics of the present tense in many languages reflects the speaker's intuition that the present is not fully observable – because, generally, while we are in the present we cannot view events in their entirety. Past situations can, however, be seen even in their details, or from beginning to end. Hence, the Simple Past in English is thus, to a large extent, neutral because it does not favour certain meanings at the expense of others, as is the case with the Simple Present Tense. Another suitable medium for explicating the meanings of verbs and verb phrases in Vendler's classification is the simple (non-progressive and non-perfect) infinitive. The Indefinite Future is only to a certain extent appropriate, for it often contains modal nuances (the future may be expected, but also desired, necessary, etc.) which can blur the basic meanings of verbs and verb phrases in particular sentences or contexts.

Thus Vendler's classification is not so much about verbs and verb phrases as about their basic, (proto)typical meanings. These meanings are, as a rule, explicated, not, say, in the Simple Present or in the Past Progressive Tense, but in neutral conditions among which, first and foremost, is the Simple Past Tense. Hence, in translating simple sentences with a Simple Past Tense verb form in English into a Slavic language, only the basic, the typical meanings of the English verbs and verb phrases ought to be conveyed through the corresponding aspectual verb forms. In the case of Bulgarian, these will be forms that combine the aspect of the separate lexical verb entry (perfective or imperfective) and the tense-aspect verb form – Aorist or Imperfect. That is, in denoting past actions in Bulgarian, perfective or imperfective verbs are additionally marked for either the Aorist (also called Past Completed Tense) or the Imperfect (also called Past Non-Completed Tense). However, out of the four possible verb forms derived in combining the two grammatical distinctions, basic and typical are only two of them: the perfective Aorist (for example, $izjade_{pfvAor}$ 'ate' [completely on a particular occasion]) and the imperfective Imperfect ($jadeše_{impfvImp}$ 'ate' [was in the process of eating; ate habitually]). The imperfective Aorist ($jade_{impfvAor}$ 'ate' [as when complemented with *for a minute*]) and especially the perfective Imperfect ($izjadeše_{pfvImp}$ 'ate' [a completed act indefinitely repeated]) are rather specific – and will be considered in some more detail later on in the book. But before proceeding to the translation of some English sentences into the Bulgarian (meta-)language to check the meanings of English verbs and verb phrases it is worth recalling that the explication of aspect in English depends on the presence of adverbials and certain grammatical entities in the sentence, as in sentences (10a) and (11) through (14), already used earlier.

(10) a. He suddenly hated that man
(11)   At times he wrote stories unworthy of him
(12) a. Peter sang a song
     b. Peter sang in the church choir
(13) a. Peter sang songs
     b. Peter sang a song from time to time
(14) a. Suddenly I remembered the letter
     b. I shall remember that moment until I die

Therefore, the sentences that will be used below to check the semantics of certain verbs and verb phrases ought to have a minimal structure. Ideally, they ought to have only a subject designating an agent or a bearer of a state. But, as already shown with sentences like (23a) and (23b), even the semantic structure of the subject can influence the aspectual interpretation of a sentence:

(23) a. Noise   was   heard
     b. A noise was   heard

For this reason, such type of sentences will be constructed in which, first, a subject (*X*) will be assumed to be typical of and corresponding to the prototypical meaning of the verb. Second, wherever an object to the verb is necessary for a sentence to be acceptable, this object (*Y*) will also be assumed to correspond to the prototypical meaning of the verb. Wherever it is difficult to imagine a typical subject or object, a common noun will be used.

The necessity to check the aspectual relevance of Vendler's classification against Slavic material is not maintained here just because of the tendency on the part of some linguists (including Verkuyl 1993: 49-50) to try and disprove the relevance of Vendler's classification for the study of structural aspectual meaning. These attempts are made on theoretical grounds, in order to propose a simple aspectual contrast in terms of a "pure" perfective/imperfective (be it called bounded/non-bounded, or terminative/durative, or telic/atelic, etc.) distinction. The old dogma that aspect in languages like English is not necessarily exactly the same phenomenon as the one found in the Slavic languages underlies the necessity. The dogma is, unfortunately, still shared by many, if not all, investigators of aspect, tense and similar phenomena in non-Slavic languages. As already noted, while Vendler's classification is taken to be the basis of practically all of modern Western aspectological thought, it is hardly ever used in studies of aspect in Slavic languages carried out by native (non-Western) Slavists. And when occasionally it is taken account of, this is done within a general theoretical framework and not as a basis on which Eastern-Western (e.g. Slavic-Germanic) language comparisons should be made: see, e.g., Bulygina (1982), Seliverstova (1982a; 1982b). In an attempt to disperse the dogma, which has proved extremely detrimental to obtaining an adequate understanding of aspect as a cross-language and universal phenomenon, let us here translate into Bulgarian sentences with verbs and verb phrases of the 'state' type constructed in the way described above (impfvImp stands for imperfective Imperfect):

(30) a. X knew/loved Y
X poznavaše$_{impfvImp}$/običaše$_{impfvImp}$ Y
b. X ruled Y [by Y objects like *the country* are subsumed)
X upravljavaše$_{impfvImp}$ Y
c. X had/wanted Y [e.g. *the car* or *the umbrella* is subsumed]
X imaše$_{impfvImp}$/iskaše$_{impfvImp}$ Y
d. X was present/absent
X prisăstvaše$_{impfvImp}$/otsăstvaše$_{impfvImp}$
e. X was healthy/ill
X beše$_{impfvImp}$ zdrav/bolen
f. X played chess/wrote books
X igraeše$_{impfvImp}$ šah/pišeše$_{impfvImp}$ knigi
g. X smoked [i.e. *was a smoker* is subsumed]
X pušeše$_{impfvImp}$
h. X painted [i.e. *was a painter* (*an artist*) is subsumed]
X risuvaše$_{impfvImp}$

The translation of English sentences into Bulgarian that typically designate states is carried out through imperfective Imperfect verb forms which is the prototypical imperfective form. Used in different types of sentences, under the influence of various aspectualisers, some of the verbs and verb phrases in sentences like (30) may obtain different meanings and, hence, will fall under the categories of accomplishments and achievements. In these cases, the corresponding Bulgarian forms to English verbs and verb phrases that are otherwise states are the perfective Aorist (pfvAor) or the perfective *da*-construction here (the Bulgarian *da*-construction is similar to the English infinitive but is marked for person and number):

(31) a. I knew the answer at once
'Vednaga razbrah$_{pfvAor}$ otgovora'
b. I believed the story
'Povjarvah$_{pfvAor}$ na razkaza'
c. Let me have a look
'Neka da pogledna$_{pfv}$'
d. I liked the painting at once
'Haresah$_{pfvAor}$ kartinata vednaga'
e. Teach your daughter how to cook before she is married
'Nauči dăšterja si da gotvi predi da se omăži$_{pfv}$ [*da*-construction]'

Conversely, below are examples of activities in English (32) that are then turned into accomplishments in (33) through the introduction of an object to the verb (all the sentences are given along with their Bulgarian counterparts):

(32) a. X pushed a cart
'X tikaše$_{impfvImp}$ količka'
b. X worked/smoked/painted
'X raboteše$_{impfvImp}$/puseše$_{impfvImp}$/risuvaše$_{impfvImp}$'
c. X swam/walked/ran
'X pluvaše$_{impfvImp}$/vărveše$_{impfvImp}$/bjagaše$_{impfvImp}$'

Note that actions rendered through the English Simple Past Tense are in this case equal to actions rendered through the Past Progressive: that is, *pushed* is roughly equivalent to *was pushing*, *swam* is roughly equivalent to *was swimming*, etc. The Bulgarian correspondences here are necessarily imperfective Imperfects. However, the introduction of a certain type of object can change the meaning of the verb, and the whole phrase can become an accomplishment. As a result, the Bulgarian equivalents become perfective Aorists.

(33) a. X walked/ran a mile
'X izvărvja$_{pfvAor}$/probjaga$_{pfvAor}$ edna milja'
b. X worked a miracle
'X izvărši$_{pfvAor}$ čudo'
c. X smoked a cigarette
'X izpuši$_{pfvAor}$ edna cigara'
d. X painted a flower
'X narisuva$_{pfvAor}$ cvete'

(The rest of the book will centre on the mechanism of this change and will deal thoroughly with it.)

If English states and activities are rendered through imperfective Imperfect verb forms in Bulgarian, accomplishments and achievements are conveyed through the perfective Aorist. See (34a) – (34b) and (35a) – (35b), respectively:

(34) a. X built a house/made a chair/drew a circle/played a game of chess/ wrote a letter/read a novel
X postroi$_{pfvAor}$ kăšta/napravi$_{pfvAor}$ stol/narisuva$_{pfvAor}$ krăg/izigra$_{pfvAor}$ partija šah/napisa$_{pfvAor}$ pismo/pročete$_{pfvAor}$ roman
b. X grew up/got ready
X porasna$_{pfvAor}$/se prigotvi$_{pfvAor}$
(35) a. X won the race/crossed the border
X spečeli$_{pfvAor}$ nadbjagvaneto/preseče$_{pfvAor}$ granicata
b. X lost/found Y [by Y, e.g. *a watch* is subsumed]
X zagubi$_{pfvAor}$/nameri$_{pfvAor}$ Y

It has been assumed again that *X* is a typical subject and *Y* is a typical object. Some of the sentences represent examples of typical subjects and objects (represented by common nouns), and, as a rule, their referents are singular physical entities –

human individuals or material objects. Plural subjects or objects that are unspecified with respect to quantity are, conversely, considered as atypical. Used instead of the typical ones, plural subjects or objects unspecified with respect to quantity change the meaning of the verb from an accomplishment or an achievement to a state or an activity. In other words, the situations denoted change from perfective to imperfective. This is also reflected in their translation into Bulgarian, where a change in the choice of the tense-aspect form occurs, from the perfective Aorist into the imperfective Imperfect:

(36) a. X built houses/made chairs/drew circles/read novels/wrote letters
X stroeše$_{impfvImp}$ kăšti/praveše$_{impfvImp}$ stolove/risuvaše$_{impfvImp}$ krăgove/četeše$_{impfvImp}$ romani/piseše$_{impfvImp}$ pisma
b. Children grew up
Deca porastvaha$_{impfvImp}$
c. X won races/lost pencils/crossed borders
X pečeleše$_{impfvImp}$ nadbjagvanija/gubeše$_{impfvImp}$ molivi/presičaše$_{impfvImp}$ granici
d. Babies were born/People died
Raždaha se$_{impfvImp}$ bebeta/Umiraha$_{impfvImp}$ hora

Although it is **potentially** present in the classification considered here, especially with respect to the type of object to be used in any sentence, it is worth noting that this extremely important regularity was neglected (or remained partly unnoticed) by Vendler. It is also worth asking why, in spite of the enormous popularity of Vendler's classification and similar descriptions of 'situations' in Western European and American studies, Slavic aspectological research has rarely employed these as analytical tools.

Naturally, classifications of Vendler's type followed the implications of the peculiarities of the languages investigated. Although Slavic aspect is not consistently marked in the morphological system (generally, Slavic aspect has no inherent morphological markers, and the Slavic distinction does not coincide with the supposedly universal perfective/imperfective contrast), the Slavic perfective/imperfective opposition has almost always been taken for granted as a starting point for a linguistic analysis of (allegedly) aspectless languages – but not as a necessity to distinguish between bounded and non-bounded situations. It can be maintained that this approach, overwhelmingly dominant, hindered the development of Slavic aspectology. A good all-round comparison between Slavic languages and a language like English will ultimately show that the presence in the Slavic languages of a perfective/imperfective opposition can hardly be regarded as an idiosyncrasy or as a kind of advantage to these languages since, as will become perfectly clear later on, a Non-Slavic language like English can also be said to feature sufficient devices for the explication of both perfectivity and imperfectivity.

The incompatibility between Slavic and Non-Slavic approaches towards aspect forced Dahl (1981: 80-81) to draw a methodological distinction between the so-called Eastern view, dominating in the Slavic world, and the so-called Western view, emanating from Aristotle and ultimately associated with Vendler's classification and similar descriptions. As already emphasised, Slavic aspectological studies rarely used Vendler's or similar classifications as an analytical tool. And even when these have been taken into account (see, e.g., the contributions in Seliverstova 1982a), an essential circumstance is usually ignored, viz., that the grounds in Vendler's classification (and in similar approaches) for distinguishing between states, activities (processes), accomplishments, achievements, etc., are not only semantic but also formal. This important methodological difference tended and still tends to remain unnoticed, probably for being deemed insignificant. Actually, it is decisively essential for clarifying the reasons behind the incompatibility between the two methodologies.

Let us analyse the difference. For instance, the two classifications of situations denoted by Russian 'predicates' proposed by Seliverstova (1982b) and Bulygina (1982) are restricted to:

i) verbs;

ii) verbs and verb phrases with *byt'* 'be' combined with different adjectives and nouns.

Predicates in Seliverstova's and Bulygina's classifications are 'verbs and verb phrases with *byt'* 'be' or its zero form' (see Seliverstova 1982a: 3). Vendler's classification, on the other hand, may be said to handle:

iii) verbs in isolation;

iv) verbs and verb phrases with *be* combined with different adjectives and nouns (as in Seliverstova's and Bulygina's classifications);

v) other phrases made up of different verbs and nouns.

Terminological differences set aside, the two approaches, the Russian one, of 'predicates' and Vendler's, of verbs and verb phrases, could be taken to be identical or at least very similar, as (i) above contains in itself, at least at first sight, (v). But an assumption of this kind would in fact be erroneous because Vendler's classification features the important distinction between (iii) and (v). In other words, Vendler's classification rests on the following additional formal (syntactic) criterion: whether a particular verb under analysis is used in isolation or in combination with a noun is something that is necessarily taken into account. Moreover, as has been already shown, classifying an item in Vendler's classification as an imperfective one (as a state or an activity) or as a perfective one (as an accomplishment or an achievement) also crucially depends on the type of noun complemented to the verb.

This can be regarded as a general fundamental difference between the Eastern (Slavic, Russian, etc.) and the Western (American, Western European, etc.) linguistic traditions, along with some of the basic notions employed in them. For instance, from the very beginning of the development of transformational-generative theory, *a phrase* could be defined both as a combination of words or an isolated word (e.g. a noun) syntactically realised. Thus both *a book* and *books*, for instance, are phrases (noun phrases) that can be major sentence components (subjects, objects) used either with a determiner (quantifier, etc.) or without a determiner/quantifier (i.e., with a zero determiner/quantifier), etc. Of course, it makes perfect sense to describe *a book* as a phrase also in a Slavic approach, for *a book* consists of two words. But in mainstream Slavic linguistics, which studies mostly languages without articles and where, hence, bare nouns are very common and even prevail, considering subjects and objects unaccompanied by adjectives, determiners, quantifiers etc. as phrases can hardly be termed a standard description.

This fundamental methodological difference also arises from other specific features of the two groups of languages (the Slavic group and the Western European one, barring exceptions). Slavic verbal aspect is certainly among these features. Recall the general attitude of Western linguists towards Russian aspects, so ingeniously described by Issatschenko (1974: 141), as awe-inspiring and mystical categories to be treated only by the native speaker. The strong impact of the Slavic verb, both in discourse, at the sentence level, and at the level of the overall language system, involves concentrating within a single sentence element (the verb within the verb phrase in the sentence, the verb as a lexical entry) not only aspect, i.e., the perfective/imperfective distinction, but also the general semantics of situations in Vendler's terms, stripping nouns of their function or, say, responsibility, for its explication. This forms a stark contrast with languages like English where, as already shown to a certain extent, and as will be shown later on in this book, aspect and the overall situational meaning of a phrase or a sentence is to a large degree dependent on the contribution (in complex semantic, grammatical and even pragmatic terms) of the noun complemented to the verb.

Hence, in the Slavic (or "Eastern") approach it is only natural for nouns to remain outside the scope of aspectual analysis. What Slavic researchers intuit is that nouns, in principle, do not and could not change the aspect of the verb they are complemented to, nor could they change other possible types of situational meanings. The present work, apart from dealing with its own objectives, will aim to remedy this deficiency of the Slavic tradition with respect to the treatment of situational meanings. As already shown elsewhere (see Kabakčiev 1987; 1989), Slavic nouns are in fact not only capable of contributing to the explication of the aspectual meaning in certain sentences. Occasionally, they can even change it dramatically.[7] On the other hand, it can be assumed that at the level of the overall language system lexical meanings of verbs are formed under the influence of situational meanings of

---

[7] Consider the two Bulgarian sentences below in which the meaning of an overtly marked imperfective verb form is dominated by the situational meaning of the noun (*projava* 'act', *zakăsnenie* 'delay'):

Vratar-jat   imaše$_{impfvImp}$ otlična   projava i   uspja   da spasi   duzpa-ta
Goalkeeper-the had   excellent   act   and managed to save   penalty-the
'The goalkeeper acted excellently and managed to save the penalty'

Zakăsnenie-to   ti   mi struvaše$_{impfvImp}$ cjalo   săstojanie
Delay-the   your me cost   whole   fortune
'Your delay cost me a whole fortune'

Note that in both cases the verb is imperfectively marked twice! First, with the imperfective aspect of the lexical entries *imam* 'have' (a very strong, prototypical, lexical stative) and *struvam* 'cost'; second, with the imperfectivity of the Imperfect (Past) Tense.

nouns – and vice versa. The contribution of nouns to the explication of aspect in English will be considered in much more detail in Chapter Ten, *Meanings of nouns and noun phrases, and aspect in English*, but, more importantly, the parallels made between Slavic and English data and the implications of the way nouns influence the explication of aspect will show that the significance of Vendler's classification, in spite of its popularity, has not been properly understood in linguistics so far – both in the East and the West.

To sum up the discussion in this chapter, plural subjects or objects unaccompanied by a determiner or a quantifier change the meaning of the verb in a simple English sentence from an accomplishment or an achievement to a state or an activity. This extremely important regularity did not receive Vendler's attention, although it was potentially present in his classification, at least with respect to the type of object used in a sentence. The probable reason was that Vendler's major theoretical concerns were philosophical rather than linguistic. The regularity in question was investigated in depth in the early 1970s by Henk Verkuyl, whose theory revealed, for the first time in linguistics, the outlines of the overall mechanism for explicating the perfective/imperfective contrast in languages like Dutch and English.

CHAPTER 3

VERKUYL'S THEORY OF COMPOSITIONAL ASPECT

A CORNERSTONE IN THE DEVELOPMENT OF ASPECTOLOGY

Verkuyl's work *On the compositional nature of the aspects* appeared as a dissertation in 1971 and was published a year later (Verkuyl 1972). It was to turn into a cornerstone in the development of aspectology. The linguistic analysis in it is based on the author's mother tongue, Dutch, but the English translation equivalents supplied throughout show that the regularities revealed are also valid for English, and for other languages as well.

Compositional aspect was recognised as a very important general language phenomenon immediately after the publication of Verkuyl's work. Back in 1974 Friedrich, who, unlike Verkuyl, actually used the term 'compositional aspect', wrote:

> "Since all languages have compositional aspect, but only a subset have thematic aspect, the former must be seen as the more general and defining phenomenon. Speaking more generally, aspect is fundamentally not a problem of morphological form but of a theory of semantics and morphosyntax, where it deserves to play a central role"

(Friedrich 1974: 37). Unfortunately, however, despite the fact that a number of other authors also recognised the importance of Verkuyl's work (in broad terms) and his exclusive contribution in describing its mechanism (see Zydatiß 1976: 54); Heinämäki 1978: 10; Dowty 1979: 63-64; Markkanen 1979: 54-57; (L.)Carlson 1981; Mourelatos 1981; Schopf 1974: 56-58), the essence of compositional aspect as a language phenomenon was to remain largely misunderstood, neglected and unexplored in the literature for many years. It was not until the appearance of two articles more than a decade later (Kabakčiev 1984a; 1984b), that a close parallelism between the expression of aspect through the verb only, as for example in the Slavic languages, and through compositional means was for the first time explicitly shown to exist in cross-language terms. Verbal aspect was seen as a mirror image of compositional aspect – or, vice versa, compositional aspect could be seen as a mirror image of verbal aspect. The two articles also argued that the parallelism of aspect in verbal and compositional terms can significantly advance our understanding of aspect as a general language phenomenon. Why compositional aspect is to be viewed as a mirror image of verbal aspect will be made clear in some of the following chapters in this book, more specifically in Chapter Six, *The mechanism for mapping the temporal values of subjects and objects* and Chapter Seven, *The interdependence between markers of boundedness in verbs and in nouns*.

Following the postulates of the transformational grammar of the 60s, Verkuyl managed to isolate the meanings of perfectivity and imperfectivity at the level of the sentence. In his theory, aspect meanings cover, generally speaking, certain configurations of categories within the sentence, subsumed under two schemata. In other words, aspect is expressed within the whole sentence, and not (or, rather not only) at the level of isolated verbs of verb phrases, as in Vendler's classification. It has already been shown how different sentence components can influence aspectual readings of sentences by virtue of their grammatical markedness for tense, number or definiteness in terms of the article/zero article distinction. As mentioned earlier, many observations concerning the relationship between various sentence components and the expression of aspect were actually made earlier by different scholars. In Verkuyl's work, however, these kinds of observations, along with the recognition of the separate dependencies and interdependencies in the functioning of sentence components (with their grammatical markedness and semantic structure) for the ultimate expression of aspect acquired the systematicity that was necessary for a full-blown theory to emerge: the theory of compositional aspect.

THE SCHEMATA FOR PERFECTIVITY AND IMPERFECTIVITY

In building up his theses, Verkuyl (1972) employed a certain logical and mathematical machinery that hindered the adequate interpretation of his theory. Besides, Verkuyl based it on the ideas of transformational-generative grammar of that time, shrouded in bizarre phraseology. These two factors probably constitute the major reasons why the results of the author's analysis of certain major linguistic problems remained either ignored, misunderstood or were left undiscovered for a long time. To illustrate the specificity of Verkuyl's approach and terminology, his two schemata are given below, displaying the means for explicating perfectivity and imperfectivity at the level of simple sentences containing a subject, a verb and an object:

SCHEMA FOR PERFECTIVITY (terminativity, in Verkuyl's terms)
(37) S[NP1[SPECIFIED QUANTITY OF X]NP1 + VP[V[VERB]V + NP2[SPECIFIED QUANTITY OF X]NP2]S

SCHEMA FOR IMPERFECTIVITY (durativity, in Verkuyl's terms)
(38) S[NP1[(UN)SPECIFIED QUANTITY OF X]NP1 + VP[V[VERB]V + NP2[(UN)SPECIFIED QUANTITY OF X]N

As a first step to clearing up the confusion of problems related to the expression of aspect in some basic types of English sentences (and hence, practically, in English in general) the formulae above are in need of analysis. Below is a list of what the symbols stand for. The first three are abbreviations of basic syntactic notions but the fourth and fifth represent the bones of contention:

S – sentence;

NP – noun phrase (consisting of either a group of words around a noun plus the noun itself, or of a single noun);

VP – verb phrase (consisting of either a group of words around a verb plus the verb itself or of a single verb, be it simple or marked by an auxiliary/auxiliaries for tense, voice, etc.);

SPECIFIED QUANTITY OF X – by 'specified quantity of X' a certain type of a semantic entity is meant "giving the bounds of the temporal interval in question" (see Verkuyl 1972: 59);

UNSPECIFIED QUANTITY OF X – by 'unspecified quantity of X' a certain type of a semantic entity is meant "not giving the bounds of the temporal interval in question" (see Verkuyl 1972: 59).

Consider now the following simple sentences, Verkuyl's own, containing only a subject, a verb and an object and explicating a completed/perfective action:

(39) a. Katinka knitted a Norwegian sweater
     b. Arie ate a herring
     c. Greetje walked from the Mint to the Dam[1]

The three sentences in (39) fall under the heading of (37) above. At a superficial glance it can easily be established that each of them contains two NPs denoting 'specified quantity of X' – in contrast to the sentences in (40) and (41) below. The sentences in (40) and (41) explicate imperfectivity of the action, and either the subject-NP, or the object NP, or both NPs have to be assigned the semantic feature 'unspecified quantity of X'. As far as the crucial question of what exactly the semantic features 'specified quantity of X' and 'unspecified quantity of X' stand for is concerned, it will be dealt with in the following pages and chapters of the book.

(40) a. Katinka knitted Norwegian sweaters
     b. Women knitted Norwegian sweaters
(41) a. Arie ate herrings
     b. Policemen walked from the Mint to the Dam

By incorporating the subject into the analysis of aspect meanings Verkuyl expanded the perspective of the observations already made by a number of scholars who took into account the interrelationship between a quantified object (an object with an article) and the explication of perfectivity and an unquantified (bare) object and the explication of imperfectivity. Including the subject in the analysis of the type of sentences in question turned out to be an extremely important step in the process of acquiring a better understanding of the interdependency between the type of NPs (or, viewed from another angle, nouns) in the sentence and the explication of aspect. It is astonishing how natural and easy to grasp this regularity appears, when, once

---

[1] *The Mint* and *the Dam* are squares in the central part of Amsterdam.

recognised, it is presented in detail. But, as the history of linguistics shows, it spent the efforts of many aspectologists in the course of several decades.

And so, Verkuyl managed to overcome the fragmentary approach of linguists up to the beginning of the 1970s who saw the connection between the devices for expressing aspect and the type of the NP only with respect to the object – with the exception of Ridjanović who, however, failed to transform his observations on the subject into an important generalisation. So far, according to Verkuyl's theory, both the subject and the (syntactic) object in certain types of sentences play a role in the explication of perfectivity and imperfectivity depending on whether they signify singularity or plurality of an object, whether the objects are count or non-count and whether they have articles (are quantified) or not. Before proceeding to the other aspects of Verkuyl's aspect theory, this point is worth exploring further.

ON SOME OF THE MAJOR THESES AND PROBLEMS IN VERKUYL'S WORK

Firstly, it can be seen that Verkuyl's examples contain only verbs in the Simple Past Tense in English. This is natural, because, as already mentioned in the previous chapter, the Simple Past Tense supplies relatively neutral conditions for expressing aspect distinctions (cf. also Bybee et al 1994: 83-84). It should not be forgotten, nevertheless, that the regularities are valid for many other grammatical forms of the verb as well (non-finite forms and other finite forms – for example, different moods or other tenses).

Secondly, it is worth noting that sentences containing a subject, a verb and an object represent a significant structural model through which the following situation can be denoted: there is an agent involved; the agent performs a certain action; the action is transferred onto an object. The object is usually either affected or created by the action, which can either be a perfective or an imperfective one. There exists a certain tendency, even across languages, for an action transferred onto an object to be perfective, and for an action not transferred onto an object to be imperfective (cf. Hopper and Thompson 1980). Compare the difference between the aspect readings of the (a) and (b) sentences below, in which, when an object of a certain type is present to the verb, it "measures out" the action:

(42) a. The woman ironed
b. The woman ironed the skirt
(43) a. John wrote
b. John wrote a book

The term 'measuring out' has been used independently by Tenny (1994) and Glasbey (1994) to refer to a transfer of boundedness in the spatial domain to boundedness in the temporal domain. Or, in other words, the spatial boundedness of *the skirt* or *a book* in (42b) and (43b), respectively, underlies the temporally bounded reading of *ironed* and *wrote*. However, as far as the whole sentences are concerned, note that, on the one hand, sentences of type (42a) and (43a) could, of course, in a certain context, signify actions that were terminated without being perfective (perfected, completed). Such is, for example, the action also in a sentence like *Have you eaten?* But it is clear, on the other hand, that sentences of type (42b) and (43b) can much more readily describe perfective actions than sentences of type (42a) and (43a).

Thirdly, in connection with the problem mentioned in the previous passage, it is important to note that the perfectivity of (42b) and (43b) and the imperfectivity of (42a) or (43a), construed according to Verkuyl's theory, should be regarded as default, basic, or primary, not as invariable. In other words, the perfectivity of (42b) and (43b) or the imperfectivity of (42a) and (43a), though basic or primary, are only potential, not the only possible aspectual readings of the sentences in question. This peculiarity of the aspect semantics has already been noted. In Chapter One, *On the essence of aspect*, it was observed that sentences of type (17a) and (17b) could sometimes be used with an imperfective meaning if they form part of a more complex sentence like, for example (17c):

(17)   a. He wrote the letters
        b. I checked the addresses
        c. While he wrote the letters, I checked the addresses

But what does this complexity of the aspectual readings of sentences amount to? It means that if a certain sentence is put into a context which contradicts its own aspectual reading, the sentence could acquire a reading different from its default (primary, basic, prototypical) one. Sentences like (42b) or (43b) above signify perfective actions. However, placed in a context explicating non-bounded iterativity, the action turns into an imperfective one under the influence of this context. Compare again sentence (43b) and the same sentence put in the discourse sequence in (44b). Compare also sentence (44a), perfective in isolation, and the same sentence incorporated in the discourse sequence in (44b):

(43)   b. John wrote a book
(44)   a. When I visited my friends [...]
        b. When I visited my friends, I always found them busy doing serious things. Peter usually worked on a new play. John wrote a book

Hence, when defining sentences of type (42a) or (43a) as imperfective and sentences of type (42b) and (43b) as perfective, these aspectual readings should be regarded as default, basic, primary or (proto-)typical, but by no means the only possible.

Fourthly, although this problem has been dealt with neither in Verkuyl's (1972) work, nor in his second book (1993), the specificity of the general pattern of the use of the article in English has to be taken into account, especially with respect to number and semantic type of the noun. It will be dealt with in the following chapter and pertains mainly to the differences in the use of nouns with or without articles. Observed in isolation, nouns accompanied by either the definite or the indefinite article tend to imply definiteness in general quantitative terms, whereas nouns without articles tend to imply indefiniteness, again in general quantitative terms – a point to be further clarified in the following chapters.

Fifthly, it is common knowledge that definiteness can be expressed not only through the definite article. Proper names, demonstrative and possessive pronouns in English also imply definiteness. Hence, obviously, these will usually imply quantitative definiteness/boundedness too. On the other hand, the implication of quantitative definiteness/boundedness is also associated with the use of other quantifiers (i.e., if the article is taken to be a quantifier) and indefinite pronouns. This is another point to be discussed in the following chapter.

Sixthly, the meaning of the verb (even in isolation, and in general lexical terms) does, of course, play a significant role in the explication of perfectivity or imperfectivity. As shown by Verkuyl, if a sentence like (45a) below describes a perfective action, a sentence like (45b) describes an imperfective action or, rather, a state:

(45) a. Fritz played Schumann's cello concerto
b. Fritz hated Schumann's cello concerto

It is evident that the aspectual reading is in this case predetermined by the verb since the other components in the two sentences are identical. As already mentioned in Chapter One, *On the essence of aspect*, a so-called 'telicity' component could be located in the verb, and identified as an important part of its lexical (including dictionary-entry) meaning. Or, if we stick to Vendler's terminology, *play Schumann's cello concerto* is an accomplishment, whereas *hate Schumann's cello concerto* is a state. Hence, since the whole sentence (45a) signifies an accomplishment, and sentence (45b) signifies a state, and since both sentences represent typical uses of their respective verbs, it can be conjectured that the verb *play* contains in itself 'telicity', the aspectual potential for explicating perfectivity, at a much higher degree than a verb like *hate* might be said to possess it. Recall also that the use of the verb *hate* is not incompatible with the explication of perfectivity, as in sentences like (10a):

(10) a. He suddenly hated that man

This shows that, apparently, telicity and atelicity are a matter of an important semantic potential, tendency, typicality or non-typicality in the way a certain verb is used, and by no means constitute fixed, invariable, lexical features.

Thus, judging from the overview of the history of aspectology and the analysis of language data presented so far, Verkuyl's contribution in the explanation of aspect in Dutch and English could be summed up along the following lines. The expression of perfectivity and imperfectivity is carried out at the level of the sentence. Within the framework of a simple sentence containing a subject, a verb, and an object (this kind of sentence representing a major and very productive semantico-syntactic pattern), aspect meaning is dependent on all the components of a sentence, on their grammatical form (this is also valid for NPs and it makes a large difference whether they contain or do not contain articles or other types of quantifiers), and on the lexical meanings of the words that take part in the composition of the sentence as a whole. Compare two groups of sentences given below explicating perfectivity and imperfectivity of the actions according to the two schemata (37) and (38), respectively: sentences like (46a), (46b), (45a), on the one hand, and sentences like (40a), (40b), (47), and (45b), on the other hand. Sentences like (46a), (46b), (45a) meet the requirements of the perfective schema (37):

(46) a. Katinka knitted two Norwegian sweaters
b. A tourist climbed the mountain
(45) a. Fritz played Schumann's cello concerto

Their NPs can easily be associated with boundedness (quantitative, in broad terms): the nouns are either accompanied by an article (*a tourist, the mountain*), or contain some other word (*two*) defining the bounds of the quantity, or contain proper nouns (*Katinka, Fritz, Schumann's cello concerto*) implying boundedness – note that in *Schumann's cello concerto* the proper noun is in a possessive function, again giving the bounds of the quantity, as is the general case with possessive pronouns. In all these sentences the verb meets the requirement in Verkuyl's perfectivity schema for a semantic 'telicity' potential to be present.

Conversely, sentences like (40a), (40b), (47) and (45b) meet the requirements of the imperfective schema (38):

(40) a. Katinka knitted Norwegian sweaters
b. Women knitted Norwegian sweaters
(47) Tourists climbed the mountain
(45) b. Fritz hated Schumann's cello concerto

They either contain at least one NP the referent of which implies non-boundedness in general quantitative terms – see (40a), (40b) and (47) above, or a verb lacking a telicity potential in the type of sentences in question – see (45b). The sentence component implying non-boundedness could be the subject, as in (40b) and (47), or the object, as in (40a). But it is also possible that both the subject and the object imply non-boundedness, and then the imperfectivity of the action in the sentence is even marked to a higher degree – cf. sentence (40b).

So far, the relationship between boundedness or non-boundedness in NPs and the aspectual reading of the sentence, as well as the connection between the type of the verb as a lexical entity and its aspectual reading explained by Verkuyl have emerged as comparatively straightforward and simple. Boundedness (or 'specified quantity', to use Verkuyl's term) is explicated through an article, quantifiers, certain types of pronouns, etc., whereas non-boundedness (or 'unspecified quantity', Verkuyl's term) is explicated through the lack of these elements. Hence, this is a clear case of a formal marking which, as will be maintained later, amounts in the long run to marking certain basic aspectual readings at the level of the sentence grammatically.

But the mechanism of this marking will turn out to be complex and explainable not only in the domain of grammar.

It is worth noting that most linguists dealing with the problem treated the aspect mechanism – as revealed by Verkuyl in the fashion described so far – in what has here been called 'general quantitative' boundedness/non-boundedness terms. It will be argued in the forthcoming chapters of the book that this was the major reason why Verkuyl's powerful insight into the aspects, made known to the linguistic audience as early as 1971/1972, remained misunderstood and underestimated for more than a decade. His notions of 'specified quantity of X' and 'unspecified quantity of X' (that are equated with the notions of boundedness and non-boundedness, respectively) failed to intrigue the aspectologists. The actual reason, as will gradually become clear, is not that the notions are inadequate – they are just a bit too broad to serve as an in-depth aspectological explanation. In fact, as already pointed out earlier, what Verkuyl's terms 'specified quantity of X' and 'unspecified quantity of X' actually stand for is "giving the bounds of the temporal interval in question" and "not giving the bounds of the temporal interval in question", respectively (see Verkuyl 1972: 59). That is, boundedness (bounded quantity) and non-boundedness (non-bounded quantity) are notions directly associated with the time axis.

Unfortunately, apart from the fact that in Verkuyl's work the definitions of 'specified quantity of X' and 'unspecified quantity of X' remained overshadowed by the general exposition of the aspect mechanism and the somewhat heavy formalism imposed by the transformational-generative trend, apparently the Dutch linguist simply leaned on a general assumption that both NPs (nouns) and VPs (verbs) are capable of signifying temporal entities. As a result, he failed to describe properly a basic component of the aspect phenomenon related to the way temporality features of NPs are to be interpreted. In view of the rigid methodology of the approach assumed this is understandable. But the regularities revealed in Verkuyl's (1972) book will be shown to go far beyond the restrictions of "a pure science" built up in an 'art-for-art's-sake' logico-mathematical fashion. They will turn out to be of considerable importance not only for the theory of linguistics in general, but also to various applied fields such as language and foreign language teaching, translation theory and practice, lexicology and lexicography, and so on.[2] The major ideas in Verkuyl's book will be closely investigated in the following three chapters. In Chapter Seven, *The interdependence between markers of boundedness in verbs and in nouns*, another theory will be put forward, which will be based on Verkuyl's theory, will revise and develop some of its major assumptions and will transfer these onto the structure of other languages revealing some fundamental cross-language regularities. Of course, the theory in question will be the object of attention only in so far as it touches upon the problem of the way aspect distinctions in a language like English are explicated.

---

[2] Later on in the book it will be seen that the regularities in question are closely linked to such fields of grammar as, to mention but a few, the use of articles and tenses (probably the two major problem fields of English grammar), the semantics of verbs, the semantics of abstract nouns, the use of temporal adverbials, etc.

The basic tenets in a contemporary theory of aspect for languages like English are to incorporate the view that the explication of aspect can be carried out not only through verbs but also through NPs and, in the long run, through the functional and semantic characteristics of nouns as parts of NPs. A statement of this kind may sound surprising, strange, even shocking. But, as already shown in the beginning of Chapter One, *On the essence of aspect*, the aspectual meaning of a verb in a sentence may have to do with what is expressed through the object and the subject in the sentence even in an "aspect" language like Bulgarian. A similar kind of connection was established with English language data as well – in this and in the previous chapter. To illustrate the point more clearly, let us go back to the question of boundedness and non-boundedness on the time axis, discussed insufficiently in Verkuyl (1972).

To any native speaker of English it would be a wholly trivial observation that, in the two sentences below, the objects *Schumann's cello concerto* (45a) and *Schumann's cello concerto* (45b) have a lot more to do with the time axis than, say, the subjects *Fritz* in (45a) and (45b). While Fritz is a human being, that is, represents a non-temporal, physical object remaining fairly constant in time, *Schumann's cello concerto* is conceived of as an object which is primarily temporal.

(45) a. Fritz played Schumann's cello concerto
      b. Fritz hated Schumann's cello concerto

Still, as noted by Verkuyl, *Schumann's cello concerto* can be viewed in two ways. Firstly, as something which is located in time, which happens once, and which cannot possibly be regarded as existing outside its temporal limits. This is the **performance** of Schumann's cello concerto, described in (45a) – given during a particular period of time and in particular circumstances. Secondly, however, *Schumann's cello concerto* can also be viewed as something which is relatively stable in time and does not depend on any particular performance at a given time interval and in particular circumstances. This is the **composition** 'Schumann's cello concerto', an abstract entity that can be reproduced in various ways and which represents something more than just an average of the ordinary sum of all or most particular performances. It is this meaning of 'Schumann's cello concerto' that is present in sentence (45b), and the distinction described here will undoubtedly be available not only in English, but also in many other (and probably all) natural languages.

Indeed, in analysing the two sentences in (45) above the two meanings of *Schumann's cello concerto* will not always be distinguished by speakers and may actually be rarely conceived of as separate. At first sight it even seems as if this distinction has nothing to do with the aspectual reading of the action denoted by the verb and that it plays no role in ordinary language communication. Clearly, upon hearing the two sentences, people are able to realise the difference between *Schumann's cello concerto* in (45a) and *Schumann's cello concerto* in (45b), but they do not necessarily realise it immediately. The reasons behind the phenomenon and its relevance to the problem of explicating aspect distinctions in English and similar languages will be considered in the following chapters.

Let us, however, make the natural conclusion, potentially present in Verkuyl's (1972) thesis, that whereas *Schumann's cello concerto* in (45a) is an object bounded in time, *Schumann's cello concerto* in (45b) is an object which is non-bounded in time. Doesn't a conclusion of this kind have something to do with the ways actions or states are expressed – that is, with situations (in the Vendlerian sense), usually associated with the meanings of verbs, **not** nouns? As will be shown later, the difference between the two slightly veiled meanings of *Schumann's cello concerto* actually to a large degree amounts to the essence of aspect – for in the explication of the aspects in English it is not primarily the verb that takes part but, largely speaking, the verb **along with** nouns/NPs – (syntactic) subjects, objects.

We have thus seen that 'specified quantity of X', which in Verkuyl's definition is equivalent to boundedness on the time axis, can be said to enter into the meaning of the phrase *Schumann's cello concerto* in (45a) and that 'unspecified quantity of X', being equivalent to non-boundedness on the time axis, can be said to enter into the meaning of the phrase *Schumann's cello concerto* in (45b). Recall, however, that 'specified quantity of X', i.e. boundedness in time, ought to be implied, according to Verkuyl's schemata, also by the subject in any sentence of this type explicating a perfective action/situation. And vice versa, 'unspecified quantity of X', i.e. non-boundedness in time, ought to be implied by either the subject or the object (or by both) in sentences of this type explicating imperfectivity of the action/situation. It follows, therefore, that the (referent of the) subject *Fritz* in a sentence like (45a) will imply boundedness **in time** and that the (referent of the) subject *tourists* in a sentence like (47) will imply non-boundedness **in time**.

(45) a. Fritz played Schumann's cello concerto
(47) Tourists climbed the mountain

How could it be that a value pertaining to boundedness in time should be assigned to the cello player *Fritz* in (45a) and how can one make sense of the non-boundedness in time of *tourists* in a sentence like (47)? Verkuyl neither asked, nor gave an answer to a question of this kind – in both his (1972) monograph and in his 'extended theory' (Verkuyl 1993). In his first book (Verkuyl 1972) he simply assigned the values in question to the sentence components in question; at that time the values seemed to have arisen as a result of some logical operations, and the author did not deem it necessary that a common-sense explanation of the origin of these values should be given. It is precisely this kind of explanation that will be proposed in the following chapters of this work.

Let us for the moment, on the one hand, only assume that the cello player *Fritz* in (45a) implies 'specified quantity' in broad quantitative terms, since *Fritz* constitutes **one** person. That is, *Fritz* is an exponent of definite quantity, in contrast to the NP *tourists* in (47), a form which is held to imply 'indefinite, unspecified quantity' since it denotes an indefinite, non-bounded number of entities. A thesis of this kind can easily be accepted because when we say or hear the phrase *a tourist* or *the tourist* what we have in mind is precisely **one** tourist; and when we say or hear the phrase *the tourists* we also take this to be a definite, bounded quantity, although the exact range of the quantity may be unknown to us. Conversely, when we say or hear the noun (the bare plural NP) *tourists* what we usually have in mind is an unspecified, non-bounded number of tourists. Non-boundedness should, of course, not be conceived of as an instantiation of 'eternity': it should be conceived of as an absence of indication with respect to the bounds/limits of quantity.

It is furthermore clear, on the other hand, that English features concrete grammatical markers for the denotation of 'specified/bounded quantity' and 'unspecified/non-bounded quantity'. In the former case, when 'specified/bounded quantity' is expressed or explicated, it is the article (both the definite and the indefinite) that serves as its exponent. Of course, various other exponents of 'specified/bounded quantity' can be added to the list: quantifiers, demonstrative and possessive pronouns, proper names, etc., capable of performing the function. And in the latter case, when 'unspecified/non-bounded quantity' is expressed or explicated, there is also a formal marker – it is the absence of an article or of other markers of 'specified/bounded quantity'. Just like the absence of a plural marker in English (usually a suffix *-s*) signifies singularity, the very absence of a marker of boundedness is a marker of non-boundedness.

It should be noted also that the regularities in the explication of aspect revealed by Verkuyl do not encompass the subject, the verb and the (direct) object only. The indirect object can also take part in the explication of aspectual meanings. Here are the two sentences exemplifying this side of the aspect phenomenon given in Verkuyl (1972):

(48)   a.   Den Uyl gave the Labour Party badge to a congress-goer
           b.   Den Uyl gave the Labour Party badge to congress-goers

While a sentence like (48a) refers to a singular completed act, a sentence like (48b) refers to an indefinite/non-bounded plurality of acts. Hence, clearly, Verkuyl's schemata are also valid for sentences with an indirect object. When the indirect object (in this case *a congress-goer*) contains an article, it is specified with respect to quantity and the sentence explicates perfectivity of the action – see (48a) above. And vice versa, when the indirect object is a bare plural (that is, a plural unaccompanied by an article or other marker of quantity, *congress-goers* in this case), and, hence, unspecified with respect to quantity, the sentence explicates imperfectivity of the action – see (48b).

To sum up the preliminary analysis of some of the basic points in Verkuyl's theory, it is worth pointing out that his two books, Verkuyl (1972) and Verkuyl (1993), notwithstanding their overall considerable contribution to aspectology, suffer from certain deficiencies which will be dealt with later in the book. Apart from the inadequacy in the treatment of the feature 'specified quantity of X' (here termed 'boundedness') in NPs, some of the other deficiencies pertain to the role of negation in the composition of the aspects, to the problem of whether certain types of adverbials take part in the formation of aspectual meanings, and if they do, how.

Now that the major assumptions in Verkuyl's theory and his role in the description of the devices for the explication of perfectivity and imperfectivity in English have been outlined in the present chapter, there is one central issue that remains to be settled. For the correct understanding of the aspect mechanism the notions of 'specified quantity of X' and 'unspecified quantity of X' are to receive an adequate interpretation. It is worth recalling the definitions of these categories that will later be shown to be fundamental:

'specified quantity of X' – "giving the bounds of the temporal interval in question";
'unspecified quantity of X' – "not giving the bounds of the temporal interval in question"

(Verkuyl 1972: 59). Following these definitions and the overall mechanism as described in Verkuyl's (1972) initial theory, it is both the subject and the object in sentences like (39a) below that ought to be regarded as bounded in time, and in sentences like (47) below it is both the subject and the object that ought to be regarded as non-bounded objects in time – although, at first sight, while *tourists* is an NP explicating non-boundedness, *the mountain* is an NP that ought to explicate boundedness:

(39) a. Katinka knitted a Norwegian sweater
(47) Tourists climbed the mountain

How is it that *Katinka* and *a Norwegian sweater* can be regarded as temporally bounded objects, and *tourists* and *the mountain*, respectively, as temporally non-bounded objects? Rather surprisingly, Verkuyl hardly addresses this problem in both the initial and the extended theory. Or at least to the extent that he addresses it, he does this in a framework different from the one chosen here. This point will be discussed in Chapter Five, *Extension in time of subjects and objects from a "common-sense" point of view*, where it will become clear that Verkuyl (1972) was really justified in assigning the values of 'specified quantity of X' and 'unspecified quantity of X' to physical objects. But in his extended aspectual theory Verkuyl (1993) assumed an approach different from the one in Verkuyl (1972). While Verkuyl (1972), through the definitions of 'specified quantity of X' and 'unspecified quantity of X' given above, fostered an assumption that the referents of NPs could be conceived of as temporal, in Verkuyl (1993) he started to regard the information from NPs as purely atemporal and separated from the temporal information provided by the verb component. In Verkuyl (1993) the major aspect of the aspect mechanism appeared to be such that the temporal quantitative information in the verb component is somehow derived from the quantitative but atemporal information of the NPs. Besides, a distinction was made in Verkuyl (1993) between stages at which the transfer of the temporal information from the verb is made to the internal argument (i.e., the object in the sentence) and the external argument (i.e., the subject). Thus

Verkuyl's position in Verkuyl (1993) will be shown to differ not only from the model that will be put forward in the following chapters of this book but also from his own previous model. But before considering the problem of the extension in time of objects that are otherwise (normally) conceived of as physical, a more comprehensive description of the grammatical entities bearing on the explication of aspect in English is to be made – so that a more detailed picture of the devices effecting this explication should be constructed.

CHAPTER 4

THE ARTICLE AND THE RELATED MARKERS OF QUANTITY IN THE EXPRESSION OF ASPECT IN ENGLISH

THE ARTICLE/ZERO ARTICLE CONTRAST AND THE BOUNDEDNESS/NON-BOUNDEDNESS DISTINCTION

Verkuyl's (1972) understanding of aspect, if properly studied and interpreted, supplies ample opportunities for a conclusion to be reached that the article in languages like Dutch and English has a lot to do with the mechanism for explicating aspect distinctions. For some unclear reason, however, the author abstained from giving this problem proper consideration in his first book. Nor did he remedy the situation in the extended theory (Verkuyl 1993). What is more, the thesis that the article is a marker of 'specified quantity', bearing an extremely strong heuristic potential, constitutes a single minor statement in the original version of the theory:

"[the category] SPECIFIED is provisionally located in the Determiner"

(Verkuyl 1972: 59).

It seems to be a basic notion of modern universally-oriented grammar based on a language like English that NP determiners include, among other things, two outwardly insignificant elements called the definite and the indefinite article and subsumed under the generic name *article*. As the commonplace name itself suggests, the presence of a definite and an indefinite article in a Western European language (Germanic or Romance) is something taken for granted, something more than natural. Linguists who are native speakers of these languages are usually reluctant to pay special attention to this allegedly insignificant element. They also seem to have difficulties in taking into account and properly interpreting the fact that a language could either have or not have articles. But English does feature articles, and the general pattern of their use ought to be properly understood in terms of the contrasts it manifests with respect to patterns of article use in other languages. For example, although Bulgarian, unlike other Slavic languages, features an article system comprising a definite article and a very irregular pattern of forms reminiscent of the European type of indefinite article, considerable differences can be observed between the use of the definite article in English and in Bulgarian.

The tables below show certain details of the specificity of the use of articles in English – some of which (in Table 4 below) are usually absent in the types of descriptions proposed in grammars. Articles manifest significant differences in their use with respect to nouns denoting countable and non-countable objects, concrete (physical) and abstract objects, generic and non-generic notions. In a rather broad fashion, the use of articles with respect to count and non-count nouns can be represented in the following table:

Table 3

COUNT NOUNS

	definiteness	**indefiniteness**
singular	the	a (an)
example:	the book	a book
plural	the	–
example:	the books	books

NON-COUNT NOUNS

	definiteness	**indefiniteness**
	the	–
example:	the water	water

This table, considered alongside the major postulates of Verkuyl's compositional aspectual theory, facilitates a conclusion that the article in English (that is, both definite and indefinite article) is used in those cases when a noun is associated with the denotation of boundedness, conceived in a broad, abstract sense. Conversely, the lack of an article can easily be observed in cases when a noun is associated with the denotation of non-boundedness, again conceived in a broad, abstract sense. Cf. Table 4:

Table 4

	ARTICLE boundedness	NO ARTICLE (ZERO ART.) non-boundedness
count nouns	the book a book the books	books
non-count nouns	the water	water

Thus if the meanings of NPs like *the book, a book, the books* comprising count nouns and the meanings of NPs like *the water* comprising non-count nouns are contrasted (in isolation) to the meanings of NPs comprising bare nouns like *books* and *water*, the following can be established. While the former are generally conceived of as something specified/bounded with respect to quantity, the latter are conceived of as something unspecified/non-bounded with respect to quantity. The NP *the book* typically represents **one** book, definite, known to the speaker and the hearer – or at least identifiable by the latter within the context of utterance. Conversely, *a book*, although indefinite, unknown to both speaker and hearer, also normally represents **one** book. As far as plural forms are concerned, an NP like *the books* typically represents a specified quantity/range of books as well, and although the books may be unspecified with respect to their exact number, normally *the books* stands for a bounded number of books, in contrast to an NP like *books* which typically represents books that are not only unspecified with respect to their exact number but are also non-bounded (in broad spatial terms).

The same regularity can be observed with non-count nouns. While an NP like *the water* is generally conceived of as pertaining to a spatially bounded volume or stretch of water, the bare noun *water* is typically conceived of as referring to a spatially non-bounded volume or stretch of water. Similar observations have often been made in the literature. But while parallelisms between the temporal domain, namely the bounded/non-bounded distinction, and the spatial domain (as expressed by the mass/count distinction) are taken into account, the two domains are usually kept apart (cf., e.g. Tenny 1994: 24-26). The trivial fact that the mass/count distinction holds for nouns referring to physical entities, as well as for nouns referring to abstract, including purely temporal entities, is properly interpreted only rarely (see in this respect Langacker 1987). The implications of the use of nouns in reference to abstract entities will be explored in Chapter Ten, *Meanings of nouns and noun phrases, and aspect in English*.

Another important point to be made is that the broad notion of quantitative non-boundedness should not, of course, be understood to refer to 'eternal' quantity but should be regarded as a lack of indication of bounds of the quantity subsumed under the lexical denotation. Data from other languages featuring articles yield to a similar kind of analyses and conclusions, including data from Bulgarian with its specific pattern of article usage, and it is really surprising why so many grammars (including most grammars of English) fail to pay the necessary attention to the fundamental distinction between boundedness and non-boundedness. Perhaps only partly surprising, because, as will become clear later on, the fundamental distinction in question escapes the attention of the ordinary speaker of a language – for being too abstract and impracticable in terms of the immediate goals of everyday communication.

GENERIC AND NON-GENERIC

The pattern of the article used with count and non-count nouns should be complemented with the pattern of use of generic and non-generic nouns. Awareness of the specificity of these two patterns in English is important for the correct understanding of the aspect mechanism. Generic notions in English are expressed, for example, by subjects like *the cat*, *a cat* and *cats* in sentences like (49a) through (49e) below. Broadly speaking, the subjects in these sentences refer (or may refer) not to an individual representative or to some individual representatives of the genus 'cats' but to the genus as a whole.

(49) a. The cat drinks milk
 b. The cat is an animal
 c. A cat is an animal
 d. Cats drink milk
 e. Cats are animals

Conversely, non-generic are, for example, the subjects in sentences like (50a) through (50e). They refer to individual representatives or sets of individual representatives of the genus 'cats':

(50) a. The cat is drinking milk
 b. A cat is drinking milk
 c. The cats drink milk
 d. The cats are drinking milk
 e. Cats are drinking milk

Generic and non-generic meanings lack their own markers in English but with plural and non-count nouns the following regular pattern of correspondence between meaning and use is observed:

generic meanings → nouns without an article
non-generic meanings → nouns with an article

Generic and non-generic meanings arise as a combination of various factors, including the presence of the Progressive which excludes genericity. The following table shows the pattern of the article in English used to express generic notions.

Table 5

	GENERIC NOTIONS	
	COUNT NOUNS	
	singular	plural
article:	a, the	—
example:	a cat, the cat	cats
	NON-COUNT NOUNS	
article:	—	
example:	water	

The pattern of use of the article in English for the denotation of generic and non-generic notions is rather idiosyncratic, as translation equivalents of sentences like (49) in other European languages can show. For instance, the Bulgarian equivalents of (49) are different with respect to the use of the article, (49a) being the only exception. Cf. the English sentences in (49) and their Bulgarian correspondences in (51):

(49) a. The cat drinks milk = (51a)
 b. The cat is an animal = (51b)
 c. A cat is an animal = (51c) [(51c') and (51c'') are non-grammatical]
 d. Cats drink milk = (51d) [(51d') is only non-generic]
 e. Cats are animals = (51e) [(51e') is non-grammatical]
(51) a. Kotka-ta pie mljako
  Cat-the drinks milk
 b. Kotka-ta e životno
  Cat-the is animal
 c. Kotka-ta e životno
  Cat-the is animal
 c'. *Kotka e životno
  Cat is animal
 c''. *Edna kotka e životno
  One cat is animal
 d. Kotki-te pijat mljako
  Cats-the drink milk

    d¹. Kotki pijat mljako
        Cats   drink milk [only non-generic]
   e. Kotki-te sa   životni
      Cats-the are animals
   e¹. *Kotki sa   životni
       Cats   are animals

There is no way for the English sentences (49c), (49d) and (49e) to be literally translated through (51c'), (51c''), (51d') and (51e'). If rendered literally, preserving the corresponding articles, they are either ungrammatical or fail to convey the meaning of the original sentences. Thus (51c'), (51c'') and (51e') are totally ungrammatical, and (51d') can by no means make a generalisation with respect to the characteristic milk-drinking feature of cats. In Bulgarian, as well as in other languages, generic meanings in sentences similar to the English sentences in (49) are signified mainly through the definite article – both in the singular and in the plural. The true Bulgarian translation equivalents of the English sentences in (49) are sentences (51a), (51b), (51c), (51d), and (51e).

However, if the subject in Bulgarian usually requires a definite article to convey a generic meaning, the generic object can be with or without an article. Compare the following sentences:

(52)   a. Marija   običa knigi-te
          Maria   loves books-the
          'Maria loves books'
      b. Marija   običa knigi
          Maria   loves books
          'Maria loves books'
      c. Marija   običa zlato-to
          Maria   loves gold-the
          'Maria loves gold'
      d. Marija   običa zlato
          Maria   loves gold
          'Maria loves gold'

If the meaning of *knigi* 'books', *knigite* 'the books', *zlato* 'gold', and *zlatoto* 'the gold' in (52a) through (52d) above is to be regarded as invariably generic, the sentences in (52a) and (52b) are semantically equivalent, as are (52c) and (52d). But if in (52a) and (52c) a particular set of representatives/a particular amount of the genus can be referred to (= 'the/these books', 'the/this gold'), in (52b) and (52d) it is clearly only the genus itself ('books', 'gold') that is referred to.

The (syntactic) objects in the English translation equivalents (53) of the Bulgarian sentences in (52) above display a different regularity. While Maria in (53a) and (53c) below loves a particular set of books or amount of gold known to the speaker and hearer, in (53b) and (53d) Maria necessarily loves books and gold in general only:

(53) a. Maria loves the books
      b. Maria loves books
      c. Maria loves the gold
      d. Maria loves gold

In other words, in sentences like (53a) and (53c) an object-NP with a definite article is only non-generic; in sentences like (53b) and (53d) a bare object-NP is only generic. This regularity is different from the one that can be observed in the subjects of sentences like (49d) and (50c) – repeated below. With an article, the subject-NP is only non-generic; without an article, it can be generic or non-generic:

(50) c. The cats drink milk
(49) d. Cats drink milk

But there is a difference with respect to the object-NP, too. While bare object-NPs in sentences like (53b) and (53d) can only be generic, bare object-NPs in sentences like (50c) or (49d) can be either generic or non-generic. This difference is due to the impact of the lexical meaning of the verb.

Even closely related languages may differ with respect to the ways of explicating generic meanings in NPs with or without articles. If in English the zero article is used for the explication of generic meaning with plural nouns, and this is a general rule with very few and negligible exceptions, in German this rule has a narrower scope and many exceptions are allowed (in German plural nouns with a definite article often have generic or near-generic meanings). Besides the differences across languages, 'generic meaning' escapes the precise definition of a linguistic analytical tool. Rather than forming a clear-cut semantic contrast, the distinction between reference to a genus and reference to a representative/representatives of a genus ought to be seen as occupying the two extreme ends of a continuum. Factors like indefiniteness, tense, aspect, adverbial elements, repetition, non-specificity (cf. Stephanides-Diósy 1982), as well as others, exemplified above, like, for example, the syntactic realisation of NPs (as a subject or as an object), the lexical meaning of the verb in the sentence, etc., intertwine in a very complex fashion to produce a generic or a non-generic reading of an NP in a sentence. Thus, on the one hand, if what is predicated of *cats* in the English sentence (49d) involves the whole genus, this is not the case in the Bulgarian sentences (52a) and (52b), since *Maria* is unlikely to love all kinds of books; on the other hand, it can be doubted whether all cats drink milk, while all cats are certainly animals, etc.

(49) d. Cats drink milk
(52) a. Marija običa knigi-te
         Maria loves books-the
         'Maria loves books'
      b. Maria običa knigi
         Maria loves books
         'Maria loves books'

Generic meanings certainly call for a better explanation in view of their strong context dependency. Cavedon and Glasbey (1996) have recently proposed to model the context of generic sentences in terms of a theory of channels – linking the degree of specificity or generality of the reference of different sentence components within the intentions of the speaker to the opportunities given to the hearer to receive the information correctly.

The generic/non-generic grammatical contrast has theoretical linguistic implications as well as practical significance. Good acquisition of English by a foreign learner would be hard to achieve without a proper understanding of the patterns of article use in the expression of generic and non-generic meanings. This is especially valid for native speakers of languages which lack articles or in which articles are used differently to produce generic and non-generic NPs. Furthermore, the fact that the English language itself displays a rather specific pattern of the use of articles has to be taken into account in its description. Unfortunately grammars of English generally fail to address the problem adequately.

Although at a superficial glance the generic/non-generic distinction seems to have little to do with the perfective/imperfective distinction or even with aspectual meanings in general, these two semantic distinctions are in fact closely related. Consider the problem of explicating boundedness and non-boundedness **on the time axis**. According to Verkuyl's original (1972) theory in which (syntactic) subjects and objects display 'specified' or 'unspecified' quantity, *Katinka* and *a Norwegian sweater* in Verkuyl's sentence (39a) below ought to be regarded as implying what is here called 'bounded quantity' or 'boundedness on the time axis'. However, although this property is part of the perfectivity schema given in the previous chapter, it has not been made clear so far whether temporal boundedness should be seen as a purely syntactic feature arising from the presence of articles/determiners/quantifiers or whether it should mainly be regarded as a feature of the referent of the NP, only partly explicated by an article, a determiner or a quantifier. This is a result of the inadequacy and insufficiency in the treatment of this problem in Verkuyl's original theory.

Consider, for example, sentence (39a) below. Certainly, without a detailed analysis at least, it is very hard to conceive of (the referents of) *Katinka* and a *Norwegian sweater* as temporal entities – being, furthermore, bounded!

(39) a. Katinka knitted a Norwegian sweater

But if we follow Verkuyl's definition of 'specified quantity of X' as "giving the bounds of the temporal interval in question" and the definition of 'unspecified quantity of X' as "not giving the bounds of the temporal interval in question" (Verkuyl 1972: 59), then in all sentences patterned according to Verkuyl's perfectivity schema both the subject and the object (or their referents) will have to be regarded as temporally bounded entities. In (54), for instance, *the cats* and *the milk* will also have to be regarded as bounded in time:

(54)   The cats drank the milk

Indeed, it is hard for *the cats* and *the milk* in (54) to be regarded as time entities, let alone as entities bounded in time, because they are "seen" by the native speaker as physical objects that typically persist through time. Consider, however, the way *cats* in (49d), where the subject refers to the genus of 'cats', ought to be "seen":

(49)   d.   Cats drink milk

This sentence refers to a characteristic feature in the **behaviour** of all or most cats, not of their physical nature. Hence, the physical nature of 'cats' remains in the background of the meaning of the sentence, though this may not be easy to realise straight away. Since the **behaviour** of 'cats' is in question, it can be argued that *cats* in (49d) refers to a very abstract notion of 'cats' occupying an indefinite and non-bounded stretch of time, and not to the notion of 'cats' as physical objects.

But in that case is it not worth asking: don't *Norwegian sweaters* being knitted by Katinka in (40a) refer to a similar notion? Don't *Norwegian sweaters* refer to an abstract notion of 'Norwegian sweaters' occupying an indefinite and non-bounded stretch of time?

(40)   a.   Katinka knitted Norwegian sweaters

NATURAL AND ATYPICAL SITUATIONS

If we return to the problem of genericity discussed above, indeed, the phrase *Norwegian sweaters* could, to a certain extent, be considered a generic notion. The quantity, the number of Norwegian sweaters is not specified, therefore it is non-bounded. And, of course, it is non-bounded **in time**, since the sentence gives no indication of the length of the period in which the action took place. But before establishing the way 'non-boundedness in time' of the NP *Norwegian sweaters* in sentence (40a) is to be interpreted (the relevant analysis will be carried out in detail in the forthcoming chapter), let us go back to Verkuyl's imperfectivity schema above (38) and try to assess the degree to which it is valid for the object and the subject in the sentences.

SCHEMA FOR IMPERFECTIVITY (durativity, in Verkuyl's terms)
(38) S[NP1[(UN)SPECIFIED QUANTITY OF X]NP1 + VP[V[VERB]V + NP2[(UN)SPECIFIED QUANTITY OF X]N

This schema and the examples presented so far show clearly that many simple English sentences with a subject, a verb and an object can explicate imperfectivity of the action in case the object is not accompanied by an article or some other marker of bounded quantity[1]. An article or a similar determiner may be absent in two cases: when the object is plural or when it is non-count. Compare the sentences in (40a) and (41a) below (some of them are Verkuyl's own, some are slightly changed), in which the actions, contrasted with the actions in sentences like (39), very clearly explicate imperfectivity. Imperfectivity becomes especially marked if the article is removed from both the object and the subject, cf. (40b):

(40) a. Katinka knitted Norwegian sweaters
      b. Women knitted Norwegian sweaters
(39) a. Katinka knitted a Norwegian sweater
      b. Arie ate a herring
(41) a. Arie ate herrings

Now consider again the perfective schema:

SCHEMA FOR PERFECTIVITY (terminativity, in Verkuyl's terms)
(37) S[NP1[SPECIFIED QUANTITY OF X]NP1 + VP[V[VERB]V + NP2[SPECIFIED QUANTITY OF X]NP2]S

According to Verkuyl's schemata (38) and (37), sentences explicating imperfective actions ought to be automatically derived if the article is removed only from the subject. But if we try to do this to the sentences in (39), the procedure will yield strange or (at least) atypical sentences (55), on the basis of which it will be hard to draw adequate conclusions related to aspectual meaning.[2]

(55) a. Women knitted a Norwegian sweater
      b. Men ate a herring

---

[1] Cf. in connection with this the discussion of quantity in Harlig (1983).

[2] The same is also true of the Bulgarian equivalents. Cf. the possible aspectual readings of the English sentences and the way these should be rendered in Bulgarian – it is not clear whether the imperfective Imperfect or the perfective Aorist would be more appropriate, though both aspectual forms are possible in the translation equivalents:
(55) a. Women knitted a Norwegian sweater
          'Ženi ?pletjaha$_{impfvImp}$/?izpletoha$_{pfvAor}$ edin norvežki pulover'
      b. Men ate a herring
          'Măže ?jadjaha$_{impfvImp}$/?izjadoha$_{pfvAor}$ edna heringa'

It is clear now that if the removal of the article in the syntactic objects in sentences of type (39) is generally possible, and that if after the removal of the article the sentences remain entirely acceptable and natural, elimination of the article and hence the non-boundedness of the syntactic subject does by no means always (and automatically) lead to natural sentences, fully acceptable to the native speaker's ear (see similar conclusions in Shi 1990).

Now consider the following ten sentences denoting typical everyday actions and corresponding to Verkuyl's schema of perfectivity:

(56) a. A/The boy threw a/the stone
 b. A/The child ate an/the apple
 c. A/The soldier crossed a/the street
 d. A/The girl ironed a/the skirt
 e. A/The woman cleaned a/the room
 f. A/The mechanic repaired a/the car
 g. A/The housewife prepared a/the lunch
 h. A/The passer-by signed a/the appeal
 i. A/The secretary typed a/the report
 j. A/The journalist read a/the newspaper

On the basis of these ten sentences, clearly denoting actions bounded on the time axis, it is not difficult to establish that, indeed, English features a formal pattern for explicating perfectivity. At the purely syntactic level, it is based on the SVO pattern, and at the semantico-syntactic level, it is effectuated through an agent, an action and an object to the action. The agent performs a certain action which affects or, less frequently, effects, an object; the action is necessarily brought to an end; out of the action usually a certain pragmatically definable (in terms of knowledge of the world) result emerges.

The variety of situations described in the sentences in (56) above makes it clear that sentences denoting similar actions can be constructed (and actually exist) in hundreds and thousands. For example, a child can peel or draw an apple, the girl can soil or wash or tear or sew the skirt, a secretary can type or bring or send a report, etc. The actions can be physical or abstract: the soldier may forget the street, the woman may like the room, the passer-by may support the appeal, the journalist may overlook the newspaper, etc. If these and many similar kinds of actions are to be described in English, the same semantico-syntactic pattern will be used, only the verbs will be different. Subjects and objects in the pattern can, of course, also be changed: the boy can throw not a stone but a ball or a bag, the child may eat not an apple but a sandwich, the secretary may type not a report but a letter, etc. In most cases physical actions would conform to Vendler's accomplishment type; certain psychological events (cf. verbs like *forget, like, disapprove, spot, overlook*) would tend to conform to the achievement type.

The variety of situations pertains also to the agents in the sentences. They can perform actions that are different in the length and fashion of their accomplishment, and these actions can affect various objects. Thus a forester can fell a tree, a shoemaker can mend a shoe, a thief can steal the money, a teacher can give a lesson, a researcher can make an experiment, etc., etc. Of course, all these actions can be perfective, but they can be imperfective as well. In languages that in the past were traditionally called aspect languages, e.g. the Slavic ones, the notions of perfectivity or imperfectivity will be expressed through the verb itself. But, given the assumptions made so far, it seems only natural that there should be a way for all these actions to be expressed as either perfective or imperfective in any language. If we compare Slavic languages and a language like English, it will become evident that the explication of imperfectivity is, in principle, much easier, since for the expression of perfectivity special markers will always be needed. As already pointed out, it was in Verkuyl's schema for perfectivity that the mechanism for the expression of this type of action/situation was revealed for the first time in the history of linguistics. But some of the aspects of the aspect mechanism remained unclear then, and some other basic issues are still far from settled in the literature.

If the aspectual reading of the actions in sentences like (56) is to be changed, the article in the objects can always be eliminated. Given this change, actions in most cases turn from perfective into imperfective:

(57) a. A/The boy threw stones
      b. A/The girl ironed skirts
      c. A/The woman cleaned rooms
      d. A/The mechanic repaired cars
      e. A/The secretary typed reports

Of course, this transformation, too, will not always yield natural sentences. Not all the sentences in (57) describe ordinary events that are perfectly natural and easy to visualise in their details.

The problem, already touched upon above, will turn more severe if we try to eliminate the article in the subjects of these sentences, without eliminating the article in the objects. Natural, though perhaps not so typical, will then be only some of the resulting sentences. Compare, for example, the following sentences:

(58) a. Soldiers crossed the street
      b. Women cleaned the room
      c. Mechanics repaired the car
      d. Passers-by signed the appeal

The reason for the unnaturalness of some of these sentences has to do with the reasons why certain situations are regarded as typical and others as atypical. Largely normal and typical is, for example, a situation in which a given agent performs an action directed towards a number of objects – cf. the situations described in sentences like (57) above. It is a much rarer situation, however, for a number of agents to perform an action directed towards a single object, as is the case in (58).

Therefore, although not abnormal, a situation in which a concrete object is acted upon by an indefinite and quantitatively unspecified multiple agent, the action itself being temporally non-bounded, is to be regarded as generally atypical. Hence, not all sentences like those in (56) can easily be transformed from explicating perfective actions into explicating imperfective actions through the elimination of the article in the subject. In an effort to carry out such a transformation for analytical linguistic purposes, there is a high probability that it will contradict the native speaker's intuitions about correctness and incorrectness of language expressions or the typicality and atypicality of situations denoted by sentences.

On the other hand, if the sentences in (58) above are analysed in detail, it can be established that some of them (or even all of them) can be interpreted as designating **either** imperfective or perfective actions. Still, if the illustrative material in (58) is compared to that in (56), it will be seen that the probability for the sentences in (58) to designate imperfective actions in a given discourse is much higher than for the sentences in (56).[3] And if the article is missing in both the subject and the object, as in sentences like (59) below, the aspectual reading much more definitely changes into an imperfective one:

(59)   a. Boys threw stones
      b. Children ate apples
      c. Mechanics repaired cars
      d. Passers-by signed appeals
      e. Secretaries typed reports

But, in the long run, it is a certain integrity or non-integrity of the situation in the problematic sentences of type (58) that is at issue. This is only natural, because sentences like (58) refer to situations that can rarely be independent from a larger context. As Tenny (1994: 27) puts it, sentences with count noun objects and bare plural subjects are often "awkward". It also seems that the past tense of the described situation adds to the ambiguity – and to the suspicion that since a sentence with a non-bounded subject and a bounded object does not fit in easily with Verkuyl's imperfective schema, this might refute the general regularity. Sentences with non-bounded subjects and bounded objects explicating imperfectivity are indeed rare in the literature. Verkuyl (1972) and Verkuyl (1993) offer just a handful of such examples, like those in (60a), (60b), (41b) below.

---

[3] It is true a sentence like *Mechanics repaired the car* is not at all unnatural in its perfective reading. This point was made by an anonymous reviewer, as well as by other people in personal communication. Therefore, it is probably worth emphasizing the following again. First, it is just a **general tendency** for sentences with a bare plural like those in (58) to be read imperfectively, not that they are to be regarded as **always** imperfective. Second, in spite of this tendency, probably **all** sentences of this kind could be perfective in actual discourse, depending on a very large number of factors: type of quantification of NP constituents, the lexical semantics of nouns and verbs used, the semantic effects of combining words together, and, first of all, context. Third, vice versa, all perfective sentences can be read imperfectively (an already trivial observation in aspectology). Fourth, as will be shown in Chapter 14, 'knowledge of the world', an additional factor, plays a specific role in determining the aspect of many types of sentences, overriding other rules.

(60) a. Water streamed out of the rock
    b. Children came in
(41) b. Policemen walked from the Mint to the Dam

A good example of this kind, (61a), is offered by Dowty (1979: 63). However, to be able to count as typical, it desperately needs the time adverbial *for years* – or something similar. Otherwise it has an equally possible perfective reading, compare (61b):

(61) a. Tourists discovered that quaint little village for years
    b. Tourists discovered that quaint little village

Shi (1990: 49) even provides an example with a bare plural *tourists* as subject which can obviously be read as primarily perfective because the sentence contains an *in*-time phrase, considered to be the standard test for perfectivity:

(62) Tourists drank the milk in an hour

But in his attempt to exclude the role of the subject in the composition of perfectivity Shi goes too far by claiming that also the subject in a sentence like (63a) below does not play a role and that a sentence like this should be viewed as perfective. As already pointed out earlier in Chapter Three, *Verkuyl's theory of compositional aspect*, it should not be forgotten, however, that the imperfectivity of a sentence like (63b) is just a default, primary reading, not the only possible one.

(63) a. Tourists wrote a/one/the letter in an hour
    b. Tourists wrote a/one/the letter

Hence, it can be argued that the interpretation of (63b) that allows (63a) to be read perfectively is the secondary one. Furthermore, the semantic content of a sentence like (63a) appears too strange anyway for the sentence to be interpreted aspectually in a definite and precise way.

Sentences with a marked imperfectivity and with subjects that are non-bounded can sometimes easily be constructed out of sentences with bounded subjects explicating perfectivity. For instance, Harlig's sentence (64a) below with an *in*-time adverbial, about which he argues that it can only be true after all five hundred ants are in the pantry (see Harlig 1983: 166-167), can be changed into (64b) – to explicate imperfectivity:

(64) a. Five hundred ants trailed into John's pantry in two days
    b. Ants trailed into John's pantry

It could be argued, however, that imperfectivity here is not so much a result of a global semantico-syntactic mechanism, as of the inherent properties of the situation, including knowledge of the world (the impossibility to count so many ants).

A REVEALING EXAMPLE OF A NON-BOUNDED SUBJECT

To avoid the problem of the non-integrity in the description of a given situation, and supply another illustrative example of non-boundedness of an action with a non-bounded subject, a case of a special sentence in English will be considered here. The original authentic sentence was constructed in a wrong way by a non-native speaker of English – as if to illustrate marvelously the interdependence between aspect and subjects with or without articles. Here is the setting in which the authentic and wrongly constructed sentence was used.

To use an in-town bus, a trolley-bus or a tram service in Bulgaria one is usually obliged to buy a ticket before boarding and then perforate the ticket in a perforating device within the vehicle. For several years in the past, all the buses in the Black Sea resort of Varna, Bulgaria, contained a message for tourists in Bulgarian – reproduced below as sentence (65a). The Bulgarian message was translated into English through sentence (65b) – which is a wrong translation. The correct translation of the Bulgarian sentence (65a) is (65c), not (65b)!

(65) a. Pătnici-te trjabva da si kupuvat$_{impfv}$ bileti predvaritelno i da gi perforirat$_{biasp}$ v avtobus-a
Passengers-the have to *prt.* buy tickets beforehand and to them perforate in bus-the

b. The passengers have to buy tickets beforehand and perforate them in the bus

c. Passengers have to buy tickets beforehand and perforate them in the bus

Let us consider these sentences in more detail.

Certainly, for the native speaker of English, both sentences, (65b) and (65c) above, are entirely grammatical and perfectly acceptable. But they mean two completely different things. If a native speaker of English receives the instruction in (65b), he/she will normally conceive of the situation in approximately the following way. This is a particular occasion on which a certain group of passengers are to travel by bus. They have to buy tickets beforehand and perforate them in the bus if they want to have a ride without committing an offence and being fined. That is, the sentence with the subject with an article would be acceptable in the following kind of circumstances. An English-speaking group of tourists has arrived in Varna and has to use a bus. Without explaining the rules for paying the fare in detail, the Bulgarian guide addresses the person in charge of the group by giving him the instruction in (65b), beginning with a subject accompanied by an article. But if the authentic instruction, contained in the Bulgarian sentence (65a), is to be adequately rendered in English, sentence (65c), with the bare-noun subject, is to be used. It is this sentence, and not (65b), that conveys the message that all possible passengers who might want to travel in the bus at any time are to buy tickets beforehand and perforate them in the bus. The essential difference in meaning is a direct consequence of the use and omission of the article in the subject with a noun in the plural. Note that this use is characteristic of the English language – in similar sentences in other Western European languages the subject would tend to be accompanied by an article.

The use of a plural bare-noun subject in an English sentence of this kind is reminiscent of the generic use discussed above. It is for the whole "genus of passengers" who want to travel in this particular bus (or in this particular resort) that the following rule is valid: whoever wants to travel, has to buy a ticket beforehand and perforate it in the bus. Alternatively, in case an article (a definite article) is used, the attention of the hearer is immediately directed to a situation in which a particular group of passengers, not a particular "genus of passengers", is referred to.

The interdependence between the quantitative characteristics of the plural subject and the aspect of the action in a sentence is not occasional or accidental. It is a general rule of the semantics and grammar of English. But this rule can hardly be convincingly exemplified by context-independent sentences like those given earlier or in (58b), (58c) and (59a) below – that is, by sentences used outside a context free of ambiguities and familiar to the recipient of the message.

(59) a. Boys threw stones
(58) b. Women cleaned the room
c. Mechanics repaired the car

On the other hand, when the (potential) context of a particular isolated sentence is transparent, unambiguous, easy to reconstruct, as in Verkuyl's sentence (41b) or in sentences like (47) and (58d) below, the ability of the sentence to explicate imperfectivity of the action is not subject to any doubt whatsoever.

(41) b. Policemen walked from the Mint to the Dam
(47) Tourists climbed the mountain
(58) d. Passers-by signed the appeal

OTHER MARKERS OF BOUNDEDNESS

So far, sentences of a particular kind have been discussed, in which the explication of perfectivity or imperfectivity depended on the presence or absence of an article in the subject and/or the object implying what has already been termed 'boundedness'. But the article is not the only marker that can be associated with the explication of boundedness. A similar function is performed by other elements of the language. Consider the sentences in (66) below in which certain changes to some of the sentences used so far have been introduced:

(66) a. John/He threw a stone
 b. Ann's sister cleaned the room
 c. The soldier crossed this/that street
 d. The mechanic repaired my car
 e. Twenty passers-by signed the appeal
 f. The secretary typed some/many reports

In the first sentence, (66a), the former subject *the boy* has been replaced by *John*. The aspectual meaning remains the same. Proper names contain in themselves the meaning explicated by the definite article (whatever its definition). Every proper name can be viewed as a reconstruction of a phrase containing *the*. Thus *John* is a reconstruction of the phrase *the man named John*. The fact that proper names preserve the contribution of the article to the aspectual meaning of the sentence is significant with respect to the description of the semantic and functional characteristics of the article but has (almost) never been dealt with in the literature.

Personal pronouns can also be used to substitute nouns explicating definiteness, hence boundedness, and their use does not contradict the aspectual meaning, at least in the sentence (66a) under discussion. Thus both proper names and personal pronouns in English are capable of preserving the aspectual meaning due to their capacity to explicate or imply definiteness and maintain the import of the article. But if proper names naturally refer to unique singular objects persisting through time that cannot easily be seen as an indefinite number of objects or an indefinite quantity of a substance, personal pronouns, despite their name, are able to refer in certain cases to generic nouns as well. Cf. the pronouns *them* and *it* in sentences like (67a) and (67b):

(67) a. John likes dogs and Mary likes them too
 b. John likes whiskey and Mary likes it too

If languages like English, German and Bulgarian were found earlier to differ in their ways of referring to generic and non-generic concepts through articles, the examples below will show that all these three languages display the capability of personal pronouns to refer to either generic or non-generic concepts. For instance, the German sentence (68a) below, presented by Krifka (1989: 34), and its translation equivalents in Bulgarian (68b) and English (68c) show the interesting phenomenon that pronouns are so flexible that they can not only refer back to either the boundedness or non-boundedness of the antecedent, cf. (67a) and (67b) above. They can also be used with a reference different to the one present in the antecedent when the antecedent is represented by a noun unaccompanied by an article:

(68) a. Anna hat Gold gekauft, weil es wertvoll ist (German)
 Ann has gold bought because it valuable is
 'Anna bought gold because it is valuable'

b. Ana kupi_pfvAor zlato, tăj kato to e cenno (Bulgarian)
   Ann bought   gold   because   it is valuable
   'Anna bought gold because it is valuable'
c. Anna bought gold because it is valuable (English)

German *es*, Bulgarian *to*, and English *it* here refer **semantically** to gold in general, not to the gold Ann bought, although **nominally** the three pronouns do refer to the gold mentioned in the previous clauses. Note, however, that if the antecedent is made definite, as in (69) below, the pronouns in all the three languages can hardly be said to refer to gold in general.

(69) a. Anna hat   das   Gold gekauft, weil   es wertvoll is (German)
        Ann has   the   gold bought   because it valuable is
        'Anna bought the gold because it is valuable'
     b. Ana   kupi_pfvAor zlato-to, tăj kato to e cenno (Bulgarian)
        Ann   bought   gold-the because   it is valuable
        'Anna bought the gold because it is valuable'
     c. Anna bought the gold because it is valuable (English)

Although certainly gold in general is valuable, *es*, *to* and *it* here refer only to the particular gold bought by Ann. But in spite of the possibility of having such special cases, personal pronouns can be defined as generally conforming to the meaning of the antecedent that contributes to the explication of the aspectual reading of the sentence.

In a sentence like (66b), repeated below, the subject NP *the woman*, as in the previously used sentence (56e), is replaced by *Ann's sister*:

(56) e. A/The woman cleaned a/the room
(66) b. Ann's sister cleaned the room

Ann's sister preserves the definiteness of the antecedent. It can be supposed that it is the ability of the proper name to explicate definiteness that influences the explication of definiteness in phrases like *Ann's sister*. But this phenomenon, again, is a language-specific feature of English, not a universal trait. In Bulgarian, a proper name in a possessive function loses the status of a marker of definiteness characteristic of the separate proper name. It must always be accompanied by a definite article for definiteness to be signalled. Cf. the following correspondences between Bulgarian and English:

Bulgarian			English
Anina sestra		=	a sister of Ann's
Anina-*ta* sestra[4]	=	the sister of Ann/Ann's sister [as with a definite article]

Definiteness is also displayed by demonstrative pronouns, hence boundedness of the original NP, if it is present, is, as a rule, preserved. If *the street* is substituted by *this/that street*, as in (56c) – (66c), the change produces no shift in the aspectual reading of the derived sentence – both (56c) and (66c) are perfective:

(56) c. A/The soldier crossed a/the street
(66) c. The soldier crossed this/that street

The same is valid if plural definite subjects are substituted by demonstrative pronouns: the aspectual reading of sentence (70a) remains the same (perfective) in the derived sentence (70b):

(70) a. The soldiers crossed the street
     b. These/those soldiers crossed the street

This could be accounted for by the trivial observation that definiteness is a basic feature of demonstrative pronouns. However, as already shown, definiteness and boundedness (in broad quantitative terms), although overlapping considerably in semantic space, are different notions. Hence, confirming the preservation of the aspectual meaning does not seem to be superfluous, also in view of the fact that it is generally ignored in the literature.

Possessive pronouns in English are also able to express definiteness or to preserve it from the original sentence with a noun accompanied by a definite article. In (66d) the perfective aspectual reading is also preserved with respect to (56f), presumably due to the ability of English possessive pronouns to signal definiteness.

(56) f. A/The mechanic repaired a/the car
(66) d. The mechanic repaired my car

The preservation of definiteness by possessive pronouns, again, is a special feature of English and some similar languages. Other languages, including Bulgarian, distinguish between definite and indefinite possessive pronouns – possessive pronouns can be accompanied by articles like ordinary nouns:

Bulgarian			English
moja kola		=	a car of mine
moja*ta* kola[5]	=	my car

---

[4] -*ta* is a postpositioned definite article.
[5] -*ta* is a postpositioned definite article.

There are many words in English designating quantity and termed 'quantifiers'. Their syntactic location and behaviour are similar to those of articles and other determiners, like demonstratives. Their use in NPs also leads to the explication of what Verkuyl called 'specified quantity', i.e. bounded quantity. In sentences like (66e) and (66f), repeated below, the quantifiers *twenty*, *some* and *many* directly designate the boundedness of the quantity, and more specifically the number of agents or objects taking part in the action:

(66) e. Twenty passers-by signed the appeal
    f. The secretary typed some/many reports

The contrast to be made is between sentences like (66e) and (66f) and sentences in which there is no indication of quantity in the (syntactic) subject and/or the (syntactic) object. Compare (66e) and (66f) with (58d) and (57e):

(58) d. Passers-by signed the appeal
(57) e. A/The secretary typed reports

While the absence of an article or some other quantifier leads to the explication of non-boundedness in the subject- or object-NP in the sentence, determiners and quantifiers serve to explicate boundedness. With its potential to explicate 'bounded quantity', the article could also be considered a quantifier, and the same would be valid for demonstratives, etc., and even for proper nouns. It can be generalised that when an action in a sentence is performed by a subject explicating boundedness and affects an object also explicating boundedness, the action itself will be bounded, perfective. However, firstly, recall that for an action to be perfective, telicity should also prevail in the lexical semantics of the verb or in the particular meaning of the verb involved in a particular case. Secondly, the generalisation made above will be shown later to be valid indeed, but its place within the overall aspect mechanism should be (and will be) much more precisely defined.

Clearly, in the explication of perfectivity and imperfectivity in simple sentences of the SVO type in English discussed so far an essential role is played by quantifiers and NP determiners. Hence, it can be argued that quantifiers are not only words directly designating quantity but also such that are capable of explicating or implying bounded quantity, in contrast to the non-bounded quantity explicated by the absence of an article, a quantifier and a determiner. Therefore, the absence of an article, the zero article, can subsume lack of other elements in the NP designating quantity. For example, NPs like *women*, *blonde women*, *beautiful blonde women*, *beer*, *delicious beer*, *cold delicious beer*, etc. can be (and will be henceforward) referred to as NPs without an article, NPs with a zero article or, since they also lack other markers of quantity of the type described above, unquantified NPs. Conversely, NPs containing an article (definite or indefinite) or other determiners and markers of quantity can be (and will be henceforward) referred to as quantified.

Lastly, the language entities called quantifiers here play a decisive role for the explication of aspectual distinctions specifically in simple sentences of the type discussed so far. As already mentioned, these sentences constitute an important semantico-syntactic pattern which allows significant generalisations to be made with respect to aspect meaning and the functions that different language elements perform in its explication. But the role that quantifiers play in the expression of aspect is not restricted to this simple type of sentences. As the examples (65b) and (65c) above with the passengers and the tickets showed, it is also valid for more complex sentences, and it will gradually be shown to be valid for sentences used in larger contexts as well. Verkuyl's theory (in both its 1972 and its extended 1993 version) pays enormous attention to various kinds of quantifiers. But it almost entirely neglects the role of the article for the expression of aspect. The article is unjustifiably considered in it as only one among many other determiners that have to do with aspect. This may be a natural decision for a Western-European approach towards the problem, since the article is viewed as an integral part of an NP. However, from the point of view of Slavic languages for example, which lack articles (Bulgarian is only a partial exception), the role of the article assumes a major importance. Consider the trivial fact that the article in English (or in any other Germanic or Romance language) is the major determiner. Actually, as we have already seen, the article is a quantifier, and, statistically speaking, it is **the major** quantifier. Other markers of bounded quantity (proper names, personal, possessive and demonstrative pronouns, ordinary quantifiers, etc.), if compared to the article, turn out to form an insignificant part of the number of functional (closed-class) words actually used in discourse to explicate or imply boundedness.

A comparison between the role of the article in English and similar languages to explicate boundedness (and, hence, perfectivity of an action), the general structure of Slavic languages and the principles underlying their overall aspect mechanism will be made in Chapter Seven, *The interdependence between markers of boundedness in verbs and in nouns*. Before that, the following chapter will deal with the features 'boundedness' and 'non-boundedness' **in time** – or, in other words, with the crucial problem of how NPs denoting physical entities are to be conceived of as temporal entities. As already mentioned, in his initial theory Verkuyl (1972) assigned somewhat ambiguously these features to referents of subjects and objects, but he did this by necessity, from a certain logical point of view. He neither offered an account of how and why boundedness and non-boundedness actually emerge, nor did he propose an explanation of the phenomenon from the point of view of the ordinary speaker of a language – that is, from a common-sense point of view which forms the basis of the semantics of natural language. An explanation of this kind will be offered in the forthcoming chapters. Furthermore, an ontological distinction will be proposed, valid at least for aspectological studies, according to which the referents of subjects and objects in all sentences in a language can be viewed as either bounded or non-bounded temporal entities. The model is similar to Carlson's (1980) well-known tripartition between kinds, individuals and stages. Carlson's tripartition has already been used in a large number of studies and is thought to underlie a certain organisation of man's abilities to process data from reality. No claim will be made here that the distinction between bounded and non-bounded entities (to be proposed) is necessarily relevant outside aspectology. But since boundedness and non-boundedness are phenomena also found in other language spheres (tense and temporality in general), the distinction may as well turn out to be applicable as an analytical tool in other linguistic spheres.

The "common-sense" explanation of the temporality of NPs denoting physical entities will facilitate the understanding of the phenomenon of aspect in English and in language in general and will put the potential of Verkuyl's model in its proper perspective. Gradually, an entirely novel and comprehensive theory of aspect will emerge, and a large number of regularities will be uncovered within and beyond the scope of language structure – aspect will be analysed as a phenomenon based on mechanisms governing the perception of reality, storing and processing of data from it and modelling it according to human needs.

CHAPTER 5

EXTENSION IN TIME OF SUBJECTS AND OBJECTS FROM A "COMMON-SENSE" POINT OF VIEW

MEASURING OUT EVENTS THROUGH SPATIAL PARAMETERS OF OBJECTS?

The prevailing bulk of aspectological studies using data from English and similar languages (like e.g. German) take it as their points of theoretical departure prototypical sentences of type (71) below when considering the expression of perfectivity. In this kind of sentences, already described, a typical singular agent performs an action directed towards a singular physical object which, after the completion of the action, undergoes an observable and identifiable change. In the first case the object is consumed, in the second created:

(71)   a. John ate an apple
       b. John built a house

The following quotation is a description that fits in with the prevailing trend of explaining the reasons why the semantics of phrases like *eat an apple* or *build a house* (given a typical singular subject) accommodates the completion of the event:

> "In [*eat an apple*], the eating event is understood to progress through the internal argument, the apple, until the end of the apple and of the eating event are achieved. Some quantity of apple is consumed during each interval of eating, until the apple is entirely consumed. In this way the apple provides a measure, in a sense, of the eating event. Verbs of creation as well as verbs of consumption can have incremental themes [...] The verb phrase in [*build a house*] describes a building event that progresses through the house in its various stages of completion. When the house is complete, then the house building is also complete. The final stage of the completed house provides a temporal terminus for the event. The apple and the house in the examples above [(71a) and (71b)] are incremental themes because increments of the house or the apple, as they are created or consumed, correspond to the temporal progress of the event. Moreover, there is a final increment which marks the temporal end of the event"

Tenny (1994: 15). Objects like *an apple* and *a house* (and similar objects) have also been called 'gradual patients', and the phenomenon has been referred to as 'mapping' – to objects or to events (Krifka 1992; Glasbey 1994: 276-278). Tenny uses the notion of 'measuring out' that applies to quantified direct objects of: (i) so-called incremental-theme verbs like *build* and *eat* (*build a house*, *eat an apple*); (ii) so-called change-of-state verbs like *ripen* and *explode*; and (iii) so-called route verbs like *walk* or *climb* (*walk a distance*, *climb a ladder*).[1] The term 'measuring out' has also been used by Glasbey (1994: 282-283). Referring to an alleged weakness in Verkuyl's theory, Glasbey points out one apparent problem of the approach discussed here: if in *eat an apple* the apple is gradually consumed to the end, in a phrase like *drive a car* there is nothing intrinsic to the car that can be measured that corresponds to the progress of the event, unless an expression such as *to Glasgow* is added (Glasbey 1994: 274). Hence, if perfectivity is to be explained at a systemic linguistic level that is not purely semantic, exploring the meanings of verb phrases as a combination or even some complex build-up of simply the semantics of the lexical components could hardly be expected to offer a satisfactory non-trivial solution.

Clearly, verb phrases containing a verb and a direct-object noun with an article can be either perfective (*build the house*, *eat an apple*, *paint the car*) or imperfective (*hate the house*, *carry an apple*, *drive the car*), and there have been many attempts to account for the different behaviour of the two types of phrases and the different types of relationships between the referents of the verbs and the nouns. Glasbey (1994: 274-278), reviewing some of the major attempts (mainly Verkuyl's and Krifka's 1992) to deal, formally or less formally, with the difference between the two types of phrases, admits that what she and other authors call 'a gradual patient' or 'an incremental theme' is a highly intuitive notion "which nevertheless seems to elude precise definition" (Glasbey 1994: 278). According to the approach in the present work, what notions like 'gradual patient', 'incremental theme', 'mapping to objects and events' or 'measuring-out' (of the event) all share in common is that they all try to find the true origin of the perfectivity of certain language expressions without resorting to the temporal parameters of the participants in the situations.

As a rule, if temporal properties of an event are discussed in the aspectological literature as built around the semantics of the verb and derived from the combination of the verb and an object and a subject, the properties of the object being consumed or created are regarded as purely or at least predominantly **atemporal**. If the object, as already argued in the preceding chapter, could in a way be viewed as having certain temporal properties, these properties either escape the attention of investigators or are ignored – probably for being judged as irrelevant. This holds for most of the larger descriptions of aspect in English (cf., e.g., Dowty 1979; Quirk et al 1985: 175-213; Tenny 1994; Smith 1994, to quote but a few). On the other hand, in those rare publications in which temporal properties of subjects and objects in sentences like (71a) and (71b) above are indeed taken into account, the temporal properties are considered alongside spatial ones and other, atemporal, properties (see Cooper 1985; Hinrichs 1985; Krifka 1989). The problem with the mixed, spatio-temporal approach will be discussed later on in this chapter, after introducing the

---

[1] See also Krifka (1989) for another aspectological model based on prototypical cases of perfectivity as represented in phrases like *build a house* or *drink a glass of wine*.

temporal approach for interpreting participants in situations – the thesis assumed as fundamental for the present work.

There is at least one reason why an explanation of the perfectivity of events like *eat an apple* or *build a house* along the lines of e.g. Tenny's model (outlined above) can be considered insufficient, if not completely inadequate. There is nothing necessarily inherent in merely the overall semantics of the phrases *eat an apple* and *build a house* that presupposes perfectivity. Apple-eating and house-building can be represented as non-completed not only through the use of the Progressive, through the use of tenses different from the Simple Past, and, as already mentioned in earlier chapters, the Simple Past itself allows the expression of imperfectivity, provided certain lexical markers of indefinite repetition are present in the sentence or in the general context. In fact, Tenny herself admits repeatedly that such "canonical" perfective phrases like *eat an apple, climb the ladder/the bridge, play a sonata* could be interpreted as describing non-completed actions (Tenny 1994: 17, 24, 32). However, she assigns this primarily to idiolectal differences, without assuming two different possible aspectual readings for all or most sentences **in principle**.[2] Lastly, any appropriate comparison with a language in which perfectivity and imperfectivity are part of the grammatical structure (the verb paradigm), can easily corroborate the idea that the actions of *eat an apple* and *build a house* are not as strictly perfective as they can be when perfectivity is marked on the verb. Any translator of English into a Slavic language (e.g. Bulgarian, Russian) or any translator of a Slavic language into English will have no hesitation confirming that the following equivalents containing either a perfective or an imperfective verb in Slavic are perfectly legitimate as they are, out of context, and that they are fairly often realised in discourse with the verb in English in the Simple Past Tense form:

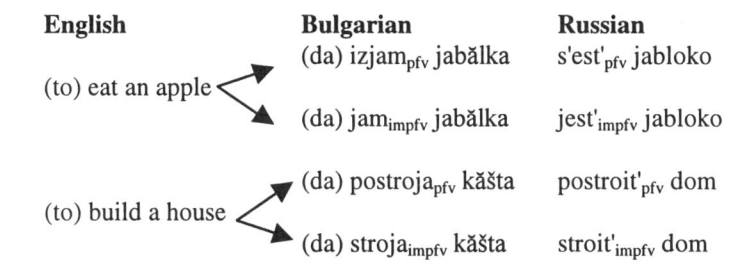

English	**Bulgarian**	**Russian**
(to) eat an apple	(da) izjam$_{pfv}$ jabǎlka	s'est'$_{pfv}$ jabloko
	(da) jam$_{impfv}$ jabǎlka	jest'$_{impfv}$ jabloko
(to) build a house	(da) postroja$_{pfv}$ kǎsta	postroit'$_{pfv}$ dom
	(da) stroja$_{impfv}$ kǎsta	stroit'$_{impfv}$ dom

---

[2] The following quotation reveals this point:

"Incremental-theme and change-of-state verbs (with the exception of achievement verbs) can for some people, with varying degrees of effort, be understood as describing non-delimited events. That would be the sense in which someone ate an apple or built a house for an extended period of time, but never finished the house or the apple. (They were eating *at* the apple, or building *on* the house, to put it colloquially.) Or they were ripening a banana or melting an ice cube as a kind of activity, without actually having a ripe banana or a melted ice cube to show for it."

(Tenny 1994: 33).

In the preceding chapter, ten sentences in English of the SVO type (56) expressing perfective actions were analysed.

(56) a. A/The boy threw a/the stone
b. A/The child ate an/the apple
c. A/The soldier crossed a/the street
d. A/The girl ironed a/the skirt
e. A/The woman cleaned a/the room
f. A/The mechanic repaired a/the car
g. A/The housewife prepared a/the lunch
h. A/The passer-by signed a/the appeal
i. A/The secretary typed a/the report
j. A/The journalist read a/the newspaper

As already pointed out, in Verkuyl's (1972) original aspectual theory subjects and objects in sentences of this kind are to be regarded as implying 'specified quantity', defined as "giving the bounds of the temporal interval in question" (Verkuyl 1972: 59). This means that the referents of these (syntactic) subjects and objects should be viewed as temporally bounded entities. Unfortunately, as already mentioned, Verkuyl's position with respect to whether subjects and objects of sentences like (56) are to be always regarded as temporal entities was rather ambiguous. Compare the following passage:

> "the semantic information 'UNSPECIFIED QUANTITY OF X' or 'SPECIFIED QUANTITY OF X' pertains directly or indirectly to the Time axis. That is, the quantities of X involved are expressible in terms of linearly ordered sets of temporal entities" [capitals in the original text]

(Verkuyl 1972: 96-97).

This passage, as well as the whole of Verkuyl's original work made it unclear how and when 'unspecified quantity of X' and 'specified quantity of X' would pertain **directly** to the time axis and how and when they would pertain **indirectly** to it. Therefore, it was not entirely surprising that in his extended aspectual theory Verkuyl (1993) took a step backwards and started to regard the (so-called there) SQA, that is, 'specified quantity of A', information at the NP level as **purely atemporal**, maintaining that this atemporal information is capable of contributing to the structuring of the temporal information at the level of the verb phrase or the whole sentence. But if the ambiguity of the original theory of Verkuyl is resolved in favour of the temporal interpretation of NPs, this automatically raises certain serious issues (which Verkuyl did not address) for the interpretation of sentences expressing imperfectivity in which either the subject or the object is unquantified. In this type of sentences the subject or the object represented by an unquantified NP ought to be regarded as implying 'unspecified quantity', i.e. temporal non-boundedness. Compare again the sentences in (57) and (58), repeated below, where, in the former, the (syntactic) objects are non-bounded and this matches the non-boundedness (the imperfectivity) of the action, and, in the latter, the (syntactic) subjects are non-bounded and this matches the non-boundedness (the imperfectivity) of the action:

(57) a. A/The boy threw stones
 b. A/The girl ironed skirts
 c. A/The woman cleaned rooms
 d. A/The mechanic repaired cars
 e. A/The secretary typed reports
(58) a. Soldiers crossed the street
 b. Women cleaned the room
 c. Mechanics repaired the car
 d. Passers-by signed the appeal

But what about the (syntactic) subjects in (57) and the (syntactic) objects in (58) which are accompanied by an article and, hence, ought to be associated with boundedness – which would then stand in contrast with the non-boundedness (imperfectivity) of the action?

This problem has not remained unnoticed in the literature, though it has not been dealt with from the point of view of the (possible) temporality of NP referents.[3] Jackendoff (1992: 25), analysing boundedness as a cross-categorial feature that can characterise both events and physical objects, made the observation that while in sentences like *Will you mop up that water, please?* and *The boys were impressed* the determiner or the article (*that water, the boys*) can be associated with the expression of boundedness, conversely, in sentences like *That water kept spurting out of the broken hose* and *The boys arrived for hours on end* the determiner or the article fail to associate themselves with the expression of boundedness. Jackendoff here apparently analysed the parameters of the subjects in the sentences in question in spatial (not temporal) terms, but the observation was made in connection with the potential of sentences to express boundedness also as a feature of events. It is interesting to note, first, that Jackendoff made the important point concerning the non-boundedness of *that water* and *the boys* (in the second pair of sentences above) from the point of view of the referent of the NP (*that water* "denotes a contextually identifiable medium, not a fixed amount"), and not from the point of view of the referent of the verb. Second, he emphasised that in the second pair of sentences

> "definiteness contributes only the content "contextually identifiable"; the determination of boundedness depends on other constraints"

(Jackendoff 1992: 25). But while the difference between the boundedness of *that water* and *the boys* in the first pair of sentences and the non-boundedness of *that water* and *the boys* in the second pair of sentences is easily conceivable in spatial terms (and, hence, perhaps also in temporal terms – for at least *the boys* can easily be thought of as "boy-arrivals"), the non-boundedness of the referents of singular subjects like *a boy, a girl, a mechanic*, etc. in sentences like (57a) through (57e)

---

[3] To the author's knowledge.

above (that will be argued for in this work) is much more difficult to grasp from the point of view of the ordinary speaker of the language. This is because if in a sentence like *The boys arrived for hours on end* the referent of the plural subject allows of spatial **and** temporal unbounding (i.e., it lends itself to the "boy-arrivals interpretation"), the referent of a singular subject in sentences like *The boy threw stones* or *The boy threw stones all day long* somehow escapes a non-bounded characterisation – because of the convention for *the boy* to be regarded as a spatially bounded entity, persistent, unchangeable through time.

In the preceding chapter it was established that *Katinka* and *a Norwegian sweater* (or the referents of these NPs) in the sentence (39a) below could, in a certain sense, be regarded as temporally bounded entities.

(39) a. Katinka knitted a Norwegian sweater

If this is taken for granted, the same ought to hold for many or all other similar syntactic subjects and objects, or, rather, their referents. For example, *the cats* and *the milk* in (54) should somehow be conceived of as temporally bounded, despite the fact that they are normally thought of as physical objects persisting through time:

(54) The cats drank the milk

Meanwhile it was established that *cats* in (49d), repeated below, refers more or less to the 'genus' of cats, and that in this sentence the physical nature of cats somehow remains in the background. Therefore, it seems perfectly natural to assume that *cats* in (49d) pertains to the abstract notion of 'cats' associated with an indefinite, unspecified, non-bounded stretch of time, rather than to the physical nature of cats:

(49) d. Cats drink milk

There is a vast logico-linguistic tradition of analysing sentences of this kind in which *cats* (and also *milk*) is considered to have two possible readings: the first one is called universal (which is more or less equal to generic); the second one is called existential (which is approximately equal to non-generic). The existential reading presupposes some concrete spatio-temporal existence of 'cat' or 'milk' exemplars. It is to be noted, however, that whether *cats* and *milk* in (49d) are interpreted as having a universal or existential meaning, they are certainly different from the participants of the event in (54) in which *the cats* and *the milk* are to be viewed as quantitatively identifiable exemplars – in contrast to *cats* and *milk* in (49d). Hence, as in the previous chapter, the question arises whether in a sentence like (40a) *Norwegian sweaters* (knitted by Katinka) does not refer to something that is in a similar fashion unspecified/non-bounded in time:

(40) a. Katinka knitted Norwegian sweaters

A conclusion was reached that the phrase *Norwegian sweaters* in (40a) does probably refer to something non-bounded in time – in terms of the fact that the sentence lacks any specification about the length of validity of the action described.

A PHYSICAL AGENT VIEWED AS A TEMPORAL OBJECT?

To try to explain how this temporal non-boundedness arises, let us analyse (58a), a sentence already used:

(58) a. Soldiers crossed the street

Compare (58a) to sentences like (72a) and (72b):

(72) a. A soldier crossed the street
       b. The soldier crossed the street

Let us first imagine the situation revealed before the eyes of the person (an observer/speaker) who would utter (72a) or (72b).

At a particular moment in the past the observer/speaker looked out of the window and saw a soldier cross the street. The action was performed from its natural beginning to its natural end; the observer saw the soldier cross the street from one pavement to the other. Note that in (72a) the entity 'a soldier' is introduced in the (imaginary/possible) discourse. This entity is unknown to both speaker and hearer and, therefore, the indefinite article is used. If the soldier were familiar to the speaker (or if he were already introduced earlier in the discourse), sentence (72b) would have been used, with a definite article in the subject. In both cases, however, the use of a definite or indefinite article, as already established, does not lead to differences in the interpretation of the aspectual meaning. It is perfective, brought to its natural end.

Now let us picture what should be revealed before the eyes of the observer/speaker so that he would be likely to produce sentence (58a). There are several possible situations that could be covered by a sentence of this kind. For example:

a) the action could be, broadly speaking, imperfective – and ambiguous with respect to whether it is habitual or current – due to the absence of a bounding expression (an article, another determiner or a quantifier);

b) the sentence could denote a perfective action, provided the context permits it or imposes it;

c) the sentence could denote a habitual action, that is, it could describe what the speaker observed on an unspecified number of occasions in the past (soldiers crossing the street from time to time, as in times of war); this interpretation version would then be equivalent to the meaning of sentence (73a) below and would contain two subversions – in the first one the street is crossed every time by a group of soldiers, and in the second the street is crossed every time by one soldier but all the soldier-crossings are merged into the overall situation denoted;

d) lastly, the sentence could, of course, also denote a situation taking place on a particular occasion – and then the meaning of (58a) would be equivalent to the meaning of (73b) with a verb in the Progressive.

(73) a. Soldiers used to cross the street
b. Soldiers were crossing the street

Clearly, sentence (58a) is rich in meaning and nuances of meaning, especially in its imperfective interpretation in which the non-completion of the action can be interpreted in various ways: from a progressive-like reading to one in which the action spans an hour or a day or a week, all the way through to the largest possible span in which the street in front of the observer's house may have been crossed all his life up to the moment of the utterance of the sentence.

Let us however, outline what the observer has most probably seen to be able to utter truthfully (58a) in its non-perfective reading. In an unspecified interval of time, whether it ranges over a few moments or many decades, the speaker observed the street. Soldiers were seen in it forming, literally or metaphorically, a sort of a file. The first part of the file is hidden behind one corner, the second part of the file is hidden behind a second corner. What is essential is that the soldiers are moving – and in fact constitute the action, which can also be described as 'a procession'. It is the verb in the sentence that is responsible for the direct denotation of the action. But it can be maintained that when the referent of the verb *cross* in its Simple Past Tense form is associated with a subject like *soldiers*, it transfers its feature 'movement' onto the subject itself. Especially important is that the moving group of soldiers is a non-bounded one: for the observer it is partly hidden behind the two corners, and he does not know where it starts and where it ends. Thus it is natural that the action itself (not only the group of soldiers) should be conceived of as non-bounded and, therefore, non-completed. Or, in other words, an action performed by a non-bounded agent moving in time and space is non-bounded itself.

Thus the referent of the subject *soldiers* in (58a) may be said to assume temporal parameters. Its spatial non-boundedness is associated with the meaning of the action *crossed* and transforms into temporal non-boundedness. But if the moving group of soldiers – given an appropriate explanation as the one offered above – could, with some mental effort, be "seen" by the native speaker as an object located in time, how could the referent of the subject *the soldier* in a sentence like (72b) be regarded as temporal?

(72) b. The soldier crossed the street

What is more, to fit Verkuyl's (1972) schema of perfectivity, the subject *the soldier* in (72b) is to be necessarily viewed not only as temporal, but also as bounded in time. Recall again, however, that in Verkuyl (1993) the (referent of the) subject in sentences of this kind is regarded as an atemporal entity which somehow contributes to the temporal properties of the sentence (more on this serious problem in Chapter Ten, *Meanings of nouns and noun phrases, and aspect in English*).

THE 'TELEVISION REPRESENTATION'

Let us, for the sake of convenience, use the term 'participant' to refer to both the agent/the source and the recipient of an action, whether they are animate or inanimate. To explain the temporal value of participants like *Katinka, the soldier, a Norwegian sweater* etc., a special technique will be used here, provisionally called 'a television representation'. To apply the technique, consider sentence (74):

(74)   The boy threw a stone

According to Verkuyl's theory and to the present approach, this is a sentence that explicates perfectivity. The problem to be solved through the 'television representation' is: how can in this sentence the action of throwing, along with the participants in it, be shown on a television screen?

This is how the 'television representation' can proceed.

The camera is fixed on a boy and a stone. Thereafter, the participant 'the boy' (familiar to the observer) and the participant 'a stone' appear on the television screen, the boy holding the stone in his hand. Here is where the "existence" of the two participants arises. The boy throws the stone. The stone flies, describes a trajectory and falls to the ground. The action is completed. The camera is shifted to a different direction. The boy and the stone disappear from the screen. Here is where the short-time existence of the participants in the action is brought to an end.

And so, what do the participants *the boy* and *a stone* constitute in this 'television representation' of the action? They constitute nothing more than two moving pictures on the screen that last so long as the action itself lasts. Moreover, they are entities that are bounded in time – since the beginning and the end of their "existence" are exactly determined. This is the explanation of the temporal status of participants like *the boy* and *a stone* in a sentence like (74).

A counterargument to the 'television representation' and its implications could run in the following fashion. The camera may have been fixed on the participants in advance, they can be shown on the screen much earlier than the action of throwing the stone takes place, as well as after the completion of the action. The answer to such a counterargument will be the following. If the camera is fixed on the boy and the stone before and/or after the throwing of the stone, and, generally, if the participants are present on the screen beyond the scope of the action described in (74), then they are taking part not only in the action described in (74) but in other actions (or states and other types of situations) as well. In this case, the actions and their participants ought to be described, according to the language rules, through a different sentence or through different sentences. Compare, for example, the following description of several actions (consecutive or simultaneous) among which the action described in sentence (74) is also present:

(75)   Some girls and a boy were playing in the street with stones. Suddenly a cat appeared from behind the corner. The boy threw a stone. The stone hit a policeman. The boy ran away

OTHER INTERPRETATIONS OF TEMPORAL 'SLICES' OF PHYSICAL OBJECTS

The possible temporal status of 'participants' has been discussed in linguistics outside Verkuyl's work – in which it is in fact only peripherally considered. The discussion can be traced back (at least) as far as the early 1960s in Quine's postulation of 'stages' of objects (Quine 1960). Later G.N.Carlson (1977/1980) extensively dealt with the problem and put forward a three-way division between 'stages' of objects, 'objects' (that is, ordinary objects, also called 'individuals'), and 'kinds' (like 'boys', 'stones' or 'gold'). Without going deeper into the technical details of G.N.Carlson's ontological tripartition, the following correspondences could be proposed. The entities *the boy* and *a stone* in (74) are 'stages' of ordinary 'objects' ('individuals') like 'the boy' and 'a stone' – such as they are dealt with in, for example the short narrative in (75). The 'ordinary objects' 'the boy' and 'a stone' could, of course, also be treated in a much larger narrative. A 'kind', then, is, roughly speaking, what was referred to earlier in this book as a 'genus'.

G.N.Carlson did not make a distinction between stages of objects/individuals that are bounded and stages that are non-bounded in time. He advanced, however, an important hypothesis, viz., that a distinction between stages, individuals and kinds might be a mode of organisation of man's cognitive potential. In his extended aspectual theory Verkuyl (1993: 131-132) loosely referred to 'categories' (Carlson's 'kinds') and to 'individuals' making up 'categories' but did not employ the distinction in his formal analysis. It is worth noting that in contrast to Quine's position, who dealt with the 'stage' issue in a broader philosophical framework, in Verkuyl's (1972), and especially in G.N.Carlson's work the problem was placed in a narrower linguistic perspective. Later, gradually, the notion of stage (whatever the particular term employed) began to appear useful for the description of certain regularities in the expression of temporal relations through language (see, e.g., Kabakčiev 1984b; Hinrichs 1985; Cooper 1985, Vlach 1993).

There is a certain tradition for the analysis of the temporal values of referents of NPs in sentences like (76):

(76)   a. Every fugitive is now in jail
       b. Every admiral graduated from Annapolis
       c. Most college students were lazy in highschool

For (76a) see Vlach (1993), for (76b) see Hinrichs (1988), for (76c) see (Musan 1999). Sentences like these pose certain interpretation problems (different for the different types of sentences) in that the face temporal value of the referent of the particular NP enters into a contradiction with the temporal information supplied by the rest of the sentence. Thus in (76a) a fugitive who is in jail again is not a fugitive any more. In (76b) an admiral who graduated from Annapolis was not an admiral then. In (76c) a college student was not yet a college student in highschool. Vlach (1993: 258) states that a previous paper of his (Vlach 1981b) may have been the first to recognise this problem and that it was Enç (1981) who also tackled it, though from a somewhat different perspective. It will be seen, however, that this analysis of the possible temporal values of NP referents is different from the approach assumed in this work. Furthermore, not all authors dealing with the temporal properties of NPs aimed at describing aspectual properties of sentences.

It is Hinrichs' (1985) model that may be said to come closest to the major thesis about temporality to be maintained in this book (cf. also Kabakčiev 1984a; 1984b), namely, that referents of subjects and objects are to be viewed as temporal entities. Hinrichs used Carlson's ontology of 'kinds', 'individuals' and 'stages' and described in detail the properties of sentences involving 'stage'-level events. 'Stages' in his theory are, however, not just temporal but **spatio-temporal** instances of 'individuals', and this is one point in which his approach differs from the one assumed in the present work. Instances of 'individuals' being viewed as **spatial** in addition to temporal, there was no way for Hinrichs (1985: 256) not to suggest that, for example, the stage of an agent performing a sonata in a particular auditorium must be present somewhere in that auditorium.

This proves to be a serious problem, however. On the one hand, actions are not always associated with physical locations. If somebody performing a sonata in an auditorium may or must, indeed, somehow be associated with a location in that auditorium, this can hardly be the case when, for example, somebody guesses, remembers or realises something. Another, though less severe, problem is that Hinrichs explains aspectual properties by the so-called homogeneous and heterogeneous properties of actions, represented by VPs. Thus, in his phraseology, any part of *eating* or *eating cake* is still eating or eating cake, whereas no part of *eating a cake* is eating a cake (that is, when *eating a cake* is taken to be an accomplishment). To distinguish homogeneous from heterogeneous actions Hinrichs had to resort to a division of stages of events:

> "in order for a sentence whose verb phrase is modified by a *for*-phrase to be true there have to be at least two homogeneous substages of the event denoted by the verb phrase that is modified. By homogeneous substages we mean event stages that realise the same type of event as the event as a whole"

(Hinrichs 1985: 286). However, a division of this kind seems to be somewhat counterintuitive. In principle any simple action like, for instance, walking in the park, that basically appears homogeneous, can certainly be viewed both as a homogeneous and as a heterogeneous event depending on the particular circumstances: location, destination, participants, etc.

But, to come back to Hinrichs' thesis, since events and the stages of individuals taking part in them are closely related, stage of individuals are furthermore also divided into substages:

> "... proper substages of an event have to involve substages of the individuals that are involved in the event as a whole. Since this is still rather abstract, let us give a concrete example. Consider a plane flying from San Francisco to Columbus via Indianapolis. Then the stage realising the plane for the event stage of flying from San Francisco to Indianapolis has to be a proper substage of the individual stage realising the plane for the entire flight, and the event stage of the first leg of the flight has to be a proper stage making up both legs of the flight"

(Hinrichs 1985: 255). That is, in Hinrichs's thesis, the artificial division of events is carried over to an even more artificial division of stages of their participants. Reference to such stages of individuals, firstly, brought to Hinrichs the necessity to produce awkward examples describing a plane flight from one place to another not directly but by via a third, in-between place. And, secondly, how is a bounded event that is, according to many aspectological definitions, to be viewed as an indivisible whole, to be accounted for – for example a flight of John's from San Francisco to Columbus **directly**, as in *John flew from San Francisco to Columbus*?

Hinrichs takes it that stages of ordinary objects are homogeneous just like activities are and asks why it is that sentences such as (71b) and (77) are accomplishments.

(71) b. John built a house
(77)   John ate a cake

Here is his answer:

> "... their accomplishment property can obviously not be derived from the semantics of the object NPs, since their reference properties are not heterogeneous as far as their stage realisations are concerned. If an accomplishment property cannot be attributed to the object term, then the only other alternative is that [it] has to originate with the verb semantics. In other words, the fact that *build a house* is an accomplishment follows from the nature of building rather than from the semantics of the term *a house*."

(Hinrichs 1985: 264). Or, in other words, although Hinrichs views subjects and objects as temporal entities (alongside their being spatial ones), he refuses to assign the ultimate expression of boundedness to a property of the object (or the subject or both the subject and the object). What is in the approach assumed here referred to as temporal boundedness in the referents of subjects and objects, in Hinrichs' terms is a feature called 'unique'. Consider (71b) again:

(71) b. John built a house

In a sentence like this, according to the author, event stages realising the event of building, the stage realising the agent of the event and the stage realising the effected object are **unique**, that is, "they can have no substages that stand in the same relation and realise the same objects" (Hinrichs 1985: 265).

Another serious problem for Hinrichs' thesis is that at times his theory is inconsistent with respect to the temporal scope of participants in an action. He argues, along with Cooper (1985), that, for example, in the case of a sentence like (78) below it is not clear whether Bill's and John's 'stages' coincide. For Bill, Hinrichs argues, might first call his agent to authorise the sale of his house, then Bill's agent might call John's agent and bring about the sale, etc.

(78)   Bill sold his house to John

But this difficulty in the interpretation, as envisaged by Hinrichs (and also by Cooper 1985), is mainly worsened by the fact that, as already mentioned, stages of individuals are regarded not only as temporal slices but as spatio-temporal 'locations'. Or, to use Hinrichs' and Cooper's gastronomic metaphors, 'slices', or 'sausages'. Here is Hinrichs' precise argumentation in the attempt to resolve the issue:

> "In this case [(78) above] it seems once again difficult to pinpoint the exact location of the event of the sale. It is temporally restricted to the time span that it took the two agents to reach a legally binding agreement and thus involves along the spatial dimension the location of the two agents, but not the location of the buyer and seller? Or does the location at which the sale takes place include also the buyer and seller? Does it temporally begin with Bill's phone call to his agent and end with John's agent calling John? The answer will once again depend on the context in which the event is reported. In a court of law, the "smaller" location that includes only the agents may be sufficient to prove that a sale has transpired. But regardless of whether we identify the location of the sale in a broader or a narrower sense, the individual stages of the buyer and the seller, which play a role in the event, will not coincide with the event stage that realises the sale as such"

(Hinrichs 1985: 192). It must, indeed, be admitted that in a description of the global semantics of sentences of this kind spatial locations ought to be, of course, accounted for as well. But along the line of reasoning quoted above it is to be expected that there will arise many other problematic cases in which the degree of non-coincidence of stages of event participants could be increased even further. Thus in Hinrichs' sentences (79) and (especially) in (80) below the stages of the agent and the recipient allegedly diverge – in an even more significant manner. Because Nixon's order to bomb Hanoi – Hinrichs argues – comes earlier than the actual bombing; and if John made Bill a millionaire in his will, Bill's becoming a millionaire happens after John's death (Hinrichs 1985: 191-192).

(79)   Nixon bombed Hanoi
(80)   John made Bill a millionaire

But difficulties of this kind can, in fact, easily be avoided. Spatial dimensions of the action or of the participants in it are not discarded in the present approach. They are simply not taken into account. A pure temporal dimension is abstracted from, or rather before, the possible pragmatic inferences concerning the existence of the participants outside the scope of the action. Otherwise the inconsistency with the allegedly different locations in time of Nixon and Hanoi could be transferred onto many other sentences, with the consequence that the picture of systematicity already presented in the previous chapters would be blurred.

Consider the following. If we analyse the participation in the action of entities like *a boy* and *a stone* in a sentence like (81) below in Hinrichs' fashion, paying special attention to the proper distribution of energy emitted and energy received, we could reach a similar conclusion about different locations in time of the two participants:

(81) A boy threw a stone

Because in normal circumstances the expenditure of energy by the boy has to take place first for the stone to be set in motion. Then the stone receiving the energy starts on its way describing a trajectory, and if there is some overlapping movement between the two entities at first, fractions of a second later the boy may (and will probably) actually be stative while the stone is still in motion and continues to be before finishing the trajectory and falling to the ground. The seemingly nasty problem is that this kind of analysis is, of course, valid as a possible truthful description of the action of throwing a stone by a boy. But it fails to capture the generalisation outlined above that actions and the time slices of their participants coincide in their temporal properties and grammatical representation, and that this is true also in the more "literal" sense, as in sentences like (72b) and (82) below in which subjects move along an object, and hence the temporal slices of both the moving subject and the object being traversed coincide in a natural way.

(72) b. The soldier crossed the street
(82)   The boat crossed the river

As can be seen in a sentence like (82), in which the spatial and the temporal configurations of the referent of the object (the river can, and usually does, move in a direction different from the direction of movement of the boat) are subtly intertwined with those of the referent of the subject, delving into the spatio-temporal complexities of moving and interacting objects and trying to work out all the combinations of temporal and spatial parameters is hardly what the observer/ speaker does when he perceives an action of this kind and encodes it in linguistic form. Compare, in connection with this, Langacker's concept of 'summary scanning' of, for example, a falling object, which guarantees that a single gestalt be built up out of the separate phases of perception of the movement of the falling object (Langacker 1991: 79-80).

It was apparently questions of this kind that led the majority of investigators of aspect to ignore the stage-status of participants (cf. Tenny 1994: 30) or to maintain that they are better avoided than tackled. The following passage is revealing in this respect, and also with respect to the fact that temporal properties of typical subjects and objects as those in the sentences adduced above are very rarely dealt with at all:

> "Following G.Carlson, Cooper distinguishes *individuals* from their *stages*. While statives involve the former, non-statives involve the latter. One way of capturing this

> distinction is to treat stages as located individuals. But [this] introduces the seemingly artefactual problem that we must constrain histories so that the individuals involved are located precisely where the relevant situations are. [...] An alternative approach presented by Cooper is to utilise simple individuals throughout but to constrain histories so the individuals involved in a history are *present* at the relevant locations. From the point of view that it seems *necessary*, not merely contingent, that the participants in a history coincide with that history, this is hardly any better a solution"

(Binnick 1991: 334).

However, there are certain studies of the meanings of noun phrases that analyse their temporal values only. Musan (1995; 1999), dealing with sentences like her own (76c), uses Carlson's distinction between individuals and stages.

(76) c. Most college students were lazy in highschool

Musan's approach is different from the one assumed here because the aim is different – to describe certain **overt** temporal values of NPs, not those covert ones linked to the compositional explication of aspect in the sentence. Hence, the argumentation in Musan's study is restricted, as e.g. in Hinrichs' work, by some pragmatic considerations concerning temporal values of NP referents that would be inapplicable in an investigation of the aspectually relevant temporal values of NP referents.[4] But some of the conclusions reached as a result of Musan's analysis tie in with the general model proposed here. The author, arguing for the linguistic relevance of Carlson's differentiation between individuals and stages and taking into account some of the effects of the exponents of definiteness, indefiniteness and quantification on the temporal properties of the NPs, maintains that:

> "if [...] entities that are quantified over by determiner-quantifiers are stages of sufficiently restricted length, then [...] there should be more restricted temporal interpretations of noun phrases"; "a stage that is introduced by a noun phrase is not larger than necessary, i.e., does not reach beyond the situation time of the noun"

(Musan 1999: 652).

So the tradition of dealing with the temporal values of referents of NPs represented by the above mentioned studies is generally different from the present approach in which the temporal values of the referents of NPs are in the enormous number of cases held to be covert, totally invisible to the speaker/hearer and arising out of the interplay between a number of factors: mainly the temporal values (grammatically or semantically marked) of the referents of the other NPs in the sentence and the temporal value (grammatically or semantically marked) of the referent of the verb in the sentence. The temporal values of the referents of NPs in the above-mentioned tradition are overt elements of anaphoric relationships arising in the discourse, entirely visible to the ordinary speaker. Conversely, the temporal values

---

[4] In a sentence like *Diana is talked about*, the analysis is based on the argument that the referent of *Diana* is "Diana's lifetime" (Musan 1999: 625, 655). This can hardly be justified even from what is here called the "common-sense" point of view – of the ordinary speaker – for talking about a person does not necessarily involve talking about this person's lifetime, let alone his/her lifetime taken in its entirety.

that are here argued to exist fall outside of the field of anaphoricity and are covert for the ordinary speaker.[5]

MORE ARGUMENTS IN FAVOUR OF THE TEMPORAL STATUS OF 'PARTICIPANTS'

For an explanation of the temporal status of participants from a more "common-sense" point view, there is at least one more argument available – which divorces pragmatic inferences from the proper semantics of the sentence in question in a sufficiently convincing manner. It can be maintained that in cases like (79) Nixon's order for Hanoi to be bombed as part of Hinrichs' (1985: 191-193) description of the meaning of this sentence does not at all fall into the meaning scope of sentence (79) – because the meaning in which Nixon orders Hanoi to be bombed is to be captured by a sentence such as (83) below rather than by a sentence such as (79):

(79)   Nixon bombed Hanoi
(83)   Nixon ordered that Hanoi be bombed

But even without taking into account the language options represented in (79) and (83), it is fairly reasonable to assume that the stage of Nixon ordering the bombing of Hanoi and the (metaphorical) stage of Nixon bombing Hanoi are completely different stages of the same individual that should be kept apart whatever the fashion of their language encoding. On the one hand, since stages are what makes up an individual, if Nixon's order for the bombing of Hanoi is taken to fall directly within the semantics of sentence (79) above, this would irreparably blur not only the difference between stages and individuals (cf. Langacker's example of how an event can be construed linguistically in various ways – Langacker 1991: 214) but also the possible consequences of the events described referred to by the speaker. After all, if Nixon bombed Hanoi, Hanoi was truthfully bombed (with all the gruesome practical effect), whereas if Nixon only ordered the bombing of a city, this does not yet effect the actual bombing of the city. On the other hand, in the sentence describing the stage of Nixon ordering the bombing of Hanoi and the bombing of Hanoi as two different stages, that is, sentence (83), language offers us the opportunity to separate the two stages on the basis of the grammatical structure of the sentence itself. In a

---

[5] Anaphoricity is a mechanism by which entities in discourse are assumed to be identical or non-identical, whereas in the framework used in this study temporal entities in discourse have more complex configurations and may be unrelated to one another in terms of identity or nonidentity. Unlike the anaphoric relationship of identity between *the man* and *he* in the discourse sequence *I saw the man, he was eating a sandwich*, the ultimate temporal values of *the man* and *he* within the approach used in this work are totally different. Although identical in anaphoric terms, *the man* and *he* cannot be said to be identical in the present analysis: *the man* is a temporally bounded entity and *he* is a temporally non-bounded entity, these two values arising as a result of a very complex interplay (already discussed in detail) between certain components in the two sentences. Of course, identity in anaphoric terms does not in any way interfere with boundedness or non-boundedness as temporal values and, vice versa, boundedness and non-boundedness do not in any way interfere with the identity value in anaphoric terms. These are two distinct fields of reference.

linguistic representation of this kind Nixon's stage of ordering is covered by the subject *Nixon*, the action is covered by the verb *ordered*, and the essence of the order is covered by the object *that Hanoi be bombed*.

Furthermore, first, *Hanoi be bombed* itself can be analysed as a clause describing an action different from the action of the ordering. Second, although *Hanoi be bombed*, as a whole entity constituting the essence of the order, can be said to coincide as a stage with the stage of the order (designated primarily by the verb *ordered*), it, third, describes an essentially different action (of bombing) from the action of ordering the bombing, and the action of bombing is embedded in the essence of the order described by the phrase *Hanoi be bombed*. And, finally, fourth, in *Hanoi be bombed* the temporal slices of the subject *Hanoi* and the action *be bombed* again (necessarily) coincide.

It should be noted that such a relatively complex differentiation of time slices can take place not only between clauses but also, for example, within a *verb + to + verb* sequence. In this case the subject receives a double-stage interpretation which (and this is especially noteworthy) is **overt** – and completely evident not only for the semanticist but also for the ordinary speaker. Furthermore, the aspectual distinction can be realised without any restriction in both parts of the sentence. Compare all the English sentences in (84) and (85):

(84) a. John wanted to see the film
 b. John wanted to watch the film
(85) a. John expressed a desire to see the film
 b. John expressed a desire to watch the film

In all of these sentences the subject *John* clearly has a double stage-meaning. The first one refers to *John* as a possessor or utterer of a desire and is associated with the main verb in each of the sentences. The second refers to *John* as the agent of an action of seeing or watching the film and is associated with the infinitival part of each sentence. These two stage realisations of a ("longer") individual 'John' necessarily have different locations in time and, perhaps, place. For example, John's wanting to see the film will normally be prior to John's seeing the film. The two stage realisations can, furthermore, have different aspectual values. This is the case in (84a) and (85b). John's wanting to see the film in (84a) is a non-bounded temporal slice of the individual 'John', whereas John's (possible, future) seeing the film in the same sentence is a bounded temporal slice of the individual 'John'. John's expressing a desire in (85b) is a bounded temporal slice of the individual 'John', whereas John's (possible, future) watching the film is a non-bounded temporal slice of the individual 'John'. In the infinitive both aspectual values can be explicated (*to see* is realised as a perfective, *to watch* as an imperfective), but they can be explicated also in the main verb, as is shown by the difference between (84) and (85): *wanted* in *John wanted* in (84a) and (84b) is a non-bounded temporal entity, and *expressed* in *John expressed a desire* in (85a) and (85b) is a bounded temporal entity.

To sum up, the analysis above reveals that the decision to treat *Nixon* in (79) and referents of similar subjects as not coinciding with the action described is unconvincing, and a fairly artificial one.

(79)   Nixon bombed Hanoi

First, considering *Nixon* in (79) as a stage of the individual 'Nixon' that actually ordered the bombing of Hanoi but did not (literally) bomb Hanoi is a (largely plausible) **pragmatic inference**, not a **proper interpretation** of the basic aspects of the semantics of the sentence. And, second, as metaphor is a fundamental and extremely widespread feature of natural language, there is no reason for *Nixon* in this sentence not be viewed metaphorically as the agent of the action *per se*.

The necessity to treat a given participant as consisting of two (or more) different stages is also, and perhaps even more clearly, seen in cases of conjoined clauses – as in (86) below, a sentence discussed by Derzhanski (1995: 9):

(86)   The girls met at breakfast and were wearing their golden earrings

According to Derzhanski's observation, the subject *the girls* in (86) is to be treated differently in the two conjoined clauses. More specifically, in his terms, *the girls* in *the girls met at breakfast* is to be treated as a 'group', while *the girls* in *the girls were wearing their golden earrings* are to be interpreted as a 'sum' over which the predicate can distribute (Derzhanski 1995: 9). Compare the inadequate subevent **Mary* [one of the girls] *met* and the adequate subevent *Mary* [one of the girls] *was wearing her golden earring*. Whatever the exact scope of the two stages of *the girls* from a more pragmatically-oriented temporal point of view (for example, *the girls* in *the girls were wearing their golden earrings* ought to precede temporally *the girls* in *the girls met at breakfast*), aspectually *the girls* in *the girls met at breakfast* is a temporally bounded entity, while *the girls* in *the girls were wearing their golden earrings* is a temporally non-bounded entity – according to the analysis proposed in this chapter.

Thus stages of individuals conceived of as lying outside the action they take part in should simply be regarded as entirely separate from those that fall within the scope of the action, even if these stages coincide in (are represented by) one syntactic entity. Many other examples could be given in favour of such a solution. Viewing stages of individuals that take part in actions as dead, as not yet born, as absent, etc. should be considered to be reasoning in pragmatic terms which is irrelevant to the proper semantics of the sentence and to the way stages of individuals are (probably) perceived and later processed in memory as taking part in the corresponding actions. Consider sentence (87) below, reporting a fact from Bulgarian history:

(87)   The judge sentenced General Stefanov to death

In the situation described in (87), the general sentenced is, actually, dead at the moment he is sentenced! The background behind the semantics of this sentence, which covers a true legal case, is the following. After the invasion of the Soviet Red Army in Bulgaria at the end of World War II tens of thousands of people, most of them innocent, uninvolved in previous persecutions of communists, were brutally massacred – without any prior legal proceedings. Many months later, special communist tribunals, the so-called People's Courts, were established. These tribunals not only sentenced living political opponents to prison or death, but also, in an attempt to attribute a legal facade to the new regime and to justify further reprisals upon the families of the political opponents, knowingly ruled numerous death sentences on people who had already been murdered. In the case of (87), General Stefanov, a chief commander of the Bulgarian army, was murdered in the street by a well-known female communist leader after he and his troops returned from the war fighting the Nazis. Given this particular historical situation, as authentic as the situation described in the Nixon example above, could we say, for instance, that there is no stage of the individual 'General Stefanov' in (87) simply because, as we know, General Stefanov was sentenced to death **after** having been killed? Certainly not. For, first, there were many serious practical consequences (including legal) of the death sentences so imposed that the families of people sentenced in this way had to face. All their property was confiscated, they were sent in exile, the defendants' children were not allowed to study at a university, etc. And, second, if there is no identifiable (in some way) stage of a defendant in a court case of this kind, arguably, a sentence could not be passed.

But in fact, though the case in question is highly revealing, it is not really necessary to resort to such specific facts of history. Many other examples can be given of similar events happening any time, in any country. Heroes are awarded medals after dying in war. Offenders sometimes get sanctioned, fined, sentenced, etc. *in abscentio*. Very often people are talked about without their knowledge, etc. Consider sentences like (88a) or (88b) below in which the existence of a 'stage' of an individual 'Smith' could not, simply, be denied:

(88) a. Smith was awarded a medal after his heroic death
b. Smith was fined for fast driving on the basis of a video recording. He learned about it a month later

These examples raise another important question relevant to the problem of stages of individuals. Is there any reason in pragmatic terms, or from some linguistic analytical point of view, to account for a **spatial** location of *Smith* in the two sentences? Obviously not. And hence, there is no reason not to assign a stage value, purely temporal and equal to the value of the action, to *the judge* and to *General Stefanov* in (87) and to *Smith* in sentences (88a) and (88b), as well as to *Nixon, Hanoi, John* and *Bill* in sentences (79) and (80).

CHAPTER 5

MORE ON THE MIXED, SPATIO-TEMPORAL APPROACH

To go back to Hinrichs' thesis again, the author did not take into account some highly relevant structural language phenomena already discussed here – for example, the fact that NPs referring to stages of objects are systematically marked for boundedness and non-boundedness through certain types of grammatical devices. This, probably, is a consequence of his failure to assign the property of boundedness to referents of subjects and objects – and of his reluctance to see them as properly coinciding with the stages of the actions they take part in. Nevertheless, placed in an appropriate theoretical perspective, Hinrichs' idea of viewing stages of objects and events as temporally coinciding remains a considerable contribution to the understanding of aspectual phenomena.

It can be argued that building an appropriate theoretical perspective should involve, first and foremost, discarding spatial parameters of participants in situations. Spatial parameters are, no doubt, present in many sentences as semantic properties or as parts of certain pragmatic inferences. But they are otherwise irrelevant with respect to aspectual values, and the failure to abstract the temporal from the spatial properties of participants in situations apparently impedes the disclosure of certain major language regularities.

Finally, and this has already been pointed out as regards Verkuyl's theory, sometimes the arcane jargon of linguistics, and especially logic, burdens the communication of ideas that are otherwise fruitful. Compare the following passage:

> "The reason why verb phrases with bare plural argument terms receive a coherent semantic interpretation when they are modified by *for*-phrases is essentially the same as the one pointed out above for mass term arguments. Unlike ordinary objects which have unique stage realisations at any given interval, bare plurals and mass terms denote kinds, which do not have the same restriction. Thus, after one stage realising a kind has undergone the change denoted by the verb in question, due to the non-uniqueness of stage realisations for kinds there will be others available to undergo the same change"

(Hinrichs 1985: 286-287). What Hinrichs is saying here, on the one hand, is that bare plurals and mass terms are to be considered as referring basically to generic entities – an assumption tacitly assumed and rarely spelled out by linguists dealing simultaneously with verbal and nominal reference. On the other hand, if the stage realisations of ordinary objects are to be viewed as unique at any given interval, clearly uniqueness in Hinrichs' model is not to be equated with boundedness in the approach assumed for the present study.

Cooper (1985) also referred to G.N.Carlson's stages, and made a suggestion similar to Hinrichs', according to which 'statives' (stative verbs, stative relations) involve (G.N.Carlson's) 'individuals' and 'non-statives' (non-stative verbs, non-stative relations) involve (G.N.Carlson's) 'stages' – treated as 'located individuals' (Cooper 1985: 11-13). Such an attempt to distinguish between temporal entities according to their participation in different types of situations was unconvincing to Krifka (1989: 139-140), who points out that, on the one hand, mere location of individuals could be relevant in stative situations and that, vice versa, location of individuals could play no role in non-stative situations, on the other hand. Thus, for example, in a non-stative sentence like (89) in German the location of the participants in the event has little or nothing to do with the semantics of the sentence (cf. also the English translation):

(89)　　Otto heiratet Anna
　　　　'Otto marries Anna'

Krifka himself offers a solution to the problem concerning the relationship between the meaning of the verb and the NPs along the following lines: verbs like *trinken, bauen, lesen* in German, or the corresponding *drink, build, read* in English, are directly related to the meaning of the NPs associated with them as a direct object in the sense that the NP referent is either consumed or created from beginning to end. But Krifka's solution is also largely identical to Cooper's and Hinrichs' in that the temporal stretch of the referent of the verb and the spatial stretch of the referent of the NP merge in his analysis (Krifka 1989: 159). Strangely, however, in Krifka's diagrammatic representations phrases like *wein trinken* 'drink wine' and *ein Glas Wein trinken* 'drink a glass of wine' do not differ significantly, in spite of the fact that Krifka makes a distinction between the two in terms of 'telicity' and 'atelicity' (Krifka 1989: 159) – equivalent to 'boundedness' and 'non-boundedness' in the terminology employed here. A position of this kind is, indeed, in line with the native speaker's conception: *a house* in *build a house* is viewed temporally in the sense that *a house* can easily be taken to refer to a 'house-stage' beginning at the point where the building starts and ending at the point where the building of the house finishes. Similarly, *a glass of wine* in *drink a glass of wine* can, with some further intellectual effort, be "seen" as beginning where the drinking begins and ending where the drinking stops. Such a theoretical model invariably leads, however, to the assumption that in verb phrases in which the object is not created or consumed there is no merging of spatial and temporal values. And Krifka apparently makes this assumption by arguing that there is no similar merging between the spatial and temporal values in *Wein sehen* 'see wine' and *ein Glas Wein sehen* 'see a glass of wine' (Krifka 1989: 159-160). Indeed, there is a difference between the verb *see* in English and the verb *sehen* 'see' in German in the sense that German *sehen* resembles *watch* in English (cf. German *fernsehen* 'watch television'), and thus the German verb *sehen* could be said to belong to the group of aspectually ambiguous verbs like English *push* (cf. Verkuyl 1993: 329-338) – to be discussed below. However, later in his book Krifka (1989: 212) argues that the verb *sehen* 'see' could also be regarded as (what he calls) a telic predicate, as in the expression *sieben Elefanten sehen* 'see seven elephants'.

The aspectual nature of the verb *see* is not unproblematic in English either. It is obviously through the influence of context, through pragmatic implications and, generally, on the basis of knowledge of the world that the aspectual meanings of phrases like *see a glass of wine* or *see wine* will be explicated. The marked capability of the verb *see* to denote perfective actions was observed as early as 1949 by Hornby who noted that this verb can refer to a single act of perception (Hornby

1949: 173). However, the compositional mechanism does not seem to work smoothly for expressions like *see wine* and *see a glass of wine*. Both phrases could equally well be interpreted in English as perfective. But whether *see wine* and *see a glass of wine* are interpreted as aspectually different or not, there is no reason for not assigning a temporal status to *wine* and to *a glass of wine*, exactly corresponding to the temporal value (whatever it is – bounded or non-bounded) of the action of seeing. Hence, it becomes clear that verbs like *see*, to the extent that they are able to explicate perfectivity, are not and cannot be different from verbs like *eat* or *build* – in which, to use Tenny's (1994) term, allegedly, a 'measuring-out' of the event on the part of the object occurs. There remains the problem, however, of what it is that predicts that singular count objects of verbs like *see* or *push* or *drive* are different from objects of verbs like *eat* or *build*. This problem is dealt with in the forthcoming chapters.

It is worth here making a comparison with Slavic, where, for example in Bulgarian, the counterpart of the verb *see* can be either perfective/bounded (*vidja*, referring to a single act of perception) or imperfective/non-bounded (*viždam*, referring to a state or process of perceiving). And both can, of course, easily combine with object-NPs accompanied or unaccompanied by an article, cf. the Bulgarian sentences in (90) and (91):

(90) a. Ivan   vidja$_{pfvAor}$ vino
          Ivan   saw   wine
          'Ivan saw wine'
     b. Ivan   viždaše$_{impfvImp}$ vino
          Ivan   saw   wine
          'Ivan saw wine'
(91) a. Ivan   vidja$_{pfvAor}$ vino-to
          Ivan   saw   wine-the
          'Ivan saw the wine'
     b. Ivan   viždaše$_{impfvImp}$ vino-to
          Ivan   saw   wine-the
          'Ivan saw the wine'

Not surprisingly, Krifka (1989), who tried to give an account of the relationship between perfectivity/imperfectivity and object-NPs in Slavic (but not subject-NPs: cf. Kabakčiev 1984b), used examples in Czech corresponding to (English) *drink (the) wine* but ignored examples like *see wine* and *see the wine*.

To sum up the proposals made by Hinrichs (1985), Cooper (1985) and Krifka (1989), what they share in common is that they assign to participants in actions not only temporal but also spatial values. As already mentioned, such a mixed spatio-temporal approach has probably something to do with the strong aptitude on the part of the speaker of a natural language to view participants in actions in spatial terms at the expense of temporal ones. But the approach could also be said to be based on linguistic tradition. The mainstream of linguistic thought had never seriously attempted to divorce the temporal parameters of participants in actions from the spatial ones. Arguing that

> "for any event the locations of the participants have to temporally overlap the event stage which realises the event that these individuals are engaged in"

Hinrichs (1985: 194-195) admits that this property had earlier been noted in Geis (1975a; 1975b). What Geis himself argued was that

> "The function of place adverbials is to locate one or more of the participants of actions and states of affairs and the like in space"

and that

> "The functions of time adverbials and of some elements of the auxiliary is to locate actions and states of affairs and the like in time"

(Geis 1975b: 18). Geis did not, however, merge these two theses into a unified spatio-temporal view of participants in actions. Clearly, Hinrichs' line of reasoning was to borrow the spatial parameter from Geis and amplify it with a temporal one (not entirely based on Geis'). And this was a natural step to make: if Geis' idea is followed, that is, if place adverbials locate participants in space, as in (92) below (Geis' own example), in a tensed sentence like (92) the participant *John* can, first, easily be said to be also located in time, in this particular case prior to the moment of speech, and, second, *John* can very easily be viewed as a stage of a "longer" entity 'John' that is not miserable outside New York.

(92)   John was miserable in New York

The idea of the spatio-temporal property of participants can then less problematically be transferred to sentences without adverbials, like Hinrichs' (71b), and generalised over all participants (also syntactic objects, not only subjects), and all sentences.

(71)   b. John built a house

Certainly, participants in actions, and situations in general, possess spatial parameters, and these spatial parameters can, in principle, be added to the temporal ones. But the question to be asked once again is: are spatial parameters relevant in discussing temporal properties of a sentence as a whole, including the crucial contribution of the semantics of the verb as a lexical entry? The answer is no. Provided the action in a sentence like (71b) is perceived by the speaker of a language as in the 'television representation' described at the beginning of this chapter, given the fact that in the perception of an action of this kind in reality (that is, not on a TV screen) the spatio-temporal configurations of the participants in the action are extremely complex, given the fact that in many sentences participants have no identifiable spatial properties relevant to the action, given the fact that the boundedness/non-boundedness distinction is clearly explicated in English through the article/zero article contrast, there is no option for an adequate account of the aspect mechanism but to separate the spatial parameter from the temporal one – if certain linguistically valid generalisations are to be made. This is done in the present work.

Apart from the unnecessary association of the temporal with the spatial dimension, Hinrichs (1985), Cooper (1985) and Krifka (1989) failed to pinpoint the difference between stages of individuals taking part in bounded situations and stages of individuals taking part in non-bounded situations. Indeed, Cooper (1985) assigns the so-called (by him) temporal ungroundedness to states and activities, temporal groundedness to accomplishments and punctuality to achievements, and Hinrichs (1985) makes a distinction between 'unique stages' and 'non-unique stages' to refer to more or less the same phenomena (as mentioned earlier, somewhat inconsistently). But the trade-off between the temporal parameters of actions and participants and the corresponding language entities at the syntactic and paradigmatic level remained insufficiently clarified in the three works cited.

Of course, the criticism levelled here does not imply that these publications gave wrong interpretations of the language data they dealt with. On the contrary. Firstly, Cooper's, Hinrichs' and Krifka's works offer an abundance of careful analyses and valuable insights into the problems in question that could promote any investigation of verbal and temporal reference of natural language entities. Secondly, their contention – made independently from and simultaneously (at least as far as Hinrichs and Cooper's works are concerned) with Kabakčiev (1984a; 1984b) – that temporal parameters of participants in situations do play a role in the overall semantics of many English sentences lends additional support to the thesis of the interplay between properties of verbal and nominal constituents in sentences in English and other languages. It is this thesis (put forward in Kabakčiev 1984a; 1984b) that has been developed in the present chapter and that forms the basis of the overall theory presented in this book.

To test the perfectivity or imperfectivity of a certain verb phrase or sentence in English, linguists usually resort to the compatibility/incompatibility with *in*-time and *for*-time phrases. But this test does not work or works inefficiently in many cases, e.g., with sentences containing the verb *see* and other verbs and verb phrases – see also Chapter Eleven, *The impact of adverbials in the sentence, and aspect in English*, below. The comparison between English and Bulgarian with respect to the verb *see* can be made feasible through the introduction in the sentence not of *in*-time or *for*-time phrases but of an adverbial like *suddenly*. Cf. again (90):

(90) a. Ivan vidja$_{pfvAor}$ vino
 Ivan saw wine
 'Ivan saw wine'
 b. Ivan viždaše$_{impfvImp}$ vino
 Ivan saw wine
 'Ivan saw wine'

The meaning of Bulgarian (90a) can best be captured by adding *suddenly*, as in (93a) below, whereas the meaning of Bulgarian (90b) is ambiguous and can be rendered either through the use of the Progressive, as in (93b) below (not entirely acceptable for some speakers of English), or through adverbials of indefinite repetition, as in (93c):

(93) a. Ivan suddenly saw wine
b. ?Ivan was seeing wine
c. Ivan occasionally/often/from time to time saw wine

Cf. here Filip's (1993) atemporal analysis of NPs in the verb-NP interplay.

It is obvious that reasoning along the lines of, and sticking only to, the everyday experience of the ordinary speaker of a language (that is, the one not versed in its intricacies), as in Cooper's and Krifka's argumentation concerning the importance or lack of importance of temporal locations, does not, on the one hand, yield a sound theoretical solution of the problem in question. Recall Binnick (1991: 334) who also, apart from Krifka, finds Cooper's solution that the participants in a history should coincide with that history unconvincing. Indeed, without a special way of reasoning, besides being inaccessible to the ordinary speaker of the language, temporal parameters of participants in situations remain theoretically unanalysable. On the other hand, the basic difficulty with the idea of the temporal parameters of participants in situations is that it cannot easily be explained from a common-sense point of view. But why should the "everyday" point of view of the native speaker be disregarded? If the idea of the temporal parameters of the participants has a certain significance for the study of grammar, why should it remain a reserved territory for a handful of specialists – who will always tend to disagree about the exact parameters of temporality anyway, and this will add up to the theoretical confusion?

Although in a somewhat different perspective, the idea of the temporal status of participants in situations has recently also been discussed by Bartsch (1995: 117-123). The author goes so far as to maintain that an ontology is possible with only situations, and not individuals, as basic entities. In contrast to the approach in this book, which is based on certain structural language exponents of properties of participants in situations, Bartsch recognises time slices of individuals generally, arguing that individuals can be presented not *per se*, as basic entities, but as having life-histories and holding roles. The ontology with individuals with their roles and life-histories is discussed as a possible formal analytical tool; no linguistic justification for assuming such an approach is provided. Furthermore, although less markedly than Hinrichs and Krifka, Bartsch (1995: 117) also seems to merge the temporal dimension with the spatial one, and, like Hinrichs, argues that the shortcomings of the approach (she lists several of them) seem to render its applicability to linguistic investigations dubious. Clearly, if the whole of the semantics of a language is to be described, the spatial dimension could by no means be discarded and would have to be incorporated into the temporal one at a certain level of analysis, including the analysis of sentences. But it is unjustified for the spatial dimension to interfere with the interpretation of aspect anyway, for this category has to do with only the temporal and not the spatial properties of a situation and the participants in it.

TEMPORAL SLICES OF 'PARTICIPANTS' VIEWED AS PART OF MAN'S COGNITIVE ORGANISATION

Of course, the temporal features of participants in situations *are* hidden for the native speaker. If we ask people in the street what they make out of entities like *the boy* and *a stone* in a sentence like (74), repeated below, their answers run approximately like this. *The boy* is a human being at a young age and possesses certain typical outward features (cf. the concept of 'boy' as described by Smith and Medin 1981: 19-20). *The boy*, judging from this particular sentence, is supposed to be naughty, and his naughtiness is likely to bring about negative consequences, e.g. a broken window, angry neighbours, etc. The entity *a stone*, on the other hand, is an inanimate object with certain physical and chemical properties. It has an approximately identifiable size and a weight – such that they correspond to the possibility for it to be thrown by a boy.

(74)　　The bow threw a stone

Furthermore, certainly these are not features of the English sentence or of the corresponding proposition in (74) that are language-specific. The equivalent Bulgarian sentence (94) below, when subjected to the same kind of linguistic experiment, yields the same results – and the same kind of answer is elicited also from students and lecturers of linguistics who might otherwise be expected to "know more".

(94)　　Momče-to　　hvărli$_{pfvAor}$　　kamăk
　　　　 Boy-the　　 threw　　　　　　stone
　　　　'The boy threw a stone'

It is clear why native speakers' responses do not contain even the slightest trace of some temporal parameters of the 'objects' *the boy* and *a stone* corresponding to their extension in time **during** the accomplishment of the action of throwing. Even if these temporal parameters exist somewhere in the mind of the native speaker, they are irrelevant pragmatically. When specifically instructed to analyse the features of *the boy* and *a stone* in sentence (94) only, native speakers (including linguists) resort to generic features and not to spatially and temporally relevant features – that is, to features associated not with *the boy* and *a stone* as depicted in (94) but with the generalised concepts of 'boy' and 'stone'. Even when specifically asked to comment on the extension of time of the entities *the boy* and *a stone* in the Bulgarian sentence (94), native informants usually give, approximately, the following answer:

> *Momčeto* 'the boy' was born about a decade ago. He will grow up and thus will one day no longer correspond to the description of the subject in sentence (74). *A stone*, on the other hand, is something that took hundreds or thousands of years to assume its present shape; and it will probably continue to exist in its present physical configuration for a long time to come.

Again, what is referred to is the generalised concept, not the time slice of the (ordinary) individual and the physical object taking part in the action.

But in spite of these native speakers' responses, it can be assumed that the objects *the boy* and *a stone* in sentences like (74) do exist for some time in the speaker's/hearer's memory precisely as temporal entities, bounded on the time axis – just as many covert grammatical entities like, for example, (syntactic) subjects and objects can certainly be assumed to be present in the speaker's/hearer's mind. It can be supposed that after the perception of objects like *the boy* and *a stone* taking part in the action in sentences like (74) or (94) they are initially stored in the memory and processed precisely as temporal entities – in so far as they are regarded as participants in the action. With the passage of time and the fading of memory they are later gradually transferred to the concepts of 'boy' and 'stone'. Reasoning along these lines, it could also be argued that if 'the boy' is later transferred to the concept of a particular young individual, 'the stone' is more likely to fade in the memory of the observer of the action depicted in (74) – (94) both as a time slice and as an individual object – for being, unlike 'the boy', unimportant from a practical point of view. Compare this to an object like 'a chair', again thrown by a boy, say, in a burst of anger, which is going to be used again. It will, arguably, be also mentally processed as a participant in the action of throwing, i.e., as a time slice, but will, unlike the stone, remain in memory as a "long-term" individual physical object that will be of future practical importance to the household.

Let us illustrate further this hypothetical psycho-physiological mechanism by considering features of human participants in situations. Sentences of type (74) denote actions performed by a human being about whom we may know nothing more. But what does the notion of a particular human being in our minds consist of? That is, what lies behind the concept of an individual in the common-sense meaning of the word? Suppose at the department where John works there is a new colleague, Mary. John does not know Mary very well as of yet. He has talked to her only once, has seen her on a couple of other occasions – reading a book in the library, telephoning somebody – and has also heard someone saying that she liked classical music. All this is enough for John to build up some concept of the individual Mary, whose personality is undoubtedly much more complex, but who nevertheless constitutes for John at that moment little more than the sum total of the occurrences (stages) in John's vision and hearing. If John and Mary later get to know each other better, John will probably be unable to reconstruct exactly the several occasions on which he saw or heard of Mary, unless some of them are important. Most of the occasions will have merged into John's generalised concept of Mary.

Making up concepts of our closest friends and relatives is obviously not a very different process, although the number of occasions of seeing them and hearing about them is much greater. The ability to construct generalised concepts of human individuals and other physical objects over a wide time-span thus helps people's memory get rid of a vast amount of unimportant information. But it is undoubtedly such separate occurrences, that is, stages of individuals, on which concepts of individuals are based. And since here it is mostly stages of individuals and objects that is at issue, it could be assumed that the so-called television representation of physical entities as time stretches is only the technical equivalent of a cognitive phenomenon: things, no matter what their physical nature in the real world or their representation in memory is, seem to be perceived and initially stored in people's minds as temporally distinct stages when taking part in different situations. In other words, what happens on the television screen can be supposed to be analogous to what goes on in our heads. Compare in connection with this the role of the ego in the perception of motion in Koffka (1935: 285) and the fact that continuity of perception arises out of the discontinuous stages of the various complex physiological processes. This observation was central among the numerous cognitive phenomena dealt with in Gestalt psychology. It is also worth noting that the establishment of the figure/ground distinction, one of the major findings of this scientific trend, has been found to underlie the perfective/imperfective opposition in language by a number of aspectologists (see e.g. Wallace 1982; Leinonen 1982: 82-84). The general importance of the discoveries of Gestalt psychology has also been stressed by Jackendoff (1983). On the other hand, in so far as these issues presuppose a considerable departure from linguistic analysis proper, it would be better here to leave them as a subject open for future research.

But, to consider the problem of memory containment in some more detail, Miller and Johnson-Laird (1976) argued, in defence of the thesis for a differentiation between episodic, person, and semantic memory, that the semantics of proper nouns is so different from the semantics of common nouns that "combining them into a single semantic domain seems inappropriate" (Miller and Johnson-Laird 1976: 310-311). The authors also maintained that:

> "The kind of information people associate with various persons they know, like the kind of information they associate with various episodes they have lived through, differs from the kind of perceptual and functional information they associate with common nouns in semantic memory"

(Miller and Johnson-Laird 1976: 310). However, viewed in the way described above, concept formation of persons does not seem to be so entirely different from concept formation of other physical objects, especially if one focuses on the importance of mobility characteristics of physical objects, and is certainly not totally divorced from information contained in episodic memory.

In the following chapter, a mechanism for mapping the temporal values between the major syntactic components in the sentences will be described, according to which the boundedness or non-boundedness of NPs can be transferred from NPs to verbs or vice versa. If, behind this mechanism as a model for explicating aspectual phenomena, some psychological reality could be posited, then episodic memory might be viewed as a vehicle for storing information not only about situations but also about the 'stage' characteristics of participants in situations. It would be logically inconsistent to maintain that episodic memory will contain information only about particular situations anyway, since particular situations cannot normally occur or be thought of independently of their participants. A proposal of this kind is in fact complementary to the idea of the close functional interrelationship between the different kinds of memory emphasised, e.g., by Miller and Johnson-Laird (1976: 151-153). Therefore, it seems tempting to suggest that information about stages, objects and kinds (as proposed by G.N.Carlson), each of these entities being an indispensable tool for the encoding of reality, will be stored in episodic, person and semantic memory respectively and will be addressed according to need.

Of course, in spite of this neat division, various problems may arise with a suggestion of this kind. However, as has already been shown, it is supported by language (including cross-language) data, and also by common sense: when people perceive or picture mentally actions like those in (74) or (94) they remain unaware of the way the stages in their perceptions or recollections merge into larger wholes since, on the one hand, the process bears no pragmatic significance of its own and, on the other hand, should people be permanently aware of the merging process, this would probably have a disastrous effect on their ability to build up more generalised and time-extended concepts of persons and other physical objects (see also G.N.Carlson 1982: 168-169). The need for a suggestion of this kind to be verified by psychological and/or psycholinguistic test procedures is here (for the present) left out of consideration due to obvious difficulties with the identification of the appropriate procedures. Or, as G.N.Carlson himself and Tanenhaus put it:

> "What a concept is remains something of a puzzle (see, for instance, Norreklit (1973) for a lengthy discussion of this issue), and we certainly cannot resolve this question here"

(Carlson and Tanenhaus 1984: 46). The authors go on to say that:

> "...we might make the claim that concepts are not to be thought of as composed of other concepts. While there is little psychological evidence to distinguish between these two views, there does seem to be some support for the notion that lexical items are not decomposed during language processing. For instance, Fodor, Fodor and Garret (1975) and Kintsch (1974) failed to find any evidence that verbs that might be thought of as complex predicates, for example, *kill* or *break*, take longer to recognise or integrate into a sentence than "simpler" predicates"

(Carlson and Tanenhaus 1984: 48-49). From the point of view of the thesis put forward here an idea of this kind can be seen as complementary. The concept of a situation with the participants in it and the boundedness or non-boundedness parameters associated with both the situation and the participants is, indeed, to be analysed in a simple, visual manner, and not in terms of the semantic complexity of a lexeme, as, for example, present in the results of different componential analyses.

But let us return to the problem of the temporal properties of the participants in an action in a sentence like (74). The 'television representation' would have to be regarded as a technical metaphor of what happens in the mind of the observer/speaker.

(74)   The boy threw a stone

Even when the participants in an action like the one in (74) are directly observed in reality, that is, say, in the street, not on the television screen, it seems that they are perceived precisely as temporally bounded entities and remain such for some time. Ultimately, it should not make any difference whether the participants in an action are perceived from reality, from a television screen or are just a product of one's imagination. To be able to utter sentence (74) or its equivalent in another language, the observer/speaker should have perceived this action as a completed, bounded one, together with its participants that are also bounded within the scope of the action. And if the psycho-physiological mechanism of perceiving and reproducing actions and their participants through language approximates the one described here, it is obvious that it corresponds to structural data of languages as far as the presence of certain markers of boundedness is concerned. The problem of language structure will be dealt with in more detail in the following chapters.

Note that, in contrast to most other approaches, temporal status will here not be assigned to participants in accomplishments like crossing a street or throwing a stone only. Carlson (1980) assigns a 'stage' status to the referents of subjects and objects in accomplishment sentences like (74) but an 'individual' status, which is atemporal, to the referents of subjects and objects in state-denoting sentences like (30a) or (30b):

(30) a. X knew Y
b. X loved Y

In the approach assumed in this work, **all** participants in all kinds of situations labelled as events, actions, activities, states, accomplishments, achievements, etc., expressed through sentences in natural language, will be said to possess temporal values that can be adequately analysed and described. Thus *cats* (when drinking milk) or *Norwegian sweaters* (when being knitted by Katinka) can be seen as temporal stretches of the corresponding larger individuals/objects present in our memory beyond our awareness. The temporal stretches can have different lengths, different properties and configurations. For instance, besides being bounded and non-bounded, they can be singular and plural, the members of these two distinctions can be combined with each other, etc.

To sum up the whole of the discussion in this chapter, the explanation of the temporal status of referents of (syntactic) subjects and objects in the appropriate types of sentences should be placed in conjunction with the following requirement. The temporality of participants should not be seen as a purely theoretical construct but should be considered from the point of view of the common sense of the language speaker. A requirement of this kind is dictated, first, by the necessity for the mechanism of the explication of aspect to be understood in an adequate fashion by both the linguist and the ordinary speaker of the language, as well as by the learner of English (native or foreign alike) – and by learners of other languages as well. Second, an elegant solution to the problem of aspect would advance the state of the art in this linguistic sphere, would clear up the considerable confusion reigning in the field of aspectology, and would thus help linguists also address adequately other, non-aspectological issues that are essential for the understanding of the way language works.

But the problem of the temporal status of participants in situations does not only involve an explanation from a "common-sense" point of view. Participants in actions possess other properties as well – including the spatial ones discussed above, and others that may or may not remain hidden for the ordinary speaker. These properties are derived from various semantic and formal entities and factors in the sentence and its components, and are located at different levels of functional structure. They are intertwined in a complex fashion and influence each other. The mutual influences are valid with respect to the temporal properties of verbal and nominal components in the sentence: the following chapter will outline the so-called mechanism of mapping the temporal values of subjects and objects onto the referent of the verb. The postulation of such a mechanism is a logical consequence of assigning temporal values to the referents of subjects and objects in the sentence. But it should also be viewed as a real language phenomenon, given the fact that it is the verb that is ultimately conceived as the major structural entity denoting a situation.

CHAPTER 6

THE MECHANISM FOR MAPPING THE TEMPORAL VALUES OF SUBJECTS AND OBJECTS

THE TEMPORAL STATUS OF QUANTIFIED EXPRESSIONS IN IMPERFECTIVE SENTENCES

At least two serious problems arise in connection with the various characteristics of the referents of subjects and objects in the sentence, as described in the previous chapter. According to Verkuyl's peripheral statement mentioned earlier, the boundedness information (which is to be understood as temporal boundedness) of the subject or the object in the type of sentences under consideration is provisionally located in the determiner (Verkuyl 1972: 59). It is worth noting again that in Verkuyl's work it is not the article but the determiner in general that is held responsible for the explication of boundedness. In other words, apart from the article, personal, possessive and demonstrative pronouns, and some similar elements mark boundedness. Thus the telicity component in the verb in the sentence and the explication of temporal boundedness in the subject and the object(s) somehow remain separated, without any connection between them. That is, if we analyse sentence (74) below again, we ought to conclude that the referents of the subject and the object do indeed constitute temporally bounded entities, but it is not clear how their boundedness relates to the feature 'telicity', undoubtedly present in the lexical meaning of the verb:

(74)   The boy threw a stone

(Consider the contribution of the verb *throw* to the explication of perfectivity in this sentence in contrast to an atelic verb like *carry* – the two verbs will be compared in more detail below.)

The second essential problem has to do with the explication of imperfectivity in sentences with the structure under consideration. According to Verkuyl's model, the explication of imperfectivity in a given sentence can become possible due to the lack of a determiner or a quantifier in both the (syntactic) subject and the object, as in a sentence like (40b):

(40) b. Women knitted Norwegian sweaters

The lack of a determiner or a quantifier here explicates unspecified/non-bounded quantity which, in combination with the meaning of the verb, is transferred into the temporal domain and the corresponding "physical" objects are transformed into stretches of time, non-bounded at both the left and the right side of the temporal axis. The subject *women* and the object *Norwegian sweaters* in (40b) are part of the series of pictures that will arise in the mind of a speaker who made occasional visits to a knitting shop in which 'women knitted Norwegian sweaters'. *Women* in this sentence refers to a perceptual entity (received by an observer/speaker) consisting of a temporally non-bounded chain of knitting women, and *Norwegian sweaters* refers to a perceptual entity (received by the observer/speaker) consisting of a temporally non-bounded chain of sweaters being knitted by women.

If sentences like (95a) and (95b) below are analysed from this point of view, it will be established that they do not differ substantially from (40b).

(95) a. A woman knitted Norwegian sweaters
b. The woman knitted Norwegian sweaters

Again, this is a case of imperfectivity of an action induced by the lack of a quantifier/determiner in the object; again, this a case of a reception of a perceptual entity consisting of a temporally non-bounded chain of Norwegian sweaters being knitted, and of a recurring picture of a woman knitting sweaters, respectively.[1] It is to be noted that the woman denoted by the subject in (95a) may be one woman, but it

---

[1] An anonymous reviewer expressed reservations with respect to the relevance of the notion of 'perceptual entity' proposed here – as well as, in fact, to the whole enterprise of assigning the temporal values of boundedness and non-boundedness to the referents of subjects and objects. A perceptual entity is whatever it is that the observer/speaker perceives – and needs this to be able to encode the aspect of a sentence, along with other similar (or dissimilar) semantic parameters. Thus in the imperfective (habitual or habitual-like) interpretation of sentences like *The boy threw stones* or *The boy would throw a stone* the perceptual entity is of a recurring picture of a boy (there is indefinite repetition). Conversely, in the (prototypical) perfective interpretation of a sentence like *The boy threw a stone* the perceptual entity will not be of a recurring picture of a boy but of a single (moving) picture of a boy. And to produce truthful sentences with adverbials of definite repetition (or similar markers) like *The boy threw a stone three times*, there must be a perceptual entity comprising three (moving) pictures of a boy. Or, to put it in more common-sense terms, although participants like *a boy*, *a stone*, etc. (agents, patients) are thought of as stable physical entities, it is hardly debatable at all that a speaker will have to have observed: (a) a single moving picture of a boy to be able to utter a sentence like *The boy threw a stone*; (b) three moving pictures of a boy to be able to utter a sentence like *The boy threw a stone three times*; (c) an indefinite number of moving pictures of a boy to be able to utter sentences like *The boy threw stones* or *The boy would throw a stone*. And all this in spite of the fact that in all these sentences the agent is encoded as a singular and is otherwise thought to represent a stable physical, non-temporal, entity.

Of course, it must be borne in mind that in many cases things may be complicated. For example, in the (prototypical) perfective interpretation of a sentence like *The woman knitted a sweater* the perceptual entity of "a woman" could be argued to consist of (at least) several pictures of a woman, because one cannot knit a sweater to the end without stopping to rest. But this kind of complication does not invalidate the necessity for there to be a certain type of perceptual entity representing the participant(s) in the situation for the aspect of a sentence to be correctly encoded (along with other parameters).

could be an entity consisting of more than one woman as well. And, what is more, the woman referred to in this sentence may be unfamiliar to both the speaker and the hearer – the woman could be familiar to the speaker but not to the hearer or even vice versa. It could be, as already mentioned, "the same woman", but it could also be "not the same (not one) woman". These additional meanings have to do with the potential of the indefinite article to explicate them all. But the possibility for the woman to be "not the same woman" is present also in sentence (95b) in which a definite article is used. Hence, if the subject in (95b) does not denote one and the same woman, the referent of *the woman* in this sentence again, in spite of the outward (grammatical) singularity, amounts to a temporally non-bounded chain of women – not of one woman. Here 'definite' (made through a definite article) is not the woman as a particular personality but the notion of 'somebody performing the action of sweater-knitting'. Compare the similar kind of referent contained in the subject of a sentence like (96):

(96)   The sentry was replaced every two hours

So far so good. If Verkuyl's schema of imperfectivity is considered again and its implications are followed to the end, it will be established that for imperfectivity to be explicated it is enough if only one of the two components in the sentence is associated with temporal non-boundedness. But if sentences like (95a) and (95b) are the object of analysis, this amounts to saying that, on the one hand, the presence of an indefinite or a definite article in the subject presupposes the explication of boundedness on the time axis. Yet, on the other hand, as has already been seen, the entity behind a sentence component (in this case a subject) like *a woman* or *the woman* in sentences (95a) and (95b) in fact comprises a non-bounded chain of separate 'stages' or ('segments' or 'slices') of a woman knitting sweaters (who may even otherwise, despite the type of article, be familiar or unfamiliar to the speaker and/or hearer). It could hardly be argued that the occurrence of a non-bounded entity of this kind would be less frequent in actual discourse or that it would only occur in those cases in which the subject *a woman* or *the woman* does not refer to the same personality, but to different women performing the action of sweater-knitting. Or, to spell out the problem, in sentences like (95) there arises a certain contradiction between the outward boundedness of the referents of subjects like *a woman* or *the woman* marked by an article or some other language element with a similar bounding function and the necessity for the observer/speaker to have perceived a recurring, that is, non-bounded, picture of a woman knitting sweaters.

To solve the problem of the identity or non-identity of the person performing the action, it would be useful to compare sentences (95a) and (95b), on the one hand, and Verkuyl's sentence (40a), already considered on a number of occasions, on the other hand.

(95) a. A woman knitted Norwegian sweaters
 b. The woman knitted Norwegian sweaters
(40) a. Katinka knitted Norwegian sweaters

Sentence (40a) has the same structure and a similar meaning, but the subject in it is a proper noun and cannot, therefore, in normal circumstances, refer to different persons.[2] The question is: does the type of the agent in (40a) with its temporal characteristics differ substantially from the type of the agent in sentences like (95a) and (95b)? According to Verkuyl's schema for imperfectivity, *Katinka* in (40a) should be assigned the value of 'specified quantity of X', that is, temporal boundedness. But then Katinka would have the same temporal status as Katinka in (39a) has – an assumption which is rather unacceptable, since sentence (39a) denotes a single completed action whereas sentence (40a) denotes an indefinitely repeated non-bounded one. Compare the two sentences:

(39) a. Katinka knitted a Norwegian sweater
(40) a. Katinka knitted Norwegian sweaters

Apparently, this is a serious problem for which an appropriate solution must be found.

And so, could we assume that the subjects *Katinka* in (40a) and *the boy* or *a boy* in sentences like (57a) ought to be assigned the feature 'temporal boundedness' simply because they contain structural language elements with a bounding function – a proper name and an article (definite or indefinite), respectively?

(40) a. Katinka knitted Norwegian sweaters
(57) a. A/The boy threw stones

The answer to this question, obviously, has to be negative. As already established, the subject in (40a), *Katinka*, represents a perceptual entity (received by the speaker and conveyed to the hearer) which constitutes a recurring picture (in the past) of a performer of a certain action. And if the referent of the (syntactic) object *Norwegian sweaters* in sentence (40a) also constitutes a recurring 'stage' ('stages') of objects, then the participants in the action in (57a) could not be different, since the sentence and its components display the same structure in terms of the principles of aspectual composition discussed so far. Hence, once such a view is accepted, it turns out that, in fact, the temporal values of the participants in an action will have to be regarded as always equivalent one to another. And more – since the verb is what ultimately denotes the action in the sentence, it would have to be assumed that the temporal values of the participants in an action are equivalent also to the temporal

---

[2] To consider a non-normal case, one could construct a situation in which several women all named Katinka take part in the action covered by sentence (40a). This is a possible but at the same time a relatively unusual reading for a sentence like (40a).

value of the action, denoted, largely speaking, by the verb component in the sentence (in so far as very simple sentences are discussed).

The idea of the equivalence of the temporal values of the participants in an action or (generally) a situation is indeed in consistence with the thesis put forward above about the way one conceives of actions and their participants. It is also similar to the treatment proposed by Hinrichs (1985), discussed earlier. But let us analyse the consequences that an assumption of this thesis would have for the interpretation of the grammatical data and of other phenomena observed on the basis of the characteristics of the types of sentences analysed so far.

The comparison between Slavic languages (including Bulgarian in particular) and a language like English leads to the conclusion that within the perfective/imperfective distinction it is perfectivity that is more difficult to express. In Slavic languages it is expressed mainly through prefixes and suffixes in the verb, cf. Bulgarian *piša*$_{impfv}$ 'write' – *napiša*$_{pfv}$ 'write' – *napisvam*$_{impfv2}$ 'write', *prepiša*$_{pfv}$ 'rewrite' – *prepisvam*$_{impfv2}$ 'rewrite', *četa*$_{impfv}$ 'read' – *pročeta*$_{pfv}$ 'read' – *pročitam*$_{impfv2}$ 'read', *izčeta*$_{pfv}$ 'read thoroughly' – *izčitam*$_{impfv2}$ 'read through', *padam*$_{impfv}$ 'fall [repeatedly or be in the process of falling]' – *padna*$_{pfv}$ 'fall', etc. Taking into account the importance of signifying the distinction between completed/perfective and non-completed/ imperfective actions, deeply rooted in both individual and collective mentality and hence necessary for any language, a question arises with respect to the global expression of aspect in languages like English. If imperfectivity has at least a partial overt expression in the English verb system through the Progressive, it is apparently useless to look for a formal element in the English verb for the expression of perfectivity similar to the Slavic perfective aspect. Still, as has already been established and as the theory of Verkuyl shows, many sentences can be constructed in English which explicate perfective actions. But if Verkuyl has outlined the global mechanism of perfectivity, we could also ask where exactly the compositional mechanism is derived from and what it is based on.

To the representatives of the Russian school who introduced the key notion of *predel'nost'* 'telicity', and perhaps even for most other linguists around the world, the answer to this question is self-evident. It is the verb that the ultimate expression of perfectivity is derived from and based on. But from the large number of sentences with the same verb (in the same tense form, mainly the Simple Past Tense) which can explicate either perfectivity or imperfectivity, and this is only due to the absence of an article or a determiner or a quantifier in the subject and/or the object, it can be concluded that the verb only **contributes** to the explication of perfectivity. Hence, it is possible for the ultimate explication of perfectivity in English (and similar languages) to originate in the verb, but it is not the verb on which perfectivity is mainly based. On the other hand, we have already seen that Verkuyl's minor and rather provisional statement that the temporal boundedness of the participants in an action is located in the determiner (that is, in the article, some other closed-class lexical items, etc.) enters into a contradiction with the conclusion made above that subjects and objects containing articles (or certain personal, possessive, and demonstrative pronouns, proper names, etc.) in fact do not explicate temporal boundedness in a sentence with an imperfective meaning.

To facilitate the discussion, recall the following detail of the compositional aspect mechanism. Subjects and objects like *Katinka, a Norwegian sweater, a boy, the boy, a stone, John, he* are temporally bounded in sentences (39a), (56a) and (66a), and their temporal boundedness is (perhaps) explicated through the article or other elements that are functionally similar:

(39) a. Katinka knitted a Norwegian sweater
(56) a. A/The boy threw a/the stone
(66) a. John/He threw a stone

But if this is so, then why do the article and the similar elements **not** explicate temporal boundedness of the respective subjects in (40a) and (57a)?

(40) a. Katinka knitted Norwegian sweaters
(57) a. A/The boy threw stones

In the search for an adequate answer to this question recall also that the article and the similar elements cannot **directly** express temporal boundedness, at least in the sentences of the type analysed so far. According to the terminology employed in this work, they do not signify or denote or express temporal boundedness. They only explicate or imply it. Temporal boundedness is covert in them, and they may be said to transfer it to the referents of NPs which take part in situations. But temporal boundedness, generally inaccessible to the native speaker, was proved to exist, through an appropriate analysis.

Therefore, the solution to the problem could be put forward along the following lines. The article and the similar elements are really able to imply or explicate temporal boundedness of referents of subjects and objects in sentences of a certain type, as in Verkuyl's schema of perfectivity. But in sentences in which they are present and which explicate imperfectivity due to the absence of an article (or a similar element) in another major sentence component, their ability to imply boundedness is suppressed. In these cases subjects and objects that contain these elements may start to imply temporal non-boundedness under the influence of another part or other parts of the sentence.

What is considered here is certainly not an isolated phenomenon in the grammars of languages, and in the expression of aspect in particular. In Bulgarian, for instance, the basic function of the imperfective aspect is, naturally, the denotation of imperfective, non-completed actions. But in a sentence like (97) below the aspectual meaning of the verb *pija*$_{impfv}$ 'drink' is suppressed, so that the imperfective verb form *šte pija* 'will drink' in this sentence is actually forced to explicate a perfective action:

(97)   Šte   pija$_{impfv}$ čaša   bira   i   šte   izljaza$_{pfv}$
       Will   drink-I   glass   beer   and   will   leave-I
       'I'll drink a glass of beer and leave'

Conversely, the basic function of the perfective aspect is to denote single completed actions, as, for example, in sentences like (98a) and (98b):

(98) a. Izpih$_{pfvAor}$ čaša   bira
        Drank-I   glass   beer
        'I drank a glass of beer'
     b. Iskam$_{impfv}$ da izpija$_{pfv}$ čaša   bira
        Want-I   to drink   glass   beer
        'I want to drink a glass of beer'

But this basic, prototypical meaning of the perfective aspect can not only be suppressed, it can be radically changed. Consider sentences like (99a) and (99b) below where the perfective verb *izpija* 'drink' denotes an indefinitely iterative action and hence, actually, describes a situation which is imperfective:

(99) a. Izpieh$_{pfvImp}$ li   čaša   bira,   se   razveseljavah$_{impfvImp}$
        Drank-I   prt.   glass   beer,   prt.   cheered-up-I
        'Whenever I drank a glass of beer, I cheered up'
     b. Izpija$_{pfv}$ li   čaša   bira,   se   razveseljavam$_{impfv}$
        Drank-I   prt.   glass   beer,   prt.   cheer-up-I
        'Whenever I drink a glass of beer, I cheer up'

Of course, many other examples of sentences in different Slavic languages can be given in which the basic meaning of aspect is suppressed under the influence of various other elements within a sentence or the context of its use.

Therefore, there is nothing strange in the fact that the article and the similar bounding elements in English are capable of explicating temporal boundedness in certain types of sentences and incapable of doing this in other types of sentences. Still, an explanation of this phenomenon ought to be given. Obviously, the existence of a specific mechanism for distributing and redistributing the temporal features of NPs will have to be assumed: it will allow certain components to explicate temporal boundedness in certain types of sentences and will not allow these components to explicate temporal boundedness in other types of sentences.

THE IMPACT OF THE VERB AND THE ADVERBIAL

But let us go back to the question of the meaning of the verb component and its contribution to the aspectual reading of a sentence. It was assumed that in sentences like (74) the verb is of such a type that, taken as a lexical entry, possesses the feature 'telicity'. That it is true of certain verbs that they do possess this feature – in contrast to other verbs which lack it – can easily be exemplified through the comparison between a sentence like (74), which explicates perfectivity, and (100a) below, which explicates imperfectivity. However, it could hardly be said of a verb like *threw* in (74) that it expresses or explicates perfectivity of the action by itself. Apparently, it does contribute to the explication of perfectivity, but it only conveys perfectivity as a default interpretation, or the possibility for the ultimate explication of perfectivity, **indirectly**, without denoting it. Neither does a primarily atelic verb like *carry*, as in a sentence like (100a) explicate imperfectivity of the action by itself. Compare sentence (100a) and a sentence like (100b) where in the latter the destination of the action of carrying contributes to the explication of perfectivity. Moreover, even in the presence of an article in both the subject and the object in some similar sentences, the verb *threw* may still be unable to explicate or imply perfectivity of the action. Compare, for example, sentence (100c) in which, in contrast to (74), the action is made indefinitely repetitive, hence non-bounded:

(74)   The boy threw a stone
(100) a. The boy carried a stone
      b. The boy carried a stone into the basement
      c. The boy often threw a stone
      d. The bow threw a stone three times

Repetition does not necessarily mean non-boundedness, cf. (100d) above where the action is bounded again, as in (74), but it is also repetitive.

Of course, as has already been shown, the bounded or non-bounded meaning of a certain verb in the Simple Past Tense can entirely depend not on the verb itself but on another component of the sentence. In contrast to sentence (74), sentences like (57a) and (59a) explicate imperfectivity:

(57) a. A/The boy threw stones
(59) a. Boys threw stones

But what is the change from the perfectivity of (74) to the imperfectivity of (100c) due to? Obviously, it is a consequence of the introduction of the adverbial *often*. And if an adverbial is capable of transforming the aspectual reading of a sentence, then there is a complex mechanism through which temporal boundedness and temporal non-boundedness are distributed and redistributed among the different components in the sentence.

So far, the problem of the crucial meaning of the adverbial for the explication of aspect at the level of the sentence has not been considered in detail. This will be done in Chapter Eleven, *The impact of adverbials in the sentence, and aspect in English*. But let us here make use of the example (100c) – which is very appropriate for the illustration of the mechanism for redistributing temporal boundedness and non-boundedness.

THE MAPPING MECHANISM; MAPPING FROM THE 'PARTICIPANT(S)' ONTO THE VERB

Let us call this a mapping mechanism[3] and go back to sentence (74):

(74)   The boy threw a stone

This sentence explicates a perfective action. Sentence (100c), however, in which only the adverbial *often* has been added, explicates an imperfective action, an indefinitely iterative one:

(100) c. The boy often threw a stone

It is obviously the adverbial *often* that is responsible for transforming the perfectivity of the original sentence into the imperfectivity of the derived one. And it is to be assumed that the meaning of non-bounded iterativity is contained in the word *often* as a lexical entry, for imperfectivity here does not arise in some special way in the sentence – as does, for example, the perfective reading of a sentence like (74). Moreover, after the introduction of *often* into sentence (74), which explicates a single bounded action, *often* maps its own meaning of 'non-bounded iterativity' onto the entire aspectual meaning of the sentence. The non-bounded iterativity is mapped, in particular, also onto the temporal values of the subject and the object. As the analysis above showed, *the boy* and *a stone* in (74) should be viewed as temporal entities, singular and bounded. In (100c), if *the boy* and *a stone* are to be viewed again as temporal slices, then here each of them ought to constitute an indefinite series of temporal stretches. That is, (100c) ought to invoke not only an indefinitely recurring picture of a throwing action but also an indefinitely recurring picture of *the boy* and *a stone*, respectively. And after the conclusions made above concerning the way situations and their participants should be regarded, it is now easier for the temporal status of participants in the situations to be also conceived of in more "common-sense" terms: to utter truthfully sentence (100c), an observer/speaker has to have perceived time slices of a (familiar) boy and a (non-familiar) stone taking part in the action of throwing an indefinite number of times.

As far as the notion of iterativity itself is concerned, note that it can be either non-bounded or bounded, as already exemplified through the action in sentence (100c) vs. the action in sentence (100d):

(100) c. The boy often threw a stone
      d. The bow threw a stone three times

---

[3] Although the notion of mapping introduced here bears a certain resemblance to Krifka's 'mapping to objects' and 'mapping to events' (Krifka 1992), the difference is considerable – in the sense that what is mapped here are purely temporal properties. On the other hand, the proposal to view the mechanism of mapping in temporal terms was made earlier, in Kabakčiev (1984b).

Thus if in order to utter (100c) truthfully an observer/speaker has to have perceived time slices of a (familiar) boy and a (non-familiar) stone taking part in the action of throwing an indefinite number of times, in the case of (100d) the perception is of three time slices of a (familiar) boy and a (non-familiar) stone taking part in the action of throwing.

But the verb in a sentence like (74), too, could not explicate the perfectivity of the action by itself. On the other hand, the article, definite or indefinite, explicates temporal boundedness in the referents of the two NPs. Therefore, in this sentence the two NPs are in a sense marked for temporal boundedness to a higher degree than is the verb. What is more, whereas the verb contains the feature 'telicity' in its lexical meaning only and assists the two NPs in their explication of temporal boundedness, the subject and the object are **grammatically** marked through the article. In other words, while the subject-NP and the object-NP in the sentence are formally marked, the verb is not. We can, therefore, assume that in sentences of type (74) the temporal boundedness in the subject and in the object, marked by the article, is mapped onto the verb. Temporal boundedness will here and henceforward be represented by a straight line, closed at the two ends, as in (101a) below, and the lack of marking of temporal boundedness (or temporal non-boundedness itself) will be represented by a wavy line, as in (101b):

Temporal boundedness (101a) and temporal non-boundedness (101b)

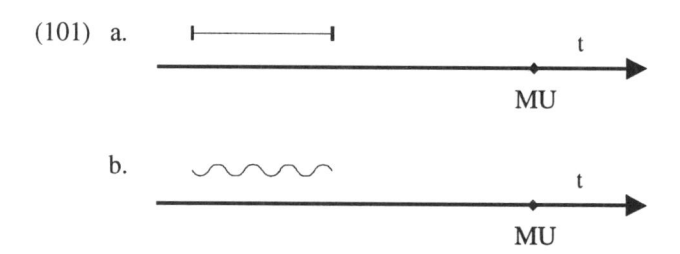

(101) a.

b.

Here MU stands for 'moment of utterance'; t for 'time'.

Given this representation, the aspectually relevant meaning of sentence (74) can be described through the diagram in (102) below:

(74) The boy threw a stone

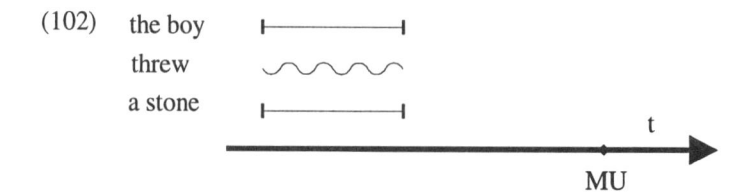

(102) the boy
threw
a stone

It is to be noted that this diagram differs essentially from Verkuyl's schema for perfectivity. Verkuyl's schema treats both [SPECIFIED QUANTITY OF X] and [ADD TO] as plus-values – no account is given of the fact that while the node SPECIFIED finds a surface language (grammatical) realisation, [ADD TO] is just a lexical feature. Diagram (102) here makes a distinction between these two kinds of language data. While the subject and the object (*the boy* and *a stone*) are overtly marked for temporal boundedness through the article, the verb (*threw*) is not. Hence, *the boy* and *a stone* receive a straight line; *threw* a wavy one.

And within this kind of diagrammatic representation, the mapping of temporal boundedness could be displayed in the following way:

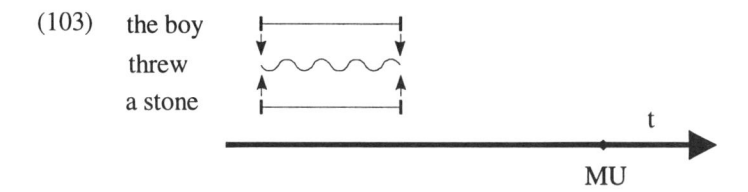

(103)   the boy
        threw
        a stone

                                    t
                    MU

Recall again that the mechanism of mapping is also inaccessible to the intuitions of the native speaker. This follows from the inaccessibility of the mechanism for assigning temporal values to physical referents of subjects and objects as, for example, those in sentences like (74). But if a "common sense" explanation of the assignment of temporal values to "physical" subjects and objects can be given, the mechanism of mapping could also be explained in similar terms.

Again, the question arises: if certain sentences explicate perfectivity, and other sentences explicate imperfectivity, isn't it the verb that has to be represented as the ultimate exponent of perfectivity or imperfectivity? From the point of view of Slavic grammar, and also from a general theoretical point of view, this question is to be answered positively. In English, however, it turns out, it is not the verb that directly denotes perfectivity and imperfectivity. The verb only assists in their explication in compositional terms. Temporal boundedness is explicated by the participants in an action, and is then mapped onto the referent of the verb. And it is eventually only then that the verb – that otherwise denotes most of the general characteristics of the action/situation – can be said to imply or, rather, explicate perfectivity. But this only happens after boundedness has been mapped onto the referent of the verb from the referent of another sentence component or from the referents of other sentence components.

Certainly, if the kind of mechanism of mapping described here can be assumed to exist with respect to sentences explicating perfective situations, it will have to be assumed also for sentences explicating imperfective situations. If we take it that subjects like *Katinka*, *a boy*, *the boy*, etc., display a tendency to assist the explication of perfectivity in actions like *knit*, *throw*, etc., then it would be normal for these subjects to be regarded as bounded singular temporal slices that are indefinitely multiplied along the time axis in sentences like (40a) and (57a):

(40) a. Katinka knitted Norwegian sweaters
(57) a. A/The boy threw stones[4]

It is also natural to reason that the action in a sentence like (40a) above will contain in itself the action in a sentence like (39a) below. That is, in the situation described in (40a) the action of (39a) is indefinitely serialised through the multiplication of the referent of the object *a Norwegian sweater*. And the multiplication of the referent of the object itself is realised by the lack of quantification and by the overt, grammatical, pluralisation:

(39) a. Katinka knitted a Norwegian sweater

Hence, multiplied indefinitely is not just the (separate) action of knitting a Norwegian sweater but also the temporal (preliminary bounded) slice of the 'individual' Katinka. Diagrammatically, this reading of sentence (40a) can be represented in the following fashion:

(40) a. Katinka knitted Norwegian sweaters

(104) Katinka ◄ |―――| |―――| |―――| ►
      knitted ◄ ∼∼∼ ∼∼∼ ∼∼∼ ►
(Norwegian) sweaters ◄ |―――| |―――| |―――| ► t

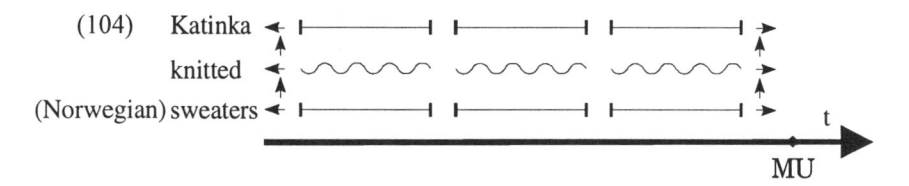

MU

The left and right pointing arrows designate the 'indefinite recurrence' feature (indefinite repetition/indefinite iterativity) of the referent of the subject or the object and the indefinite iterativity of the action. But besides non-bounded, indefinite, the iterativity of an overall action can be a definite, bounded one, as in (100d) or in sentences of the type (105a) below. Note that iterative boundedness can also be designated by a sentence like (105b) in which, however, the boundedness of the action is clearly different from that in (105a). The difference between these two types of action is important but it will be dealt with later on, in Chapter Thirteen. *On aspectual classes in English*.

(100) d. The bow threw a stone three times
(105) a. Katinka knitted many/a lot of Norwegian sweaters
      b. Katinka knitted Norwegian sweaters for a week

---

[4] These and similar subjects are, so to say, "regarded" as temporal slices only in terms of the linguistic analysis undertaken. In psycho-physiological reality, however, they are truly "regarded" (perceived) by the native speaker as such, although they are not "grasped" (conceived) in this manner. Were we to conceive of the temporal status of physical objects too, our memory would have been burdened to a degree where it would not be able to function (cf. Smith and Medin 1981: 1).

To return to the diagram in (104) above, the lower row of upward pointing arrows represents the mapping of non-boundedness (in this case it is an indefinite, non-bounded, open series of temporal stretches) from the referent of the object to the referent of the verb, and the upper row of upward pointing arrows represents the mapping of boundedness (again an indefinite open series of temporal stretches) from the referent of the verb (or the whole verb phrase *knitted Norwegian sweaters*) to the referent of the subject.

However, there are certain problems with this representation. For example, sentence (40a) does not really tell whether each of the separate actions that constitute the overall indefinitely repetitive action in the sentence is completed/bounded or not. Compare Verkuyl's (1993: 154) extensive reasoning about the way a sentence like (106a), or (106b) for that matter (see Verkuyl 1993: 143-154), leaves the addressee in the dark as to how exactly the action described is performed.

(106) a. Three children came in
b. The three men lifted four pianos

Did the three children come in together, or one by one, or two and then one, etc.? Even more are the possibilities for distributing the action and the participants in a sentence like (106b). Similarly, in a sentence like (40a) both the object *Norwegian sweaters* and the action, the essence of which is broadly designated by the verb *knitted*, could be alternatively represented as an indefinite series of non-bounded stretches (wavy lines in the diagram), the indefinite repetitiveness of the overall action being again generated by the indefinite recurrence of the object. As in the previous diagram, this can be designated by the lower row of arrows. This kind of representation certainly makes sense from the point of view of the difference between the referents of *Katinka* and *Norwegian sweaters*. While the referent of *Norwegian sweaters* is originally temporally non-bounded, the referent of *Katinka* is originally temporally bounded, and this difference is not present in the diagram in (104) above. Compare diagram (107) below, where the referent of *Katinka* is bounded in its separate-slice representation (but not in its repetition) and the referent of *Norwegian sweaters* is non-bounded in both its separate occurrences and in its iterativity:

(40) a. Katinka knitted Norwegian sweaters

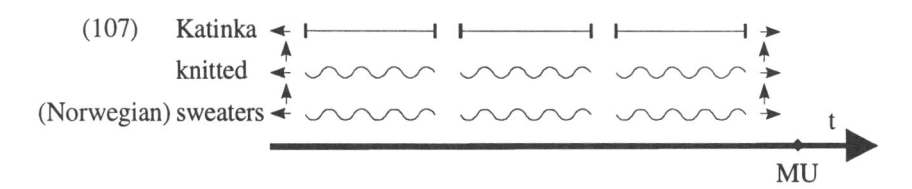

(107) Katinka
knitted
(Norwegian) sweaters

MU

It has to be decided, however, whether the action in a sentence like (40a) should be regarded as an indefinite multiplication of the entity *knitted a Norwegian sweater*, as described at first, or as a process of sweater-knitting in which it is not necessary even for a single sweater to have been made? Compare, for example, knitting sweater parts in a knitting shop by a single knitter or doing a ceaseless knitting exercise on many sweaters without finishing a single one. Clearly, sentence (40a) does not by itself inform us which of these two possibilities is to be assumed. Knowledge of the world and of the typical behaviour of human beings counsel us, however, to accept a 'normal interpretation' in which Katinka has knitted whole sweaters. (Compare the discussion along these lines in Chapter Fourteen, *On 'knowledge of the world' in the explication of aspect in English*.) In both interpretations of the action, the one in which there is an indefinite repetition of a bounded act and the one in which there is an indefinite repetition of a process, the referent of the subject *Katinka* should be assigned temporal non-boundedness (non-bounded iterativity). But in the case of the more unusual interpretation in which Katinka is doing a ceaseless knitting exercise on many sweaters without finishing a single one, it appears more natural to assume that the referent of the verb *knitted* in its separate occurrences is not as large as the referents of *Katinka* and *sweaters* in their separate occurrences. This is because, first, the representation of *Katinka* and especially *sweaters* as 'whole' stretches is already reserved for the perfective action in a sentence like (39a), repeated below – which is generally identical to the action described in (74) and represented in (102) and (103) – or for the 'normal' interpretation of (40a), as represented in (104) above.

(39) a. Katinka knitted a Norwegian sweater

Second, if we compare the action of knitting a whole sweater to the action of knitting part of it, obviously the length of the time stretch of knitting part of a sweater will be shorter than the length of the stretch of knitting a whole sweater.

Therefore, the referent of *knitted* in sentence (40a) in the more unusual interpretation defined above should be regarded as a shorter stretch of time than that of *Norwegian sweaters* (and also *Katinka*) in the normal interpretation of (40a), in (104) and in (107). This is shown in diagram (108) below. But the non-boundedness of *knitted* arises out of the non-boundedness of *Norwegian sweaters* in the first place – that is, the referent of *Norwegian sweaters* maps its non-bounded iterativity and the non-boundedness of its separate occurrences onto the referent of the verb *knitted*. Thereafter, the non-bounded iterativity and the non-boundedness of the separate occurrences of the referent of the verb *knitted* are mapped onto the referent of the subject *Katinka*, as shown in (108):

(40) a. Katinka knitted Norwegian sweaters

(108) Katinka
       knitted
(Norwegian) sweaters
                                                            MU

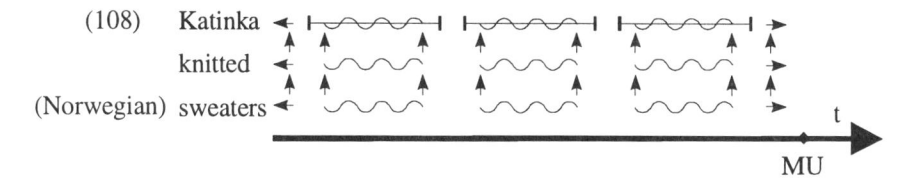

This seems to be the optimal representation of the unusual reading of (40a) but it would be natural for the possibilities for diagrammatic representation to remain as open as are the possibilities for interpreting the action in sentences of the type considered. What is relatively fixed is the overall imperfectivity (indefinite iterativity) of the action. But, again, it is worth remembering that the non-bounded one is the primary, the prototypical, but not the only possible interpretation of the sentence. Consider, for example, sentence (105b), already used above, and contrast it to (40a):

(105) b. Katinka knitted Norwegian sweaters for a week
(40)   a. Katinka knitted Norwegian sweaters

The adverbial *for a week*, although it is generally considered to be a very good test for the imperfectivity of a sentence or phrase it is applied to, actually bounds the action explicated by the rest of the sentence. Hence, clearly, (40a) itself could have a meaning identical to the one in (105b) provided the context of use of this sentence contains indications as to the week's duration of the action of Katinka's knitting Norwegian sweaters. Observations of this kind make a considerable detour from most aspectological studies which usually ignore the semantic influence of *for*-time adverbials on phrases or sentences they are applied to. But this point will be considered in more detail in Chapter Thirteen, *On aspectual classes in English*.

MAPPING FROM THE VERB ONTO THE 'PARTICIPANTS'

Despite certain problems, sentences like (74) or even (40a) relatively easily allow a diagrammatic representation of the mapping mechanism. But with other kinds of sentences the diagrammatic representation can be more difficult. Consider sentence (100a) below, which is similar to (74) but is imperfective. The verb in it, without being overtly marked for imperfectivity (as, for example, are progressive verb forms in English or imperfective verbs in the Slavic languages), imposes a non-bounded reading on the sentence. Compare the perfective (74) and the imperfective (100a), differing only in the verb:

(74)   The boy threw a stone
(100) a. The boy carried a stone

Generally, entities denoted by definite NPs or by NPs quantified otherwise, that is, non-generic, specific entities, ought to be taken as basically implying temporal boundedness or, in more common-sense terms, implying limited existence in time relative to the time span denoted by the lexical meaning of the verb. The limited existence in time of *the boy* and *a stone* in (100a) below relative to the lexical meaning of the verb can be, broadly speaking, two-fold, and such that it can either cover a particular moment of time or a more extended period of the possible lifespan of the two participants. In the first case it is equivalent to a sentence with a verb in the Progressive. That is, (100a) is equivalent to (109):

(100) a. The boy carried a stone
(109) The boy was carrying a stone

In the second case, the extended period of time referred to by the sentence can be a relatively short period, as in (110a), or a larger period covering the whole (or a significant part of the) existence of the entity in question, as in (110b).

(110) a. The boy carried a stone in his hand during the picnic
b. The boy carried a stone in his hand whenever I saw him in the street

Here arises a problem with respect to the interpretation of the length of existence of certain entities. Thus *a boy* is an entity whose life span is roughly (conventionally) limited to a period of not more than two decades. But, of course, there are many sentences like (111) which, in a way, prolong the life span:

(111) The boy became a president/an archbishop later

Cf. Musan (1999). Again, it is clear that these kinds of sentences should be treated as special metaphorical descriptions (compare the 'stage' of Nixon bombing Hanoi in the previous chapter) and that the length of existence of objects (both animate and inanimate) relevant to the action or state these objects take part in is either directly denoted or implied by context.

But while the meanings of certain verbs are vague with respect to the length of the period they cover, the meanings of other verbs are such that these verbs typically imply extended periods and do not normally refer to moments or short periods of time. The properties of the verb *hate*, for example, have often been discussed in the linguistic literature. *Hate* is normally used to refer to extended time spans, as in (112a) below, a typically imperfective sentence, in contrast to a sentence like (112b), a typically perfective sentence:

(112) a. John hated Mary
b. John kissed Mary

On the other hand, the use of *hate* in sentences like (113a) and (113b) below is treated as special – as stylistically marked, metaphorical or as equivalent to verbs or verb phrases with a somewhat different meaning. For example, the meaning of the verb *hated* in (113a) and (113b) below can be paraphrased by the expression *felt hatred*, as in (113d), (113e) and (113f), with a slight change in meaning. The phrase *feel hatred* is different from the verb *hate* in that, first, it can more easily present the action as inchoative (making reference to the beginning of the action) and perfective, cf. (113c). Second, in contrast to the verb *hate*, the expression *feel hatred* can easily imply shorter periods of time and even moments, cf. (113d), (113e) and (113f).

(113) a. John hated Mary at that moment
 b. John hated Mary yesterday/that evening
 c. John felt hatred towards Mary
 d. John felt hatred towards Mary at that moment/yesterday/that evening
 e. John was feeling hatred towards Mary at that moment
 f. John was feeling hatred towards Mary yesterday/that evening

Note that in the case of adding an adverbial like *at that moment* to a sentence like (112a) the verb can be interpreted as referring to a different kind of situation. The verb *hated* in this case, (113a), acquires an inchoative meaning – cf. Glasbey (1994: 249-256) for an analysis of the interplay between the use of the temporal preposition *at* and the expression of states and/or their inception.

In both (100a) and (112a), however, it is precisely the meaning of the verb that prevents the explication of perfectivity in spite of the initial boundedness of the NPs marked through an article or, in the second case, through a proper noun (the two sentences are given below). This is easily seen with respect to the verb *hate* when it is substituted and contrasted with the phrase *feel hatred*, as in (113c) above. Therefore, the verb in (100a) and (112a) below can be said to be marked lexically for atelicity to a higher degree than many other verbs already discussed. The lexical feature of atelicity itself can be said to be realised as non-boundedness at the level of the sentence and to dominate the initial boundedness of the subject- and object-NPs in sentences like (74) or (112b). Diagrammatically, the transfer of non-boundedness from the referent of the verb onto the referents of the NPs can be represented by specifying the higher degree of markedness of atelicity in the verb as a lexical entry. But note that unlike grammatical non-boundedness, as represented, for example, by the Progressive, lexical non-boundedness is flexible. Two extreme situational readings and possibilities for intermediate readings are generally allowed. The first one, at one extreme, is the most natural reading for (100a) – the 'activity'/'process' (progressive-like) reading. The second one is the true 'state' reading, the most natural one for (112a):

(100) a. The boy carried a stone
(112) a. John hated Mary

But both (100a) and (112a) are capable of accommodating also the two less natural readings. The expression of a 'state' (habitual) reading of (100a) is context-dependent, and the expression of an 'activity' (progressive-like) reading in a sentence like (112a), though rather atypical, is not impossible – through the support of adverbials or the neighbouring context, as, for example, in the non-inchoative reading of (113a) below, equivalent in meaning to (113e):

(113) a. John hated Mary at that moment
e. John was feeling hatred towards Mary at that moment

All this, along with the relevant lexical (not grammatical) property of the verb complicates the diagrammatic representation of the transfer of non-boundedness from the verb onto the subject-NP and the object-NP. If we take it that NPs with an article like *the boy* and *a stone* display a tendency to refer to bounded entities in a sentence like (74) and in many similar sentences (as argued extensively in the previous chapters), then their primary boundedness, implied by a grammatical entity, the article, ought to be reflected in the diagrammatic representation of a sentence like (100a) too. This will be displayed again by a bounded straight line, as in the diagrammatic representation (102) of sentence (74), repeated here for the sake of clarity:

(74)   The boy threw a stone

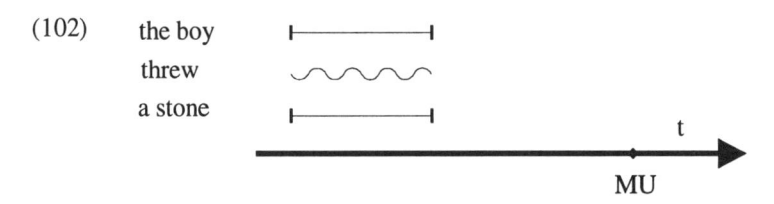

(102)   the boy
        threw
        a stone

Thus, a possibility for a diagrammatic representation of the activity reading of sentence (100a) will be the one given in (114):

(100) a. The boy carried a stone

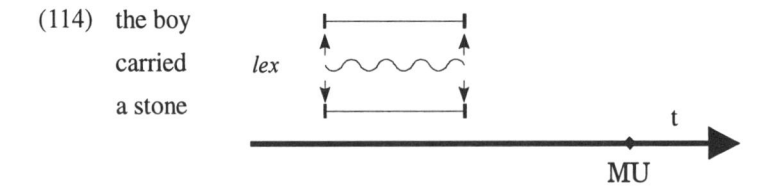

(114)   the boy
        carried   lex
        a stone

The lexical non-boundedness of *carried* can be said to be mapped onto the initial boundedness of the referents of the subject and object NPs, thereby cancelling it. But the meaning explicated in (100a) is largely identical to that in sentences with a verb in the Progressive. Hence, the diagrammatic representation of the basic aspectual reading of (100a) ought to be given in a fashion similar to the one for the sentence with a progressive form of the verb, (109) – and it will turn out to be different from (114), see Chapter Eight, *The Progressive in English*.

(109)   The boy was carrying a stone

However, since the meaning of the Progressive is in need of further analysis in semantic terms and in terms of certain cross-language regularities, both the representation of the progressive meaning proper, as in (109), and the representation of the basic (progressive-like) reading of sentences like (100a) will be dealt with later on, in Chapter Eight, *The Progressive in English*.

As far as the state-like (habitual) reading of (100a) is concerned, obviously it ought to receive a representation similar to the one given above for a sentence like (40a).

(40)   a. Katinka knitted Norwegian sweaters

That is, when the activity in (100a) turns into a state, the participants in it acquire non-boundedness at two levels – at the level of the separate occasion on which the boy is observed carrying a stone, and at the level of the situation as a whole in which there is a non-bounded series of the action of 'carrying a stone' performed by a boy.

Both types of non-boundedness in (100a) – at the level of the separate occasion and at the level of the repetition of the action – can be regarded as being mapped from the lexical property of the verb onto the referents of the subject and the object. In diagram (115) this is designated by the two types of vertical arrows – those representing the transfer of the non-bounded repetition (the two extreme pairs of arrows) and those representing the unbounding of the referents of the subject and the object at the level of the separate occasions:

(100) a. The boy carried a stone

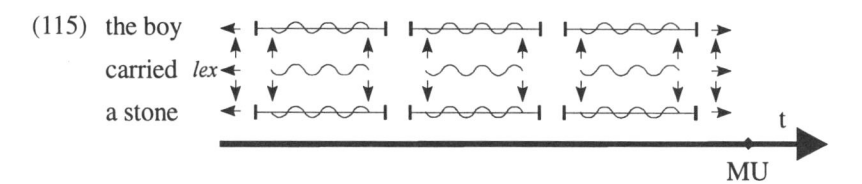

(115)   the boy
        carried *lex*
        a stone

There is also enough common-sense reasoning to assume that at both levels the stages of *the boy* and *a stone* are conceived of as non-bonded stretches of time coinciding with the essence of the action itself. To be able to utter (100a) truthfully, one has to have observed a boy carrying a stone an indefinite number of times, and on each occasion the boy and the stone have to have been non-bounded in the sense that they always took part in an activity that did not reach a natural endpoint. Hence, in the diagrammatic representation, non-boundedness is to be shown as transferred from the verb not only onto the total temporal configurations of the participants making them a non-bounded series of temporal stretches, but also onto the separate slices of the participants. These, being bounded initially through the article, are unbounded, and this is reflected in the diagram (115) above by the wavy lines imposed onto the separate straight time lines of the participants. In many ways, this reading of sentence (100a) is actually similar to the basic reading in a sentence like (116a) with a bare plural (syntactic) object explicating a non-bounded recurring referent. In this case the bare plural obviously does not contribute greatly to the composition of the aspectual meaning because the imperfective meaning of the sentence has already been composed. Compare (100a) and (116a):

(100) a. The boy carried a stone
(116) a. The boy carried stones
       b. The boy often carried a stone into the basement

SIMULTANEOUS REVERSE MAPPING

There is, however, a somewhat rarer case in which the separate occasions of stone-carrying in (100a) could actually involve an endpoint. This kind of reading is identical to the situational reading of sentence (116b) given above. In it, the separate stages of *the boy* and *a stone* will have to be represented as bounded, though in the situation as a whole they, again, will be non-bounded – for they will constitute an indefinite number of (recurring) time stretches. The following is a diagrammatic representation of this specific reading of (100a), identical to the normal reading of (116b):

(100) a. The boy carried a stone

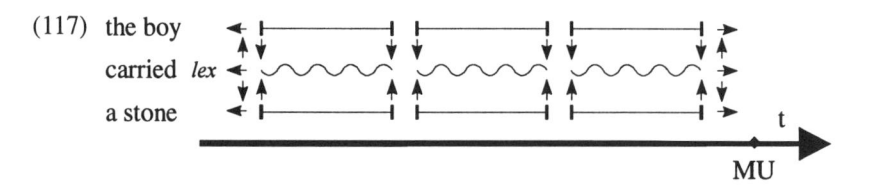

(117) the boy
      carried *lex*
      a stone
                                                                    t
                                                                   MU

Diagram (117) displays the reverse direction of the two types of mapping of temporal values. At the level of the separate occasions of the overall iterative action, boundedness is mapped from the referents of the subject-NP and the object-NP onto the referent of the verb; and at the level of the indefinite repetition, non-boundedness can be said to be mapped from the referent of the verb (explicating the essence of the action) onto the referents of the subject-NP and the object-NP. Needless to say, this secondary reading of (100a), identical to the primary one in (116b) above will be explicated through the influence of context – when it is explicated at all. The primary reading, covered in diagram (115) above, would not normally need contextual support.[5]

PHYSICAL VS. TEMPORAL SINGULARITY AND PLURALITY OF 'PARTICIPANTS'

Another problem concerning the diagrammatic representation of (100a) in its reading similar to sentence (40a), repeated below, or to (116b) is that the singularity of the object *a stone* – in contrast to the plurality of the object *Norwegian sweaters* in (40a) – should be taken into account.

(40) a. Katinka knitted Norwegian sweaters

Although singularity or plurality of the referent of the object is overtly expressed anyway (grammatically, through the category of number), one way of dealing with the problem would be to introduce an additional designation *sing* or *pl* – similar to the designation *lex* in the diagrammatic representation (117) of a sentence like (100a). See diagram (117') below – in which the mapping mechanism within the separate occasions of carrying out the overall action is not represented.

(116) b. The boy often carried a stone into the basement
(100) a. The boy carried a stone

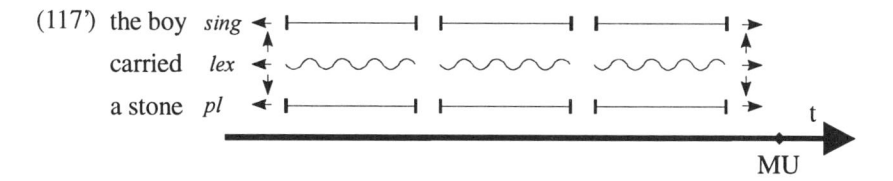

(117') the boy *sing*
carried *lex*
a stone *pl*

MU

As already partly observed earlier, outward (grammatical) singularity of the object may conceal physical and temporal plurality of its referent. Note, however, that while the temporal plurality of the referent of the object *a stone* is not immediately in view, but is still relatively accessible to the ordinary speaker, the temporal plurality (recurrence) of the referent of the subject *the boy* is generally inaccessible (or is much less accessible) to the ordinary speaker. Hence, as can be seen in the diagram,

---

[5] A contrastive analysis would show that in Bulgarian the two meanings are usually directly expressed – through the use of either a primary or a secondary imperfective verb in the Imperfect. Compare the two Bulgarian sentences below:
Momče-to   noseše$_{impfv1Imp}$ kamăk
Boy-the   carried   stone
'The boy carried a stone'
Momče-to   donasjaše$_{impfv2Imp}$ kamăk
Boy-the   carried   stone
'The boy brought a stone (repeatedly)/used to bring a stone'
In the former, a primary imperfective verb is used, a secondary imperfective one in the latter.

designations like *sing* and *pl* would have to be applied to the subject also, not only to the object, because the referent of the subject can also be singular or plural outside its outward grammatical characteristics. In the diagram above, the designations *sing* and *pl* cover the physical singularity or plurality of the participants, whereas their temporal parameters are represented by the straight or wavy lines. Clearly, the interplay between singularity or plurality in the physical sense and singularity or plurality in the temporal sense, taking place at different levels, may be extremely complicated. All the possibilities could not be handled here, of course, and they do not bear directly on the main aspectological issue.

MAPPING IN 'STATE' SENTENCES

Now there remains the problem of the possible diagrammatic representation of a "state proper" like the one in sentence (112a), repeated below. It ought to be similar to the representation of sentence (100a) in (114). The designation *lex* in the diagrams (114) above and (119) below, in contrast to the mapping of values that originate in grammatical structure as in (103) above, should be understood also as signifying that the time extension presupposed by the lexical meaning of the particular verb is to (broadly) determine the time extension of the participants. Thus while in a case like (100a) the referents of *the boy* and *a stone* are normally conceived of as taking part in a separate short stretch of time, in a sentence like (112a) what is referred to is a much larger period of time, a more substantial slice of the possible life-span of the individuals (the referents of the subject *John* and the object *Mary*) involved. Since it has already been taken for granted that all referents of subjects, verbs and objects should be viewed as temporal, and since NPs with articles and NPs represented by proper nouns tend to refer initially to bounded entities (not only in abstract quantitative terms but also in temporal terms), it will be natural for them to be originally represented through a bounded straight line. To support this thesis, sentence (112a) can most effectively be contrasted with a sentence like (112b), as already done above:

(112) a. John hated Mary
b. John kissed Mary

Sentence (112b) will, of course, receive a diagrammatic representation identical to the one for sentence (74) in (102) above. In it, see (118) below, the referents of the three sentence components coincide, John and Mary mapping their boundedness (presupposed by their 'quantified' status of proper names) onto the referent of the verb, non-marked grammatically for perfectivity, lexically marked for 'telicity':

(112) b. John kissed Mary

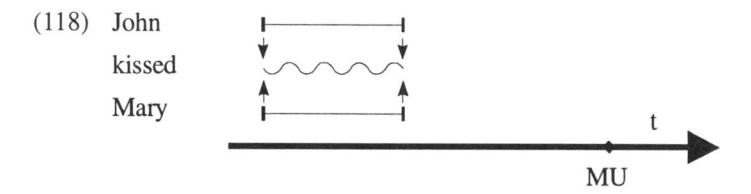

(118) John kissed Mary [diagram with timeline, MU]

Clearly, the contribution of an atelic verb to the explication of the aspect of a sentence in the face of boundedness implied by the referents of NPs has to be represented as higher than that of the verb in sentences like (74) or (112b). In other words, while in sentences like (74) or (112b) telic verbs (in the sense defined in this work) only assist in the explication of perfectivity, perfectivity being composed mainly through the mapping of boundedness from the referents of the subject- and object-NPs onto the referent of the verb, in sentences like (100a) and (112a) the composition of the aspectual meaning works in a different way. As already established for the activity reading (the usual one) of a sentence like (100a), the verb dominates the explication of its aspectual value: the lexical atelic aspectual potential of the verb is realised as non-boundedness which is then imposed onto the otherwise (initially taken to be) bounded referents of the NPs. Obviously, the same would happen in sentences like (112a) in which the verb mainly belongs to the group of 'state' verbs. Thus the most natural solution for both types of cases, (100a) and (112a), is for the verbs to be considered as marked in their lexical aspectual potential in a stronger way than telic verbs like *threw* or *kissed* are in sentences like (74) or (112b). The referent of the verb in a 'state' sentence like (112a) must, again, be said to map its non-boundedness onto the boundedness of the referents of the subject-NP and the object-NP:

(112) a. John hated Mary

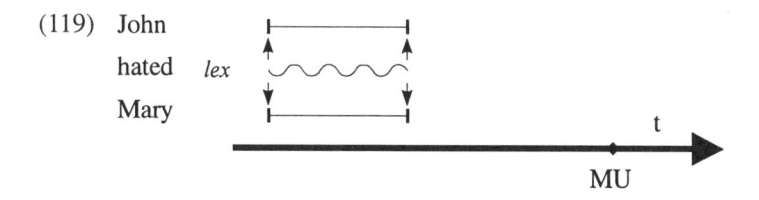

(119) John hated *lex* Mary [diagram with timeline, MU]

In the long run, however, the essential properties of the participants that have to do with aspect, their boundedness and non-boundedness, are mainly determined by the complex interplay between the grammatical features and the semantics of verbs and nouns and, in the present approach, boundedness and non-boundedness are abstracted over real-life extension of objects. It should be noted also that the semantics of language is reflected in an enormous number of various sentences with various structural (grammatical, including syntactic) and semantic characteristics that are furthermore normally embedded in contexts making an additional semantic impact. Hence, sentences like (100a) or (112a) must be regarded as only prototypical cases of the abstract mechanism of mapping non-boundedness from the (referent of the) verb onto (referents of) subjects and objects. In the real functioning of language for interpersonal communication, in actual discourse, the mechanism described and the structural entities taking part in it ('boundedness' and 'non-boundedness' of participants, types of configurations of participants, lexical features of verbs, etc.) are concealed under the pragmatic import of language and the functional meanings of traditional grammatical entities like verbs, tenses, subjects, objects, articles, etc.

In (112a) the boundedness, or, rather, the tendency to explicate boundedness, of the (referents of the) subject and object is suppressed, and their initial boundedness is replaced by the non-boundedness of the (referent of the) verb. Hence, the two rows of arrows in (119) are going from the verb in two opposite directions: towards the subject and towards the object. This mapping makes sense from a certain point of view which has to be formulated first before being accepted as a "common-sense" one: the stage of 'John' that hated 'Mary' is as indefinite and non-bounded in time as is John's hatred; and the stage of Mary that is hated by John is as indefinite and non-bounded in time as is John's hatred.

Thus, led by the pragmatic import of the meaning of sentences, the aspectologist might here be tempted to present the stages of the 'individuals' John and Mary as larger than the stage of hatred – which, intuitively, is an adequate solution from an "ordinary-life" point of view (one cannot hate all his/her life). Here is the diagrammatic representation of this solution:

(112) a. John hated Mary

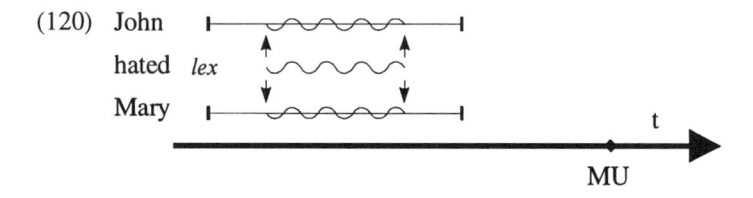

(120) John
      hated *lex*
      Mary
                                    MU → t

But, as already argued in the description of the 'television representation' in which the stage of the boy running away after throwing the stone is different from the stage of the boy throwing the stone, the stage of John that falls outside the hating stage is to be seen as another, totally different, stage of John that might, in common-sense terms, be indifferent to, or even love, Mary. (We know very well that love and hate sometimes replace one another.) Similarly, the stage of Mary that falls outside the hating stage of John is another stage of Mary that might be indifferent to or even loved by John. Furthermore, the diagram in (120) bears resemblance to another one which is given later on in the book, in Chapter Eight, *The Progressive in English*, for a sentence with a progressive verb form. There it will be argued that the representations for sentences of type (112a) and for sentences with the Progressive ought to be different, and an answer to the question why diagram (120) is not good as a description of the mapping mechanism for sentences like (112a) will be given.

The solution will also be shown to differ from the one in Carlson (1977/1980), who was the first to discuss extensively the distinction between individuals and stages. As already mentioned, Carlson would view *John* and *Mary* in sentences like (112a) as referring to the 'individuals' John and Mary, and in a sentence like (112b) Carlson would assign a 'stage' status to the participants. This approach is found in the prevailing number of studies on aspect and related matters in which states are understood as something entirely different from actions and involving totally different properties of sentences and characteristics of participants. In particular, states are viewed either as situations involving time spans that are "too long" to have anything to do with the expression of boundedness or perfectivity or as forming a class of their own that falls outside "true" aspectual distinctions (recall Smith's 1991 theory discussed earlier).

However, as previously noted, perfectivity and imperfectivity should by no means be associated with notions like 'shortness' or 'large extension'. This point has already been manifested by the Bulgarian sentence (9b) in which the special perfective counterpart *prebăda* 'be' of the otherwise normal imperfective verb *băda* 'be' is used.

(9) b. Čoveška-ta civilizacija šte prebăde$_{pfv}$ văv vekove-te
Human-the civilisation will be in centuries-the
'Human civilisation will be preserved for centuries'

Many English sentences can also be found denoting extended periods of time but explicating perfectivity, cf. (121a) and (121b):

(121) a. John lived a nice life
b. John outlived Mary

MORE ARGUMENTS IN FAVOUR OF THE TEMPORAL STATUS OF PARTICIPANTS

Again, allegedly, in (121b) the problem of the non-coincidence of time slices of participants arises, *Mary*, in a certain sense, constituting a shorter slice than *John*. But the stretch of Mary's possible life until John's death is also taken into account at the moment of comparing the two life-spans, and so the semantics of the verb presupposing (and requiring) different length of the participants simply remains outside the analysis carried out according to the stage-coincidence thesis. Note, moreover, that, first, an imperfective reading is not at all available for this sentence (unless it is a case of a very, very special iterative meaning), and that, second, (121b) does not necessarily mean that John is dead at the moment of assessment. Hence, sentence (121b) can be analysed in a way that is similar to the analysis of standard sentences in which the participants are viewed as entities that are equal in temporal terms. Both *John* and *Mary* fall within it as bounded and equal time stretches and bear an additional meaning to the effect that in pragmatic terms John's time stretch is longer than Mary's. The other pragmatic circumstance that holds for this sentence, viz. that one NP-referent (Mary) is not alive and the other NP-referent (John) is either still alive or not alive, is also an important part of the semantics but is not relevant to the overall aspectual meaning.

Recall that temporal extension of participants in the present framework does not cover real-life temporal constitution of entities as intuited by ordinary speakers. Thus, following the analysis made above of sentences like (74), both *John* and *a house* in (71b) will be bounded temporal entities that coincide with the time the action takes place. This reasoning evades the circumstance that *a house* immediately after the beginning of the action in (71b) is not a house at all but a couple of stones, bricks, planks, etc. arranged with the intention of building a house eventually.

(71) b. John built a house

Indeed, viewed from a certain standpoint, *a house* in (71b) is not a house during the whole time the action is carried out. It becomes a real house **after** the action in (71b) is completed: still, *a house* in (71b) is the object of the essence of the action denoted by the verb – cf. the analyses in Harlig (1983: 166-167); Hinrichs (1985: 265); Hoepelman (1981: 45-46).[6] The analyses of the temporal status of the participants in (121b) according to the present approach and according to common-sense reasoning yield rather different results. However, certain arguments can be put forward, showing that "common-sense reasoning" is not always what it seems to be.

Actually, it is not very clear why in so many publications a solution is favoured in which the semantics of a sentence like (71b) above is said to involve either the final point or the consequences of the event. Indeed, there are scholars (Parsons 1989: 225) arguing that if Mary was building a house but was struck down by lightning and the house remained only one fourth finished, it is correct to say that there is a house. Parsons (1989: 226-227) maintains this even for sentences with a futurate like *I'm making a cake* but from a different standpoint. According to the model proposed here, what sentences like these primarily refer to is not the consequences of the act, but the whole act, along with the accompanying circumstances. This certainly means that sentences like these do not mainly refer to the temporal stage of the house and the circle **after** the act is completed or exactly and only at the point where the objects come into existence. Furthermore, if the intuitions of the ordinary speaker about these two sentences are taken into account, certain results can be obtained that are rather different from some linguists' expectations. If it is assumed that in *John was building a house* or *Mary was drawing a circle* there is as yet no house and no

---

[6] Also according to an anonymous reviewer, many publications point out examples like *Mary drew/ was drawing a circle*, where no circle exists until the event is over (up until then it is just an arc). Hence, to quote the reviewer, "it doesn't make sense to talk about the circle-stage as beginning when the drawing begins. That is, we only start having circle-stages once the circle is complete."

circle, this ought to mean, e.g., that reactions like *How did John know he was building a house?* or *How did Mary know she was drawing a circle* would be fine. Consider also reactions like *How do you know you are building a house?* or *How do you know you are drawing a circle?* to statements like *I am building a house* and *I am drawing a circle*. Certainly, they are not fine. A speaker knows that he is building a house or drawing a circle, simply because the house or the circle, etc. are in his head. The same would be valid also for sentences with inanimate subjects and verbs of consumption/destruction (like *The storm was destroying the house*) – where the observer/speaker foresees the consequences. Thus the idea that the complements of verbs of creation simply do not refer to the whole of the objects (i.e., before their "real-world completion") should not be taken for granted. It is also worth noting that in developing this idea semanticists prefer to use verbs of creation at the expense of verbs of consumption – where the argumentation would apparently be much less felicitous.

The necessity for certain specific analytical tools to be used in aspectology, such as 'perceptual entities' (stages, in the terminology that has already become traditional), i.e., entities that can be either bounded or non-bounded, may be worth explaining further. In linguistic studies it is usually taken for granted that the referents of, for example, *John* and *the door* in *John opened the door* are physical objects that, even though they undergo some change, are stable and enduring through time. Indeed, when sentences like *John built the house* or *The boy ate the apple* are discussed, although *the house* and *the apple* are taken to be different in the different phases of the actions associated with them (while the house is being made and the apple is being eaten), it is again assumed that they are entities that are physical and atemporal. That is, they are persistently regarded as entities existing outside time and outside the action they take part in. It could be argued that if an observer/speaker standing on the pavement produces a sentence like *A child crossed the street*, the entity 'child' would be a moving entity and the entity 'street' would be a stable entity. From a certain point of view it can also be argued that for an observer/speaker walking along a street and producing a sentence like *I walked along the street* the entity 'street' would be a moving entity – rather than the entity 'I', which could be seen as stationary from the point of view of the observer/speaker. But in spite of the large diversity of such considerations, it can also be taken for granted that all referents of subjects and objects taking part in a particular situation (be it a state, a process or an achievement, etc.) are entities necessarily moving in time. And, by moving in time, they feature certain temporal parameters, among which boundedness and non-boundedness appear to be the most important ones (at least from the aspectological point of view). It is worth recalling here the popular thesis in studies on children psychology and on early language acquisition, according to which what a newly born child perceives of a mother is a passing wave. It is only later that the child develops the concept of a mother as a physical object, stable and identical in all its occurrences. Of course, many questions remain open as to the manner in which language, through its structure and general semantics, reacted to the need to process those waves (stages, time slices) of individuals and physical objects (if it did). But the idea that with the development of concepts the perception of people and other physical things as time slices is hampered (for memory not to be overburdened) is hardly questionable.

THE MECHANISM OF MAPPING TEMPORAL VALUES IN THE SENTENCE: A SUMMARY

The representations for sentences of type (100a), (112a) are similar in that there is a mapping of a value from the (referent of the) verb onto the (referents of) subjects and objects. Mapping of non-boundedness from the (referent of the) verb onto the (referents of) subjects and objects also takes place when the Progressive is used (to be considered in Chapter Eight, *The Progressive in English*), as in a sentence like (27b).

(100) a. The boy carried a stone
(112) a. John hated Mary
(27) b. John was reading the newspaper

But these three types of mapping of non-boundedness constitute the only mapping of a value in the direction from the verb towards the (referents of) subjects and objects. In contrast to Slavic languages (see Chapter Seven, *The interdependence between markers of boundedness in verbs and in nouns*), boundedness in English cannot generally be mapped in this way. According to the major thesis in this book, in English, supported by the lexical semantics of the verb, boundedness originates in the referents of NPs that are arguments of the verb (syntactic subjects, objects), in certain basic semantico-syntactic configurations.[7]

In the present study states are treated on a par with activities and other possible non-bounded situations, and participants in all kinds of situations are regarded as bounded or non-bounded time stretches however long or short the length of these stretches may be from a real-life point of view. Thus, to sum up, as has become clear from the parallel made in the preceding chapter between the English sentence (74) and the common-sense interpretation of its meaning, certain language regularities exist that have to do with the temporal constitution of the action and the participants in it. These regularities are not language-specific but have a universal nature. To illustrate their cross-language validity, they can be found, for example, in (94), the Bulgarian equivalent of (74), in which the temporal constitution of the participants in the action can also be said to coincide with the temporal constitution of the action itself:

---

[7] It could be argued, however, that in certain peripheral types of phrases the telic potential of the verb is so strong that boundedness is imposed in the sentence mainly through the telicity of the verb. This point is discussed below, in Chapter Ten, *Meanings of nouns and noun phrases, and aspect in English*.

(74) The boy threw a stone
(94) Momče-to hvărli$_{pfvAor}$ kamăk
Boy-the threw stone
'The boy threw a stone'

(cf. Kabakčiev 1984a; 1984b). The difference, which is a difference in language typology, is that while in Bulgarian the temporal constitution of the action is explicitly given and is transferred onto the participants, in English the temporal constitution of the action is composed, partly, out of the temporal status of the nominal components in the sentence and, generally, through a complex interplay between the referents of the verb component and the nominal ones. Of course, the transfer (mapping) of temporal values within the sentence is inaccessible to the ordinary speaker of a particular language.

As mentioned at the very beginning of this book, even without a special analysis like the one undertaken here, it could be supposed that in a language like English there ought to be certain devices available for the expression of a distinction between perfectivity and imperfectivity similar to the one found in Slavic verbs. A thesis of this kind can be said to be based on the trivial piece of reasoning that, if in languages like the Slavic ones there exist numerous sentences that denote typical perfective or imperfective situations belonging to the reality experienced by human beings, these situations ought to find some kind of adequate expression in other languages as well, including English, and presumably in all natural languages. After the parallel drawn between the compositional mechanism for explicating aspect distinctions in English at the level of the sentence and a hypothetical psycho-physiological mechanism of perceiving actions and their participants, the following generalisation can be made. The opposition between perfectivity and imperfectivity should not be seen as a specific or exotic feature of Slavic languages. The perfective/imperfective opposition is not only present in English but will, most probably, be found in all other languages in different types of structural disguise. The following chapter gives the outlines of a theory explaining the regularities behind the direct denotation (expression) of aspect or its explication (in compositional terms) in different languages. This theory may, at first sight, seem to go beyond the peculiarities of the grammar and semantics of the English language that are the primary object of investigation in this work. But, in fact, it will be shown to be closely related to them. What is more, ignoring the major import of the theory – it will be argued – could seriously hamper the proper understanding of aspect in English and in similar languages.

CHAPTER 7

THE INTERDEPENDENCE BETWEEN MARKERS OF BOUNDEDNESS IN VERBS AND IN NOUNS

MARKERS OF BOUNDEDNESS FROM A CROSS-LANGUAGE POINT OF VIEW

The analysis of the data in the preceding chapters showed that English features systemic devices to mark the perfective/imperfective contrast, which in languages like the Slavic ones is located in verbs and is represented morphologically, though not in a straightforward manner typical of the realisation of some other grammatical categories. These devices can be described within the structure of the sentence, most revealingly within the SVO semantico-syntactic pattern. Only implicit in Verkuyl's (1972) theory (and absent in his 1993 extended theory) is the requirement that for a certain sentence to be regarded as perfective its subject and its object should be exponents of temporal boundedness – besides the necessity for the verb to possess the lexical aspectual potential of 'telicity'. Generally speaking, again according to Verkuyl's theory, for imperfectivity to be explicated in the SVO type of sentence, either the subject or the object (or both) should be associated with non-boundedness or the verb as a lexical entry should lack the 'telicity' feature.

It was established that a sentence like (74) in English explicates perfectivity as a primary aspectual reading, and that in this reading it is semantically equivalent to the Bulgarian sentence (94):

(74) (English)
The boy threw a stone

(94) (Bulgarian)
Momče-to hvărli$_{pfvAor}$ kamăk
Boy-the threw stone
'The boy threw a stone'

It was, on the one hand, also found that:
a) the participants in the actions described in sentences (74) and (94) should be regarded as temporally bounded entities, as temporal slices of some larger temporal

entities 'the boy' and 'a stone' – of which these sentences hardly inform the hearer anything more besides the fact that they took part in an action;

b) temporal boundedness of the action, although covert for the ordinary speaker, is, hence, marked in a grammatical fashion, through the article, and is not a semantic component occurring through some accidental interplay of sentence components.

On the other hand, the verb component in the semantico-syntactic pattern examined is not formally marked for boundedness. Therefore, for the action, denoted primarily by the verb, to be conceived of as temporally bounded, a mechanism should be present within the language system capable of transferring the temporal boundedness of the participants onto the referent of the verb. Diagrammatically, the temporal configurations of the participants were presented in the following fashion:

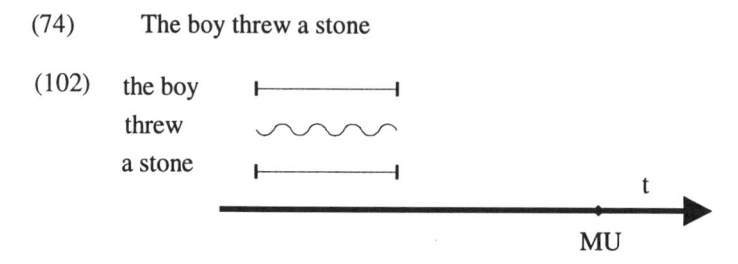

(74)   The boy threw a stone

(102)   the boy   ├──────────┤
        threw   ∿∿∿∿∿
        a stone   ├──────────┤
                                              t
        ──────────────────────────────▶
                            MU

This diagram may be said to outline the way perfectivity is explicated not only in English but also in many other languages like English. In comparison with Verkuyl's (1972) model it offers a much better account of the mechanism of explicating perfectivity. Even if we take it that in Verkuyl (1972) a certain temporality is assumed for the referents of subjects and objects (cf. again the definition of 'specified' as "giving the bound of the temporal interval in question" in Verkuyl 1972: 59), the entities signified by the two NPs remain linearly located on the time axis (one after the other) in Verkuyl's account – or, at least, no suggestion is given that they could be regarded as temporally parallel to each other, as in the diagram above. That is, there is no indication that they could be regarded as coming into and ceasing their existence simultaneously – referents of (syntactic) subjects, verbs and objects in Verkuyl's theory are not given a diagrammatic representation and no explanation is offered as to whether there is some correspondence between the temporal configuration (including the boundedness) of the referents of the subject and the object, on the one hand, and the referent of the verb component, on the other. (Some indications of the possibility for such relationships to exist are mentioned in Verkuyl's extended theory, which is critically analysed in this book, mainly in Chapter Ten, *Meanings of nouns and noun phrases, and aspect in English*.) Therefore, diagram (102) above, complemented with an explanation of the temporal status of the participants in the action in sentences like (74) from a "common-sense" point of view and taking into account a (possible) psycho-physiological mechanism for perceiving and storing information about situations, enables the formulation of a much more precise definition of the contribution of the article in English (and similar languages) for the explication of perfectivity.

But, on the one hand, articles are not present in all languages. And, on the other hand, it may sound astonishing, and for grammarians with a more traditional background even shocking, if it is argued that in English and in similar languages the explication of aspect distinctions could, in the long run, be effected through the article – that is, through a language element which to the ordinary speaker of a language has absolutely nothing to do with the conception of the time extension of objects, let alone with the conception of the time extension of actions. Compare now, however, the way aspect is explicated in sentences of the type already discussed in English with the way aspect ought to be expressed in a language in which articles are absent.

Let this language be Russian. The translation equivalent in Russian of sentence (74) is sentence (122a) below, in which the perfective verb $brosil_{pfv}$ 'threw' denotes a perfective action, in contrast to $brosal_{impfv}$ 'threw' which denotes an imperfective action (122b).

(English)
(74)   The boy threw a stone

(Russian)
(122) a. Mal'čik $brosil_{pfv}$ kamen'
         Boy   threw   stone
         'The boy threw a stone'
      b. Mal'čik $brosal_{impfv}$ kamen'
         Boy   threw   stone
         'The boy threw repeatedly/was throwing a stone'

After making the cross-language comparison between sentences like (74) and (122a), what could be the conclusion to reach about the way perfectivity is expressed in Russian? Diagrammatically, in contrast to the explication of perfectivity in English, it ought to be represented in the following fashion:

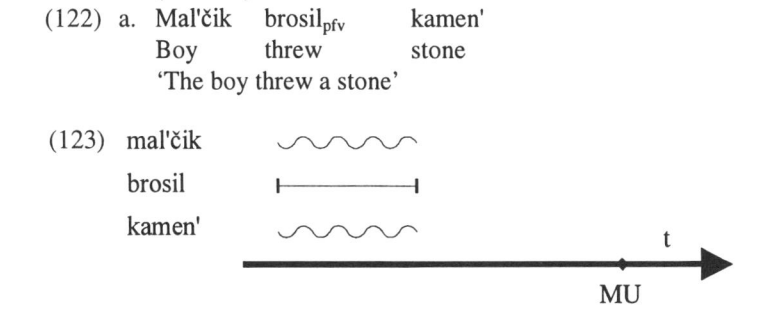

(Russian)
(122) a. Mal'čik $brosil_{pfv}$ kamen'
         Boy   threw   stone
         'The boy threw a stone'

(123) mal'čik
       brosil
       kamen'
                                           t
                                    MU

This diagrammatic representation reflects the fact that, in contrast to English, where perfectivity is the result of a complex systematic interplay between different semantic and structural elements in the sentence, in Russian a perfective action is directly expressed by the verb: it is formally (grammatically) marked through the perfective aspect. Note that since in Russian there are no articles, the subject and the object NPs in the sentence, represented by the nouns *mal'čik* 'boy' and *kamen'* 'stone', do not directly signify definiteness and indefiniteness, although the subject in this sentence is normally taken to be definite and the object indefinite. But the mechanism for the explication of the meanings of definiteness and indefiniteness in a language without articles will not be dealt with here. What is at issue, instead, is the other, extremely important, function of the article, namely, its ability to explicate temporal boundedness of NPs. It is only natural that a function of this kind should be revealed not only in an analysis of a language with articles but also through a comparison between languages with and without articles.

Given that perfectivity of the action in the Russian sentence (122a) is directly denoted by the verb (it is marked grammatically), and the subject and the object are not marked for boundedness in general quantitative terms or for temporal boundedness through an article (hence the wavy line in front of these sentence components), it can be assumed that there exists a cross-language regularity that can be formulated in the following way:

> Languages display an inverse relationship between markers of boundedness in verbs and nouns. When a certain language lacks markers of boundedness in the verbs, they are present in nouns; and vice versa, when a language lacks markers of boundedness in nouns, they are present in verbs.

The findings supporting the existence of this universal regularity were reported a long time ago in a number of articles (English publications include Kabakčiev 1984a; 1984b). So far, for almost two decades, the findings have neither been challenged as incorrect (on any language data), nor has the model of analysis employed been found to be (at least partially) defective. A fact of this kind justifies a conclusion that the theory of the interrelationship between markers of boundedness in verbs and in nouns ought to be considered valid.

The model outlined above can be used as a heuristic procedure for the description of languages the structure of which has not been fully analysed. It allows making predictions with a high degree of certainty that, for example, verbs in a given language will be likely to have a grammatical distinction between perfectivity and imperfectivity or that nouns in another language will be likely to have articles or similar markers of boundedness in the nominal system. It is to be noted that, on the one hand, the explication of perfectivity and imperfectivity in the different languages around the world can be realised in different ways and through various types of categories in verbs (cf. two extensive studies of the varieties of tense-aspect systems across languages – Dahl 1985; Bybee et al 1994). On the other hand, the explication of temporal boundedness in (referents of) nouns and NPs is also different in the different languages. It is not always effected through articles. For instance, in Finnish, a language without articles and verbal aspect, some of the sixteen cases of the noun (namely, the nominative and the accusative vs. the partitive) are specialised in the explication of boundedness and non-boundedness in a fashion very similar to the article/zero article contrast in English. This grammatical feature of Finnish was described a long time ago and is standard in the description of Finnish in most linguistic studies, grammars and textbooks. But boundedness explicated by nouns/ NPs through a case marker has always been interpreted in general quantitative terms, not in terms of the temporal features of referents of nominal sentence components, as proposed here and in the preceding two chapters of this book. Taking into account the fact that the explication of aspect is interpreted through markers of quantity in the case system in Finnish, it is really surprising why English grammars should concentrate their description of aspect solely on the distinction between progressive and non-progressive forms (or even, incorrectly, on the distinction between perfect and non-perfect verb forms). Whatever the reason for this, English grammars fail to interpret the explication of aspect adequately (but see Kabakčiev 1998), because, as already shown, this explication is effected not solely through the verbal system but through a complex interplay of various components within the sentence in which the system of nominal determination and the article in particular play a major role.

CHAPTER 7

COMPOSITIONAL ASPECT AS A MIRROR IMAGE OF VERBAL ASPECT – OR VICE VERSA

To sum up the cross-language regularities discussed above, now compare the two diagrams representing the way aspect is expressed in languages of the type of English and languages of the type of Russian:

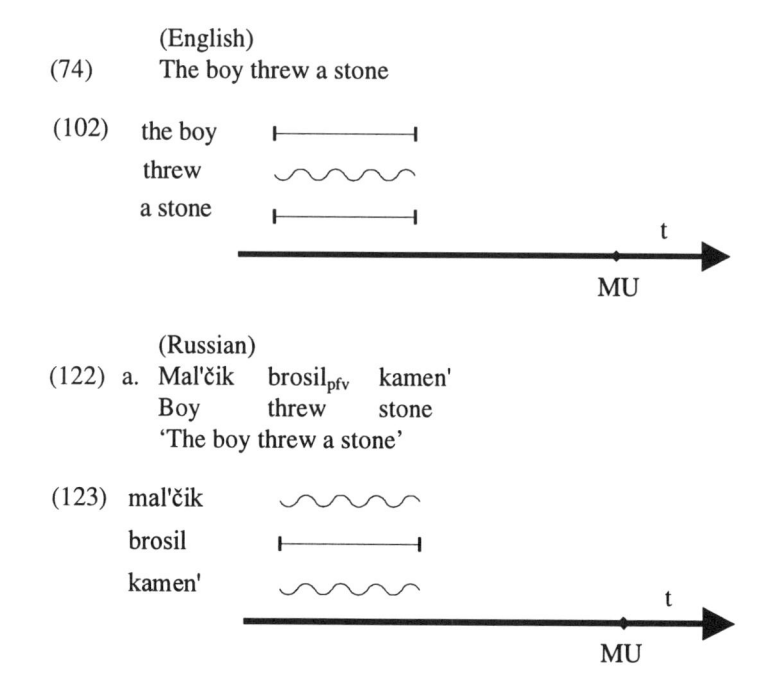

(English)
(74)   The boy threw a stone

(102)   the boy
        threw
        a stone
                                            t
                                    MU

(Russian)
(122) a.   Mal'čik   brosil$_{pfv}$ kamen'
           Boy   threw   stone
           'The boy threw a stone'

(123)   mal'čik
        brosil
        kamen'
                                            t
                                    MU

The two diagrams show the reverse proportion of the distribution of markers of boundedness in verbs and nouns in the two languages without taking into account the mapping mechanism, described in the previous chapter for English. Recall that the verb and the noun are two of the most fundamental language universals, nouns and verbs being available in any language. Hence the validity of the interdependence assumes an even larger theoretical importance.

Of course, English and Russian are just two extremes of the distinction between languages that express aspect through the verb system and those that explicate it mainly through the nominal system. It can be hypothesised that there can be no language without markers of boundedness in both verbs and in nouns – or at least a language of this kind ought to have **some** kind of system to mark the perfective/imperfective contrast. The first possibility that springs to mind is for a language to have adverbials explicating (or, rather, expressing) the contrast – but these adverbials would eventually have to be classified as verbal markers anyway. Obviously, apart from English, the rest of the Germanic languages will fall into the group of languages explicating aspect through the nominal system and most Slavic languages will fall into the group of languages expressing aspect directly through the verbal system.

There are many other languages, however, that should be viewed as borderline cases – featuring markers of boundedness in both verbs and nouns. Bulgarian is one of these languages – with the presence of a perfective/imperfective opposition in verbs and a definite article in the nominal system. Bulgarian lacks an indefinite article or, rather, a regular pattern of an indefinite article – of the kind observed in Western European languages. This lack of an indefinite article in Bulgarian can be accounted for by the presence of the perfective aspect in verbs which renders the regular pattern of a definite and an indefinite article redundant: boundedness in Bulgarian is directly marked by verbs and is mapped onto the subject NP and/or the object NP in the sentence (as is shown below for Russian). But there is still another grammatical phenomenon in Bulgarian which makes it a language of the borderline group, i.e. occupying a place in the region between the two extremes (in this description Russian and English). It is the past tense Aorist/Imperfect distinction which in a way, broadly speaking, repeats the aspect distinction between perfectivity and imperfectivity in verbs as lexical entries. These peculiarities of Bulgarian need not be considered here; they have already been dealt with in a publication showing that there exists a certain link between the presence in Bulgarian of both a definite article and an Aorist/Imperfect distinction (Kabakčiev 1984b). Among Western European languages, the Romance languages could also be said to belong to languages of the internal borderline group – with the presence in them of a regular pattern of articles and a past tense distinction between terminated and non-terminated situations similar to the Aorist/Imperfect distinction in Bulgarian.

As far as the problem of explicating temporal boundedness in referents of subjects and objects in sentences of the major type is concerned, it could be interpreted in cross-language terms in the following way. In Chapter Five, *Extension in time of subjects and objects from a "common-sense" point of view*, it was established that the so-called television representation of the participants in an action described through the sentence (74) is valid for English, as well as for the corresponding sentence (94) in Bulgarian (see the two sentences below). There are also reasons to assume that it is valid for all languages.

(74)　　The boy threw a stone
(94)　　Momče-to　　hvărli$_{pfvAor}$　　kamăk
　　　　 Boy-the　　　 threw　　　　　　 stone
　　　　 'The boy threw a stone'

The event described in sentences like (74) or (94) above is a common one, and as such will probably be "seen" in the same way by all people, whatever the language they speak. The meanings of sentences describing the event in other languages, as well as the semantic and pragmatic import of these sentences ought to be identical too, and the same ought to be valid for many other types of situations. Generally speaking, people observe and perceive in an identical manner various events, processes, states, etc. happening in reality. The structural devices for their expression may be different in the different languages, but for the denotation of a given type of situation a particular language would employ a concrete set of relevant grammatical, semantic and semantico-syntactic devices. It is the linguist's task to reveal which devices in a particular language serve for the encoding of a given type of situation.

Therefore, if we go back to sentence (122a) in Russian, we will have to assume that the participants in this action are temporally bounded just like the participants in (74) and (94) are. But what is especially important from a linguistic point of view is that their temporal boundedness is not marked in the way it is marked in English: it is derived from the verb. The verb in (122a) may be said to map its temporal boundedness, grammatically marked, onto the NPs, thereby making them temporally bounded. The NPs thus become equivalent in their temporal constitution to the temporal constitution of the action which is expressed directly, unlike in a language like English, by the verb. Compared to English, diagrammatically the difference can be represented in the following way:

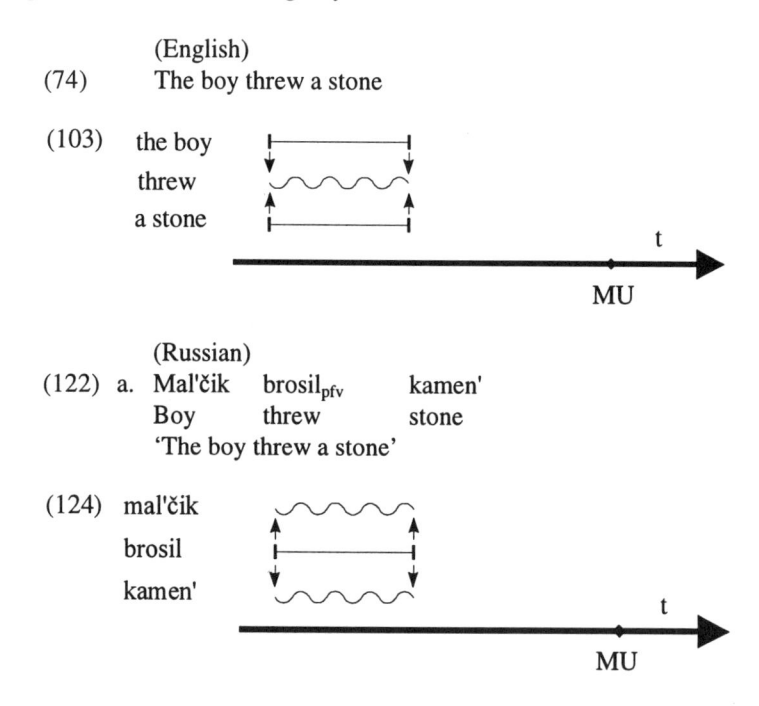

(English)
(74)   The boy threw a stone

(103)   the boy
         threw
         a stone

(Russian)
(122) a. Mal'čik   brosil$_{pfv}$ kamen'
         Boy   threw   stone
         'The boy threw a stone'

(124)   mal'čik
         brosil
         kamen'

The direction of the arrows in the two diagrams shows the direction of the mapping mechanism: in English, from the (referents of the) subject-NP and the object-NP to the (referent of the) verb; in Russian, vice versa, from the (referent of the) verb to the (referents of the) subject-NP and the object-NP. This mapping mechanism in its two variants can hence be held to be valid for many other languages, and even for all natural languages.

But note, again, the difference between the two sets of diagrams. In diagrams (102) and (123) the reverse proportion of the distribution of markers of boundedness in verbs and nouns in the two languages is represented without taking into account the mapping mechanism. These diagrams clearly show that explication of aspect in English and in similar languages in which aspect is composed at the level of the sentence is a mirror image of the expression of aspect in Russian and in similar languages in which aspect is directly expressed in the verb. Or vice versa: the expression of aspect in Russian and in similar languages in which aspect is directly expressed in the verb is a mirror image of the explication of aspect in English (and in similar languages) at the level of the sentence. Diagrams (103) and (124) display the mapping mechanism, the direction of which is opposite in the two languages: temporal boundedness is transferred from the (referents of the) subject-NP and the object-NP onto the (referent of the) verb in English, while in Russian temporal boundedness is transferred from the (referent of the) verb onto the (referents of the) subject-NP and the object-NP.

Concluding, it seems fully justified to argue that the proper understanding of the overall aspect mechanism in English and in similar languages cannot be properly understood without taking into account the typological data, the cross-language correspondences and the internal-language regularities described in this chapter.

CHAPTER 8

THE PROGRESSIVE IN ENGLISH

ON THE NATURE OF THE PROGRESSIVE

Although the distinction between perfectivity and imperfectivity in English is not, on the whole, expressed through forms of verbs, this language does feature verbal aspect as a grammatical category. It is represented by the periphrastically encoded aspectual forms '*be + ing*', as distinct from all other forms of the verb which are neutral with respect to aspect.

The aspectual nature of the English Progressive is generally taken for granted today, but not among the whole community of linguists. It is worth recalling that its basic meaning was conceived of in terms of the completion/non-completion contrast or similar distinctions long before the development of modern aspectology. Jespersen (1924: 286-289) saw the Progressive (the expanded forms, in his terminology) as exercising the function of denoting 'unfinished' actions. Hornby (1949: 172) noted that "the essence of the Progressive Tenses is the element of *incompletion*". Although his notion of completion was a little different from today's, some of the observations Hornby made at that time are in line with most modern aspectological approaches:

> "It is obvious that *see* and *hear*, when they refer to single acts or efforts of perception, do not contain the element of incompletion. They are not, therefore, used in the Progressive Tenses"

(Hornby (1949: 173). By *a single act* (of perception), undoubtedly, a perfective action (an achievement or an accomplishment in Vendler's terms) is meant.

But although the aspectual essence of the Progressive was intuited, at least by some authors, a long time ago, English grammars today generally fail to describe the meaning of the Progressive properly. This is true, for instance, of the most comprehensive grammar of Modern English available today (Quirk et al 1985). According to its authors, the Progressive is as much an aspect as the Perfect is, and its meaning can be divided into three components, not necessarily present in all examples with the Progressive:

a) the happening has DURATION
b) the happening has LIMITED duration
c) the happening is NOT NECESSARILY COMPLETE

(Quirk et al 1985: 198). According to Scheffer (1975: 21), it is precisely the meaning of duration that is found most often in analyses of aspect and the Progressive in particular. But it is natural to suppose that what is referred to above as 'limited duration' should be understood not as 'boundedness' in the sense assumed in this work but as something like "duration of a short and unspecified time" – see Scheffer's (1975: 60) discussion about the vacuousness of terms like 'limited duration' or 'restricted duration'. In any case, the description of the semantics of the Progressive given above is in need of criticism in the light of the approach to be developed in this chapter.

It can be argued that the Progressive does not usually describe an action as continuous. It generally denotes an action being performed at a particular moment or stretch of time, and this action is non-bounded, imperfective. Precisely for this reason, progressives should not be defined as expressing duration/continuity: in most cases, if it is present at all, the meaning of duration is not directly expressed. It is only implicit, inferred. For example, if duration was part of the meaning conveyed by the Progressive, it would easily combine with adverbials of duration. Consider, however, sentences like (125a) or (125c) below, which are either only partly acceptable or imply a scope of the action shorter than the time interval denoted by the *for*-time adverbial, in contrast to sentences like (125b) or (125d), in which duration of the action can be said to be explicit in the sentence or phrase without the *for*-time adverbial.

(125) a. ?John was singing for five minutes
b. John sang for five minutes
c. ?John was painting this wall for five hours
d. John painted this wall for five hours

Of course, there are other cases, like (126a), (126b) below, in which adverbials implying extended periods are not incompatible with the Progressive. Still, even in (126a) and (126b) a moment of performing the action is usually focused on within the period designated, and this moment of performing the action serves as a background to the signification of another, perfective action, as in (126c) and (126d):

(126) a. John was singing that morning
b. John was painting this wall that afternoon
c. John was singing that morning when the thunderstorm started
d. John was painting this wall that afternoon when the earthquake destroyed it

The Progressive is very often used to denote an imperfective action which serves as a background for another action which is perfective. This may be defined as the prototypical use of the Progressive. The contrast between an action designated by a Past Progressive form and an action designated by a Simple Past form is the most exemplary one and there is a consensus in aspectology that in studying the meaning of the Progressive it is to be analysed against the meaning of the Simple Past Tense. (This point is discussed further below.) Consider sentence (127), illustrating the prototypical use of the Progressive:

(127)   John was singing when I entered the house

Does this sentence mean that John's singing had a duration, i.e., that John sang/was singing "continuously"? The answer tends to be negative. It may be inferred from this sentence that John did not sing for a long time. In any case, it could hardly be argued that the observer/speaker could possibly know whether John sang for a long time or not. For the statement in (127) to be truthful, it is sufficient for the speaker to have heard John singing for a second or for some seconds (not for minutes or for hours) while entering the house – normally, entering a house takes seconds, not minutes or hours. So, how could the hearer possibly infer from a sentence like (127) that John's singing had duration, that it lasted, for example, a minute or ten minutes or an hour?

Now consider the third point in the description of Quirk et al (1985: 198). A definition to the effect that a happening signified by a progressive is not necessarily complete allows the happening to be complete sometimes. But a description of the basic meaning of the Progressive, it will be argued below, ought to include an opposite statement, to the effect that the happening is necessarily **not** complete.

According to a different, rather more convincing definition (Binnick 1991: 287), the Progressive asserts a moment but implies an extended interval. This is an explanation which is closer to the intuitions of the native speaker. Of course, it is another question whether explanations of grammatical categories that are close to the intuitions of ordinary speakers always manage to capture the essence of the categories explained. But, on the other hand, there certainly is a case in which the Progressive could be said to assert, not just imply, continuity: this is the combination of the Progressive with the Perfect in the tense paradigm (e.g. the Present Perfect Progressive and the Past Perfect Progressive forms – *have/has been writing*, *had been writing*, etc.) and in the infinitive (*to have been writing*). However, firstly, the continuity expressed here might be said to arise out of the meaning of the Perfect rather than the Progressive itself, or at least out of the combination between the two grammemes. The Perfect may be said to coerce the action into taking place between the two points inherent in the meaning of the Perfect – the event point and the reference point (according to Reichenbach's well-known description of the meaning of the Perfect – Reichenbach's 1947). It should be borne in mind that similar metamorphoses in the use of aspect verb forms are a widespread phenomenon. In Bulgarian, for instance, perfective verbs forms can be used in the denotation of imperfective (indefinitely repetitive) actions, as in the perfective Imperfect, already discussed, and, vice versa, imperfective verbs forms can be used in the denotation of perfective actions, as in the case of a sentence like (97), used earlier:

(97) Šte pija_impfv čaša bira i šte izljaza_pfv
      Will drink-I   glass beer and will leave-I
      'I'll drink a glass of beer and leave'

Furthermore, the Perfect in English as well as in many other languages remains a mystery, and a serious challenge to linguistics. In spite of the serious investigations to which it has been subjected (see, e.g., McCoard 1978, Fenn 1987; Psaltou-Joycey 1991; Bybee et al 1994, to name but some of the outstanding ones), neither its meaning, nor its functions, nor the reasons why it is present in some languages and absent in others have been sufficiently clarified. Secondly, even if continuity/duration is taken to be a possible meaning component of the Progressive itself, it could be considered to stand apart from what will below be claimed to be the fundamental functional meaning of the Progressive.

For a long time there was no consensus among linguists with respect to the general grammatical status of the Progressive. Many grammarians refused to accept the Progressive as an aspect form. However, especially after some extensive typological investigations of the distribution of tense and aspect grammemes across languages were carried out (cf. Dahl 1985, Bybee 1985: 125-126; Bybee et al 1994), the only correct assumption nowadays seems to be that the Progressive is a true aspect form, and just one of the specific verbal aspectual markers found in the languages of the world which serve to express imperfectivity. In this sense, it is entirely wrong to treat both the Progressive and the Perfect as aspects. However, the usual approach not only in grammars, see, e.g. Quirk et al (1985: 188-189), but also in many other publications nominally dealing with aspect is to treat both the Progressive and the Perfect as aspects: see, e.g., Binnick (1991), Hatav (1993), Mellor (1995: 60). Idiosyncratic aspectological approaches are not missing, too. Bartsch (1995: 36-38, 140-142) treats the Progressive in English along with German constructions of the type *im/am Laufen sein* '(literally) be in/on the running, be on the run' and *am Schreiben des Briefes sein* '(literally) be in the writing of the letter, be writing the letter' (which she calls analytic progressive) as imperfective. But Bartsch also calls the Perfect both 'the perfect' and 'the perfective' – which means that no distinction is made between the categories of 'perfect' and 'perfective' and that the major aspectual notion of perfectivity finds no adequate treatment in her approach. Furthermore, Bartsch insists that not only are the Perfect and the Progressive aspects, the Future is an aspect too:

> "PERFECTIVE [that is, perfect] is the third aspect, which can also be composed with all tenses and with the aspects IMPERFECTIVE, and WERDEN [the future auxiliary in German]"

(Bartsch 1995: 142).

Ideas of this kind not only add up to the conceptual and terminological confusion reigning in the sphere of temporal and aspectual semantics. The confusion has often been pointed out by aspectologists, see Danchev (1976); Dahl (1981: 80-81); Binnick (1991: 139, 147), and it creates a serious impediment to the proper understanding of tense and aspect phenomena. Treating the Perfect in aspectual terms is a very loose way of defining aspect, and findings of investigations of tense and aspect systems in cross-language terms do not at all support the idea of considering the Perfect an aspect form (see Comrie 1976; Dahl 1985; Bybee 1985; Bybee et al 1994). And, of course, on the other hand, analysing the Perfect as a tense, along with, e.g., past, present or future markers, causes serious problems with respect to the definition of tense itself. Therefore, the nature of the Perfect is often treated with utmost caution by linguists. Bybee (1985: 141), for example, while admitting that it is often associated with aspect, deals with it under the heading of tense, and Bybee et al (1994: 3) refuse to group it into either of the two semantic domains, stating that these domains are cognitively significant but not structurally.

The Progressive is characterised by certain features of its meaning and use which are covered in most grammars. Besides being capable of expressing (directly expressing, not just explicating or implying) an imperfective action at a particular moment or stretch of time which often serves as a background for another, usually perfective, action, as in sentence (127) below, the Progressive can be used to describe two actions that are parallel to each other in time, both imperfective (128):

(127) John was singing when I entered the house
(128) While John was singing, Mary was working in the garden

The Progressive can also signify an isolated action the exact timing of which is either contextually implied, as in (129a), or is expressly defined, e.g. by an adverbial, as in (129b):

(129) a. Mary was working in the garden
       b. Yesterday at five o'clock Mary was working in the garden

Note, again, the reference to a particular moment, not period, by the adverbial *at five o'clock* and the easily cancelable inference that Mary worked before or after that moment.

Since progressive forms express an action at a definite moment or stretch of time, there are certain restrictions in English with respect to the use of certain verbs. There are verbs designating states, for example, that could not in any way be represented as actions taking place at a definite point in time. Thus sentence (130a) is good but (130b) is ungrammatical:

(130) a. The box contained a letter
       b. *The box was containing a letter

This restriction in the use of the Progressive is valid for a large number of 'state' verbs, for example, *consist of, know, see, hear, have, possess, want*, etc., but it does not hold in those cases when a verb of this kind does not signify a state. Consider sentences (131a) and (132a) below, which are ungrammatical, with sentences (131b) and (132b), which are correct:

(131) a. *I was knowing him
 b. I was knowing him better and better
(132) a. *I was having a house
 b. I was having a meeting

The restrictions with respect to the use of certain verbs in the Progressive have been well described in the literature. There is a certain tendency for these restrictions to disappear gradually, leaving the number of verbs that are (potentially) incompatible with the Progressive even further reduced. Verbs that are supposed to be incompatible with the Progressive sometimes appear in it, for example *understand* in sentences like (133a) below, *want* (mainly in informal discourse), as in (133b), or even *have* as part of the modal substitute *have to*, as in (133c). Note that while sentences like (133b) and (133c) are, indeed, hardly acceptable in the standard English as spoken in England, they are fairly common in the language of many educated Scottish speakers of English.

(133) a. I am understanding his character more and more every day
 b. – Excuse me, do you offer accommodation?
  – You're wanting a room?
 c. I'm having to go now

The argument that the way these verbs enter such expressions is highly context-sensitive and that there is a certain change of meaning here does not seem to be very convincing and hardly explains the behaviour of some of the typical representatives of the class of verbs not used in the Progressive. If we take it that in cases like (133a) and (133b) above the verbs *understand* and *want* mean different things ('learn' and 'ask for', respectively), this would be tantamount to exploring the idea of the use of the Progressive being restricted only with respect to semantic properties, not verbs.

THE PROGRESSIVE AS A DEVICE TO ELIMINATE THE BOUNDEDNESS OF NP REFERENTS

The purpose of the present chapter is to explain the functions of the Progressive aspect in English from the point of view of the regularities already described earlier in this book. In a work dealing extensively with tense and aspect in a large number of languages, Binnick wrote:

> "The English progressive has proven intractable and its analysis controversial, as Allen (1966), Scheffer (1975), and the papers in Schopf (1974) attest. No one has ever specified in a complete and satisfactorily general way how it is used or how the progressive tenses differ in meaning from the corresponding simple tenses, though English speakers all agree that they do differ, often quite radically (*he eats lunch in the cafe*, *he is eating lunch in the cafe*), though sometimes in tantalisingly subtle ways (it looks like rain out, it's looking like rain out). No one has convincingly argued for any one basic meaning for it, but neither has anyone established that it lacks one."

(Binnick 1991: 281-282). However, the explanation of the English Progressive that will be developed here was, in fact, offered in an article published many years ago (Kabakčiev 1984b), albeit in a less detailed fashion. It is usually maintained, even by scholars who regard the Progressive mainly as an aspect (see, e.g., Scheffer 1975: 17-42; Bybee et al 1994: 138), that it displays **many** meanings, aspectual and non-aspectual. The possibility to reveal the essence of the Progressive through a 'basic meaning' is thus, directly or indirectly, denied. In Kabakčiev (1984b), an argument was put forward in favour of precisely a basic functional meaning of the Progressive. The analysis below builds on this argument.

To sum up what was discussed above, progressive forms in English are periphrastic and combine with tense grammemes. Semantically, the Progressive is usually regarded as either mainly imperfective (see Hornby 1949: Palmer 1965: 79; Scheffer 1975) or, cross-linguistically, as a type/subtype of imperfective, one restricted to the denotation of non-bounded actions performed at a particular point or interval of time only (see, e.g., Comrie 1976: 116; Bybee et al 1994: 84-85[1]). As far as the difference between progressive and non-progressive forms in English is concerned, linguists usually resort to the Past Simple/Past Progressive distinction to determine it. What is more, it is typical of certain aspectological trends, e.g. the logical one, to try to uncover the essence of the Progressive on the basis of just a handful of example – or even a single example in which forms of the same verb in the Simple Past and the Progressive Past are contrasted in otherwise identical sentences/parts of sentences. This approach is to be used here as well, as it is taken to be an adequate one.

Earlier, in Chapter Five, *Extension in time of subjects and objects from a "common-sense" point of view* and in Chapter Six, *The mechanism for mapping the temporal values of subjects and objects*, it was argued that in sentences like (74), repeated below, the referents of the subject-NP and the object-NP (*the boy* and *a stone*) map their own temporal boundedness onto the action denoted by the aspectually unmarked verb form *threw*:

(74)   The boy threw a stone

Conversely (as was shown in Chapter Seven, *The interdependence between markers of boundedness in verbs and in nouns*), when in a language like Russian the verb in the same type of sentence is marked for aspect, it maps its temporal characteristics (the boundedness) onto the referents of the subject-NP and the object NP in the sentence, as for (122a) shown in (124):

---

[1] According to some opinions (received in personal communication), language typologists are not always inclined to associate the Progressive with prototypical imperfectives (like, e.g. the Slavic phenomenon), and an anonymous reviewer of this work maintained that "Bybee et al (1994) explicitly reject the treatment of progressive as a subtype of imperfective". Compare, however, the following statement in Bybee et al (1994: 85): "the simple past may be used in combination with an imperfective gram (e.g. *was sleeping*)".

(122) a. Mal'čik brosil$_{pfv}$ kamen'
      Boy   threw   stone
      'The boy threw a stone'

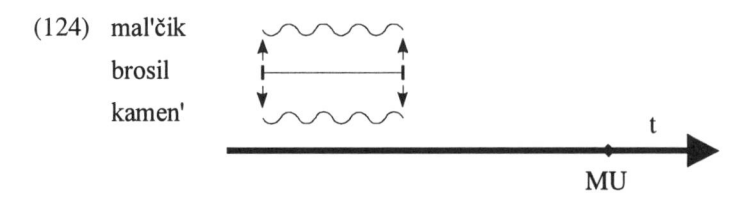

(124) mal'čik
     brosil
     kamen'

                            MU

Also, in Chapter Six, *The mechanism for mapping the temporal values of subjects and objects*, the following possibility for a diagrammatic representation of the activity reading of a sentence like (100a) was explored:

(100) a. The boy carried a stone

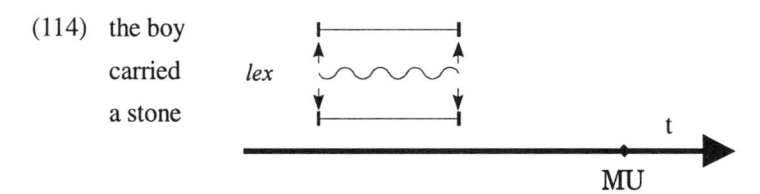

(114) the boy
     carried   *lex*
     a stone

                            MU

The lexical non-boundedness of *carried* may be said to be mapped onto the initial boundedness of the (referents of the) subject-NP and the object-NP, thereby cancelling it. The meaning explicated in (100a) is largely identical to that in sentences with a verb in the Progressive. Hence, the diagrammatic representation of the basic aspectual reading of (100a) ought to be given in a fashion similar to the one for the sentence with a progressive form of the verb, (109):

(109)   The boy was carrying a stone

Therefore, in comparing English sentences of type (74) and (134), given below, in which verb forms for the Simple Past and the Progressive Past Tense, respectively, are used, the following can be established. The temporal boundedness of the referents of the subject-NP and the object-NP in a sentence like (74) blocks the possibility for the action to be conceived of as imperfective/non-bounded and taking place at a particular point/stretch of time:

(74)   The boy threw a stone

It is necessary that this temporal boundedness of the (referents of the) NPs be eliminated. Elimination is carried out through the introduction of the Progressive:

(134)   The boy was throwing a stone

Or, in other words, the function of the English Progressive, similarly to the function of the perfective aspect in Russian, can be considered along the following lines. In structural terms, the Progressive is employed not only to mark the temporal non-boundedness of the action on the verb, but also to map it onto the referents of both the subject-NP and the object-NP in the sentence transforming them from bounded into non-bounded 'stages' of 'individuals' (in G.N.Carlson's terms). As already argued, in a sentence like (74) the subject-NP and the object-NP, marked for temporal boundedness in a covert way, transfer their temporal boundedness onto the verb. Consider again diagram (103):

(74)   The boy threw a stone

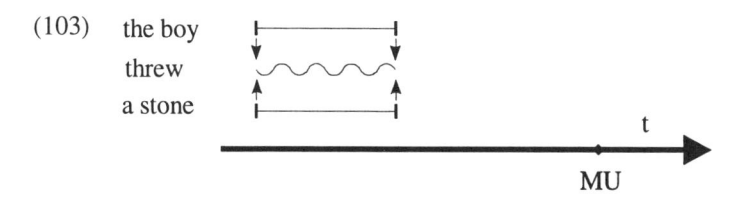

(103)   the boy
        threw
        a stone

In a sentence like (134), however, conversely, the verb, overtly marked for temporal non-boundedness, maps this temporal non-boundedness onto the subject-NP and the object-NP, which are marked for temporal boundedness in a covert fashion. Their initial boundedness is thus eliminated. Compare the diagrammatic representation (103) above of the mapping mechanism in a sentence like (74) with the diagrammatic representation (135) below of the function of the Progressive to eliminate the boundedness of the referents of the subject-NP and the object-NP in sentences like (134):

(134)   The boy was throwing a stone

(135)   the boy
        was throwing
        a stone

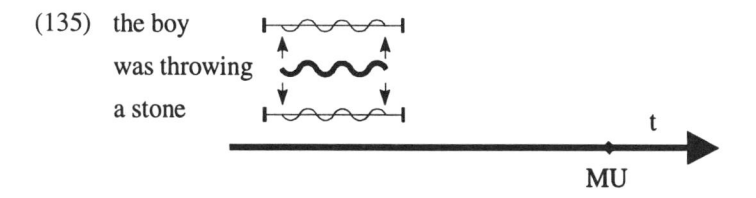

Compare also diagram (135) with diagram (124) for the Russian sentence (122) above illustrating the identical function (with an opposite value) of the Russian perfective to map its aspectual feature (boundedness) onto the referents of the subject- and object-NPs, unmarked for boundedness (due to the absence of articles in Russian).

Diagram (135) is to be read in conjunction with the thesis according to which *the boy* and *a stone* ought to be originally regarded as temporally bounded entities, as in (74), their boundedness being explicated through the article. Markedness is covert when it is not conceptualised by the native speaker. The thickened wavy line in (135) designates the markedness of the Progressive for the imperfectivity of the action – the verb is grammatically marked for non-boundedness which is then mapped onto the referents of the subject-NP and the object-NP. What is important is that the Past Progressive can be regarded as a partitive transformation in the temporal domain with respect to the Simple Past – or, rather, to its perfective interpretation. This thesis is prevalent in aspectological studies, and L.Carlson (1981: 44) was among the first who formulated it clearly. Following the idea that the referent of *was throwing* in (134) should be regarded as a partial and non-bounded stretch with respect to the referent of *threw* in (74), inevitably, the subject-NP and the object-NP *the boy* and *a stone* in (134) will have to be represented as partial temporal stretches with respect to *the boy* and *a stone* in (74) as well.

Thus, in more general terms, the explanatory procedure used in Chapter Five, *Extension in time of subjects and objects from a "common-sense" point of view* and Chapter Six, *The mechanism for mapping the temporal values of subjects and objects*, has again been used in support of a proposal to treat the grammatical expression of aspect as a consequence of the interplay between actions and their participants. However, according to a belief which is still widespread among linguists and even aspectologists, aspect is to be viewed as a category *per se* that has nothing to do with the participants in the action – in contrast to, e.g., the category of voice. This idea, entirely coinciding with the intuitions of the native speaker and most clearly worded in a famous article (Jakobson 1957), remained unchallenged for many decades. In Kabakčiev (1984b: 670) it was argued for the first time that, counter to this view, not only is verbal aspect **not** a category *per se*, precisely the opposite. The verbal grammatical category of aspect, as found in the Slavic languages, can be seen as a formal language device the basic function of which is to govern the temporal range of the participants in a given situation. The participants in a situation are most often propositionally represented as an agent and a receiver of an action, and syntactically encoded as the subject and the object in simple sentences. Naturally subsumed under this entirely novel proposal was the suggestion that the English Progressive should also be considered as a device for eliminating the boundedness of the participants in a bounded action denoted by a verb in the Simple Past Tense. Such an explanation of the Progressive, apart from being logically consistent within the framework of the theory described so far, is not an artificial invention aimed at justifying the theory by assigning it a diagrammatic facade. It will be given below also in "common-sense" terms, and will be seen as part of an entire cognitive organisation: a psycho-physiological mechanism to perceive, store and systematise information according to man's needs to model reality.

One of the problems remaining is, to use G.N.Carlson's entities again ('stages', 'objects'/'individuals' and 'kinds'), whether there is enough justification for stages of objects/individuals to be considered mentally represented as bounded and non-bounded. In grammatical terms, a historical detour could partly help clarify the point. On the one hand, the Progressive in English is supposed to have developed out of a prepositional locative construction with a (de)verbal noun (see, e.g., Andersson 1973: 20-21), where the preposition renders the meaning of the whole prepositional phrase and of the whole sentence non-bounded. And, on the other hand, as has already been observed (Heinämäki 1978: 6-9), certain prepositions can be associated with rendering the meaning of certain sentences perfective/bounded, while other prepositions can be associated with rendering the meaning imperfective/non-bounded. Compare Heinämäki's examples (136a) and (136b):

(136) a. The boy ran in/along the street
       b. The boy ran (out) to the street

But if verbal nouns, just like verbs in the traditionally so-called aspect languages, can be presented as bounded or as non-bounded depending on the context in which they are used (cf. the non-bounded meaning of the nouns in phrases like *in motion* and *in agreement with* with the bounded meaning of the same nouns in phrases like *with a motion, reach an agreement*), would not 'material' entities tend to resist this kind of further manipulation? In the semantico-syntactic configurations explicating perfectivity the role of subjects and objects in the examples given so far is generally played by nouns denoting material entities. The way in which the perfective/imperfective contrast can be explicated through the use of concrete and abstract nouns will be dealt with in Chapter Ten, *Meanings of nouns and noun phrases, and aspect in English*.

PARTICIPANTS IN SENTENCES WITH A PROGRESSIVE FROM A "COMMON-SENSE" POINT OF VIEW

But let us now try to give a more "common-sense" account of the temporal status of the participants in a sentence like (134), repeated below – along the lines of the account already given for sentences like *The boy threw a stone*.

Suppose that an observer/speaker X and a receiver/hearer Y are in a train which is moving very fast past a school yard. Suddenly X and Y see a boy outside the window of the compartment. X thinks the boy was throwing a stone at the train. To communicate his suspicion to Y, X uses sentence (134):

(134)   The boy was throwing a stone

What did X actually see from the window of the fast-running train? The observer could not see the action in its totality, so he could not be sure whether the boy threw the stone. He only saw the throwing movement of the boy's hand with the stone in it without knowing whether the boy eventually threw the stone: the boy might be threatening a dog nearby, or, perhaps, the stone just slipped through the boy's fingers and was not thrown at all. But a natural conjecture here is that the decision of the observer/speaker *X* to present the throwing movement of the boy's hand as (134) is based on his knowledge of the real world and, more specifically, on a presumption that the non-bounded situation described in (134) could alternatively be seen as an accomplished act (cf. Filip 1993: 147). Note that while this kind of action (of throwing a stone) **can** be accomplished in its entirety, there are other kinds of situations that cannot generally be transformed into accomplishments. For instance, the situation in (112a) can hardly at all be seen as an accomplishment, and it could be perfective (an achievement) primarily if the beginning is focused on – and, necessarily, through the strong support of context.

(112) a. John hated Mary

All this means that the observer/speaker has a preliminary mental picture of the action of throwing a stone as a completed one, as in (74), and that in the case of (134) he presents only one part of it, which is also a non-bounded part. Compare again (74) and (134):

(74) The boy threw a stone
(134) The boy was throwing a stone

And if the participants in an action constitute bounded entities when it is perceived or presented in language terms as completed, then naturally they will constitute non-bounded partial stretches of time when the action is presented as non-bounded and partial. Compare in this vein Langacker (1991: 79-80), who has convincingly argued in favour of a similar interpretation of a conception of an object falling to the ground in which there is a 'summary scanning', manipulable as a single gestalt, and involving a so-called build-up phase of the points in the trajectory.

A SINGLE BASIC MEANING FOR THE PROGRESSIVE OR NOT?

As already mentioned, there have been attempts at a definition of the Progressive involving a single meaning. Hornby's (1949: 172) element of 'incompletion' representing the essence of the Progressive has already been discussed. Carlson (1980: 109-110), while discussing the differences between his 'stages' and 'individuals' noted that the Progressive is typically associated with stages of individuals, not with individuals. Unfortunately, however, the possible formulation of a single basic meaning of the Progressive has been hindered by an enormous number of proposals to characterise the Progressive as featuring **a large multitude** of meanings. A good review of the possible meanings of the Progressive put forward in the literature can be found in Scheffer (1975). Of course, it is undoubtedly true that from a general semantic and pragmatic point of view the Progressive can be associated with many meanings, submeanings, nuances, stylistic effects, etc. But the result of the analysis carried out above shows that the real essence of the Progressive, its *raison d'etre*, can be seen as a single function – to cancel the boundedness of NPs functioning as subjects and objects in sentences of a particular major semantico-syntactic pattern.

THE PROGRESSIVE-LIKE INTERPRETATION OF THE SIMPLE PAST

Now recall again that in Chapter Six, *The mechanism for mapping the temporal values of subjects and objects*, sentence (100a) was discussed as a case in which a progressive-like meaning can be explicated – along with other aspectual meanings that this sentence is capable of conveying. Diagram (114) was proposed as a representation of the temporal status of participants in the action as part of the mapping mechanism between the (referent of the) verb and the (referents of the) subject-NP and the object-NP:

(100) a. The boy carried a stone

(114) the boy
carried   *lex*
a stone

                              MU

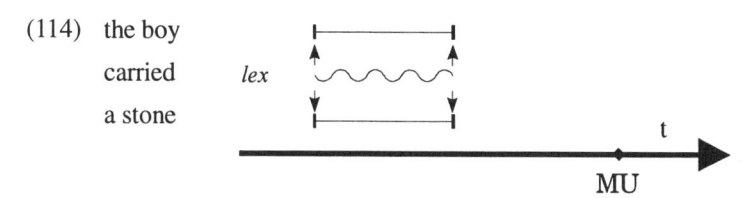

A representation of this kind now turns out to be incorrect in terms of the description of the basic functional meaning of the Progressive given above. In the progressive-like reading of sentence (100a), the non-boundedness of the verb, lexically marked, is mapped onto the presupposed initial boundedness of the participants, rendering them non-bounded. But if the Progressive can be viewed as a partitive operation in the temporal domain with respect to the Simple Past in its perfective interpretation, diagrammatically represented in (135) below, there is no reason now not to assume a similar mapping for (100a), i.e., the one given in (137):

(134)   The boy was throwing a stone

(135)   the boy
            was throwing
            a stone

                              MU

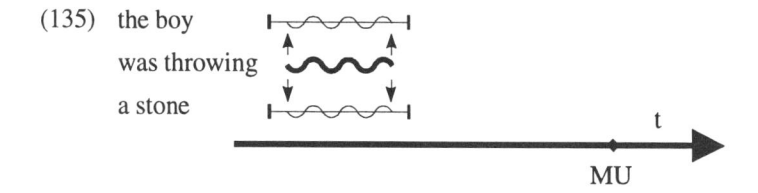

(100) a. The boy carried a stone

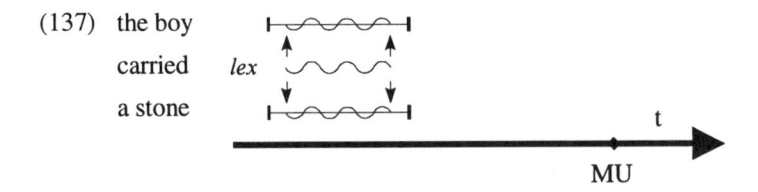

(137) the boy
carried   *lex*
a stone

MU

The difference between the type of mapping of non-boundedness in (135) and (137) is due to the difference in the expression of aspect. In the first case, (135), the mapping is achieved through the direct (grammatical) expression of non-boundedness of the action in the verb itself; the non-boundedness of the action is transferred onto the referents of the subject-NP and the object-NP eliminating their boundedness. In the second case, (137), the mapping of temporal non-boundedness is effected through the lexical meaning of the verb which overrides the tendency of (referents of) subject- and object-NPs to explicate temporal boundedness as 'stages' in similar sentences but with different lexical entries for verbs. Hence the thickened wavy line in (135) symbolizing the grammatical markedness of the verb with respect to non-boundedness and the designation *lex* in (137) with a non-thickened wavy line symbolizing lexical markedness and the lack of grammatical markedness.

Here the question arises as to the exact reason why the proper diagrammatic representation for (100a) should be (137) instead of (114) above. Because the diagrammatic representation (135) for sentence (134) was based on the Progressive/Non-Progressive contrast in the verb – that is, on the aspectual difference between sentence (134) and sentence (74). Hence, it could be argued that representation (137) for sentence (100a) is unjustifiable since no grammatical contrast similar to the contrast between (134) and (74) can be found here. However, according to the general approach developed, the representation (137) for sentence (100a) ought to be considered correct, for another reason, outside the possibility for a sentence like (100a) to be contrasted to a sentence with a different lexical entry for a verb, like e.g. (74). Sentence (100a) can be contrasted to a sentence like (100b) with the same lexical entry for the verb – whereby the action in sentence (100a) can be viewed as non-bounded and partial with respect to the bounded action carried to its natural endpoint in a sentence like (100b). Cf. again (100a) and (100b):

(100) a. The boy carried a stone
      b. The boy carried a stone into the basement

Compare this to the lack of a natural endpoint in the situation described in a sentence like (112a) – hence the (different) representation (119), already given in Chapter Six, *The mechanism for mapping the temporal values of subjects and objects*, for a state-denoting sentence like (112a):

(112) a. John hated Mary

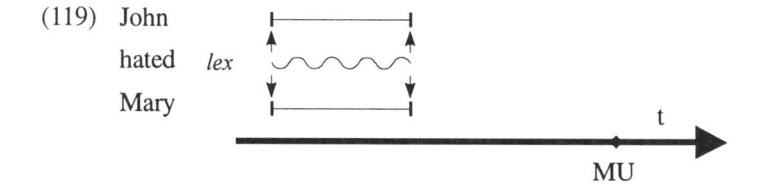

(119) John
hated *lex*
Mary

MU

PROBLEMS WITH STATE SENTENCES VS. SENTENCES IN THE PROGRESSIVE

But now there arises another problem, related to the representation of state-denoting sentences against the representation of the Progressive. Earlier, in Chapter Six, *The mechanism for mapping the temporal values of subjects and objects*, it was argued that the aspectologist might be tempted to present the stages of John and Mary in a sentence like (112a) as larger than the stage of hatred – which may be an intuitively correct decision from a common-sense point of view but is incorrect from the point of view of the approach developed. This incorrect decision here coincides with the representation for the internal-language function of the Progressive. Cf. the diagrams below, (135) and (120), for sentence (134) and for sentence (112a), respectively:

(134)   The boy was throwing a stone

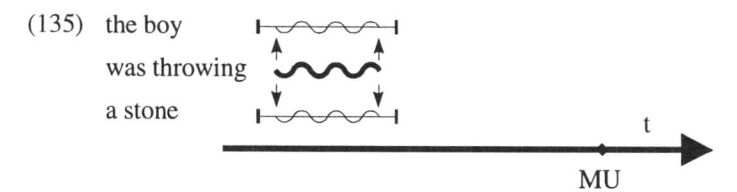

(135)   the boy
was throwing
a stone

MU

(112) a. John hated Mary

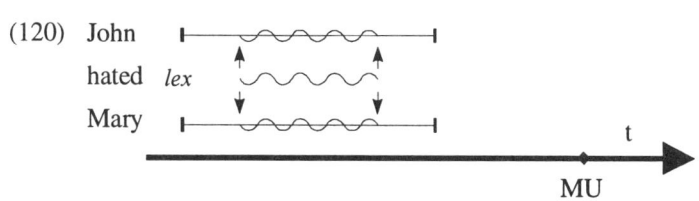

(120) John
hated *lex*
Mary

MU

To prevent confusion, the reason for the meaning difference between the two types of sentences and their representations should be explained. A state like 'hate' can be said to have no correspondence covering the stages of the participants in the situation as bounded 'wholes'. As already mentioned above, a sentence like (112a) can hardly be an accomplishment at all. The sum of all possible stages of entities like *John* and

Mary are what Carlson (1980) would call the individuals 'John' and 'Mary' – which, however, as Carlson himself rightfully noted, somehow escape proper description. What is it that embraces "all" of an individual like John or Mary? As argued earlier, the life history of a human being cannot be said to use up the contents (the essence) of the individual, for an individual can be remembered, loved, hated or, as we saw earlier, even sentenced to death after having died, and it is precisely matters like these, concerning parts of histories of individuals, that are dealt with in sentences like (112a) and many other similar sentences.[2] Hence, a (large) stage of the whole life of Mary and John cannot be held to correspond to a bounded stretch larger than the stretch of the situation described, as is actually the case depicted in (120). Conversely, in the representation of the Progressive there is a very well defined stage of the subject and a very well defined stage of the object that take part in a very well defined bounded action of throwing, identifiable in aspectual compositional terms. Moreover, the action and the participants described in (134) are identifiable as contrasting to the action and the participants in (74) in purely grammatical terms. There is no such grammatical contrast involved for the (incorrect) representation in (120). Therefore, the outwardly similar possible representation of sentence (112a) in (120) should be seen as unacceptable for the present approach and, hence, should not be considered as hindering or faulting the analysis of sentence (134) in terms of the diagram (135).

On the other hand, it may be argued that a sentence like (112a) could, in certain peripheral cases, be contrasted with sentences representing the hate as brought to some natural endpoint. Consider a sentence like (138):

(138)   John hated Mary to his heart's content

Language, as we know very well, is an extremely flexible tool for communication. Still, it would be unreasonable to generalise that it is typical for the situation in a sentence like (112a) to be contrasted to an accomplishment of the sort found in (138). Hence, the diagrammatic visualization of the mapping mechanism in (135), (137), and (119) can be taken to be fairly representative of the language reality behind them.

Another, relatively minor, problem remains with respect to the reason why *John* and *Mary* should be represented as bounded stretches in (119) above when there is no natural and typical bounded situation that *John* and *Mary* can be associated with in discussing sentences like (112a) related to a large span of individual histories. This solution is based on the initial assumption that NPs marked for boundedness through articles or other determiners and quantifiers are prototypical exponents of boundedness in sentences like (74) or (112b).

---

[2] But see Musan (1999) for a different approach, assigning 'life-time' status to nominal expressions with proper names, e.g. to *Diana* in sentences like *Diana is talked about*, according to which certain predicates can be asserted of people when they do not exist any more while others can't. But making a distinction between expressions that are applicable and expressions that are non-applicable to deceased people is a rather artificial enterprise, as proved by Hinrich's example *John made Bill a millionaire*.

(74)   The boy threw a stone
(112) b. John kissed Mary

This may not be a very elegant theoretical solution but at least it is a way of evading the vicious circle in the attempt to find the source of boundedness. Since, in terms of the structure of the English language at least, accompanied by an article and quantified are primarily nouns denoting material entities (including physical agents) in contrast to nouns denoting abstract entities, the assumption of the initial boundedness of referents of nouns/NPs denoting material entities may be said to be ultimately based on the naive ontological view that physical things are given at our disposal and we can, generally speaking, do whatever we wish to do to them, whereas abstract entities are, largely, inaccessible.

ABOUT THE LOGICAL TREND IN THE STUDY OF THE PROGRESSIVE

Finally, an account of the Progressive of the type given here ought to make at least some reference to the vast logico-linguistic literature on the Progressive in which it is treated in terms of truth conditions, points, intervals, subintervals, etc. on the time axis (see, e.g., Dowty 1979; Koenig 1980; Vlach 1981a; Goldschmidt and Woisetschlaeger 1982; Hinrichs 1983; Cooper 1985; Galton 1984; Lascarides 1988; Krifka 1989, to name but a few). The following passage from Galton's (1984) monograph, discussing the English sentence *John was walking home*, reveals a large part of the way of thinking about the Progressive within the logical trend:

> "As regards ordinary English usage, the issue is clear: John *was* walking home when he said he was [even though he was run over by a car before reaching his home]. The fact that he did not actually make it home does not render this false; rather, it tells us something about the logic of the progressive in ordinary usage. One might none the less wish to argue that, strictly speaking, ordinary usage is at fault in this matter, and that a proper logical account of the progressive should indeed deny that John was walking home if in fact he never reached home. Barry Taylor [1977] has argued just this"

(Galton 1984: 87). A distinction is made, not only in the two publications cited, between the logic of the Progressive in "ordinary English usage" and some presumably higher-order logic capable of explaining the "real meaning" of the Progressive. But the idea runs counter to the very nature of the Progressive – which is, first and foremost, a phenomenon formed on the basis of natural language mechanisms. Maintaining it conceals the failure on the part of the 'logical trend' to deal successfully with the Progressive.

CONCLUSION

To sum up, this chapter has proposed an updated version of an old explanation of the internal language function of the English Progressive. Contrary to the standard linguistic dogma, according to which aspect is a device to shape the temporal configuration of states or actions only and not the participants in them, the basic function of formally (grammatically) marked aspectual categories should be regarded as governing the temporal range of participants in situations (see Kabakčiev 1984b). Clearly, within this line of reasoning, the English Progressive can be no exception to the rule: it is an expedient for eliminating the temporal boundedness of referents of subject- and object-NPs in sentences belonging to a particular (previously defined) major semantico-syntactic pattern. This description of the basic function of the Progressive complements the general aspectual theory outlined in previous publications and in this book. According to it aspect, broadly (be it verbal or compositional), is a result of a very subtle and complex interplay between verbal and nominal referents. A major role in this enterprise is played by meanings of verbs and nouns, including lexical ones. These meanings will be analysed in more detail in the following two chapters of the book.

CHAPTER 9

LEXICAL MEANINGS OF VERBS, AND ASPECT IN ENGLISH

GENERAL REMARKS

The meanings of verbs as lexical entries play a major role in the compositional explication of aspect in English at the level of the sentence. These meanings can be classified into different groups according to the way situations are depicted. This has already been done by different authors in various publications – some of which were discussed in Chapter One, *On the essence of aspect*. But, whenever a large number of verbs in English are investigated, the results usually create the impression that verbs have too many different meanings to be effectively classified into groups. Trying to present the regularities of explicating aspect in English compositionally as invalid, the critics of the compositional theory usually refer to the variety of meanings displayed by verbs, arguing that this variety cannot be subsumed under a handful of rules. It is impossible for the verb lexicon with its enormous semantic diversity to be neatly divided into two or three major groups – this is one of the major objections.

Of course, maintaining that verbs in English are too diverse in their meanings is justified in itself; what is more, many verbs in English display more than one "basic" meaning. Meaning diversity can be viewed in two major ways: as polysemy or as homonymy. In the case of polysemy, two or more meanings are taken to belong to the same verb. For example, the verb *stand* can be considered to manifest polysemy, with its several meanings closely related one to the other, for example:

stand... 1. Have, take, keep, an upright position. *He was too weak to stand.* 2... 6. Cause to be placed in an upright position. *Stand the ladder against the wall.*

(Hornby 1974: 840). In the case of homonymy, two or more verbs of the same form but with different meanings are identified as separate lexical entries. For example, instead of presenting *rest* as a polysemous verb with two or more separate meanings, Hornby's (1974) dictionary lists two separate verbs – *rest¹*, *rest²*, the first meaning 'be still or quiet, be free from activity, movement, disturbance, etc.', as in sentence (139a), the second meaning 'continue to be in a specified state', as in sentence (139b):

(139) a. We rested for an hour after lunch
b. The affair rests a mystery

(Hornby 1974: 722). That is, according to this dictionary the semantic link between *rest¹* and *rest²* is weak – and this leads to the separation of two separate dictionary entries.

Clearly, the division between polysemy and homonymy has to do with the approach assumed towards a particular verb or a group of verbs in a given dictionary – so that a verb ends up being presented as demonstrating polysemy or homonymy. Of course, for a dictionary of English the choice of polysemy or homonymy is a serious problem that is to be attended to, but when in this chapter the various meanings of verbs are considered (the various meanings of verbs often leading also to different interpretations of the aspect of an action), the problem of polysemy and homonymy will not be taken into account. Some of the examples below will be from Hornby (1974) – and will be marked as borrowed from this dictionary. This lexicographic source was chosen because it is sensitive to the typicality of use of verbs in phrases and sentences in spoken standard English.

In discussing the contribution of verbs to the compositional explication of aspect it is worth considering what kinds of entities verbs in the different languages, and in English in particular, can refer to. On the one hand, according to a common formulation in grammars, verbs express actions and states. But on the other hand, the notion of state is in many cases simply subsumed under the notion of action – which then stands for the whole species of 'situations' that can be described by verbs. This is certainly not the most felicitous terminology but it is universally employed. Interestingly enough, while the notions of action and state are poorly explained and exemplified in grammars, their essence is conceived of unproblematically in an intuitive way by ordinary speakers of languages. If studies of English aspect are compared with studies of aspect in the Slavic languages, it will be established that in its long tradition Slavic aspectology has suffered not only from this terminological insufficiency of traditional grammar. It often simply ignores the varieties of situational meanings denoted by verbs because it is the perfective/imperfective verb distinction that is focused on. Reasoning runs along the following lines: actions can be both perfective or imperfective, so what do situational meanings have to do with aspect? And within the perfective/imperfective opposition states simply fall out of the perfective member, so why bother deal with states specifically? Conversely, in aspectological studies of English and other non-Slavic languages, it is often notions like perfectivity or imperfectivity that are ignored, or their significance is underestimated, at the expense of notions like event, accomplishment, achievement, activity, state, etc.

However, it will be shown in this book that even the distinctions between states and activities, on the one hand, and accomplishments and achievements, on the other, cannot cover all major possible types of situations. Because, for instance, states are imperfective/non-bounded situations and certainly cannot be transformed into true perfectives. But states can certainly terminate, so what about states that have terminated? For example, a sentence like (140) can be interpreted in the following two ways.

(140)   I felt tired

It may mean:

(i) 'suddenly I was overcome with fatigue' – that is, (140) describes an achievement, a transition from one state into another;
(ii) 'I was in a state of fatigue for an indefinite, non-bounded period of time' – that is, (140) describes a state.

In its first reading, describing a transition from one state into another, sentence (140) is normally incompatible with an adverbial of duration like a *for*-time adverbial. Therefore, a sentence like (141) may be said to have been derived out of the second, 'state' meaning of (140), for (141) refers to a stretch of time, not to a momentary transition from one state into another.

(141)   I felt tired for three hours

However, as is clear from the adverbial in the sentence, the state in (141) has expired: it was valid for a certain period of time. Vendler's accomplishment class cannot provide an account for this type of meaning – not only because accomplishments are generally incompatible with a *for*-time adverbial but because there is no result associated with the termination of the action in (141), no inherent endpoint. Neither can such a situation be subsumed under Vendler's activities or achievements, nor can it be accommodated in Verkuyl's compositional theory – for it takes *I was tired* to be imperfective, and treats the *for*-time adverbial simply as a good test for proving the imperfectivity of (140). It can be supposed that situations of the type described in sentence (141) usually remain unaccounted for because they are not potentially present in the meanings of verbs as lexical entries. But this is not to say that they do not exist. They will be given an appropriate treatment in Chapter Eleven, *The impact of adverbials in the sentence, and aspect in English* and especially in Chapter Thirteen, *On aspectual classes in English.*

The introductory remarks made above are meant to show that apart from the way of treating the compositional explication of aspect, the tradition of studying lexical semantics of verbs in English in terms of aspect is also far from satisfactory. It suffers from certain methodological dogmas related to the inability of aspectologists to give a correct interpretation of the compositional theory of aspect and to make a certain necessary theoretical departure from Vendler's schemata. Another weakness of the aspectological tradition of studying English aspect is the failure to make a proper generalisation with respect to the overall verbal lexicon. It has already been established in this book that there is an enormous number of sentences in English explicating (or capable of explicating) perfective actions. Therefore, for any study of aspect in English it would be important to give an assessment of the approximate size of the English verbal lexicon capable of contributing to the compositional explication of perfectivity. Obviously, the potential to explicate perfectivity is present in a very large number of verbs – and, of course, the possibility for a verb to imply a perfective action can increase within a particular sentence or discourse. Conversely, an aptitude for implying imperfective actions ought to be present in a much smaller portion of the English verb lexicon. It is to be noted that for the potential of verbs to imply perfectivity or imperfectivity to be properly determined, it ought to be examined in the so-called neutral conditions for explicating aspect distinctions, considered, e.g., in Danchev (1974) and Moens (1987: 94). As far as the more general types of meanings of verbs are concerned, mainly physical actions performed by a particular agent and affecting (or effecting) a particular object/particular objects have so far been considered. But the English language also features verbs denoting various types of other states, actions or activities that have so far remained unanalysed. For example, many verbs designate intellectual actions like understanding, thinking, remembering, etc. The question is: will verbs denoting such actions be capable of contributing to the explication of perfectivity as are, generally speaking, verbs denoting physical actions?

Of course, it would be an impossible task to try to check exactly how many verbs in English possess the potential to imply perfectivity or imperfectivity within the semantico-syntactic prototypical pattern employed so far. First, there is no such thing as the total number of verbs in a language. Second, verbs feature homonymy and synonymy. Third, there is no agreement among aspectologists about the meanings of certain major lexemes, let alone the whole verbal lexicon. Therefore, it seems best to resort to a procedure that would enable just a broad assessment of how many and which of the comparatively most frequent verbs in English would display an aptitude for explicating compositionally one or the other value of the basic aspectual distinction, and in approximately what conditions.

With this purpose in mind, Danchev and Alexieva's (1974) list of 200 most frequently used verbs in English will be employed here. Although this list is now somewhat outdated it can by no means be considered obsolete. Two decades is too short a period in the development of a language to influence the frequency of use of words. Below are the two hundred most commonly used verbs in English according to the authors:

> accept, add, advance, agree, allow, answer, appear, arrive, ask, attempt, be, become, begin, believe, belong, blow, borrow, break, bring, build, burn, burst, call, carry, catch, cease, change, close, come, consider, contain, continue, control, cook, count, cover, cross, cry, cut, dance, deal, decide, demand, desire, destroy, die, direct, discover, divide, do, dry, enjoy, enter, escape, exist, expect, explain, fail, fall, feel, fell, fill, find, finish, fix, flow, follow, gain, gather, get, give, go, grow, guard, hang, happen, hate, have, hear, help, hesitate, hit, hold, hurry, hurt, include, increase, join, jump, keep, kill, kiss, know, laugh, lay,

lead, learn, leave, lie, lift, like, listen, live, look, lose, love, lower, make, marry, mean, meet, miss, move, notice, offer, open, own, pay, pass, pick, play, please, prefer, prepare, press, prove, pull, push, put, raise, reach, read, realise, receive, remember, reply, require, rest, return, roll, row, run, rush, save, say, see, seem, send, separate, serve, set, settle, shake, shine, shoot, shout, show, sing, sit, sleep, smile, sell, smell, speak, spend, spread, stand, start, stop, succeed, suffer, suppose, suit, supply, surprise, talk, taste, thank, think, throw, tie, touch, try, turn, take, travel, understand, use, visit, wait, walk, want, wash, watch, wave, wear, win, wish, work, write.

Taking cursory glance at the list it appears that many of the lexical entries have to be classified as a group of verbs capable of implying perfectivity, and the group will be called the group of telic verbs. These will be verbs that will contribute to the explication of perfective rather than imperfective situations in the proper semantico-syntactic conditions considered so far. On the other hand, since in other conditions the same verbs would contribute to the explication of imperfectivity, it is natural that their potential for implying imperfectivity ought to be taken into account as well, as a secondary, weaker and atypical one.

A comparison between English and a language that features verbal aspect would be in place here. Clearly, in spite of the outward similarity between verbal perfectivity in Bulgarian and verbal telicity in English, both perfective and imperfective verbs in Bulgarian will correspond to telic verbs in English – because of the secondary potential of telic English verbs to explicate imperfectivity. But if the telicity of English verbs is to be indicated in bilingual dictionaries, a lexicographic convention can be established such that, for example, perfective verbs must precede imperfective ones in the enumeration of Bulgarian correspondences of English verbs, or a perfective verb must precede the imperfective one in an aspectual pair equivalent to an English verb. And vice versa, if an English verb displays atelicity as an aspectual potential, an imperfective Bulgarian verb must be given as a primary equivalent.[1]

It has already been mentioned that, as a general rule, bilingual dictionaries representing Bulgarian and a Western European language list only imperfective verbs as equivalents of the corresponding verbs in, say, English, German or French. This method is unacceptable not only from the point of view of the regularities discussed here, but also in view of the fact that, for example, there are many verbs in Bulgarian that are only perfective. All these perfective verbs are thus either doomed to be absent in bilingual dictionaries, or, if they are included, they will inevitably mystify non-Slavic users. Because Slavic verbs have no intrinsic markers of aspect and the perfective-imperfective/imperfective-perfective morphological derivational

---

[1] In Kabakčiev (1994), a concise English-Bulgarian dictionary, an attempt at such an aspectological solution of rendering the meanings of verbs has been made. Cf. the entries for *give* and *know* (Kabakčiev 1994: 43; 54):
give *vt* dam$_{pfv}$/davam$_{impfv}$
[...]
know *vt/vi* znaja$_{impfv}$, poznaja$_{pfv}$/poznavam$_{impfv}$.

machinery in Bulgarian is an extremely complicated one. Thus the necessity to represent the aspectual potential of the English verb in dictionaries is a must where English-Slavic bilingual dictionaries are concerned. But if the English verb possesses a lexical aspectual potential, such as the one described here, it ought to be covered in other dictionaries also – in specialised dictionaries, in lexicographic data bases and other descriptions of the lexicon, especially in modern scientific areas like computer linguistics, machine translation, voice data recognition, artificial intelligence, etc., where semantic precision is essential. Undoubtedly, ordinary dictionaries would also profit immensely from a more adequate and exhaustive description of the semantics of verbs. The reason why dictionaries (not only bilingual English-Slavic but also standard English ones) have so far treated aspect inadequately is at least two-fold. Firstly, in addition to the lack of consensus concerning many issues in aspectology, the major language regularities related to aspect have been discovered only recently. Secondly, lexicographic traditions take a long time to change.

VERBS WITH A TELIC ASPECTUAL POTENTIAL

Since many verbs describing physical actions have already been discussed, now consider the following lexemes denoting actions of interpersonal communication and belonging to the list of verbs most commonly used: *agree, ask, explain, offer, say*. These verbs usually require either another verb in the infinitive or a conjunct introducing an embedded object clause denoting a statement Z (of the type, say, *John was late* or *the train would leave soon*). Let X be an agent and a human being. Compare the sentences in (142) and their natural Bulgarian (metalanguage) equivalents in which the verb sounds fine in its typical perfective form (the perfective Aorist), and the imperfective Imperfect does not seem appropriate as an equivalent of the corresponding English sentence:

(142) a. X agreed that Z
 'X se săglasi$_{pfvAor}$/?se săglasjavaše$_{impfvImp}$, če Z'
 b. X asked whether Z
 'X popita$_{pfvAor}$/?pitaše$_{impfvImp}$ dali Z'
 c. X explained that Z
 'X objasni$_{pfvAor}$/?objasnjavaše$_{impfvImp}$ če Z'
 d. X offered to leave
 'X predloži$_{pfvAor}$/?predlagaše$_{impfvImp}$ da zamine'
 e. X said that Z
 'X kaza$_{pfvAor}$/?kazvaše$_{impfvImp}$, če Z'[2]

---

[2] Conversely, if the Bulgarian sentences with the imperfective Imperfect are to be rendered in English, the natural translation would normally require habitual expressions like *used to/would*:

Clearly, in this type of sentences the verbs may be said to imply perfective actions. They could also be said to explicate boundedness after the mechanism of mapping the boundedness of (the referents of) the subject and the object onto the (referent of the) verb is accomplished. There is no reason not to assume that mapping really takes place in the mind of the hearer to process the semantics of the sentence after it has been uttered – however complex the elements and phases of the corresponding psycho-physiological mechanism may be. Just like sentences with a human (syntactic) subject and an affected material (syntactic) object of type (72b) or (74), see below, sentences like (142) may be said to denote mental acts associated with an identifiable result obtained at an inherent endpoint.

(72) b. The soldier crossed the street
(74)   The boy threw a stone

The outward appearance of the result of the action in sentences like (142) may be absent or hard to visualize, in contrast to sentences denoting physical actions like building a house, crossing the street or throwing a stone. The propositions of sentences like (142) contain a concrete agent performing not a physical action affecting a material entity but a mental action effecting an abstract object. But if the events in (142) are analysed along the same lines as sentences with subjects and objects denoting material entities like (72b) or (74), it will turn out that in the compositional explication of aspect and in the type of mapping of temporal values that takes place sentences denoting mental acts do not differ greatly from those denoting physical acts.

The analysis of sentences like (142), repeated below, reveals another important feature that should be noted. The abstract object effected by the action should not only be regarded as temporal in an analytical model (as in Chapter Five, *Extension in time of subjects and objects from a "common-sense" point of view*) – it is overtly temporal. That is, it is conceived of as such by the ordinary speaker. What is more, it could even be conceived of as bounded in time, perhaps with some intellectual effort.

Suppose Z in (142b) stands for *the train would leave soon*. Since the abstract object Z constitutes an act in itself, the act of enquiry (say, *Will the train leave soon?*), overtly bounded as it is in time, it represents the content of the referent of the verb *asked*. The same boundedness is true of Z in (142a), (142c), (142e) and in an indefinite number of other similar sentences – if Z in (142a) stands for, say, *John is a fool*, or if in (142c) it stands for, say, *he had lost his way*, etc.

---

(140) a'. 'X se săglasjavaše$_{impfvImp}$, če Z'
            X used to/would agree that Z
       b'. 'X pitaše$_{impfvImp}$ dali Z'
            X used to/would ask whether Z
etc.

(142) a. X agreed that Z
b. X asked whether Z
c. X explained that Z
d. X offered to leave
e. X said that Z

In the more specific case of (142d) bounded is the referent of the verb *to leave*. Note, however, that the referent of *to leave* in (142d) has two meanings of boundedness: one at the level of its association with the boundedness of *offered*, and one at the level of its own inherent aspectual potential of telicity, realised as boundedness. The latter level can best be exemplified by substituting the verb phrase *offered to leave* in (142d) with a verb phrase like *offered to play*. In *X offered to play* the referent of *to play* can be said to have two different aspectological values: boundedness at the level of its association with the boundedness of *offered*, and non-boundedness at the level of the realisation of its atelic aspectual potential. Similar cases of infinitival aspectual complexity have already been considered in sentences like (84) and (85):

(84) a. John wanted to see the film
b. John wanted to watch the film
(85) a. John expressed a desire to see the film
b. John expressed a desire to watch the film

For detail, see again the discussion in Chapter Five, *Extension in time of subjects and objects from a "common-sense" point of view*.

To return to the analysis of sentences like (142) above, since the embedded clause Z in some of the sentences can be substituted by an NP consisting of a noun accompanied by an article or some other kind of determiner, the conception of abstract objects effected by the action of the verb as bounded in time is important for recognising the role played by nouns as lexical entries for the explication of aspect in the sentence. For example, if *whether Z* is substituted for *a question* in (142b), if *to leave* in (142d) is substituted for *his resignation* or if *that Z* is substituted for *a prayer* in (142e), the NPs *a question, his resignation* and *a prayer* would explicate boundedness through the article just as the substituted clauses do compositionally. But since abstract nouns like these contain temporality as a regular feature (a basic one) of their lexical meaning, this raises the question of whether it is the article only through which boundedness can be explicated. The problem will be dealt with in Chapter Ten, *Meanings of nouns and noun phrases, and aspect in English*.

It is clear, however, that, on the one hand, the situations described in (142) can best be defined as typically perfective and that, on the other hand, it would hardly make any difference which or what is the particular natural language that such situations would be described in. It is also but self-evident that a large number of other similar mental operations, even such that may have no outward appearance whatsoever (like, for example, *decide, learn, prove, realise,* etc.), will also very definitely be conceived of as bounded/perfective. They will be denoted in a similar type of sentences, see (143) below, in which again there must be a subject *X* denoting an agent (a human being) and an embedded clause (*that*) *Z* standing for a statement like *John was late*:

(143) a. X decided that Z
b. X learned that Z
c. X proved that Z
d. X realised that Z

In a similar vein, Tenny (1994: 64-68) deals from an aspectual point of view with so-called psych verbs in English like *fear, frighten, excite, fascinate, worry*, etc., maintaining that many of them describe changes of state, that is, explicate boundedness, as in the examples (144a) through (144h), constructed by the author, in which, however, the subject is an abstract entity:

(144) a. The truth worried John
b. The truth interested John
c. The truth attracted John
d. The truth moved John
e. The truth excited John
f. The truth fascinated John
g. The truth frightened John
h. The truth disgusted John
i. John feared the truth

But not all psych verbs describe changes of state. That is, not all of them should be regarded as having a telic aspectual potential. For example, the verb *fear* in a sentence like (144i) contributes to the explication of imperfectivity with its atelic aspectual potential. It is interesting to note that an abstract and non-bounded entity like *the truth* (see the discussion about abstract entities in the following Chapter Ten, *Meanings of nouns and noun phrases, and aspect in English*), does not prevent the explication of perfectivity in sentences like (144a) through (144h), while the semantico-syntactic pattern in (144i) with a human subject (but an abstract object) fails to explicate perfectivity. Of course, on the one hand, the definite article in the subjects of (144a) through (144h) may be said to help in the explication of boundedness which is then mapped onto the referents of the verbs according to the mapping mechanism. On the other hand, the human subject in (144i) is not an agent but a patient – in what Dowty (1991) calls a 'thematic role'. From the point of view of the aspect mechanism, in (144i) the non-boundedness generated in the verb phrase *feared the truth* (mainly through the atelic aspectual potential of the verb *fear*) is mapped onto the referent of the subject *John* making it non-bounded.

Below are some other verbs in the list of most frequently used ones that denote perceptions or psycho-physiological changes in the (referent of the) subject or object: *hear, see, notice, move, please, surprise*. They often explicate perfectivity, as is the case in all the sentences in (145):

(145) a. John heard that Mary was ill
b. John was seen to enter a restaurant
c. I noticed that he left early
d. The happy end moved the audience
e. The answer pleased the teacher
f. John's proposal surprised Mary

With verbs like *see* and *hear* an interesting distinction in English can be observed between perfective and imperfective actions, expressed systematically by the forms of the infinitive and the present participle respectively. This phenomenon has to do precisely with the explication of perfectivity and imperfectivity and is usually covered in grammars. But, on the other hand, the very notions of perfectivity and imperfectivity remain, as a rule, ignored or ill-defined and, as a consequence, grammars fail to determine the origin of the difference in aspect in sentences like (146) and (147) given below. Compare the sentences in (146), in which the phrase *cross the street* has a perfective meaning, with the sentences in (147), in which the phrase *crossing the street* has an imperfective meaning:

(146) a. I heard the soldier cross the street
b. I saw the soldier cross the street
(147) a. I heard the soldier crossing the street
b. I saw the soldier crossing the street

The explication of perfectivity and imperfectivity here could be said to be partly based on the use of the infinitive versus the use of the present participle after verbs like *see* and *hear* with their somewhat ambiguous aspectual potential. These verbs are capable of denoting what Hornby (1949: 173) called a single act of perception but they can also be associated with the denotation of physiological processes that cannot be controlled, hence with the denotation of 'states'. The phrase *cross the street*, taken as a simple infinitive, clearly belongs to the group of accomplishments (in Vendler's terms) while the present participle is not infrequently associated with the denotation of a process (an activity in Vendler's terms). However, neither is an infinitive necessarily perfective, nor is the *-ing* form (including the present participle) necessarily imperfective. Compare the perfectivity of *seeing the signal* and *hearing the signal* in (148a) and (148b):

(148) a. On hearing the signal the soldier crossed the street
b. After seeing the signal the soldier crossed the street

Hence, perfectivity and imperfectivity in sentences like (146) and (147) above are derived from the characteristics of the two types of constructions as a whole, including compositional ones (the influence of the article, the lexical potential of the verb, etc.), not from the general meaning or the typical use of the infinitive or the present participle *per se*.

Recall, furthermore, that in some passive sentences with the verb *hear* the outward structure of the subject (namely, the presence or absence of an article) is responsible for the explication of perfectivity or imperfectivity of the action. Compare sentences (22a) and (22b):

(22) a. Noise was heard
b. A noise was heard

Sentences like (22a) and (22b) are passive transformations of sentences like (149a) and (149b):

(149) a. We heard noise
b. We heard a noise

As can be judged from these four examples, the explication of temporal boundedness and non-boundedness should be associated not only with the outward structure of the subject or object NPs (the presence or absence of an article, other determiners, quantifiers) but also with the meaning of the noun as a lexical entry. The problem will be discussed in detail in Chapter Ten, *Meanings of nouns and noun phrases, and aspect in English*, but examples of type (22) and (149), along with many others, make it clear that the interrelationship between the presence of an article and perfectivity, on the one hand, and the absence of an article and imperfectivity, on the other hand, is undoubtedly valid as a global mechanism for the subject, despite arguments to the contrary (see Shi 1990; Tenny 1994: 27-28) some of which will be dealt with later. After the transformation of sentences like (149a) into (22a) and (149b) into (22b), objects appear as subjects and the initial subjects are omitted, but the sentences preserve their characteristics with respect to the different tense and aspect values.

Of course, there remains the problem whether sentences in the passive voice will always be so typical and natural for the interrelationship in question to be easily observed. For example, if sentences like (40a) and (40b) below are passivised in a similar way, the situational meaning in the resulting sentence becomes unclear. Compare (40) and (150a) with the three possible translations of (150a) into the Bulgarian metalanguage – using the perfective Aorist, the imperfective Imperfect or the imperfective Aorist, as in (150b):

(40) a. Katinka knitted Norwegian sweaters
b. Women knitted Norwegian sweaters

192   CHAPTER 9

(150) a. Norwegian sweaters were knitted
      b. Norvežki   puloveri   se   izpletoha$_{pfvAor}$/pletjaha$_{impfvImp}$/pletoha$_{impfvAor}$
         Norwegian   sweaters   *prt.pass.*   knitted

The ambiguity (or lack of clarity) of the aspectual reading in a sentence like (150a) above makes a strong contrast with sentences like (151a) and (151b) below, similar to the sentences in (65b) and (65c), already discussed, in which the setting of the event, the context, and, hence, the aspectual reading, are clear. Sentence (151a) explicates perfectivity of the actions denoted by both *bought* and *perforated*, while (151b) explicates imperfectivity of these actions:

(65) b. The passengers have to buy tickets beforehand and perforate them in the bus
     c. Passengers have to buy tickets beforehand and perforate them in the bus
(151) a. The tickets are to be bought beforehand and must be perforated in the bus
      b. Tickets are to be bought beforehand and must be perforated in the bus

All these examples show that the explication of the aspectual meaning of a sentence or a clause or a verb is based on a complex set of rules in which the lexical aspectual potential of the verb is not at all dominant. It is just one of many factors, another is, for instance, the contribution of the outward quantification of NP components in the sentence.

In spite of the comparatively clear context in certain sentences, like those in (151a) and (151b) above, so far in the analysis of aspectual meaning almost only isolated sentences have been used. But isolated sentences are not a rare phenomenon in themselves. We constantly hear or read such sentences: we come across various instructions, guidelines, warnings, orders, advertisements, we overhear parts of conversations in the street, initial or final utterances of news bulletins when switching on or off the radio or whenever our attention is diverted from what we have been listening to. This is a universal trait of the mode of functioning of language. It is therefore beyond any doubt that sentences that are isolated of their context have to receive an interpretation that is as meaningful and as adequate as possible. And the notions of perfectivity and imperfectivity represent an extremely important part of the semantic interpretation that is to be given to any utterance/sentence. Hence the necessity for isolated utterances/sentences in English to be interpreted from the point of view of the basic aspectual contrast belongs to the general requirements for successful communication between people carried out through natural language.

Below are some more examples (152) with verbs denoting mental actions (*accept, add, allow, discover*) from the list of most frequently used verbs in English. These verbs feature telicity as a lexical aspectual potential that can be (and is here) realised as boundedness/perfectivity. Z in (152b) and (152d), again, stands for a statement of the type *John was late*:

(152) a. X accepted the invitation
   b. X added that Z
   c. X allowed me to leave
   d. X discovered that Z

To sum up the discussion of verbs denoting mental actions, given the enormous variety of sentences describing situations of type (142), (143), (144), or (152) above, telicity can safely be assumed to be present as an important aspectual element in the lexical meanings of the verbs in the sentences analysed. Telicity is a potential semantic feature that is effectuated in certain appropriate semantico-syntactic conditions and is not effectuated in other conditions. When it is effectuated, this results in the explication of boundedness in the referent of the verb in the sentence and, more generally, at the level of the sentence – in sentences of a particular type. Note again, however, that, according to the mechanism of mapping proposed in this work, the realisation of the telic aspectual potential as boundedness is dependent on the contribution of the referents of NPs. They have to map their boundedness onto the referent of the verb for the telic feature to be realised as boundedness.

But what about the aspectual behaviour of verbs denoting actions that can be visualized, different from those used so far? To analyse the way these verbs can contribute to the explication of aspectual meanings some authentic sentences will be used, that is, not simple examples like most of those used above constructed for the sake of the analysis but real English sentences as spoken in everyday life. With this purpose in mind, examples from Hornby's (1974) dictionary will again be made use of (in some of the examples minor changes have been introduced to make them suitable for the discussion). Note that so far in the analysis almost only past tense forms of verbs have been used, as it was established that the Simple Past Tense, being aspectually unmarked, is the most appropriate one for the explication of aspectual meanings. But perfectivity and imperfectivity can be explicated by many other forms of the verb too. Therefore, henceforward, not only verbs in the Simple Past Tense will be used but also various other verb forms for tense, voice or mood. The non-perfect and non-progressive infinitive will be employed in the illustrations as well because many non-finite forms are also able to supply neutral conditions for the explication of aspect distinctions.

Of special interest for the analysis are verbs used intransitively. So far they have been left out of consideration. Below are some sentences (153) with verbs (*come, fall, gather, return*) capable of signifying motion that has a definite beginning and a definite end:

(153) a. John has come to this town to work
   b. The chimney fell from the top of the building to the ground

c. A crowd gathered round the football player
d. The employee returned to collect his money

It is clear that reference to motion that has a definite beginning and a definite end does not necessarily involve explication of perfectivity, for any action between two points can be represented either as completed or as in the process of taking place. In some sentences of type (153) above the initial point and the endpoint may be overtly expressed through the use of adverbials, as is the case in (153b). In other sentences the two points may be overtly unexpressed, as it is in the rest of the sentences in (153). But an initial and an endpoint of the movement can always be **inferred** to be present in the meaning of verbs like those in (153), even if viewed as lexical entries only. It is this semantic feature precisely, an initial and an endpoint of the movement, that seems to be the factor that predetermines the explication of boundedness/perfectivity of the action in the use of this type of verbs, under appropriate semantico-syntactic conditions.

So, within the semantic feature of telicity, all the verbs in (153), viewed as lexical entries, imply a beginning and an end of the action – whether these are expressly stated in the sentence through an adverbial or not. Of course, since other actions, e.g. those denoted by verbs like *realise*, *remember*, etc., are also telic but cannot be said to contain initial points and endpoints, reference to the initial point and the endpoint of movement does not exhaust the content of the notion of telicity. The possibility to refer to the initial point and the endpoint of some movement is just a subtype of telicity. Furthermore, the beginning and the end of an action should not be confused with what could be called the 'face value' of lexical meaning. For example, in a certain sense, verbs like *arrive* and *come* or expressions like *X arrived/came* can be regarded as referring to an endpoint of a certain action, whereas verbs like *leave*, *depart* or expressions like *X left/departed* can be regarded as referring to an initial point of a certain action. But in terms of the aspectual analysis carried out here, both types of words and expressions have their initial and final points whether one is explicit and the other only implied. For instance, in the perfective reading of *X arrived/came* (the normal one) the final point is explicit and the initial point is implied. In the perfective reading of *X left/departed* (the normal one) the initial point is explicit and the final point is implied. The implied initial point in *X arrived/came* is one where the agent either starts the journey or starts the final phase (the arrival) of the journey. An arrival may be said to have an initial and a final point: for instance, in everyday terms, an arrival takes place in the interval between seeing one's guest in the window of the approaching train and greeting him/her on the platform. Conversely, the implied final point in *X left/departed* is one where the final phase of the departure is reached (for instance, the interval between kissing someone goodbye on the platform and the disappearance of the last car of the train).

Other verbs capable of denoting movement in space with a fixed initial and a fixed final point (in the list of most frequently used verbs in English) are *burst, close, cover, cross, cut, escape, fill, go, hit, join, jump, lay, lift, lower, open, pass, pick, put, reach, send, shake, shoot, spread, throw, touch, turn*. The actions in sentences

(154) below are perfective in their most natural reading. They start at an initial point, take a larger or shorter period of time to develop, and finish at an endpoint:

(154) a. Close/open the door
b. Let me pass, will you?
c. The animal escaped from its cage
d. Mary laid her hand on John's shoulder

In a similar fashion, it can be argued that while in (154a) and (154b) no points are defined by adverbials, in (154c) it is only the initial point that is defined by an adverbial, and in (154d) it is only the endpoint. This is true with respect to the outward expression of the limits of the action. But for an action to finish at a particular point in space it is necessary that it starts at another point. Hence, if the endpoint is given (the more usual case), the starting point is taken for granted, or vice versa, the initial point may be given and the endpoint may be implicit, as in (154c).

Apart from the so-called psych verbs discussed above, Tenny (1994) also dealt with verbs of motion, arguing, *inter alia*, that in sentences like (155a) and (155b) below the moved object has no aspectual role (Tenny 1994: 77-78).

(155) a. John pushed the car to a gas station
b. Bill rolled the log to the top of the hill

However, one can easily construct sentences like (156a), (156b) or (156c)[3]:

(156) a. John pushed trolleys into the supermarket *in an hour/for hours/for hours on end [this was his job]
b. John pushed tubs of coal from the coal face to the bottom of the mine shaft *in an hour/for hours/for hours on end [this was his job]
c. Bill rolled logs to the top of the hill *in an hour/for an hour/for hours on end [he wanted to build a house there]

Their analysis shows that if in a sentence like (155a) or (155b) the semantic nature of the verb is such that the definite direct object does not seem to contribute to the aspectual meaning, in sentences like (156a) – (156c) the bare plural of the direct objects does contribute to the non-boundedness of the sentence, in spite of the fact that adverbials like *into the supermarket, from the coal face to the bottom of the mine shaft, to the top of the hill* are considered (also by Tenny 1994: 76-78) to perfectivise the meaning of the action. The possibility to introduce adverbials like *for an hour* or *for hours on end*, and the unacceptability of the *in*-time phrase in (156), although the *in*-time and the *for*-time tests are not absolute criteria in themselves (see below, Chapter Eleven, *The impact of adverbials in the sentence, and aspect in*

---

[3] Jim Miller, as a native speaker of English, made valuable suggestions in the process of constructing these examples.

English), support the judgement that the basic sentences in (156) have primarily non-bounded readings.

Again, the perfectivity of a particular action may be said to depend not so much on the meaning of the verb as a lexical entity – viewed as an abstraction, as a prototype of the various uses. Rather, it depends on the essence of the situation described through the whole sentence, not only through the verb. So far, mainly sentences of a very simple semantico-syntactic type, with agentive subjects, have been analysed. Compare now a more complex sentence like (157a) below, in which the verb (*pass*) belongs to the list of verbs apt to imply perfectivity, but its reading is here imperfective because of the non-boundedness of the NP *cars*. The imperfectivity of (157a) can be clearly seen in the Bulgarian equivalent of this sentence (157b) in which the verb has to be an imperfective one.

(157) a. The road was too narrow for cars to pass (Hornby 1974)
        b. Păt-iat   beše   tvărde tesen,   za da mogat   da preminavat$_{impfv}$ koli/koli-te
           Road-the   was   too   narrow   for to can-they to pass   cars/cars-the

Conversely, the addition of a definite determiner into the NP *cars* introduces the possibility for the action to be read as perfective. This, again, finds reflection in the Bulgarian equivalent (158b) of the English sentence (158a). A perfective verb must be used in (158b):

(158) a. The road was too narrow for the cars to pass (Hornby 1974)
        b. Păt-jat   beše   tvărde tesen,   za da mogat   da preminat$_{pfv}$ koli-te
           Road-the   was   too   narrow   for to can-they to pass-they cars-the

Note that in the Bulgarian translation (157b) of the English sentence (157a) above, there is no change in meaning whether the definite article is used or not in the NP equivalent to *cars* (*koli/kolite* 'cars/the cars'). And in (158b) the definite article in *kolite* 'the cars' contributes nothing to the aspectual interpretation of the sentence – because the aspectual meaning is inherent in the verb itself (*premina*$_{pfv}$ 'pass'). Furthermore, the definite article in the Bulgarian sentences does not alter the interpretation of the NP itself. Whether the noun is accompanied by an article (*kolite* 'cars') or not (*koli* 'cars'), the description of the overall situation in (157b) does not change at all. In other words, the (so-called traditionally) definite article is here stripped of its function to mark entities already introduced (or otherwise present – subsumed, etc.) in context. Conversely, the imperfective reading of *to pass* in the English sentence (157a) and the perfective reading of *to pass* in the English sentence (158a) are due to the use and the non-use of an article, respectively. But note that here the definite article, again, does not at all exercise its "proper" outward function to mark entities that have already been introduced in context or are otherwise present in it. Examples like this in English, displaying the important covert function of the article to explicate boundedness at the expense of its usual function, may not be easy to find in actual discourse (or even to construct), but they certainly exist.

In terms of the aspectual regularities at the level of the sentence that have been discussed so far in the book, indeed, the two English sentences (157a) and (158a) above belong to a rather specific semantico-syntactic pattern. But they can be said to fall unmistakably into Verkuyl's perfective and imperfective schemata, respectively, because the two prepositional objects (*the cars* and *cars*) can easily be syntactically transformed into subjects. Compare (159a) and (159b) below, where *pass* in (159a) definitely explicates non-boundedness/imperfectivity, while *pass* in (159b) could explicate (through the support of the definite article in the subject NP) both perfectivity and imperfectivity. Still, it is more readily associated with the explication of boundedness/perfectivity:

(159) a. Cars could not pass, for the road was too narrow
b. The cars could not pass, for the road was too narrow

Sentences like these show that although the aspectual role of the contrast between quantified and non-quantified nouns/NPs in the subject can be less frequently observed, the associations between quantification and perfectivity and the lack of quantification and imperfectivity in this syntactic position are not to be dismissed.

The Bulgarian correspondences of (159a) and (159b), viz. (160a) and (160b) respectively, simply reflect the aspectual readings of (159a) and (159b):

(160) a. Koli ne možeha$_{impfvImp}$ da preminavat$_{impfv}$, zaštoto păt-jat beše tvărde tesen
Cars not could to pass, because road-the was too narrow

b. Koli-te ne možaha$_{pfvAor}$ da preminat$_{pfv}$, zaštoto păt-jat beše tvărde tesen
Cars-the not could to pass because road-the was too narrow

Lexical meanings of verbs are certainly too diverse and it is not an easy task to subsume definitely a particular verb under one of the two lexical aspectual categories (telicity and atelicity), even if the problem of polysemy is somehow ignored in many verbs for the sake of clearly defining their prototypical aspectual potential. A question arises whether it can be generalised that whenever the lexical meaning of a verb is homogeneous, its aspectual potential will be clear-cut. Consider again verbs of movement in space superficially, in their lexical 'face value', denoting only one of the two points on the time axis discussed above – either the initial one or the final one. In (161) below the verb *leave* is a representative of the former kind, *arrive* of the latter, and sentences like (161a) or (161c) seem to undermine the idea that the more homogeneous the lexical meaning (lack of polysemy), the more clear-cut the aspectual potential. (These two sentences do not fall within the SVO semantico-syntactic pattern discussed so far.) While *leave* and *arrive* in sentences like (161b) and (161d) clearly have perfective readings, *leave* and *arrive* in sentences like (161a) and (161c) have imperfective rather than perfective readings.[4]

(161) a. It was time for me to leave the party
b. It was the right time for me to leave the party
c. The train was about to arrive at platform five
d. The train arrived at platform five

The sentences in (161) corroborate the thesis about the necessity to analyse aspectual readings of sentences according to the semantico-syntactic pattern they follow. These examples show that the context of use of a verb can really play a decisive role in explicating aspect even at the level of very simple sentences like (161a) or (161c). Note that what is usually very loosely referred to (in traditional grammar and in many aspectological studies) as 'context responsible for the explication of aspect' is not a mysterious construct: it can boil down to some fully analysable and identifiable entity. The following chapter will show the crucial role played by the semantics of nouns for the explication of aspectual distinctions. Here, in (161a), the NP (noun) *time*, non-bounded in itself for lacking an article, can be recognised as the source of non-boundedness which is then mapped onto the (referent of the) verb *leave*. Recall the impact of the bare noun *noise* on the aspectual reading in (23a), in contrast to the use of an article:

(23) a. Noise was heard
b. A noise was heard

Conversely, the expression *the right time* in (161b) may be said to bound the relevant temporal stretch for the action of leaving, thus perfectivising it. And in the other allegedly problematic example, (161c), it is the temporal vagueness introduced through the preposition *about* that creates the uncertainty, hence the non-boundedness, of the arrival. Note that in (161c) the arrival of the train at platform five can easily be cancelled:

(161) cɜ. The train was about to arrive at platform five. But due to some unexpected circumstances the platform was changed and it arrived at platform ten

---

[4] The Bulgarian equivalents confirm this. While sentences (161b) and (161d) are normally translated with a prototypical perfective, the perfective Aorist, (161a) and (161c) require the imperfective Imperfect:

(161) aɜ. Vreme beše da   trăgvam$_{impfv}$/?trăgna$_{pfv}$
        Time   was   to   leave-I
     cɜ. Vlak-ăt   šteše   da   pristiga$_{impfv}$/?da pristigne$_{pfv}$ na   peti   peron
        Train-the would   to   arrive   at   fifth   platform

Thus, the first sentence in the sequence in (161cэ) now even more clearly displays a non-bounded meaning – because the arrival at the inherent endpoint is not effected.[5] All this shows that if the verbs are placed in an appropriate semantico-semantic environment for the explication of a particular aspectual meaning, as the one present in (161b) and (161d), their primary lexical aspectual potential (in this case telicity) comes to the fore. In any case, sentences like those in (161) do not undermine the idea that the more homogeneous the lexical meaning, the more clear-cut the aspectual potential.

PHASE AND OTHER ACHIEVEMENT VERBS

But let us continue the review of verbs with a telic aspectual potential with the type of so-called 'phase' verbs, signifying either the beginning or the end of another action. Sentences with verbs like these are interesting when the subject is inanimate. In spite of the absence here of a typical agent with which actions are usually associated, these sentences are capable of explicating perfectivity. Consider the following three examples from Hornby (1974):

(162) a. The meeting will begin at seven o'clock
     b. The factory has ceased making bicycles
     c. The earthquake stopped all the clocks

For verbs like *begin, cease, stop*, etc. it is only natural that they should explicate perfectivity, for they refer to a more or less momentary transition from one state into another. Linguists have often asked the question whether the general meaning of these verbs can accommodate extension in time or whether it is to be regarded as a sudden, zero-time transition from one state of affairs into another. It is taken for granted in the present approach that a transition, however short, should be regarded as an interval (cf. Lloyd 1979: 28; Dowty 1979: 138-139), and not as a point. (Although even a point can be thought of as something which takes space and, hence, if transferred onto the time axis, it is to take time, albeit of a minimal value.)

Vendler's so-called achievement verbs constitute a small portion of the list of most frequently used verbs in English. Apart from the phase type (*begin, cease,*

---

[5] Although it can be argued that translation into another language is not the best proof of the aspectual meaning of a certain sentence in a certain language, note here that the Bulgarian equivalent of (161cэ) disallows the use of a perfective verb:

(161)   cээ. Vlak-ăt šteše da pristiga$_{impfv}$/*da pristigne$_{pfv}$ na peti peron, no poradi neočakvani obstojatelstva peronyt beše smenen i toj pristigna$_{pfvAor}$ na deseti peron
        'The train was about to arrive at platform five. But due to some unexpected circumstances the platform was changed and it arrived at platform ten'

This cross-language comparison supports the idea that a certain real-world situation described through ordinary language, like the one in (161c), (161cэ) or (161cээ) denoting the expected arrival of a train, has inherent temporal characteristics that can be represented through a "universal" situation – e.g. of the Vendlerian type. In other words, that is in common-sense terms, the arrival of the train in the first clauses in (161c), (161cэ) and (161cээ) is a non-bounded action in the mind of the observer, in contrast to the arrival of the train in (161d) which is a bounded action.

finish, stop), other verbs that could qualify as achievements are *die, discover, find, reach* and *realise*. When achievements are considered in terms of the approach in this book, viz., in terms of the explication of temporal values of actions and their participants, a problem inevitably arises with respect to how temporal values of participants would correspond to the temporal status of achievement verbs. If we go back to the idea of the equivalence of the temporal values of the action and the participants in it, discussed in Chapter Five, *Extension in time of subjects and objects from a "common-sense" point of view*, we will see that assigning a transition with no extension in time to the meaning of the verb would amount to a rejection of the model. Since the temporal values of actions and the participants in them were taken to be equal, if achievements had no extension in time, then the participants would also lack extension in time. And if participants lacked extension in time, this would be tantamount to saying they are non-existent.

The absurdity of such an idea is striking in sentences like (162) above. On the one hand, the stopping of the clocks is something that could be regarded as a sudden transition. But in common-sense terms this event actually takes some time: one clock stopping first, and then another, and then another, until the last one stops – due to differences in the machinery and the momentum of motion. Furthermore, there are different kinds of stopping. Stopping an engine of a car is not a sudden transition. It takes time, sometimes seconds – for example, if the octane number of the petrol is lower than required. And we all know that stopping a car suddenly can be a real ordeal – taking an eternity after treading on the brakes. On the other hand, even if the stopping of the clocks is viewed as a sudden transition, it is carried out through the application of a certain force in time, however short the time may be. Clearly, the stopping of the clocks as an act is equivalent to the action of the earthquake necessary to stop the clocks, and the earthquake could, of course, continue after the clocks have stopped. That is, in sentence (162c) we are talking of the earthquake only in so far as it was the force that caused the clocks to stop, and we are talking of the clocks only in so far as they take part in the act of stopping. Therefore, as in the case of sentences of the type *The boy threw a stone*, here too, the subject and the object can be regarded as having a temporal status identical to that of the action. The transition from one state into another is mainly derived from the meaning of the verb as a lexical entry, but in many cases the borderline between a sudden and a short transition from one state into another is a very fuzzy one.

So far, within the group of most frequently used verbs in English, almost only those verbs that display an aptitude for implying perfective actions (under certain conditions properly defined) have been considered. To sum up, perfectivity of an action is an aspectual meaning that can be observed in an extremely large number of sentences in English and the verb with its telic lexical aspectual potential takes an important part in its explication. Perfectivity is not restricted to sentences denoting physical actions performed by animate agents and affecting physical objects the action of which can easily be visualized as bounded in time. It can be explicated through many other types of telic verbs, for instance:

a) verbs of movement in space with an initial point and an endpoint expressed or implied;
b) verbs denoting mental acts;
c) achievement verbs, denoting a sudden transition from one state into another.

In all these cases the verbs take part in the explication of perfective actions provided certain other conditions in the sentence, already defined, are met.

VERBS WITH AN ATELIC ASPECTUAL POTENTIAL

But what about verbs displaying an aptitude for implying imperfective actions and states?

One of the basic groups of verbs taking part in the explication of imperfective actions, under conditions already defined, is the group denoting movement in space without an initial point and an endpoint expressed or implied. It comprises atelic verbs like *carry, dance, flow, move, roll, row, run, travel, walk*. In contrast to verbs like *escape, fall, leave*, etc., which generally imply movement in space bounded to the left and to the right on the time axis, these verbs do not contain bounds in their lexical meaning. Below are some examples with verbs of this kind:

(163) a. Let me carry your suitcase
       b. The tears flowed from her eyes
       c. Can you row a boat?
       d. The boy rolled the barrel in the cellar
       e. Ivan walked towards the old town

As can easily be seen in these examples, reference to one of the points (an initial point or an endpoint), that might be considered as potentially restricting the action in space, as in (163b) or (163e), or reference to the general location of the movement, as in (163d), is not a hindrance for the action to be conceived of as an imperfective one.

The analysis of examples given so far with verbs usually implying perfective **or** imperfective actions leads to the impression that most verbs in English are simply to be divided into telic and atelic ones. However, although sentences like (164) contain verbs from the sentences in (163) that ought to be defined as atelic ones, the sentences in (164) show that these verbs can easily be associated with perfective actions as well, depending on certain other conditions in the sentence:

(164) a. Let me carry your suitcase to the station
       b. The river flowed over its banks
       c. Can you row the boat across the river?
       d. The boy rolled the barrel into the cellar
       e. Ivan walked to the University/from the old town to the University

The difference between sentences like (163) and (164) is that while in the sentences in (163) the destination (the bound) of the action has not been referred to, and hence the action is conceived of as an imperfective one, in the sentences in (164) the bound of the action has been determined through the use of adverbials, and hence it is conceived of as a perfective one. Obviously, a major role in denoting the bounds of the action is played by prepositions. Compare, for example, the difference in the aspectual readings due to the use of the preposition *in* in (163d) and the preposition *into* in (164d); cf. Heinämäki (1974: 6-9). These examples show, first, that the typical semantico-syntactic conditions for verbs to explicate perfectivity are different from the typical semantico-syntactic conditions for verbs to explicate imperfectivity. Second, the explication of perfectivity or imperfectivity through the influence of an adverbial, whatever the lexical aspectual potential of the verb, corroborates the idea (discussed earlier) of the adverbial as the strongest aspectual marker in the sentence (Danchev 1976).

Furthermore, if we consider again verbs like *paint*, *play*, *read* or *write*, we can establish that they do not greatly differ from verbs like *carry*, *flow*, *row*, *roll*, *walk* with respect to their potential to imply perfective actions, although, when complemented by a quantified direct object, the former tend to explicate perfectivity and the latter imperfectivity. Taken in isolation, that is, without any (syntactic) objects or adverbials, the verbs in both groups are atelic, and appear capable of explicating actions that are non-bounded at both sides of the time axis. To explicate a perfective action, verbs from the former group require a quantified object (a noun accompanied by a quantifier, an article or other determiner). But complementing the latter with a quantified object only does not usually render the resulting phrase/sentence bounded. Besides a quantified object, for the explication of perfectivity an adverbial bounding the scope of the action either temporally (directly) or spatially is also needed. Through the adverbial, the spatial parameters are then transferred onto the time axis. Therefore, on the one hand, it may not appear totally justified to assign telicity or atelicity to any of the verbs in the two groups but, on the other hand, the two types of verbs clearly differ at the level of their complementation with (syntactic) objects. Assigning these verbs 'duality' of the aspectual potential when they are viewed in isolation does not help the solution of the problem, because after all, in principle, all verbs in English have a dual aspectual nature. Hence, ultimately, the assignment of an aspectual potential to verbs in English is to be made according to the semantico-syntactic patterns they appear in. In lexicological and lexicographic terms this requires that the assignment of an aspectual potential is to be made with respect to separate meanings of verbs, not to an abstraction over all or most typical meanings.

MORE ATELIC VERBS

Another group of verbs with an atelic aspectual potential consists of verbs denoting physical actions or states running in time without any movement in space, or with a movement in space which lacks a definite direction. Here belong verbs like *burn*, *dance, grow, lie, rest, sit, sleep, stand, wait, watch, wear, work*. Consider the following examples:

(165) a. Will Mary dance with John?
b. A journal lay open on the top of the desk
c. A large monument stood in the middle of the square
d. Watch the street!
e. Mary wore a nice shawl

Most of these verbs could, however, given appropriate conditions (for example, depending on the use of various prepositions, on their transitive or intransitive use, etc.), also take part in the explication of perfective actions, as in (166):

(166) a. John and Mary danced into the room
b. The worker stood the ladder against the wall
c. The boy has worn his socks into holes

Whether verbs of this kind will imply perfective **or** imperfective actions is usually entirely dependent on the conditions of their use and on the meaning they are assigned in a particular context. For example, *rest* generally appears to be a verb typically expressing a state, as in the following examples:

(167) a. The machine rested on a wooden structure
b. John's father rested in the churchyard

But there are other uses of this verb in which the action is perfective, as in the following examples borrowed from Hornby (1974):

(168) a. We shall rest this field for a year
b. He stopped to rest his horse
c. Rest the ladder against the wall
d. May God rest his soul
e. He stopped to rest

The two blocks of sentences above (167) and (168) show that the explication of perfectivity and imperfectivity often has to do with transitivity and intransitivity. But this is not the ultimate rule either, because in a sentence like (168e) the verb *rest* can be said to imply perfectivity rather than imperfectivity – in view of the pragmatic probability that the rest to be taken will be bounded on the time axis. Still, the perfective reading in (168e) can hardly be said to be much more probable than the imperfective one. Sentence (168a) above presents another specific case. On the one hand, the verb is used transitively and the aspectual reading of the sentence is definitely perfective if the temporal adverbial is excluded from it. On the other hand, doesn't the *for*-time adverbial classify the action denoted by *we shall rest this field* as an imperfective one? Not really. In Chapter Eleven, *The impact of adverbials in the sentence, and aspect in English*, certain prototypical cases of combinations between a verb used perfectively (*return, leave*) and a *for*-time adverbial will be dealt with showing that the *for*-time adverbial does not always function as a test for imperfectivity. Here, too, it could not be argued that the expression *we shall rest this field* is an imperfective one because of its association with a *for*-time adverbial. The variety of examples with the verb *rest* in which the aspectual reading (the perfective or the imperfective one) is not clearly explicated make Hornby's (1974) lexicographic decision, already discussed, to list two separate entries for the verb *rest* appear justified. But other arguments could also be given in favour of one lexical entry for *rest* which will accommodate both the telic and the atelic aspectual potential as separate meanings.

VERBS WITH AN AMBIGUOUS ASPECTUAL POTENTIAL

Thus a certain problem arises which calls for a solution. Some of the examples above show that a verb like *rest* could actually be defined as a lexical entry with an ambiguous aspectual potential. That is, *rest* may be said to belong neither to the group of telic verbs, nor to the group of atelic ones. Therefore, the discussion of verbs with an atelic aspectual potential will have to be postponed temporarily, for there appear to be grounds for establishing a third group of verbs – with a semantic nature that can be defined as aspectually ambiguous and described in two almost opposite ways:

(i) these verbs are capable of implying **either** perfective **or** imperfective actions;

(ii) these verbs impart **neither** perfectivity, **nor** imperfectivity when complemented by a quantified object NP.

Using these verbs in semantico-syntactic patterns that would presuppose the explication of one of the major aspectual values, ambiguous sentences with respect to the perfective/imperfective distinction are formed instead, in which it is hard or impossible to tell whether the action should be read as bounded or non-bounded. However, few sentences in English can clearly exemplify lexical aspectual ambiguity. Apart from the example already given with the verb *rest* (168e) above, consider the sentences in (169) below with the verbs *push*, *rest* and *hold* which easily lend themselves to either of the two aspectual readings:

(169) a. John pushed the trolley
      b. She rested her elbows on the table

c. Her eyes rested on me
d. He held her hand[6]

Verkuyl (1993: 329-333) labelled verbs similar in their behaviour to the verbs in (169) above *push*-verbs, arguing that, at least as a first observation, they constitute a large class. However, not all the verbs below, listed by Verkuyl (1993: 330) as examples of *push*-verbs, really seem ambiguous in their aspectual potential:

draw, caress, hit, iron, turn, stroke, paint, knock, drive, hammer, mow, beautify, rub, help, call

One could suspect the author's judgements for English to have been biased by his mother tongue, Dutch. Maybe the Dutch correspondences of these verbs are ambiguous. But if a class of verbs lexically ambiguous in their aspectual potential (*push*-verbs in Verkuyl's terminology) has to be established, most of the English verbs above do not seem to belong definitely to this class. Among the sentences in (170) below, given as examples by Verkuyl (1993: 330), only (170a) and (170b) sound aspectually ambiguous, (170c) and (170d) sound primarily perfective:

(170) a. John pushed the cart
b. Jessica stroked Shlomie
c. Roland painted the door
d. The council beautified the park

Recall Palmer's (1965: 79) observations, discussed earlier, about the verb *paint*. Thus among the verbs listed above as *push*-verbs by Verkuyl, *draw*, *hit*, *iron*, *turn*, *paint*, *knock*, *mow*, *beautify*, *help* and *call* seem to belong to the group of telic verbs (some of these have already been considered), *drive* [*a car*] may be said to belong to the group of atelic verbs, and only *caress* [*somebody*], *hammer* [*the metal*], *stroke* [*somebody*] and *rub* [*the medicine*] seem to be the appropriate candidates for the class of *push*-verbs. But whether judgements are subjective with respect to some verbs or not, whether verbs like *push* constitute a large or a small class, the existence of verbs in English that are ambiguous in their lexical aspectual potential could hardly be questioned.

---

[6] The rendering of these sentences into Bulgarian also reflects the ambiguity/duality of their aspectual reading. Cf. the Bulgarian sentences below, where (169a) = (169a'), etc.:
(169) a'. 'Džon ?pritika$_{pfvAor}$/?tikaše$_{impfvImp}$ količkata'
b'. 'Tja ?složi$_{pfvAor}$/?slagaše$_{impfvImp}$ laktite si na masata'
c'. 'Pogledǎt j ?sprja$_{pfvAor}$/?padaše$_{impfvImp}$ vǎrhu men'
d'. 'Toj ?hvana$_{pfvAor}$/?dǎržeše$_{impfvImp}$ rǎkata j'
That is, translation would be adequate neither through a perfective, nor through an imperfective verb form and the choice of one or the other would depend on the context in which the sentences in (169) would be placed.

CHAPTER 9

ON THE DIVISION BETWEEN TELICITY, ATELICITY AND ASPECTUAL AMBIGUITY

In any case, the divisions between atelicity and lexical aspectual ambiguity, on the one hand, and telicity and lexical aspectual ambiguity, on the other, do not appear to be neat. It could even be argued that there are different degrees of telicity, or that the distinction between atelicity, aspectual ambiguity and telicity can be represented as a continuum. Although a thesis of this kind will not be specifically explored here, it could be supported by an analysis of some of the sentences already discussed – with verbs used transitively. Thus while a sentence like (100a) explicates imperfectivity and the verb in it is definitely atelic, (170a) clearly contains a verb that is lexically ambiguous with respect to the telic/atelic distinction. But the verb *paint* in (170c) and (16a) tends to move up the scale of telicity. While a sentence like (170c) is aspectually ambiguous according to Verkuyl, a sentence like (16a) does not necessarily refer to a completed event according to Palmer:

(100) a. The boy carried a stone
(170) a. John pushed the cart
      c. Roland painted the door
(16) a. I painted the table this morning

Further up the scale of telicity, a verb like *climb* can be found, and, still higher, a verb like *build*:

(46) b. A tourist climbed the mountain
(71) b. John built a house

The verb *climb* and the phrase *climb the mountain* in (46b) seem to contribute more significantly to the explication of perfectivity than do the verb *painted* or the phrase *painted the door/the table* in (170c) and (16a). But, as will be seen later on, in Chapter Eleven, *The impact of adverbials in the sentence, and aspect in English*, a phrase like *climb the mountain* easily allows, according to some speakers, the complementation of a *for*-time adverbial, generally considered to be a good test for imperfectivity, while in a sentence like (71b) the verb *build* contributes very strongly to the explication of perfectivity. As will be shown in Chapter Thirteen, *On aspectual classes in English*, a phrase like *build the house* tends to disallow the cancellation of perfectivity through context, in contrast to phrases like *climb the mountain*.

GROUPS OF ATELIC VERBS

Finally, to return to the discussion of atelic verbs, these can be divided into two groups. The first group denotes states like possession, membership and typicality. The second group consists of verbs denoting emotions and feelings (mixed with certain nuances of attitude or judgement), other mental dispositions and states that cannot be controlled by the entity they are predicated of. Verbs like *be, contain, consist of, own* and *possess* belong to the former group, and *desire, enjoy, hate, love, miss, require, respect, seem, value, want* belong to the latter. (The verb *fear*, although it is not in the list of most commonly used verbs, has also been discussed as an example of a 'psych' verb with an atelic aspectual potential.) The verb *have* partakes of both groups and, besides, is also capable of associating itself with perfectivity in many phrases like *have a look, have a shower*, etc. – these will be dealt with in the following chapter. Below are some typical sentences with atelic verbs in which *X* and *Y* stand for an appropriate and typical (syntactic) subject and an object, respectively:

(171) a. X was/contained/consisted of/owned/possessed Y
 b. X hated/loved/respected/valued Y
 c. X missed Y

Many synonyms of these verbs, given the appropriate conditions, would also tend to imply imperfectivity. Note again that, as in the example (144i) above (repeated below), the subjects in (171) are not agents. As will be shown also later on in the book, the notion of perfectivity is most often associated with agentivity which, in its turn, is one of the prototypical features of the notion of subject.

(144) i. John feared the truth

Here the problem of how to represent the temporal values and configurations of the (referents of the) subjects, verbs and objects in sentences like (171) arises again. The difference, not exactly in temporal terms, between the referents of subjects of stative and non-stative (e.g. agentive) sentences was noted a long time ago by Miller (1970) who postulated different cases, in Fillmore's (1968) sense, for subjects and objects of stative and non-stative sentences and pointed out that the similarity of the two subject nouns *on* 'he' in the Russian sentences *On ponimaet problemu* 'He understands the problem' and *On pišet pis'mo* 'He is writing a letter' is superficial and misleading (Miller 1970: 498). Recall that according to the present approach the referent of *hated* in a sentence like (112a) is non-bounded and maps this non-boundedness, which is a temporal feature, onto the referents of the subject-NP and the object-NP.

(112) a. John hated Mary

The same would be valid for many other similar sentences with referents of subjects and objects that can be regarded as potentially bounded. Of course, in sentences like (144i) the non-boundedness of the referent of *feared* cannot be said to be mapped onto the referent of the object *the truth*, simply because the referent of the object *the truth*, in spite of the definite article, is not bounded. (The problem concerning abstract nouns and their contribution to the explication of aspectual values in the sentence will be dealt with in the following chapter.) In Verkuyl's theory, however, especially in its extended version (Verkuyl 1993), NPs like *Schumann's cello concerto* in sentences like (45b) are taken to be atemporal, in contrast to NPs like *Schumann's cello concerto* in sentences like (45a).

(45) a. Fritz played Schumann's cello concerto
b. Fritz hated Schumann's cello concerto

It may be strange why stative verbs and, consequently, their arguments, should be associated with atemporality, but this seems to be the general assumption in the aspectological literature. However, the assumption is rarely worded explicitly, as in the following passage:

> "Events seem to be in some sense temporary, while states of affairs are potentially atemporal, like the world being round, or the earth revolving around the sun"

(Hinrichs 1986: 67). On the contrary, according to the present approach, states of affairs, although they appear to be, most generally speaking, lengthier than events, ought to be regarded as temporal. A ceaseless action like the earth revolving around the sun or even a property like the world being round can be said to have some time scope, however hard this time scope may be to conceive or imagine because of its length. And, of course, other states, like hating or loving somebody or being tall, for example, are also temporal – for there inevitably comes a point in which they no longer hold. It actually seems very strange for Hinrichs to propose viewing states as being atemporal when one takes into account his analysis of stages of objects (Hinrichs 1985) based on Carlson (1977/1980). And it is really incomprehensible why such an idea should be prevalent in aspectology.

CONCLUSION

To sum up the analysis in this chapter, the inevitable and most essential conclusion it leads to is actually similar to the idea put forward by Voroncova (1948) half a century ago: all or at least most verbs in English can be said to possess a certain aspectual potential. Some other conclusions about the aspectual potential of English verbs as lexical entries are:

(i) the enormous majority of verbs in English are either telic or atelic;
(ii) most verbs in English are telic;
(iii) due to the fuzziness of the distinction, even an approximately valid percentage cannot be proposed, but, very roughly, the group of telic verbs in English is several times larger than the group of atelic verbs;
(iv) there is an extremely small number of verbs in English that can be said to be definitely ambiguous in their aspectual potential.

Of course, the aspectual potential of verbs proposed here forms part of a larger compositional aspect mechanism, whereas the aspectual nature of verbs in Voroncova

(1948) and in other publications is described in broad impressionistic terms. The lexical aspectual potential of verbs plays an important part in the aspectual composition of the sentence, whereby most sentences in English, even when isolated from a larger context, can be unambiguously interpreted as explicating either perfectivity or imperfectivity. And whether the verb in a given simple sentence contributes to a smaller or larger degree to the overall aspectual meaning, whether the aspectual meaning is presupposed by the verb or is transferred onto it through the mechanism of mapping, the verb can always be said to imply or explicate, not express, the aspectual meaning of a sentence. A general rule can now be postulated, which is valid for the compositional explication of aspect (i.e., it does not concern sentences in which the Progressive is used):

> Aspect in English is systematically expressed compositionally in almost any meaningful sentence in English viewed in isolation. In the overwhelming majority of cases its basically perfective or imperfective aspectual meaning can be unambiguously identified on the basis of a combination between the lexical meaning of the verb and the contribution of the NPs with their grammatical forms and their lexical meanings.

Meanings of NPs/nouns will be discussed in further detail in the following chapter. Verification of the rule proposed above can always be made, even without reference to translation equivalents in languages where aspect is marked in the verb. For example, check any sentence in a dictionary like Hornby's (1974), where examples are given outside real discourse but the context (the setting of the event or state) is usually transparent. The aspectual meaning of such a sentence illustrating a particular word in the dictionary will, in most cases, easily be worked out in terms of the regularities discussed in this book. Hence, what is surprising is that grammars of English have so far proved unable to describe the ability of structural language entities like verbs, phrases and sentences to distinguish between perfectivity and imperfectivity. And the failure of English grammars to describe the compositional mechanism of aspect is unfortunate also in terms of the idea that aspect forms part and parcel of the semantics of any language.

CHAPTER 10

MEANINGS OF NOUNS AND NOUN PHRASES, AND ASPECT IN ENGLISH

'HAVE A LOOK' AND SIMILAR PATTERNS FROM AN ASPECTUAL POINT OF VIEW

The analysis in the previous chapter showed that English verbs display flexibility with respect to aspect distinctions. Verbs whose basic function is to denote states could in certain conditions be associated with the explication of actions, even perfective ones. Consider the verb *have*. Although it is primarily a state verb, in English there are many interesting phrases like *have a look, have a meeting, have a listen, have a try*, which fall together with a very large number of similar expressions like *take a walk, give (something) a try, make an announcement, get a knock, commit murder, exercise power, pay a visit*, the properties of which have drawn the attention of linguists for a long time (cf., e.g. Olsson 1961; Live 1965). The verb in these phrases can be regarded as a quasi-auxiliary or as one that is deprived of a large part of its primary lexical meaning. The essence of the action in these expressions is denoted by the noun rather than the verb, and the noun often has a verb equivalent: *have a look at something (= to look at something), have a meeting with somebody (= to meet somebody), have a sleep (= to sleep)*, etc.

Sometimes the noun semantically equivalent to a verb and designating an action is not in common use and is mainly encountered in special collocations of the type in question: e.g., *listen* in *have a listen, lie-in* in *have a lie-in*, etc. This group of phrases is often referred to as the *have a look* type of phrases and several verbal lexemes are especially frequent in it: *have (a look, a meeting, a try), make (an announcement, a call, a jump), give (an answer, a cry), take (action, a dive, a step), do (a dance, a favour, one's work)*. The verbs *get (a knock, satisfaction)* and *commit (adultery, a crime)* have somewhat specialised functions: the former usually produces phrases with a passive meaning (equivalent to verbs in the passive voice), and the latter is restricted mainly to combinations with nouns denoting deplorable acts. Less frequent are a couple of other verbs like *effect (payment), exercise (power, one's rights), pay (a compliment, tribute, a visit)*, etc. The verb *have* is especially productive in forming collocations like *have a drink, have a listen, have a smoke, have a walk* that are a specific trait of contemporary English phraseology, while phrases like *make a jump, take a decision, give an answer, do a favour* are common in many other modern languages as well.

As noted long ago (see e.g. Mincoff 1958: 113, Olsson 1961, Live 1965), these phrases have to do with aspect distinctions, especially the expression of perfectivity. But the linguists who dealt with them failed to explain how the meaning of perfectivity is explicated. A peculiarity of Modern English, these phrases offer a marvellous example of the mapping mechanism already described in Chapter Six, *The mechanism for mapping the temporal values of subjects and objects*. Phrases with the verb *have* and an action-designating noun in the singular are used frequently to explicate boundedness/perfectivity because very often the verb out of which the noun is formed has an atelic aspectual potential (cf. in this respect Live 1965). Thus sentences like (172) below are perfective while sentences like (173) are imperfective:

(172) a. John had a swim in the river
    b. John had a smoke outside
    c. John had a hearty laugh [in the sense of a single act]
(173) a. John swam in the river
    b. John smoked outside
    c. John laughed heartily

Note that while the verb *have* usually displays a marked propensity towards non-boundedness, also across languages, and is mainly associated with the expression of long-lasting states like possession, membership, typicality, etc., the stative nature of *have* is suppressed in this class of expressions, and in the verb phrases in sentences like (172) boundedness is mapped from the (referent of the) NP onto the (referent of the) verb thus turning the meaning of the whole VP and the sentence bounded. Or, diagrammatically, for instance, the interaction between the NP *a swim* and the verb *had* within the VP *had a swim* in (172a) could be represented in the following fashion:

(172) a. John had a swim in the river

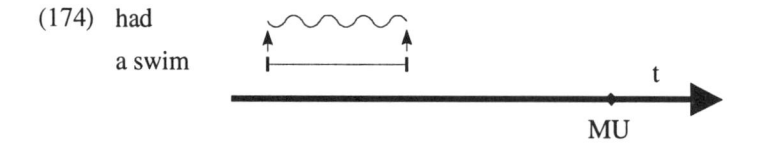

(174) had
    a swim

    MU   t

That is, the referent of *a swim* maps its boundedness onto the referent of *had*, making it bounded. Also, according to one of the major theses in this book, subjects like *John* in agentive sentences like (172a) contribute to the explication of perfectivity, and it is the article through which the boundedness of an NP like *a swim* is marked (and then transferred onto the referent of the verb). However, is it the article alone that is responsible in this type of sentences for explicating boundedness – for example, for explicating the boundedness of the object-NP *a swim* in (172a) above?

As already mentioned, the *have a look* paradigm includes not only phrases with the verb *have*, but also with *take, give, make, get, pay*, and some other verbs. In phrases of this type boundedness of the action is almost always explicated when the noun is accompanied by an indefinite article, although in many cases the verb itself of which the noun is formed may display a marked propensity towards boundedness as a lexical item. Compare, e.g., the verbs *kiss, jump* and *visit* in (112b), (175a) and (175b) below, which have a telic aspectual potential and the sentences they are used in are perfective. And the broadly equivalent sentences (176) with the phrases *give a kiss, make a jump* and *pay a visit* are also perfective:

(112) b. John kissed Mary
(175) a. John jumped the fence
       b. John visited Mary
(176) a. John gave Mary a kiss
       b. John made a jump over the fence
       c. John paid a visit to Mary

As has already been maintained, the explication or, more broadly, the expression, of perfectivity, is important for human communication, hence the existence and the relatively high frequency of use of these phrases. The analysis proposed here along the lines of boundedness and non-boundedness in the NPs transferred onto the verb differs, however, from most of the other approaches. For example, Galton (1984: 66-68) insists that a sentence like (177a) below is telic while (177b) is atelic, although, at least according to the model assumed in this work, both *a length* and *a swim* are bounded:

(177) a. Jane swam a length
       b. Jane had a swim

It can be argued that an approach of the kind proposed by Galton, based on logical considerations divorced from grammatical and typological structural reality, fails to explain where meanings like boundedness and non-boundedness or telicity and atelicity are derived from in a particular language.

Besides phrases in which the noun is equivalent to a verb, in English there also exist many expressions with a similar agentive meaning in which the noun accompanied by an indefinite article has no verbal equivalent. The boundedness of the overall action could, again, most readily be associated with the article. Consider the sentences in (178):

(178) a. John had/gave a party
       b. John had a meal
       c. John committed an offence

But for the moment let us assume that it is the article indeed that is responsible for the expression of boundedness in (172), (176), (177) and (178) above because its elimination, along with a pluralisation of the noun, normally leads to the expression of non-boundedness of the action (compare the phrases *had laughs*, *paid visits*, *gave parties*, *committed offences*, etc.), and because there are other cases where its absence will indeed be associated with non-boundedness. Compare sentences of type (179):

(179) a. John had respect [for his parents]
      b. John felt hatred [for his nasty neighbours]

Let us also assume that phrases like those listed in (180) and (181) below, quite numerous as they may be, are really an exception to the rule to have an article where boundedness is explicated in the whole expression and to have no article where non-boundedness is explicated. Obviously the verb within the expression is not the only factor to blame for the irregularity in all these cases:

VERB-NOUN PHRASES WITH NO ARTICLE, WITH A BOUNDED MEANING

	IN THE SINGULAR	IN THE PLURAL
(180)	make use of	shake hands
	give rise to	exchange glances
	take part in	take measures
	express concern	express thanks
	take advantage	offer condolences
	set foot on something	settle matters
	restore order	hold talks
	have breakfast, lunch, etc.	carry out negotiations
	show/have mercy	
	provoke laughter	
	cause destruction	

VERB-NOUN PHRASES, WITH AN ARTICLE, WITH A NON-BOUNDED MEANING

(181) have a desire
      have a sense of humour (etc.)
      serve a purpose
      owe an excuse

Could the existence of such deviant phrases be disregarded and explained away through conventionalisation, idiomatisation, economy of expression or, in the last resort, through arbitrariness, a feature most commonly found in natural language? Perhaps a more powerful explanation of the "irregular" use of the article or zero article in (180) and (181) above could be that the article does indeed mark boundedness as one of its major functions in language, but since this function is covered (cf. Kabakčiev 1984b, as well as earlier discussions here), other, more pragmatically-oriented functions like definiteness and indefiniteness, whatever they stand for exactly, eventually override its use. More on this problem later, in Chapter Fourteen, *On 'knowledge of the world' in the explication of aspect in English*.

LEXICAL MEANINGS OF NOUNS

A closer inspection of some of the phrases above will show that boundedness and non-boundedness can be identified not only as a result of the use and non-use of the article. As noted earlier elsewhere (Kabakčiev 1989), boundedness and non-boundedness can be regarded as semantic features that make up an important part of the lexical meaning of many abstract nouns (or, rather, nouns that refer to abstract entities)[1]. This point has rarely been dealt with in the literature (see, e.g., Lyons 1977: 714; Langacker 1987/1991) and usually minor observations are made with respect to it when aspect is considered. Bache (1983: 154-155) notes that while a noun like *explosion* in (182a) is "clearly punctual", a noun like *peace* in (182b) is "clearly durative":

(182) a. The explosion occurred at three o'clock
      b. Peace lasted only a couple of months

It can be argued, however, that if, taken in isolation, the entities denoted by *the explosion* and *peace* are bounded and non-bounded respectively, the entity *peace* in (182b) seems to be bounded in a certain sense, as the adverbial expression *only a couple of months* can be said to bound *peace* in time. (The problem of boundedness introduced by *for*-time phrases is dealt with in more detail in Chapter Thirteen, *On aspectual classes in English*.) Recently Bartsch (1995: 21) suggested that pairs like *destruction/destroying* and *performance/performing* should be seen as largely reflecting the perfective/imperfective distinction. But in its temporal characteristics *destruction* as a lexical entry seems to resemble *peace* rather than *explosion* above and, as will be shown below, a noun like *performance* does not necessarily (or always) denote a bounded entity. A little earlier, Zucchi (1993) analysed more extensively similar relations between verbs and nouns, but from a rather different perspective, also focusing more on the differences between gerundive and ordinary nominals than on the inherent lexical properties of ordinary nouns.

According to many of the observations already made with respect to the explication of aspect at the level of the sentence in English and the contribution of the nominal components to the aspectual reading, it can be argued that certain abstract

---

[1] Analogously, 'concrete nouns' should, of course, be read as 'nouns that refer to concrete, material entities', a 'perfective sentence' as 'a sentence with a perfective meaning', etc.

nouns refer to entities that are inherently bounded while other abstract nouns refer to entities that are inherently non-bounded. The distinction coincides to a large extent with the well-known basic grammatical distinction between countable and non-countable (also termed count and non-count) which is mainly applied to and illustrated by concrete nouns but it is valid with respect to abstract nouns as well. Material entities are countable **in space**, abstract entities are often (but not always) countable **in time**. Abstract entities are not always countable in time because not all abstract nouns refer to temporal entities – consider, e.g., nouns designating different measuring units like *inch*, *litre*, *watt*, *byte*, etc. or other operational entities like *height*, *weight*, *length* (or even nouns like *method*, *technique*, etc. in their non-temporal sense). Compare the following two groups of nouns denoting abstract entities:

ABSTRACT NOUNS, TEMPORALLY BOUNDED
(183) a. bath, concert, fall, game, instruction, jump, kick, knock, life, nod, operation, party, passage, push, smile, tap

ABSTRACT NOUNS, TEMPORALLY NON-BOUNDED
b. amusement, beauty, destruction, evil, good, grace, hate, health, imagination, laughter, love, power, strength, virtue

Rapid and purposeful movements denoted by nouns like *jump*, *kick*, *knock*, *nod*, *push*, *smile*, *tap* in (183a) can easily be seen as bounded, whereas capabilities, evils, virtues, feelings and the like, denoted by nouns like those in (183b), can easily be seen as non-bounded. The examples below confirm the conjecture. The sentences in (184) with a subject usually denoting a human agent X (X is not an agent in the second and in the fifth sentence) describe perfective actions. Those in (185), where X is human but not an agent, describe imperfective situations:

(184) a. X had a bath
 b. X had a nasty fall
 c. X made a jump
 d. X gave a party
 e. X lived a nice life
(185) a. X had power/strength/imagination
 b. X was filled with love/hate/guilt

Recall Miller's (1970: 498) postulation of different cases for subjects and objects of stative and non-stative sentences, as encountered in the difference between the two subjects in sentences like *He understands the problem* and *He is writing a letter*. Clearly, however, another difference can be found too – in the temporal boundedness of X in (184b) and (184e), on the one hand, and the temporal non-boundedness of X in (185a) and (185b), on the other, despite the non-agentivity of the subject in all these cases.

Note also again, as in the discussion of the irrelevance of the shortness or length of a situation denoted by a verb, that referents of nouns denoting more or less momentary actions like *push, jump*, etc. can be seen as bounded as the referents of nouns denoting time-consuming actions like *bath, party*, and especially *life*. That is, *push, jump, bath, party* and *life* are all bounded: they have a definite beginning and a definite end on the time axis, in contrast to the entities denoted by *power, strength, imagination, love, hate* and *guilt*, which are non-bounded, with no definite beginning and no definite end on the time axis – in the protoypical sense of all these words.

But the explication of perfectivity is, of course, by no means necessarily restricted to or dependent on the use of nouns like those in (183a). And, conversely, the explication of imperfectivity is by no means restricted to, or dependent on, the use of nouns like those in (183b). For example, sentences like those in (186) below are capable of explicating perfectivity of actions associated with nouns basically denoting non-bounded entities (*strength, imagination, guilt*), and sentences like those in (187) are capable of signifying imperfective actions associated with nouns basically denoting bounded entities (*game, film*) – at least in the progressive-like reading of (187a) and (187b):

(186) a. John increased his physical strength by exercise
 b. John used his imagination in solving the mystery
 c. John confessed his guilt
(187) a. John watched the game
 b. John enjoyed the film

Nouns like *strength, imagination* and *guilt* denoting non-bounded entities in isolation (as lexical entries) are in this case (186) forced into explicating boundedness of the referents. Conversely, nouns like *game* and *film* primarily denoting bounded entities are in this case (187) forced into explicating non-boundedness of the referents in the progressive-like reading of the sentences. This is effected through the interaction of meanings within the whole sentence or, if the problem is analysed at a higher level of abstraction, through the mechanism of mapping. Hence the general necessity to use determiners, like *his* in the case of (186), with non-bounded nouns when they are used in association with verbs explicating boundedness. Of course, as already shown in examples like those in (180) above, this is just a general tendency, not an absolute rule.

As already mentioned, the terms '(temporally) bounded' and '(temporally) non-bounded' when applied to nouns could, in a certain sense, be seen as equivalent to the usual terms 'count(able)' and 'non-count(able)'. Recall, however, that features like temporal boundedness and temporal non-boundedness in concrete nouns are inaccessible to the intuitions of the ordinary speaker, even when considered at the level of the sentence. When abstract nouns are considered, the ordinary speaker/hearer may be not fully aware of the difference between temporal boundedness and temporal non-boundedness – as exemplified in nouns like those in (183a) and (183b), respectively. But these two nominal features will certainly be much more accessible to the ordinary speaker, depending on his/her education, age, experience, intelligence, etc. Temporality constitutes a basic characteristic of the lexical meaning of many, or even most, if not all, nouns designating abstract entities, and boundedness and non-boundedness may sometimes attract the attention of the speaker or hearer – if, in a particular case, these notions bear some pragmatic significance.

Approaching the problem of lexical meanings of nouns in a broadly similar fashion, Langacker (1991: 99) admits that

"abstract nominals pose many subtle problems that have barely been explored"

See also similar conclusions in a recent article by Brinton (1998). Langacker maintains that nouns like *hope*, *fear*, and *belief* "designate the object of the imperfective process", while other "deverbal nominalisations [...] designate a single instance of the perfective process indicated by the verb stem: *an explosion, a jump, a throw, a yell, a kick, a walk*, etc." (Langacker 1991: 98-99). Langacker's approach to aspect differs substantially, however, from the present one. For instance, he regards verbs as designating perfectivity even when they are used in the Progressive and assigns perfective values to verbs like *lie* or *lack* (see Langacker 1987: 86, 94-95) – which, to use Vendler's classification, belong to the activity or state class.

A proposal of this kind is not entirely new. An aspectological analysis based on the Simple/Progressive contrast in English was offered in Hirtle (1967); similar is Smith's (1991) model, discussed in detail earlier. The objection to be raised is that an approach to aspect advanced in terms of the English Simple/Progressive contrast will fail to match the description of aspect in typological terms. It conflicts with data from cross-language or language-comparative investigations (e.g. Markkanen 1979; Lindstedt 1984; 1985; Dahl 1985; Bybee et al 1994). Even if some of these studies did not posit a universal perfective/imperfective or bounded/non-bounded contrast behind the language data they explored, they certainly showed that aspect goes beyond the Progressive/Non-Progressive distinction in the verbal system of English and that this distinction can hardly be used as a universal tool for analysing aspect. The reason can be seen in the fact that while the Progressive is clearly an aspect form (an imperfective one), its counterpart, the Non-Progressive, cannot be said to have its own aspectual value. Non-progressive forms acquire a default value through the compositional mechanism, such as the one already described in this work.

On the basis of the analysis carried out so far in this chapter it can be maintained that in English the indefinite article either supports the lexical temporal boundedness of the abstract noun, thus explicating boundedness of the action at the level of the phrase or sentence, see (178) above, or is absent in the NP when the noun lacks the semantic feature of boundedness in time, see (179) above, (cf. Kabakčiev 1989: 16-17). In other words, either temporal boundedness or temporal non-boundedness is present, and prevalent over the opposite value, in the lexical semantic structure of many nouns. There are other cases, however, in which neither temporal boundedness, nor temporal non-boundedness can be found as an inherent lexical feature of a noun. Recall *noise*, as in the sentences (23) and (149), already discussed:

(23) a. Noise was heard
 b. A noise was heard
(149) a. We heard noise
 b. We heard a noise

In these cases the article can be said to mark boundedness directly on the noun – and again, at the level of a phrase or a sentence, perfectivity is explicated.

Compare now some similar cases of a lack of a lexical feature 'boundedness' or 'non-boundedness' in the nouns in the examples below. In the expressions in (188a) the object NP contains an article and they are perfective (bounded). Conversely, in the otherwise similar expressions in (188b) the object NP does not contain an article and they are imperfective (non-bounded):

PERFECTIVE (BOUNDED) EXPRESSIONS
(188) a. have a nice time [somewhere]
 [the ability to] learn a language
 dance/play a tango
 play a ball
 kick an ass

IMPERFECTIVE (NON-BOUNDED) EXPRESSIONS
 b. have time [to do something]
 [the ability to] learn language
 dance/play tango
 play ball
 kick ass[2]

Verb expressions like those listed in (188) appear to be infrequent in English and, furthermore, at a first glance they create the impression that an article (be it definite or indefinite) could rarely be used or omitted in patterns similar to those in (188) for the expression of perfectivity vs. imperfectivity. However, a closer investigation, especially of texts that are more technically or scientifically oriented, may reveal a much larger degree of availability of means in English to express perfectivity and imperfectivity through the use or the omission of an article. Cf. the (a) and (b) sentences or phrases below extracted from texts in the social, medical and technical sciences. It can easily be felt that the (a) sentences/phrases in (189) through (195), containing an article, are either used perfectively or are at least likely to be read in this way. Conversely, the (b) sentences below describe imperfective situations. Each of the (b) sentences denotes either an action that is repeated an indefinite number of times or a more or less permanent state obtaining within an indefinite (non-bounded) period of time. It was precisely the imperfective (b) sentences, i.e., the ones that

---

[2] The availability of pairs like *kick an ass/kick ass* in substandard English was pointed out to me by Gerald Mayer.

would be felt to be less likely to appear, that were registered in texts, while their (a) counterparts were constructed:

(189) a. The temperature dropped quickly
b. Temperature dropped quickly
(190) a. [This is a way to] avoid the pressure
b. [This is a way to] avoid pressure
(191) a. [the necessity to] prevent the inflation
b. [the necessity to] prevent inflation
(192) a. The fatigue was caused [by the wrong dosage]
b. Fatigue was caused [by the wrong dosage]
(193) a. The most marked suppression was seen in the therapeutic dose ranges
b. Most marked suppression was seen in the therapeutic dose ranges
(194) a. [By using a good antenna you can] raise the input signal level
b. [By using a good antenna you can] raise input signal level
(195) a. The frequency response can be determined electronically
b. Frequency response can be determined electronically

Consider also a sentence like (196a) below, borrowed from Hornby (1974: 802). The concrete count noun *table* in it is unaccompanied by an article – bringing about the imperfective reading of *sit* in this particular sentence. Sentence (196a) forms a very clear contrast with a sentence like (196b) in which the verb *sit* refers to a single act on a particular occasion, that is, perfectivity is explicated.

(196) a. The child is not big enough to sit at table yet
b. The child is not big enough to sit at the table yet

Although it would rather be a task for native speakers of English to assess the validity and the exact scale of the phenomenon described above, the authentic examples here demonstrate that not only is it valid; it could hardly be regarded as accidental or restricted to a handful of sentences.

Obviously, the bounded/non-bounded distinction does not reside in abstract nouns the way features like 'animate' or 'inanimate' (or even to a certain degree 'countable' and 'non-countable' for that matter) are either present or absent in the semantics of concrete nouns. In addition to the data presented in (189) – (195) and the four sentences with the noun *noise* in (23) and (149) discussed earlier, let us formulate in some more detail the way an entity like 'noise' can be perceived or conceived of. The temporal entity 'noise' can be perceived or conceived of:

(i) as a bounded interval, with a definite beginning and an end, as, for example, the banging of a door or the roar of a passing train – short or long as it may be; or,

(ii) as non-bounded, without a definite beginning and an end, like, for example, the permanent hum of machines in a factory or of motor vehicles in road traffic.

Or take the noun *movement*. The temporal entity 'movement' can be perceived or conceived of as:

(i) bounded, cf. the movement of one's hand to wave somebody through; or,
(ii) non-bounded, cf. in the incessant movement of one's fingers when, say, knitting, typing, or playing the piano.

Compare now a sentence like (197a), which explicates non-boundedness of the action denoted by the NP *movement*, and a sentence like (197b), which explicates boundedness of the action denoted by the NP *a movement*:

(197) a. The animal lay in the grass without movement
 b. The children noticed the bird in the tree because it made a movement

If the contrastive metalanguage test is employed again, the difference imposed by the two prepositional phrases *without movement* and *without a movement* in English would have to be rendered in Bulgarian through verbs that have to be perfective and imperfective, respectively. Compare the Bulgarian sentences (198a) and (198b) which are translation equivalents of the English sentences (197a) and (197b), respectively:

(198) a. Zivotno-to ležeše_{impfvImp} v treva-ta bez da pomrădva_{Imp}
 Animal-the lay in grass-the without to move
 'The animal lay in the grass without movement'

 b. Deca-ta zabeljazaha_{pfvAor} ptica-ta v dărvo-to, zaštoto tja napravi_{pfvAor} dviženie
 Children-the noticed bird-the in tree-the, because it made movement
 'The children noticed the bird in the tree because it made a movement'

Translating an English sentence like (197a) into Bulgarian literally, that is, through an adverbial like *bez dviženie* 'without movement' would yield an ungrammatical sentence (199):

(199) *Zivotno-to ležeše_{impfvImp} v treva-ta bez dviženie
 Animal-the lay in grass-the without movement

This cross-language comparison may seem superficial at first sight. Actually, it favours an important conclusion, namely, that English constructions of the type found in (197a) and (197b), that are also, undoubtedly, fairly productive, perform an essential function. They serve to explicate aspectual values in the sentence through the use of quantified vs. non-quantified nouns/NPs.[3] In English, the explication of

---

[3] Conversely, in Bulgarian, a noun like *dviženie* 'movement' does not at all take part in the explication of aspect, because aspect is not explicated – it is directly expressed by the verb(s) in the

the aspectual value is effected not only through the aspectual potential of the verb (cf. the verbs *lay* and *made* – the former with an atelic, the latter with a telic potential), but mainly through a subtle interplay between the structure of the noun phrase (presence vs. absence of an article) and a semantic feature in the lexical meaning of the noun (lack of temporal boundedness or non-boundedness).

The productivity of the constructions mentioned above can be exemplified by phrases like those in (200) and (201) below. *A motion* is bounded in (200a), *motion* is non-bounded in (201a). A large number of other nouns in English are capable of following identical semantico-syntactic patterns. Compare the temporal boundedness of *a swing* in (200b) and the temporal non-boundedness of *swing* in (201b); the temporal boundedness of *a conversation* in (200c) and the temporal non-boundedness of *conversation* in (201c), the temporal boundedness of *a performance* in (200d) and the temporal non-boundedness of *performance* in (201d):

(200) a. make a motion
 b. make a swing
 c. have a conversation
 d. offer a theatrical performance
(201) a. be in motion
 b. be in full swing
 c. be in conversation
 d. offer optimal performance [of a machine, product, etc.]

In (200), a completed act (an accomplishment, in Vendler's terms) on a particular occasion is signified, whereas the phrases in (201) refer either to a current or a permanent state (see also Kabakčiev 1989: 16-17).

Of course, it should not be forgotten that, while the patterns of (200) and (201) are productive and aspectologically relevant, there are many "exceptions to the rule" of having an article in the explication of boundedness and having a zero article in the explication of non-boundedness. First, recall the bounded/perfective expressions without an article (or any other determiner/quantifier) in (180) and the non-bounded/ imperfective expressions with an article in (181):

---

corresponding sentences, cf. (198), (199). It is especially noteworthy that in Bulgarian, on the one hand, there is no construction similar to the *without movement* phrase in English in (197a), and, on the other hand, the NP *dviženie* 'movement' in (198b) and in similar constructions is not accompanied by the pseudoarticle *edin* 'one' or by some other determiner/quantifier. This is a perfect illustration of at least two major theses advanced earlier in the book: (i) the lack of necessity to have an indefinite article in the Bulgarian nominal system, because perfectivity is expressed directly by the verb; (ii) in English, the situation is different, and the indefinite article is essential – it serves to mark boundedness which must then be transferred onto the referent of the verb. Actually, these two theses merge into one (sweeping) generalisation, already made: in language, you need to have a marker of temporal boundedness either in the verb or in the noun.

(180)   make use of   shake hands
          give rise to   exchange glances
          take part in   take measures
          express concern   express thanks
          take advantage   offer condolences
          set foot on something   settle matters
          restore order   hold talks
          have breakfast, lunch, etc.   carry out negotiations
          show/have mercy
          provoke laughter
          cause destruction

(181)   have a desire
          have a sense of humour (etc.)
          serve a purpose
          owe an excuse

Second, some of the reasons for the explication of boundedness and non-boundedness in many cases may rest in the verb or at least the verb may be held partly responsible. Thus while *make* in the phrases in (200a) and (200b), repeated below, contributes to the explication of boundedness/perfectivity with its telic aspectual potential, the string *be in* in (201a) and (201b) imparts stativeness, i.e., non-boundedness/imperfectivity, to the whole expression. Hence, the lack of an indefinite article could also be regarded as a consequence of the imposed/required imperfectivity:

(200) a. make a motion
       b. make a swing
(201) a. be in motion
       b. be in full swing

The non-boundedness/imperfectivity of the expressions in (201a) and (201b) may be said to be due to the atelic aspectual potential of the verb *be* combined with the general semantics of the preposition *in*. Recall the similar case of explicating imperfectivity through the semantics of prepositions in a sentence like (136a), in contrast to the perfectivity in (136b) or (166c):

(136) a. The boy ran in/along the street
       b. The boy ran (out) to the street
(166) c. John and Mary danced into the room

Compare also the perfectivity of phrases like those in (202) below with some "exceptions" – given above and repeated below in (181).

(202) express a desire
dislike John's sense of humour [on a particular occasion]
fulfil a purpose

(181) have a desire
have a sense of humour (etc.)
serve a purpose
owe an excuse

The differences may be compositionally established or pragmatically determined within the discourse (for more detail about the latter, see below, as well as Chapter Fourteen, *On knowledge of the world in the explication of aspect in English*). In compositional terms, they are due either to the impact of the verb with its aspectual potential (*express, fulfil* are predominantly telic; *have, serve, owe* are predominantly atelic) or to the all-round content of the situation depicted. As far as the nouns are concerned, while they are accompanied by an article in (202) but are non-bounded lexically, each verb-noun collocation as a whole is temporally bounded there because the aspectual telic potential of the verb is imposed onto the whole expression. As a result, boundedness/perfectivity is explicated.

This raises the problem whether boundedness in English cannot systematically be mapped from the referent of the verb onto the referents of subjects and objects. It certainly seems to be the case with *fulfil a purpose*, where, if, e.g., the whole expression is perfective, then the referent of *a purpose* is bounded because the boundedness of the verb *fulfil* is mapped onto the original non-boundedness of *a purpose* as a lexical entry. Indeed, it can be argued that, from the point of view of lexical semantics, *a purpose* is clearly non-bounded, while, for example, *a desire* is not necessarily. The noun *desire*, viewed as a lexical entry, can denote either 'the content of what is wanted', which is non-bounded, or, perhaps somewhat less frequently, 'the act of wanting something', which is bounded. If to these possible complications (which arise because of the impact of the semantics of abstract nouns) the contribution of the subject in possible sentences with phrases of this kind is added, the overall compositional construal might turn out to be rather complicated. Therefore, the implications of the possibility to have boundedness mapped from the verb onto a subject-NP or an object-NP in English will not be investigated here. It will only be argued that what seems to appear as mapping of boundedness from the verb onto the noun in *fulfil a purpose* may, at the level of the sentence, appear as mapping of boundedness from the referent of the subject onto the referent of the whole verb phrase, as in *His early resignation fulfilled a purpose* where the boundedness of *his early resignation* dominates the meaning of the rest of the sentence.

Third, as mentioned above, a deviant aspectual reading may also be established by 'pragmatic factors'. Compare sentences (203a) and (203b) below which follow the same (outwardly identical) agentive pattern, and, hence, both ought to be perfective:

(203) a. John preached the sermon
      b. John preached the Gospel

But they differ aspectually. Sentence (203a) is perfective, while (203b) is imperfective and the difference is established according to our 'knowledge of the world'. It tells us that if *the sermon* in (203a) is a temporal entity bounded in time, *the Gospel* in (203b), despite the definite article, is an abstract non-bounded entity that amounts to 'the contents/ideas of the first four books of the New Testament'. Furthermore, if the referent of *the sermon* in (203a) clearly coincides with the referent of the verb, even from the point of view of the ordinary speaker, the non-boundedness of *the Gospel* in (203b) is mapped onto the referent of the verb, rendering the referent of *preached* non-bounded. Similarly, while *the Gospel* in (203b) is an abstract non-bounded entity, *the Gospel* in a sentence like (204) below amounts to a concrete, physical entity which is to be regarded (from a certain theoretical point of view inaccessible to the ordinary speaker and discussed at length in previous chapters) as bounded in time after the application of the so-called mapping mechanism.

(204)   John printed the Gospel

Note here that a simple and straightforward distinction between concrete and abstract entities cannot easily cover, or help instantiate, the difference between temporal boundedness and non-boundedness in nouns. Compare the abstract entity *the Gospel* 'the contents/ideas of the first four books of the New Testament' in the imperfective sentence (203b) above and the equally abstract entity *the Gospel* 'the contents/ideas of the first four books of the New Testament' in perfective sentences like (205a) or (205b):

(205) a. John read the Gospel
      b. John learned/understood the Gospel

Taking into account the fact that abstract nouns are generally used with the indefinite article when referring to bounded entities and with no article when referring to non-bounded entities lends considerable support to the thesis that the article has a lot to do with the expression of boundedness – whether it should be considered in temporal or in broad spatial terms. The universal possibilities for presenting any concrete noun as referring to a bounded or to a non-bounded spatial entity have, of course, been repeatedly noted in the literature (see, e.g., Bach 1986: 10; Galton 1984: 155ff; Krifka 1989). But the alternative use of the article and the zero article with abstract nouns described above and its relevance for the expression of aspect have generally escaped the attention of linguists dealing with these problems (see, however, Kabakčiev 1989).

Recall that in the previous chapter verbs were provisionally classified into three groups: verbs with a telic aspectual potential, verbs with an atelic aspectual potential, and verbs with an ambiguous aspectual potential (like *push*). It seems now that there are grounds to assume a classification of nouns similar to the one for verbs. Nouns in a classification of this kind will be bounded, non-bounded or ambiguous with respect to boundedness and non-boundedness. The first two groups have already been exemplified by the lexemes given in (183a) and (183b), repeated here; the third group would contain nouns like those listed in (206) below.

ABSTRACT NOUNS, TEMPORALLY BOUNDED
(183) a. bath, concert, fall, game, instruction, jump, kick, knock, life, nod, operation, party, passage, push, smile, tap

ABSTRACT NOUNS, TEMPORALLY NON-BOUNDED
b. amusement, beauty, destruction, evil, good, grace, hate, health, imagination, laughter, love, power, strength, virtue

ABSTRACT NOUNS, AMBIGUOUS WITH RESPECT TO TEMPORAL BOUNDEDNESS AND NON-BOUNDEDNESS
(206) conversation, desire, inflation, motion, movement, noise, order, performance, pressure, response, suppression, temperature

The nouns in (206) could by no means be regarded as fully representative of the (possible) group of nouns ambiguous with respect to temporal boundedness and non-boundedness in English. Nor could any other list of lexemes of this kind be easily labelled as representative or exhaustive. Any classification of abstract nouns according to their lexical potential to denote temporally bounded entities, temporally non-bounded entities or entities that are ambiguous with respect to temporal boundedness and temporal non-boundedness will inevitably resemble Vendler's classification in which some preconceived 'prototypical' meaning of a verb is taken into account identifying the verb as, say, a state, an activity or an accomplishment, while clearly the same verb is also capable of explicating dissimilar situational values. Just like a verb can have a telic, an atelic or an ambiguous aspectual potential, so can an abstract noun, too, have a certain prototypical temporal meaning and be coerced into explicating a different or even an opposite value. In the complex compositional aspect mechanism the explication of a value by a verb generally depends on the arguments (subjects, objects) with their lexical characteristics and grammatical structure. Although, ultimately, the two pairs of notions, perfectivity/imperfectivity and boundedness/non-boundedness, are identical or at least very similar, unlike perfectivity and imperfectivity the values of boundedness and non-boundedness explicated by nouns should be called temporal rather than aspectual. Like telicity and atelicity, temporal boundedness and non-boundedness in nouns are dependent on factors outside their own primary lexical content: presence of determiners and quantifiers in the NP they take part in, the lexical meaning of the verb they are associated with, as well as various complex combinations of grammatical and semantic factors, including the impact of adverbials and 'knowledge of the world' (these will be dealt with in forthcoming chapters).

This ends the discussion of the temporal values of nouns (mainly abstract nouns) – as lexical entries or as NP components – mainly from the point of view of the aspectual readings of sentences they take part in. Within the mechanism of the compositional explication of aspect, nouns and NPs were shown to be capable of explicating boundedness or non-boundedness in temporal terms and it was demonstrated that these two values can either be transferred onto the referent of the verb in a phrase or a sentence, or (less frequently) acquired from it. The overall description of aspect in English in this book was initially based on the compositional mechanism of aspect as proposed by Verkuyl, but then it made a considerable departure from the latter, primarily in the way the contribution of nominal entities in the sentence to the explication of aspect was handled. However, Verkuyl's extended theory, in spite of the different treatment of NPs, dealt extensively with their impact on the explication of aspect. Therefore, the following sections of this chapter will deal with the way Verkuyl's extended theory handles nominal entities in the sentence and will examine in more detail the differences between the two models.

THE TREATMENT OF NOUNS AND NPS IN VERKUYL'S EXTENDED THEORY

So far the analysis in the book has shown that in languages like English the perfective/imperfective opposition is explicated compositionally and that verbal aspect (as in the Slavic languages) is a 'mirror image' of aspect explicated in compositional terms[4]. On the basis of the cross-language parallelisms already described, it has been argued that Verkuyl's (1972) initial theory is a major contribution in the development of aspectology – that was unrecognised as such at first – and is still unrecognised in many respects. Later, with the development of Montague grammar, the merits of Verkuyl's work became better understood. But what the recognition amounted to mainly concerned the way Verkuyl handled aspect, quantification and some similar problems within the framework of formal semantics; neither did it reflect the importance of compositional aspect for grammatical theory proper, nor were the implications for languages with verbal aspect dealt with at all. But as some points in Verkuyl's original theory were clearly in need of revision, the author extended his (1972) theory through a series of articles into the (1993) version. The primary version has been interpreted here as extremely revealing with respect to the nature of aspect, at least along the lines of the model developed in a number of publications (Kabakčiev 1984a; 1984b; 1993a; 1993b; 1993c). Thus it was to be expected that the extended version would be of a similar importance, both for languages like Dutch and English and with respect to the new implications it might contain for the study of languages with verbal aspect like the Slavic ones.

Verkuyl's (1993) extended theory, however, differs in several important respects from the initial one. The rest of this chapter will discuss the following topics which

---

[4] Interestingly enough, it was a long time ago that Friedrich (1974: 37) hit on with a similar suggestion, unsupported by concrete linguistic evidence, to the effect that all languages have compositional aspect, whereas verbal aspect is restricted only to some languages.

are part of Verkuyl's (1993) extended theory and essentially concern the problem of how referents of nouns and NPs should be treated in a general theory of aspect:

(1) Temporality vs. atemporality;
(2) The plus-principle;
(3) Aspect construal asymmetric?

The first topic is fundamental, for the author considers aspect to be the result of a certain interaction between temporal and atemporal semantic values.[5] The so-called plus-principle amounts to the requirement for all aspectually relevant components of a perfective sentence to have positive values. Although this requirement has already been discussed, certain problems remain that have to be solved for an adequate description of the aspect mechanism. The third thesis, viz., that aspect construal is asymmetric, can also be found in Tenny's (1994) model, which, however, focuses on the syntactic object as the only sentence component capable of governing the aspectual value of a sentence.

(1) *Temporality vs. atemporality.*
The present chapter has already demonstrated that the treatment of noun/NP referents within a theory of aspect cannot be adequate without taking into account their temporal status. At the lexical (dictionary-entry) plane, temporal and atemporal nouns can be distinguished, while some abstract nouns and all concrete nouns are atemporal. However, as already shown, at a certain level of linguistic analysis all referents of nouns (concrete or abstract) or, rather, of NPs, can be regarded as having temporal values that coincide with the temporal value of the action itself.

Partly in contrast to Verkuyl (1972), Verkuyl (1993) treats information from NPs representing major syntactic components like subjects and objects as atemporal – that is, as radically different from the information provided by the verb component in a sentence, which is temporal. As far as the quantitative information in the verb component is concerned, it is taken to be somehow derived from the quantitative, but atemporal, information of NPs representing syntactic subjects and objects. If we go back to examples like (45a) and (45b), already discussed at length above, since an NP like *Schumann's cello concerto* can easily be viewed as temporal, actually, this turns out to be a rare case in which an overtly temporal NP is dealt with in Verkuyl's theory, both in its initial (1972) version and in the extended (1993) version.

(45)   a.   Fritz played Schumann's cello concerto
         b.   Fritz hated Schumann's cello concerto

Another somewhat less revealing case in which temporality looms up in some of Verkuyl's major illustrative material concerns his contention that the referents of NPs like *the Labour Party badge, that house* and *this cat*, in sentences like (207a),

---

[5] Compare the subtitle of Verkuyl (1993): "the interaction between temporal and atemporal structure".

(207b) and (207c) below count as designs or as sorts, not as particular specimens or tokens (see Verkuyl 1972: 105-106; 1993: 132-137).

(207) a. Den Uyl gave the Labour Party badge
b. The architect built that house fifteen times
c. This cat sold well

Less revealing, because designs and sorts are not necessarily viewed by the ordinary speaker as something temporal. According to the approach assumed in the previous chapters of this book, not only is *Schumann's cello concerto* to be regarded as temporal in both (45a) and (45b), also *Fritz* is to be regarded as temporal, in both sentences. In common-sense terms, in the former case Fritz's temporality has to do with some (or most, presumably not all) of his life during which he hates *Schumann's cello concerto*. And in the latter case, much less open to the intuitions of the ordinary speaker, *Fritz* is that stage of the individual Fritz which performed *Schumann's cello concerto*.

It is a little hard to understand why Verkuyl, and other authors working along these lines, had to take it that not only *Fritz* but also *Schumann's cello concerto* are to be regarded as atemporal. Actually, arguments here run against each other. The argument in favour of viewing *Schumann's cello concerto* as atemporal in (45b) is based on the assumption that it has to stand counter to the temporality of *Schumann's cello concerto* in (45a). But, on the other hand, if *Fritz* in (45a) is not to be easily conceived of as temporal in common-sense terms, *Fritz* in (45b) could, perhaps, be conceived of so more easily. Because one hates something not **outside** but **within** time, and, to be more precise, one hates something usually *for some time*, though normally the hating time interval is indefinite, non-bounded. It is non-bounded because we do not normally know and we cannot normally say exactly how long we hated something or somebody. Also, we cannot normally define a point in time at which we started hating something or somebody and a point in time at which we stopped hating something or somebody. Nor can we normally force ourselves into hating something or somebody, start or stop hating something or somebody. All this, of course, is also valid for loving, and for many other feelings as well. Feelings, along with beliefs and convictions, are not subject to man's control, and it is not accidental that beliefs and convictions constitute some of the fundamental rights in certain societies. Compare Vendler's (1957) remarkable point that we can be held responsible for running or not running, for starting running or stopping running, but we cannot be held responsible for believing, knowing or loving. All this brings to the conclusion that the problem of assigning temporality vs. atemporality to participants in situations can most effectively be solved by eliminating it, that is, by assigning temporality to all referents of subjects, verbs and objects in simple sentences of the type analysed so far. And, as already argued, this assignment of temporal values can be justified even in "common-sense" terms, from the point of view of the ordinary speaker of a language.

It is really strange why Verkuyl (1972: 59) first defined 'specified quantity of X' and 'unspecified quantity of X', the two major aspectually relevant NP values, as "giving the bounds of the temporal interval in question" and "not giving the bounds of the temporal interval in question", respectively, and then later, in his extended theory, gave up viewing NPs as temporal. For meanwhile although Kabakčiev (1984a; 1984b) offered an account of NPs denoting physical entities in temporal terms and Verkuyl (1993: 27) reacted to some of the proposals, he avoided tackling the fundamental problem of temporality vs. atemporality. Why the temporal model is difficult to follow is unclear: Verkuyl's later analyses remained atemporal (see Verkuyl 1998); while subscribing to Kabakčiev's (1984b) temporal approach to NPs, Slabakova (1997: 692) did not assume one in her own study of aspect (on English and Bulgarian data). But whatever the exact reasons for all this, the step towards atemporality of NPs that Verkuyl took in his extended (1993) theory can only be judged here as an unfortunate step in the wrong direction.

That a temporal approach is necessary can be seen in another recent (and otherwise very interesting) article by Slabakova, dealing mainly with second language acquisition of aspect parameters. Without adopting such an approach, Slabakova (1998) admits, only in passing and without specifying any further, that "the verb imparts its temporal properties to the object NP" (Slabakova 1998: 77).

(2) *The plus-principle.*
'Plus values' in Verkuyl (1993) are aspectually relevant values of two types:

i) [+SQA], an NP value (equivalent to the category "SPECIFIED QUANTITY OF A" in the original theory) – which equals boundedness in the terminology of this work;
ii) [+ADD TO] – which, in the terminology of this work, equals telicity (a telic aspectual potential) of the verb component viewed as a lexical entity.

According to the extended theory, a sentence must conform to the plus-principle for perfectivity to obtain. That is, there must be pluses ([+SQA]-NPs and a [+ADD TO-verb]) in all the (major) aspectually significant components in the sentence for the explication of perfectivity of an action. In fairly simple sentences, these components are mainly separate noun phrases syntactically represented as the subject and/or the object (direct or indirect), and the verb within the verb phrase. Or, for sentences like (208a), (208b), (48a) or (45a) below (all these are Verkuyl's own examples), all the relevant components should have plus values for the sentence to be able to explicate perfectivity:

(208) a. Judith ate a sandwich
b. The policemen walked from the Mint to the Dam
(48) a. Den Uyl gave the Labour Party badge to a congress-goer
(45) a. Fritz played Schumann's cello concerto

And they do have plus values – some of the participants are represented by proper nouns, there is no unquantified noun (e.g., unaccompanied by an article, etc.), there is no NP referent explicating non-boundedness in some non-grammatical (semantic, pragmatic, etc.) terms, there is no verb with an atelic aspectual potential (a verb that falls within Vendler's state or activity terms).

Conversely, imperfectivity is explicated when there is, in Verkuyl's metaphoric terms, an aspectual leakage. That is, a single minus-value (e.g., one [-SQA]-value or a [-ADD TO]-verb) is enough for imperfectivity to be explicated. For instance, in each of Verkuyl's sentences in (209), (41b), (48b) and (45b) below (Verkuyl's examples) there is one aspectual leakage rendering the sentence imperfective:

(209)   Judith ate sandwiches [an object (direct object) leakage]
(41)   b. Policemen walked from the Mint to the Dam [a subject leakage]
(48)   b. Den Uyl gave the Labour Party badge to congress-goers [an indirect object leakage]
(45)   b. Fritz hated Schumann's cello concerto [a verb leakage]

The mechanism of the plus-principle for the explication of perfectivity and imperfectivity can be represented here in a tabular form similar to (but, for some technical reasons, not quite identical with) Verkuyl's (1993: 20):

Table 8

PERFECTIVITY

Judith ate a sandwich   [+SQA] + [+ADD TO] + [+SQA]

The policemen walked from the Mint to the Dam
     [+SQA] + [+ADD TO] + [+SQA]

Den Uyl gave the LP badge to a congress goer
     [+SQA] + [+ADD TO] + [+SQA] + [+SQA]

Fritz played Schumann's cello concerto
     [+SQA] + [+ADD TO] + [+SQA]

Table 9

```
                    IMPERFECTIVITY

Judith ate sandwiches    [+SQA] + [+ADD TO] + [-SQA]

Policemen walked from the Mint to the Dam
                         [-SQA] + [+ADD TO] + [+SQA]

Den Uyl gave the LP badge to congress goers
                         [+SQA] + [+ADD TO] + [+SQA] + [-SQA]

Fritz hated Schumann's cello concerto
                         [+SQA] + [-ADD TO] + [+SQA]
```

These tables represent a major idea for the proper understanding of the overall compositional explication of aspect put forward by Verkuyl. It is a simple one, but its implications are rather subtle. The idea is, simply, that it is necessary for perfectivity to be regarded as a more important notion than imperfectivity. The following three points made by Verkuyl reflect the idea, as formulated here:

> "Our theory is not a theory about durativity [...];
> Durativity is [rather] the aspectual 'garbage can' (the more sophisticated term is default) [...];
> Terminativity is more well behaved"

(Verkuyl 1993: 21). Its essence is revealed in the following passages.

Earlier in this book some attempts to invalidate the role of either the subject or the object in certain sentences were discussed. Invalidating the role of the subject or the object would, of course, disprove the validity of the general compositional mechanism. To exemplify the non-involvement of the subject and the object in the explication of aspect Shi (1990: 48-49) adduced two pairs of sentences, (210) and (211) below, that show that the subject and the object, respectively, do not, indeed, play a role in the composition of the aspect.

(210) a. John rode a bicycle for an hour/*in an hour
      b. John rode bicycles for an hour/*in an hour
(211) a. Tourists rode a bicycle for an hour/*in an hour
      b. Tourists rode bicycles for an hour/*in an hour

It should be noted, however, that the apparent non-involvement of the subject and the object in the explication of aspect in sentences like (210) and (211) above is due precisely to an aspectual 'leakage', already present in the verb: *ride* can easily be defined as a verb with an atelic aspectual potential. Shi was aware of the lexical contribution of the verb to the composition of aspect (Shi 1990: 53-55). But, trying to isolate the subject or the object (or both) from the general mechanism of assigning perfectivity and imperfectivity, he based his arguments on either the plus- or minus-value of one of the major syntactic components in the sentence (the subject or the object NPs) or on the plus- or minus-value of the verb, and not on the values of **all** the aspectually relevant sentence components **at the same time**. That is, Shi and other authors failed to draw from Verkuyl's compositional theory – on which they otherwise based their observations – an essential conclusion, namely, that, for aspect to be explicated compositionally, there is a basic principle underlying the interplay of the referents of sentence components: the so-called plus-principle.[6] This principle, although implicitly present in Verkuyl's (1972) original theory, was not expressly worded, and its proper formulation in Verkuyl (1993) helped disperse serious misunderstandings.

On the other hand, the plus-principle will be shown here to have implications that remain outside of the analysis in Verkuyl (1993). For instance, although Verkuyl proved to be well aware of possible alternative aspectual readings, the aspectual readings for some of the sentences interpreted were overstressed in Verkuyl (1993). The reason for this has already been defined. The necessity for the compositionally explicated aspect of a sentence to be viewed as only primary, or prototypical, not the only possible one, was ignored in Verkuyl's theory, in both of its versions. Compare the following argument (Verkuyl 1993: 182):

> "it is necessary to point out that there is no way in which [-SQA]-NPs may receive a [+SQA]-interpretation. That is, in sentences like [...]
>
> Judith ate sandwiches. She had all five of them in her box
>
> *them* clearly has some anaphoric relation to *sandwiches*. Yet [...] *Judith ate sandwiches* is durative and remains so even if later information makes it clear that Judith ate a finite amount of sandwiches"

It can easily be argued that creating a specific context, like the one given in the sequence *Judith ate sandwiches. She had all five of them in her box*, is in fact the very reason for disallowing the [+SQA]-interpretation. Because a sentence like *Judith ate sandwiches* can be put into a radically different context, allowing, in the long run, a [+SQA]-interpretation of the object. Compare, for instance, the sentence *Judith ate sandwiches* in the following context:

(212)   That evening there was no meal in the kitchen. Peter and John had some biscuits and beer. Judith ate sandwiches. Then she went immediately to bed

In the context of (212) the referent of the verb *ate* in *Judith ate sandwiches* acquires a proper bounded reading. The boundedness of *ate* can then be said to be mapped

---

[6] Shi also ignored the necessity for the compositionally explicated aspect of a sentence to be viewed as primary, prototypical, not the only possible one. But this circumstance remains almost totally neglected in Verkuyl's work as well.

onto the referent of the object (and also onto the subject) – along the lines of the mapping mechanism described earlier – making the referent of *sandwiches* bounded, i.e. [+SQA], contrary to Verkuyl's thesis. Hence, since creating bounding contexts like (212) for non-bounded sentences like *Judith ate sandwiches* is always (or almost always) possible, a generalisation to the effect that "there is no way in which [-SQA]-NPs may receive a [+SQA]-interpretation" (Verkuyl 1993: 182) can be said to be wrong. Of course, it is true that the boundedness of *Judith ate sandwiches* in (212) may be regarded as different from the (prototypical) boundedness of, say, *Judith ate the sandwiches* – as when the sentence is analysed in isolation. This problem is dealt with in Chapter Thirteen, *On aspectual classes in English*.

The two tables given above illustrating the plus-principle are, as already mentioned, not identical with Verkuyl's, as given in Verkuyl (1993: 20). Verkuyl assigns imperfectivity to negative sentences, that is, to sentences like (213a), (213b) or (213c) below, simply because they contain negative NPs:

(213) a. Nobody ate a sandwich
　　　b. Nobody ate sandwiches
　　　c. Judith ate no sandwich

A cross-language comparison will show, however, that a thesis of this kind is hardly tenable (the analysis will be carried out in Chapter Twelve, *On negativity and the explication of perfectivity*). This is the reason why the tables describing the plus-principle here and in Verkuyl (1993: 20) are not to be taken as identical.

But, apart from the technical reason for the dissimilarity, the plus-principle raises one serious question concerning Verkuyl's tables and the ones given here. It is not whether they are valid or not with respect to positive sentences. They are valid. The problem is that if we take *sandwiches, policemen, congress-goers* and *hated* in Table 9 above to represent minus-values, this would suggest, following the mapping mechanism described in Chapter Six, *The mechanism for mapping the temporal values of subjects and objects*, that the other sentence components ought to change their values too. In fact, occasionally, Verkuyl seemed to favour a solution of this kind. But he was neither fully explicit about it, nor did he actually offer it. (As mentioned above, no rule was proposed to the effect that the visible aspectual interpretation of any sentence is just a primary or a prototypical one.) For example, discussing his sentences (214a) and (214b) below, Verkuyl assumed a possible [-SQA]-interpretation for the overtly [+SQA]-NP *the girls* in (214b) and tacitly allowed a [+SQA]-interpretation for the overtly [-SQA]-NP *soldiers* in (214a):

(214) a. When soldiers came into town, the girls stayed indoors
　　　b. When the soldiers came into town, the girls stayed indoors

(see Verkuyl 1993: 131).

Solving this problem amounts to translating Verkuyl's model into the one developed here and involves building a comparison between the atemporal and the temporal approach. It would, in principle, be possible to assign minus-values to all the NPs associated with an atelic verb explicating non-boundedness – or plus-values to NPs that are without an article and are unquantified in cases of a bounding context. However, viewing NPs like *the Mint, the Dam, Den Uyl, Judith, Fritz, sandwiches, policemen, congress-goers* as purely atemporal is precisely what seems to have created the obstacle to the assignment of these values in Verkuyl's model. In common-sense terms, too, it would be very difficult to interpret some of the NPs listed above (*the Mint, the Dam, Den Uyl, Judith, Fritz*) as [-SQA], for they are proper names and can hardly be seen, at least from the point of view of the ordinary speaker, as non-bounded. Pure temporality is the medium in which entities referred to by proper names can acquire an entirely convincing non-bounded interpretation.

(3) *Aspect construal asymmetric?*

In his extended theory Verkuyl (1993: 21) maintains that aspect construal is asymmetrically distributed among the syntactic components in the sentence, as shown in the table below:

Table 10

Aspectual asymmetry, as seen in Verkuyl (1993)
([+SQA]   +   [+ADD TO] +   [+SQA]
[[Judith   ate]   three sandwiches]
[+SQA]   +   ([+ADD TO] +   [+SQA])
[Judith   [ate   three sandwiches]]

Or, in plain terms, *Judith ate three sandwiches* is perfective, *ate three sandwiches* is also perfective. But since *Judith ate* is imperfective, this means that aspect construal in the sentence is asymmetric. Note, however, that this argument is clearly based on a mechanistic notion, namely, on partitioning information linearly within the sentence which in this case, leaving aside focus-topic distinctions, does not seem to have anything to do with the semantics of the sentence or its constituents.

It is also worth asking why it should be argued that aspect construal is asymmetric on the basis of perfective sentences only. If imperfective sentences are taken into account, like, for example, *Judith ate sandwiches* and especially *Children ate sandwiches*, it could just as well be argued that aspect construal is symmetric because the imperfectivity of these two sentences matches the imperfectivity of the VP *ate sandwiches*. Indeed, there may be a certain obstacle with the latter approach (analysing imperfective sentences). Recall Verkuyl's (1993: 21) impressionistic claim quoted above that his theory is not a theory about durativity, that durativity is an aspectual 'garbage can' and that terminativity is more well behaved.

But let us look at the three separate arguments in favour of the so-called asymmetry of aspect construal. Verkuyl's first argument in favour of asymmetry is the *in-*

for-test, the second argument concerns idiomatic expressions, the third argument makes reference to data from the Slavic languages.

First argument. The *in*-time/*for*-time test.

Verkuyl's first argument for asymmetry says that there is "independent linguistic evidence" in favour of the asymmetry thesis and that this independent evidence is represented by the *in*-time/*for*-time test (Verkuyl 1993: 24). The author then goes on to explain asymmetry very briefly in terms of Table 10 above. However, in the opening pages of his work Verkuyl (1993: 14) made a distinction between inner aspect and outer aspect: inner aspect is aspect formed without the influence of adverbials; outer aspect concerns the changes introduced by adverbials into the aspectual semantics of the sentence. Admitting that his theory lacks a "sufficiently articulated theory of adverbial modification", he declared that he would not deal with problems concerning outer aspect because while "the study of inner aspect concerns the relationship between a verb and its arguments", his study "is crucially focused on the composition of inner aspect" (Verkuyl 1993: 14). Thus the reliability of the "independent linguistic evidence" turns out to be questionable even within Verkuyl's own theory.

Second argument. The second argument in favour of aspectual asymmetry concerns idiomatic expressions:

> "No idiomatic expressions involving a two-place predicate seem to exist that can be analysed as the result of a fusion of the verb and its subject NP"

(Verkuyl 1993: 24). According to the author's argumentation, this boils down to saying that there can be no SV idiomatic expressions of the type (215b) below, meaning 'John died' and formed by passivisation out of the idiomatic expression in (215a). However, if the assumption that sentences like *The bucket was kicked* cannot be formed in the idiomatic sense is valid, it is only to a certain extent. Because one can, as native speakers of English admit, always invent and use stylistically marked, e.g. jocular, utterances like (215b).

(215) a. John kicked the bucket
b. The bucket was kicked

Furthermore, if a general theory of aspect in which aspect is asymmetric is valid, then this theory ought to have cross-linguistic validity as well. In Bulgarian, however, idiomatic expressions of the syntactic type used by Verkuyl **can** be constructed on the basis of certain idioms. For example, from an idiom like *da razgonja familijata na nkg* 'make somebody suffer (extreme hardship) [literally: to drive somebody's family away]' a fully acceptable sentence like (216a) below can easily be derived. And in Bulgarian there are also other interesting cases in which originally one-place predicates like *potăna*$_{pfv}$ 'sink' display an ability to form idiomatic expressions like (216b) in which *potăna*$_{pfv}$ 'sink' becomes a two-place predicate and there is, without any doubt, a fusion of the verb *sa potănali* 'have sunk' and the subject-NP *gemiite* 'the boats':

(216) a. Na   men   mi   se   razgoni_pfv   familija-ta
         To   me   my   *prt.pass.*   drove-away   family-the
         'I suffered extreme hardship'
    b. Na Ivan   sa   mu   potănali_pfv   gemii-te
         To Ivan   are_PerfAux   him   sunk   boats-the
         'Ivan is in a bad mood'

Thus the second argument in favour of aspectual asymmetry seems to be invalid in cross-language terms, and not fully convincing for English.

Third argument. Verkuyl's third argument in favour of aspectual asymmetry involves data from the Slavic languages. This argument is the most important of the three, and, since it purports to bring into account, in contrast to the previous two arguments, an enormous quantity of language material, it is worth considering in greater detail. Quoting Kabakčiev (1984a; 1984b), Verkuyl concedes that:

> "by the absence of articles in Russian NPs, the verb contains clues as to [+SQA]- or [-SQA]-information expressed by its argument-NPs"

(Verkuyl 1993: 27). It is quite strange, however, that the very next moment Verkuyl suddenly takes an entirely opposite view, claiming that:

> "in general, Russian two-place predicates extend the information expressed by the perfective prefix to the object rather than to the subject"

(Verkuyl 1993: 27). And later in the book the author again contradicts himself by establishing that in the Polish example (217a), and not in (217b) below, the subject *żołnierze* 'the soldiers' may "pertain to a specific group of soldiers coming into town on one occasion" (Verkuyl 1993: 138). Apparently, this is due to the perfective aspect of the verb, the information in which (boundedness) is extended to the subject:[7]

(217) a. Kiedy żołnierze przyszli_pfv do miasta,   to   dziewczęta chowali się do domów
         When   soldiers   came   to town,   then   girls stayed-*refl* to home
         'When the soldiers came into town the girls stayed indoors'
    b. Kiedy żołnierze przychodzili_impfv do miasta,   to   dziewczęta chowali się do domów
         When   soldiers   came   to town,   then   girls stayed-*refl* to home
         'Whenever the soldiers came into town, the girls stayed indoors'

---

[7] The subjects in the Polish examples are without articles – because there are no articles in Polish.

As already shown in the previous chapters, the referents of subject-NPs and object-NPs in Slavic should be equally regarded as involving either bounded or non-bounded stretches of time according to the boundedness or non-boundedness in the verb – which is transferred from the (referent of the) verb onto the (referents of the) subject and the object. Thus, in the analysis of aspectual composition, asymmetry can be judged to be an entirely artificial notion introduced to suit some major tenets of the transformational-generative approach – in which there is an asymmetry in the tree-representation of the distribution of subject-NPs and object-NPs. But this does not correlate with the composition of aspect.

Verkuyl's idea of the asymmetry of aspectual construal resembles Tenny's (1994) approach towards aspect. Strangely enough, for Tenny actually tries to refute the whole mechanism of compositional aspect! Indeed, she refers to certain general principles of compositionality whereby certain aspectual properties are central to it (Tenny 1994: 134). But these principles of compositionality have little to do with compositional aspect as described here, on the one hand, and, on the other hand, Tenny's basic idea is that since "external arguments are compositionally 'outside' of internal arguments" Tenny (1994: 134), they do not take part in the compositional aspect mechanism. Tenny actually maintains that not only external arguments (subjects), but also indirect internal arguments (indirect objects, non-temporal adverbials) **cannot** influence the aspectual interpretation of a sentence. This view is held in this book (above and also below, see Chapter Eleven, *The impact of adverbials in the sentence, and aspect in English*) to be inadequate. Tenny's suggestion that external and indirect internal arguments should not be viewed as taking part in the composition of aspect is also a mechanistic attempt to marry certain purely syntactic properties that have little or nothing to do with aspect *per se*. Hence, not only does Verkuyl's similar idea of the asymmetry of aspect pay undue tribute to the general idea of a certain asymmetry between subject NPs and NPs within the VP, it potentially undermines the basis of his own compositional theory of aspect.

CONCLUSION

To sum up the contents of this chapter, the analysis of meanings of nouns and NPs related to the explication of aspect has demonstrated that an adequate description of the overall aspect mechanism in English at the level of the sentence is impossible without taking into account the contribution of nouns and NPs for the explication of aspectual values. This is especially valid for the description of aspect in English and similar languages in which the perfective/imperfective opposition, the major aspectual distinction across languages, is explicated compositionally – although, as already shown in Kabakčiev (1987; 1999) on Bulgarian data, 'nominal aspect' can be observed in languages with verbal aspect as well. Furthermore, neither grammatical meanings, nor lexical meanings alone can account for the contribution of nouns and NPs to the explication of aspect. It is the temporal status of their referents that is ultimately associated with the aspectual value of the entity analysed, be it a phrase, a sentence or a discourse.

An overview of Verkuyl's treatment of nouns and NPs in his extended theory has revealed certain deficiencies in the theory. More importantly, however, it has shown that these deficiencies can be overcome in such an approach to aspect in which NP referents that represent participants is situations are viewed as temporal entities.

Finally, it can be generalised that any analysis of the meanings of verbs and nouns that are relevant to the compositional explication of aspect in English is bound to corroborate the idea that language is, and has to be, an extremely flexible device to reflect, store and model reality according to the psycho-physiological potential and practical needs of the human being.

CHAPTER 11

THE IMPACT OF ADVERBIALS IN THE SENTENCE, AND ASPECT IN ENGLISH

Generally, adverbials play a major role in the explication of the aspect of a simple sentence in English. Some of the preceding chapters dealt peripherally with sentences containing adverbials of time or place. With the help of these adverbials the presence or absence of temporal bounds of a situation may be expressed or implied, depending on the type of adverbial used. For example, the employment of a place adverbial like *into the cellar* in (164d) below turns the imperfective meaning of the initial sentence *The boy rolled the barrel* into a perfective one:

(164) d. The boy rolled the barrel into the cellar

Conversely, the employment of an adverbial like *in the cellar* in (163d) below is in line with the imperfectivity of *The boy rolled the barrel*:

(163) d. The boy rolled the barrel in the cellar

(cf. also Heinämäki 1978: 6-9). Adverbials of time are generally even more capable of signifying the presence or absence of temporal bounds of a situation. Thus in (156a) below an adverbial like *for hours* (with a bare noun *hours*) helps in the explication of the imperfectivity of the rest of sentence (*John pushed trolleys into the supermarket*). Conversely, the introduction of the adverbial *in an hour*, considered to be a test for imperfectivity, is impossible, due to the imperfectivity of *John pushed trolleys into the supermarket*:

(156) a. John pushed trolleys into the supermarket *in an hour/for hours/for hours on end [this was his job]

What some adverbials do is only make the aspectual value implied by the rest of the sentence more explicit, while others change the aspect of the original sentence without the adverbial. For instance, the adverbials *in the cellar* in (163d) and *for hours* in (156a) above strengthen the imperfective meaning of the rest of the sentences, while the *in*-time phrase in Shi's (1990: 49) sentence (62) below changes the initially imperfective meaning of *Tourists drank the milk* into a perfective one:

(62)   Tourists drank the milk in an hour

But adverbials have not yet been the main object of analysis in this book, and for a good reason. It was necessary that the basic mechanism of explicating perfectivity and imperfectivity in a sentence without adverbials be clarified in the first place.

ANOTHER CROSS-LANGUAGE COMPARISON

To reveal the role played by adverbials for the compositional explication of aspect in English sentences, an analysis in terms of the aspectual correspondences in a language which features verbal aspect will be made again. Consider the English sentences (218a) – (218d). They all contain verbs in the Simple Past Tense. Clearly, the situations denoted through the verb *played* in these sentences differ considerably in the way the action takes place:

(218) a. Peter played tennis for half an hour
 b. Whenever he played a game of tennis, Peter drank a glass of mineral water
 c. Peter played a game of tennis
 d. Peter often played tennis when he was in England

Consider first the example in (218d). It describes an indefinitely repetitive (non-bounded) action imposed onto the meaning of the rest of the sentence by the adverbial *often*. Non-bounded, non-completed is also every separate occasion in which Peter played tennis. This can be established by comparing the action of playing in sentence (218d) with the action of playing in sentence (218b). The action in (218b) is also repetitive but every game is played to its end. And while the action in (218d) is non-bounded in both its separate occurrences and in its repetitiveness, in (218a) the action is non-repetitive. And although it does not reach a specific end-point with a pragmatically identifiable result, it is terminated after having been performed for half an hour. This is denoted by the adverbial *for half an hour*. In (218c), however, the action is felt to be more completed because the playing is terminated with the completion of the game. Finally, as already noted, although the all-round action in (218b) is indefinitely iterative, every subaction within its scope is a completed one.

Now compare the way these four sentences and the situations denoted by them are rendered into Bulgarian, where aspect is marked on the verb. Sentence (218a') below is the translation equivalent of (218a), (218b') is the translation equivalent of (218b'), etc.:

(218) a. Peter played tennis for half an hour
 a'. Petăr   igra$_{impfvAor}$ tenis   polovin   čas
    Peter   played   tennis half   hour

    b. Whenever he played a game of tennis, Peter drank a glass of mineral water
    b'. Štom izigraeše_{pfvImp} edin gejm tenis, Petăr izpivaše_{impfvImp} časa mineralna voda
      Whenever played one game tennis Peter drank glass mineral water
    c. Peter played a game of tennis
    c'. Petăr izigra_{pfvAor} edin gejm tenis
      Peter played   one game tennis
    d. Peter often played tennis when he was in England
    d'. Petăr često igraeše_{impfvImp} tenis, kogato beše v Anglija
      Peter often played   tennis, when was-he in England

It should be noted that not only are the translation equivalents of the English sentences into Bulgarian precise, the choice of the particular aspectual verb forms in the Bulgarian sentences is almost obligatory. The Past Simple Tense form of the verb *play* in English is rendered through the four different verb forms in Bulgarian, already discussed, mainly in the first two chapters of the book: (i) *igraeše* (218d), an imperfective (verb in the) Imperfect; (ii) *igra* (218a), an imperfective (verb in the) Aorist; (iii) *izigra* (218c), a perfective (verb in the) Aorist; (iv) *izigraeše* (218b), a perfective (verb in the) Imperfect.

 A short digression into the grammar of Bulgarian will be necessary here. Bulgarian and Slavic linguists in general have never had a consensus on the essence of the grammatical categories underlying these four verb forms. There is no disagreement, however, about which verb forms are the most frequent and natural: these are the imperfective Imperfect (*igraeše* 'played/was playing') and the perfective Aorist (*izigra* 'played'). According to the approach assumed here, they denote the two prototypical aspectual values – of perfectivity and imperfectivity. Less common than the previous two, imperfective Aorist forms (*igra* 'played') denote actions that are not completed with a particular, pragmatically identifiable result, but they are certainly terminated. Even more rare are perfective Imperfect forms (*izigraeše* 'played [repeatedly to the end]') which have a specific meaning. If their homonymous use to denote Future-in-the-Past actions is ignored, they basically refer to a non-bounded series of actions in which every separate action is a completed one. It is also worth noting that the distinction between the Imperfect and the Aorist with imperfective verbs is very often not at all expressed morphologically: many verb forms in Bulgarian outside the second and third person singular (where the distinction is made always) are homonymous for the two tenses (the homonymy is exemplified below, see Footnote 5 in Chapter 12 and the sentence (259b") it deals with).

ALTERNATING SITUATIONS

What is significant here from the point of view of English grammar is that a single verb form (*played*) in the four English sentences in (218) covers four different meanings that are easily distinguished grammatically in another language. Hence, these four sentences demonstrate very clearly that, without any doubt, it is not the verb in English that conditions the aspectual reading of each sentence, it is precisely the rest of the sentence that does this job. It remains to be seen what the exact reasons for this are.

Consider first (218c):

(218) c. Peter played a game of tennis

The perfective meaning is easy to identify as a result of the temporal boundedness of the quantified NP *a game of tennis* (with a head noun accompanied by an article) and the boundedness of the referent of the subject (constituting a proper name). The boundedness of the two participants is mapped onto the action. Recall, furthermore, that *play*, taken in isolation, viewed as a lexical entry, is a verb with an atelic aspectual potential. But if complemented with objects like *a game* it becomes bounded – because the boundedness of *a game* is mapped onto the (referent of the) verb.

Now consider (218a):

(218) a. Peter played tennis for half an hour

For the sake of clarity, let us here summarise the reasons why what is referred to by the verb phrase *play a game of tennis* is something completed, bounded in time, while what is referred to by the verb phrase *play tennis* is something non-completed, non-bounded in time. This is because while the referent of the noun phrase *a game of tennis* is an object bounded in time, the referent of the noun phrase *tennis* is an object non-bounded in time.[1] The reason why the referent of the noun phrase *a game of tennis* is bounded is that the noun *game* denotes something bounded, and *game* is, hence, accompanied by an article. (The article is capable of signalling boundedness, in contrast to the zero article which signals non-boundedness.) And the reason why the referent of the noun phrase *tennis* is non-bounded is that the noun *tennis* denotes something non-bounded. Hence, *tennis* is unaccompanied by an article or, in other words, contains the zero article capable of signalling non-boundedness. It can be maintained that there is a complex mechanism in language along the lines of which boundedness and non-boundedness, initially viewed in broad spatial terms (at least as far as concrete nouns are concerned), can be transferred onto the time axis. Language itself being part of the general human psycho-physiological potential to perceive, process and store data from reality, this mechanism should be seen as a subpart of this potential and not as a purely structural language phenomenon like, e.g., aspect (be it verbal or compositional).

The non-boundedness of *played tennis* is also one of the reasons why the overall action denoted by *played* in sentence (218d) is conceived of as non-bounded:

---

[1] Recall similar observations concerning the phrases *play a rubber of bridge* and *play bridge* made by Allen (1966), who is considered to have introduced the term 'bounded' in English linguistics.

(218) d. Peter often played tennis when he was in England

The other, primary, reason, is the indefinite repetition introduced by the adverbial *often*. Now suppose the two adverbials of time (the adverb *often* and the temporal clause *when he was in England*) are removed from the sentence. The following simple sentence would result:

(218) e. Peter played tennis

The action in this sentence would again appear to be non-bounded. However, is the action in this sentence repetitive or not? And if the referent of *tennis*, being non-bounded, imposes its temporal value onto the action, couldn't the action possibly be viewed as terminated or is it necessarily non-bounded? There do not seem to be any indications of repetition or non-repetition or of termination or non-termination. It could be reasoned that if this sentence is to describe a habitual action, the habituality would have to be explicated either within the sentence or by the context, otherwise the action ought to constitute a single occurrence. But, given a single occurrence of playing, could Peter play, so to say, indefinitely, for imperfectivity to be implied in a non-progressive reading of the sentence?

And what about the role of the temporal clause *when he was in England* in (218d)? Does it take part in the explication of the aspectual meaning or not? It doesn't seem to do so, for when (or while) Peter is somewhere, he can perform various kinds of actions (bounded or non-bounded, single or repetitive). Hence, in a Bulgarian translation (218еэ) of the English sentence (218e) neither the use of the imperfective Aorist, nor the use of the imperfective Imperfect (218f) would be favoured:

(218) e. Peter played tennis
eэ. Petăr   igra$_{impfvAor}$/igraeše$_{impfvImp}$ tenis
    Peter   played   tennis

A sentence like (218e) in English does not say anything about whether the action should be regarded as bounded (terminated) or non-bounded (non-terminated) – in the sense that we do not know whether it describes John's hobby of playing tennis or John's playing tennis yesterday. If the sentence describes John's hobby, it is to be viewed as non-bounded. But if it describes John's playing tennis yesterday, it would have to be necessarily interpreted as terminated – due to natural limitations of time, energy, etc. – but, of course, without reaching a natural endpoint.

The analysis of the sentences in (218) above, complemented by a language-contrastive analysis, invariably leads to the interesting conclusion that an action generally denoted by a single verb form like *played* in five different sentences, (218a) through (218e), can be presented in terms of several situations of the Vendlerian type, whereby perfectivity can be substituted by imperfectivity or vice versa.

Compare the following changes in the type of situation denoted in the direction from (218e) to (218b) – through (218a) and (218c). If we take it that (218e) describes a habit, the non-boundedness of (218e) is substituted by some partial boundedness[2] in (218a), the partial boundedness of (218a) is then substituted by real boundedness (an action brought to its natural endpoint) in (218c), and the boundedness of (218c) is then again changed into non-boundedness (indefinite repetition of a separate action brought to a natural endpoint) in (218b):

(218) e. Peter played tennis
↓
a. Peter played tennis for half an hour
↓
c. Peter played a game of tennis
↓
b. Whenever he played a game of tennis, Peter drank a glass of mineral water

A different order in the changes of the type of situation denoted is also possible, as, for example, from (218a) to (218d):

(218) a. Peter played tennis for half an hour
↓
d. Peter often played tennis when he was in England

This shows that the action of playing tennis for some time in (218a), that is boundedness in time with no specific endpoint reached, can be indefinitely iterativised in (218d).

The recursive change of the type of the action/situation from non-bounded to bounded and vice versa has already been revealed as a phenomenon, called *nested aspects,* by Jouko Lindstedt (1984; 1985) – on data from a large number of languages including, mainly, Bulgarian, and also English. Without going into the details of the phenomenon of nested aspects, it is worth noting that various elements in the sentence, including adverbials (especially adverbials of time), are capable of changing the initial aspectual meaning explicated by a verb, a verb phrase or a whole, relatively simple, sentence. Of course, it is also possible for the aspectual meaning to be recursively changed from bounded into non-bounded – the order of the operation can be reversed in any direction.

A similar proposal on English data, using a similar terminology ('layers of meaning') was later developed by Moens (1987: 45-47), but there the possibility for recursive application of the rule of substituting boundedness for non-boundedness and vice versa was not stressed. Verkuyl (1993: 12-14), surprisingly, rejected the significance of the phenomenon with the contention that a recursive transition from

---

[2] What is here called "partial boundedness" will be considered and more precisely defined later.

boundedness into non-boundedness or vice versa ought to be accounted for in terms of operations at different syntactic levels. It can be argued, counter to this view, that whether the formal procedures for identifying the aspectual changes take place at different levels or not, changes from boundedness to non-boundedness or vice versa do occur. There can be no doubt that the corresponding sentences are interpreted by the native speaker of the language in question as aspectually different and that he/she has different aspectual options available.

THE *IN*-TIME RULE, AND THE *FOR*-TIME RULE

So far in the book, several linguists who revealed certain language regularities for the first time (at least to the best knowledge of the author of this book) have been quoted. Of course, it often happens that a certain insight into a scientific problem later proves to have been incorrect or incomplete. Or it turns out that actually a different author described the phenomenon in question earlier. Some of the regularities described here concerning the link between nouns with or without articles and the explication of aspect in certain types of sentences revealed by Verkuyl (1971/1972) were also independently shown by Mittwoch (1971). But if Mittwoch came to the conclusion concerning this relationship, this had already been done by other authors as well, in one form or another, and, again, only with respect to the object in the sentence (Garey 1957; Vendler 1957; Allen 1966; Ridjanović 1969/1976)[3].

It is important to note, however, that Mittwoch seems to have really been the first linguist to describe not so much the relationship between the explication of perfectivity and imperfectivity through the use of the article/zero article contrast but a different, major phenomenon in the grammar of English that has to do with the general mechanism of explicating aspect. The major phenomenon in question pertains to the contribution of adverbials of time to the explication of aspect at the level of the sentence. Consider the examples given by Mittwoch (1971: 256-257) in (219) and (220) below:

(219) a. He drank a bottle of beer/the bottle of beer/the beer in two hours
     b. He ate an apple/two apples/the apple/a piece of cheese in thirty seconds
     c. *He drank (beer) in two hours
     d. *He ate (apples/cheese) in thirty seconds

---

[3] James (1969) had even argued earlier that there is a systemic correspondence between the use of the article in English and the expression of aspect in Russian. Cf. the following correspondences given by James (1969: 92-93):

(English)   (Russian)
He wrote the letters = On napisal$_{pfv}$ pis'ma
He wrote letters   = On pisal$_{impfv}$ pis'ma

James' observations coincide with what has been maintained so far in this book, but they were not made within a general framework for analysing aspect.

In sentences with *in*-time adverbial phrases, while sentences like (219a) and (219b) above are normal, sentences like (219c) and (219d) are ungrammatical. Conversely, in sentences with *for*-time adverbial phrases, while sentences like (220a) and (220b) below are normal, sentences like (220c) and (220d) are ungrammatical:

(220) a. He drank (beer) for two hours
b. He ate apples/cheese for thirty seconds
c. *He drank a bottle of beer/the bottle of beer/the beer for two hours
d. *He ate an apple/two apples/the apple/a piece of cheese for thirty seconds

(The examples represent, of course, Mittwoch's personal judgements about grammaticality and non-grammaticality.)

Thus, in accordance with Mittwoch's observations, the following two rules, the *in*-time rule, and the *for*-time rule, respectively, can be formulated:

THE *IN*-TIME RULE:

In-time adverbials in English are used in association with sentences or verb phrases explicating perfectivity, to the exclusion of imperfective ones.

THE *FOR*-TIME RULE:

For-time adverbials are used in association with sentences or verb phrases explicating imperfectivity, to the exclusion of perfective ones.

As will be seen later, these are two of the most fundamental grammatical rules of Modern English. Hence, although they are not without exceptions, they ought to be present in all grammars, textbooks and dictionaries. But what is astonishing and even shocking is that they are not! The reasons for this will be discussed in the forthcoming pages of this chapter where an attempt to clarify the essence and the functional significance of the two rules will be made.

Compare sentences like (221) and (222) below, patterned to the *in*-time rule and the *for*-time rule, respectively. The imperfective phrases in (221a) and (221b) freely combine with a *for*-time adverbial, the perfective phrases in (221c) freely combine with an *in*-time adverbial:

(221) a. She played/sang/swam/knitted/laughed/painted/walked for half an hour
   b. She played tennis/played the guitar/sang songs/swam the crawl/knitted sweaters/painted pictures for half an hour
   c. She played a game of tennis/played a sonata/sang a song/swam to the other bank/knitted three sweaters/painted the pictures in half an hour

Conversely, imperfective phrases do not combine with an *in*-time adverbial, perfective phrases do not generally combine with a *for*-time adverbial. There seems to be a consensus among aspectologists and native speakers that sentences of type (222a) and (222b) are ungrammatical or unacceptable. But not all sentences of type (222c) seem to be ungrammatical or unacceptable – if they are ungrammatical or unacceptable at all.

(222) a. *She played/sang/swam/knitted/laughed/painted/walked in half an hour
   b. *She played tennis/played the guitar/sang songs/swam the crawl/knitted sweaters/painted pictures in half an hour
   c. (*)(?)She played a game of tennis/played the sonata/sang a song/swam to the other bank/knitted three sweaters/painted the wall for half an hour

"TENSE" AND OTHER INTERFERENCES

However, the association between *in*-time adverbials and perfectivity and *for*-time adverbials and imperfectivity is not always so straightforward as it might appear in the sentences in (219), (220), (221) and (222) above. Language provides opportunities to express hosts of various states, activities or events and any attempt at a rigid description of the applicability of the two rules in question is to face problems. Thus if sentences (223a) and (223b) below conform to the *in*-time rule, the sentences in (224) and (225) do not, since they contain an *in*-time phrase and are associated with expressions (*fly/swim* and *will be flying/swimming*) that are imperfective, some of them at least at first sight.

(223) a. Maria will fly to Thessaloniki in an hour
   b. Maria will swim to the other bank in an hour
(224) a. Maria will fly in an hour
   b. In an hour, Maria will be flying to Thessaloniki
(225) a. Maria will swim in an hour
   b. In an hour, Maria will be swimming to the other bank

The difference between (223), on the one hand, and (224) and (225), on the other, is in the difference of time scope of the *in*-time phrase. It falls entirely (and necessarily) within the referent of the bounded expression *will fly to Thessaloniki* in (223), while in (224) and (225) it is either outside the time scope of the referent of the non-bounded expression, immediately preceding it, as in (224a) and (225a), or within it, representing a point within the interval designated by a progressive form, as in (224b) and (225b). In other words, in (224a) Maria's flight or flying covers a period succeeding a whole hour of non-flying, whereas in (224b) there is a point of reference which is within the flying interval. As far as the aspect of the aspectually relevant phrase is concerned, it is undoubtedly imperfective (being even marked grammatically) in (224b) and (225b), whereas in (224a) and (225a) it depends on the general intent of the speaker and will be revealed in the context of the utterance – primarily as perfective, designating the beginning of the flight/flying, or (perhaps more rarely) as imperfective, designating, broadly, the essence of the action to take place.

However, although the sentences in (226) below ought to refer to perfective actions, since *to*-place phrases imply telicity (cf. Quirk et al 1985: 677), their meaning is not actually incompatible with the meaning of (224a) and (225a). This means that the *in*-time phrase neither bans, nor precludes imperfectivity, as was the case with sentences like (219c), (219d), (222a) and (222b) above, and, furthermore, the perfective and the imperfective readings are equally legitimate in (226a) and (226b):

(226) a. Maria will fly to Thessaloniki
b. Maria will swim to the other bank

Again, the beginning of the flight may be designated in a perfective reading of (226a) or (226b), as in (224a) and (225a), or the essence of the action about to take place in an imperfective one. Note, however, that the *in*-time phrase is essential to the explication of perfectivity (when it is there) in (224a) and (225a), because if the adverbial is omitted the resulting sentences become less susceptible to a perfective interpretation. Compare (224a) and (225a), on the one hand, and (227a) and (227b), on the other:

(224) a. Maria will fly in an hour
(225) a. Maria will swim in an hour
(227) a. Maria will fly
b. Maria will swim

In (224a) and (225a) *fly* and *swim* can more easily be conceived of as perfective than can *fly* and *swim* in (227a) and (227b).

The fact that the *to*-place adverbial, as in (226a) and (226b) above, does not necessarily impart perfectivity to the basic (and primarily imperfective) sentences of type (227a) and (227b), is somewhat strange, in view of the transformation of imperfective sentences of type (228a) and (228b) below into perfective (229a) and (229b) through a *to*-place adverbial – the two sentences in (229) are much more likely than those in (226) to be conceived of as perfective and non-inchoative, that is, as "wholes" with a beginning and an end:

(228) a. Maria flew
b. Maria swam
(229) a. Maria flew to Thessaloniki
b. Maria swam to the other bank

The aspectual ambiguity of (226a) and (226b), in contrast to (229a) and (229b), is apparently due to the semantics and pragmatics of tense, which falls beyond the scope of this book. It is usually assumed, however, that tense should, ideally, be excluded from the aspect analysis, and so expressions like *fly to Thessaloniki* and *swim to the other bank* are viewed as perfective in isolation. The action can be imperfectivised by the preposition *towards*, as in (230a) and (230b) but, again, the *in*-time phrase is capable of perfectivising the action in sentences like (230c) and (230d) by making it inchoative:

(230) a. Maria flew towards Thessaloniki
b. Maria swam towards the other bank
c. Maria flew towards Thessaloniki in an hour
d. Maria swam towards the other bank in an hour

The incorporation of the *in*-time phrase into the past tense sentences (229a) and (229b), resulting in (231a) and (231b) below, does two things: it precludes the inchoative (perfective) reading (or at least makes it highly improbable), but at the same time, more importantly, perfectivises the resulting sentence to a degree where it can be read imperfectively only as a non-bounded iterative – for which a strong iterativising unbounding context would be required, as in (231c):

(231) a. Maria flew to Thessaloniki in an hour
b. Maria swam to the other bank in an hour
c. Maria swam to the other bank in an hour whenever she was in good
shape

To sum up the analysis of *in*-time phrases, complementing these adverbials to various expressions explicating perfectivity or imperfectivity shows that the *in*-time rule in English is valid only in general terms. But if *in*-time adverbials do not always ban imperfectivity to make the sentence ungrammatical and do not always impose a perfective interpretation to the sentence, they certainly tend to impart perfectivity to it – which may then be overridden by the semantics or the pragmatics of the whole sentence.

OTHER EXCEPTIONS TO THE RULES

There are other important exceptions to the rule of perfective *in*-time and imperfective *for*-time association that any linguist dealing with English aspect, lexical semantics (semantics and use of prepositions) or translation into Slavic languages will be aware of. According to some authors (see, e.g., Hinrichs 1985: 232), some of the exceptions with the *for*-time adverbial were dealt with more extensively for the first time by Dowty (1979). The most obvious one is with verbs and verb phrases with meanings that permit or even presuppose time scope of the adverbial outside the scope of the action. One such example has already been dealt with in the discussion of the (partial) aspectual ambiguity of the verb *rest*, as in a sentence like (168a):

(168) a. We shall rest this field for a year

Consider also Dowty's example *John awakened for an hour* where the so-called internal reading of the action applies (see Dowty 1979: 251). Other prototypical examples of an exception to the rule of imperfective *for*-time association would be those with verbs like *leave* and *return*, as in (232a) and (232b):

(232) a. The patient left the hospital for an hour
b. The patient returned home for an hour

In these cases the *for*-time adverbial combines freely with phrases (*left the hospital, returned home*) that are undoubtedly perfective – as shown in sentences like (233a) and (233b) in which *in*-time association is also allowed. It is also interesting to note that after a *for-in* shift if *returned home* is ambiguous between an achievement and an accomplishment meaning, *left*, at least in *left the hospital*, is not, reading mainly as an achievement, the accomplishment reading being very improbable:

(233) a. The patient returned home in an hour
b. The patient left the hospital in an hour

The second, less obvious, exception, is when a bounded expression which easily combines with an *in*-time phrase, as in (234a) below, is made indefinitely iterative, as in (235a) – this case was peripherally dealt with in (231c) above. If the *in*-time adverbial in (234a) below is the expected one, the *for*-time adverbial in (234b) yields an unacceptable sentence in the achievement reading of *recovered from the effect of the drug/restored his pulse*. In the accomplishment sense, however, though less typical, the sentence is normal. The action (read as an accomplishment or an achievement) can be transformed into an indefinite iterative, as shown by the expansion of (234b) into (235):

(234) a. The patient recovered from the effect of the drug/restored his pulse in half an hour
b. (?)The patient recovered from the effect of the drug/restored his pulse for half an hour

(235) a. Whenever given an overdose, the patient recovered from the effect of the drug/restored his pulse in half an hour
b. Whenever given an overdose, the patient recovered from the effect of the drug/restored his pulse for half an hour

The bounded-non-bounded or non-bounded-bounded shift observed here again falls within Lindstedt's nested aspects phenomenon described above.

Now compare the sentences in (236) below which illustrate an important feature of the *for*-time phrase. While the perfective (236b), i.e., (236a) complemented by an *in*-time phrase, and sentence (236c), i.e., the imperfective *Tourists climbed the mountain* complemented by a *for*-time phrase, are grammatical, sentence (236d) is, if not exactly ungrammatical, unacceptable for some speakers:

(236) a. The/some/five tourists climbed the mountain
b. The/some/five tourists climbed the mountain in a week
c. Tourists climbed the mountain for a week
d. ?Tourists climbed the mountain in a week

Although, as already mentioned, native speakers' opinions seem to vary with respect to the degree of acceptability or unacceptability of sentences like (236d), it can certainly be assumed that non-boundedness of a subject is not the best match for an *in*-time adverbial. Conversely, the English sentence (237a) below with a bounded subject seems to permit a *for*-time phrase but the meaning is transformed from a true perfective to one that is broadly equivalent to the meaning of the Bulgarian imperfective Aorist (237b), cf. (237b), the Bulgarian translation equivalent of (237a) – that is, (237a) describes an action which terminated before achieving its inherent result:

(237) a. The/some/five tourists climbed the mountain for a week (but they either did not reach the peak or reached it repeatedly in an attempt at something else which was not achieved)
b. Turistite/njakolko turisti/petima turisti izkačvaha$_{impfvAor}$ planinata v prodăžlenie na edna sedmica (no te ili ne dostignaha$_{pfvAor}$, vărha ili go dostigaha$_{pfvAor}$ mnogokratno v opit da postignat drugo, koeto ne beše postignato)

(for more detail concerning the Bulgarian Aorist/Imperfect opposition, see Kabakčiev 1984b). As far as the well-formedness of phrases like *climbed the mountain for a week* is concerned, even if sentences like (237a) are unacceptable for some speakers of English, the equivalence of the situational meaning in (237a) to the situational meaning of the Bulgarian imperfective Aorist is not to be questioned. This specific meaning, explicated by the *for*-time phrase will be considered in detail in Chapter Thirteen, *On aspectual classes in English* – because, it actually represents, as will be argued there, a separate type of situation (of the Vendlerian type).

To sum up the analysis of *for*-time adverbials, though it may seem that the characteristics of the *for*-time phrase are clear-cut and that the *for*-time rule is imposed in English as rigidly as the *in*-time rule, there are cases in which the *for*-time rule fails to take effect – due to the semantics of the verb as a lexical entry or to the ability of the *for*-time phrase to expand achievements into durative imperfective situations.

NOTES ON THE RELIABILITY AND THE APPLICABILITY OF THE *FOR*-TIME AND THE *IN*-TIME TEST

There is a very important point to be made concerning the significance of *for*-time and *in*-time adverbials for the analysis of aspect. Clearly, on the one hand, the possibility of adding a *for*-time or an *in*-time adverbial to another phrase or a whole sentence depends on the basic aspectual meaning of the phrase or sentence in question. On the other hand, the possibility of adding either an *in*-time or a *for*-time adverbial is taken to be a major test for perfectivity or imperfectivity in practically the whole of the aspectological literature from the earliest times of studying aspect in the compositional framework up to the present day (see, e.g., Verkuyl 1971/1972; Mittwoch 1971; Dowty 1979; Smith 1994; Tenny 1994). It is natural for investigators of aspect in English, when they are native speakers of the language, to rely heavily on this kind of test for determining aspectual readings of phrases and sentences. But the test proves to be very tricky in many cases, and overrelying on it can be misleading. What is more, as the examples below will show, the *in*-time/*for*-time test is far from being as universally applicable, as aspectologists would like it to be. Tenny (1994: 65-66), for example, depending crucially on the test for determining aspectual meanings, adduces the following sentences that are, in her judgement, grammatical (238a), (238c), (238d), partly unacceptable (238b), or ungrammatical (238e):

(238) a. The truth frightened John in five minutes
 b. ?John feared the truth in five minutes
 c. John feared the truth for five minutes
 d. The movie frightened the children to death
 e. *The children feared the movie to death

Obviously, verbs like *frighten* and *fear*, along with many other similar verbs, cannot be analysed as displaying a tendency to explicate perfectivity and imperfectivity, respectively, on the basis of the *in*-time/*for*-time test. Or, to put it simply, although (238a) and (238c) are possible grammatical sentences, people do not usually construct sentences of this kind: it does not make much sense to use (238a) with an *in*-time adverbial and (238c) with a *for*-time adverbial, whatever the exact reason for this. If sentence (238b), too, is unacceptable, it is not only because the imperfective expression *fear the truth* does not combine with an *in*-time phrase, but because one does not normally determine the length of time associated with one's fear. Fear does not normally have a definite beginning and (especially) a definite end. Hence, the important conclusion to make is that pragmatic restrictions (that have to do with our general knowledge of the world) require the two basic aspectual readings, perfectivity and imperfectivity, to be determined not on the basis of the compatibility of phrases or sentences with a temporal adverbial but simply on the basis of what the particular phrases or sentences mean. It can be argued here that although translation from one natural language into another may not be generally considered an entirely reliable criterion for determining the semantics of classes of sentences in a given language, translation equivalents in languages with verbal aspect could be used as a metalanguage for determining the aspectual readings of English sentences. This method has been successfully employed in many cases in the present work.

In her analysis of the aspectual readings of various types of sentences in English Tenny (1994: 27-28) also claims that the subject in a sentence like (239b) below does not change the aspectual interpretation. The verb phrase *killed the rosebush*, bounded in isolation and in (239a), remains bounded, according to Tenny, also in sentences like (239b). And in a sentence like (239c) it is to be regarded as perfective again, despite the mass-noun subject. Compare the sentences in (239):

(239) a. Mary killed the rosebush (by overwatering) in a day/*for a day
 b. Snow killed the rosebush in a day/*for a day
 c. Snow killed the rosebush

But what these sentences actually show is, again, that the *in*-time/*for*-time test cannot be viewed as a universal test for boundedness/non-boundedness. Because if Tenny is right about the grammaticality of (239a) and (239b) with *in a day* and the ungrammaticality of (239a) and (239b) with *for a day*, she is certainly wrong to make a generalisation that a mass-noun subject cannot change the aspectual meaning of the sentence. Tenny's (1994: 27-28) claim that a bare subject does not imperfectivise a perfective verb phrase and that generally "external arguments cannot measure out the event" (Tenny 1994: 62) amounts to a refutation of the compositionality of aspect beyond the level of the verb phrase. In her book Tenny failed to see Verkuyl's exclusive contribution in building up the theory of compositional aspect. His theory is regarded there as just one of the many approaches towards aspect (Tenny 1994: 24, 30, 131).[4]

But, on the other hand, Tenny is right that a sentence like (239b) above is perfective, hence (239c) could be perfective too. The issue will be addressed later on, in Chapter Fourteen, *On 'knowledge of the world' in the explication of aspect in English* where it will be shown how pragmatic inferences are capable of changing or governing the aspectual interpretation of many sentences that otherwise, on the basis of the principles of the compositional mechanism, ought to be considered as having a different aspectual reading.

---

[4] Tenny's (1996) rather favourable review of Verkuyl (1993) appears inconsistent with her refutation of compositional aspect.

One of the problems here is that, for some reason, Tenny puts sentences like (239c) above in a contextual framework similar to the one in (239a). Because if she is right about the ungrammaticality of (239a) and (239b) with *for a day*, she apparently failed to see that, placed in a very slightly different context, sentence (239c), that is, sentence (239b) without any adverbial, can easily refer to a non-bounded situation. Consider a sentence like (240):

(240)   Snow killed the rosebush every winter

Contrary to Tenny's suggestion that *Snow killed the rosebush* is perfective in spite of the non-boundedness of the referent of the subject, sentence (240) is clearly imperfective. Its contextual framework now is one in which Mary has been trying to grow a rosebush in her garden for years and has repeatedly failed because snow has been killing it (of course, *the rosebush* here represents what was earlier called a design or a sort – it is not a particular specimen or a token). Recall also another problem discussed in previous chapters, and also by Danchev (1974) and Moens (1987: 94), about the necessity to isolate a neutral context for determining the aspectual reading of a sentence. Tenny has incorrectly placed sentence (239c) above in the context of (239b), and sentence (239b) itself is placed in the context of (239a) due to the situational similarity of (239a) and (239b) and for pragmatic reasons: the nature of the action of killing a rosebush is such that if we require it to takes place within a day, then this must be a case of a completed action. However, semantically, structurally and from the point of view of the compositional mechanism, sentence (239c) may be said to belong to the context of a sentence like (240) – rather than (239b), which, in its turn, belongs to the context of (239a):

(239)   c.   Snow killed the rosebush
(240)   Snow killed the rosebush every winter

In a similar vein, Tenny (1994: 28) argues that the meaning of *surround* in the sentences in (241) below is identical and is unaffected by the quantificational structure of the subjects:

(241)   a.   Eight large oaks surrounded the house for a year/*in a year
        b.   Snow surrounded the house for one winter/*in one winter

Again, it is the imposed contextual framework that predetermines the aspectual meaning in conflict with the compositional requirements. In a different contextual perspective, cf. (242a) below, the same bare mass-noun subject takes part in the explication of perfectivity, again in conflict with the compositional mechanism. Tenny's argumentation with respect to (241a) and (241b) above involves what she calls the stative verb *surround*; thus whether in (242a) and (242b) below this is a case of a different (non-stative) verb *surround*, is another matter – note that *surround* in *Snow surrounded the house for two hours* ought to be defined as more stative than *surround* in *Snow surrounded the house in two hours*:

(242) a. Snow surrounded the house in two hours/for two hours
 b. The snow surrounded the house in two hours/for two hours

As far as the sentence (242b) with a definite mass-noun subject is concerned, again, both types of time adverbials seem to be good, depending on the aspectual interpretation assigned to the sentence without the adverbials.[5]

IN-TIME AND *FOR*-TIME ADVERBIALS: A SUMMARY

To sum up the analysis of the contribution of *in*-time and *for*-time adverbials to aspectual composition, the *in*-time/*for*-time rule, originally posited by Mittwoch (1971), can be said to be valid for English in general terms, but it is not a universal one. It should be noted, however, that whatever the aspectual characteristics of the phrase they are complemented to, time adverbials are in many cases capable of strongly influencing the aspectual interpretation of the rest of the sentence. They can also serve, within certain limits, as an important tool in linguistic analyses to assign aspectual values to verbs, verb phrases and sentences. At a first glance, it seems rather strange that a basic rule for the adequate grammatical description of the English language should remain neglected in grammars. Even the most detailed grammar of English available today (Quirk et al 1985) lists just a handful of examples of the basic uses of *for*-time and *in*-time adverbials without establishing any special relationship between them. Although the concept of a 'completed action', as well as Vendler's notions of state, activity, accomplishment and achievement are occasionally made use of in Quirk et al (1985), in connection with non-progressive tense forms, lexical semantics, adverbials like *up* (as in *drink/eat up*), a coherent explanation of the aspect mechanism is absent.

---

[5] A more serious problem concerns the notion of 'measuring-out'. In spite of Tenny's conjecture that objects are able to 'measure out' the delimitedness of the event, it is far from clear exactly how, for example, an apple, being bounded **spatially**, should delimit **temporally** the event of eating in *eat an apple*. And in view of the existence of many sentences in which the quantitative nature of the subject does influence the aspectual interpretation of the sentence (the relevant linguistic data have already been considered here and extensively dealt with in the aspectological literature), the following conclusion can be said to be simply wrong:

> "It appears to be the case that the option of translating spatial delimitedness into temporal delimitedness is only available for direct internal arguments, as these are the arguments which can measure out events"

(Tenny 1994: 29). Firstly, spatial delimitedness cannot be translated into temporal delimitedness: delimitedness/boundedness, at least according to the present approach, is transferred directly in temporal terms. Secondly, temporal delimitedness/boundedness is not "only available for direct internal arguments". As already shown, the referents of NPs are capable of transferring their (temporal) boundedness onto the referents of verbs from all syntactic positions – though, of course, the explication of the aspectual meaning of a phrase or sentence can also be influenced by other factors, e.g. pragmatic ones.

It can be concluded that the failure to formulate properly the basic *in*-time/*for*-time rule, along with its specific subrules and exceptions, manifested in different linguistic studies and in most grammars is apparently due to the lack of understanding of the global aspect mechanism to which the specific rule in question ultimately belongs. Moreover, it seems that in spite of the great progress made in aspectology in recent decades, the overall mechanism of the explication of aspect in English and in similar languages has generally remained misunderstood in linguistics. Thus, as a final generalisation concerning *in*-time and *for*-time adverbials, it appears fully justified to maintain that any description of the grammar and semantics of English that takes no proper account of the behaviour of these adverbials is doomed to be inadequate.

ADVERBIALS OF PLACE

As already shown in the discussion of verb meanings in the previous chapter, besides adverbials of time, which can be seen as a major factor for explicating aspectual distinctions, adverbials of place can also play a role in the composition of aspect in the sentence. Consider once again the sentences in (163) and (164) below. The lack of adverbials or the presence of adverbials specifying the location or the destination of the action in (163) allows the explication of imperfectivity due to the atelic aspectual potential of the verbs and the aspectual contribution of the other components in the sentences. Conversely, the presence of adverbials of place in (164) determining not merely the location of the action or the destination of the movement, but the actual point of arrival allows the explication of perfectivity.

(163) a. Let me carry your suitcase
b. The tears flowed from her eyes
c. Can you row a boat?
d. The boy rolled the barrel in the cellar
e. Ivan walked toward the old town

(164) a. Let me carry your suitcase to the station
b. The river flowed over its banks
c. Can you row the boat across the river?
d. The boy rolled the barrel into the cellar
e. Ivan walked to the University/from the old town to the University

Here it is worth analysing precisely where the perfectivity of sentences like (164b), (164c), (164d) and (164e), in contrast to the imperfectivity of sentences like (163b), (163c), (163d) and (163e), originates from. Clearly, the explication of perfectivity is due to the contribution of the prepositions (in this case *to*, *into* and *across*) which, partnered with telic verbs in the Past Simple Tense, are capable of signifying arrival at the point of destination – provided, of course, that the rest of the sentence is also in tune with the requirements for perfectivity. The problem is whether the notion of boundedness should somehow be regarded as located in the lexical meaning of the preposition, that is, whether prepositions like *to*, *into* and *across* should be regarded as having a telic aspectual potential in contrast to prepositions like *in* and *toward* which ought to be regarded as atelic, or whether perfectivity should be considered as only analysable at the semantico-syntactic level.

Since the explication of perfectivity is crucially dependent on the use of prepositions, the former solution seems to be the correct one. Thus, in the long run, prepositions like *to*, *into* and *across*, on the one hand, and *in* and *toward*, on the other hand, can be said to exercise aspectual functions in English. Compare the explication of perfectivity and imperfectivity in simple sentences like (163) and (164) through the use of prepositions in languages where aspect is expressed directly in the verb. In Bulgarian, the imperfective English sentence in (163e) is rendered through an imperfective Imperfect verb form and the preposition *kăm* 'towards', as in (163e'); the perfective sentence (164e) is rendered through a perfective Aorist verb form and the preposition *v* 'in', as in (164e'):

(163) e. Ivan walked towards the old town
     e'. Ivan vărveše$_{impfvImp}$ kăm star-ija grad
        Ivan walked towards old-the town
(164) e. Ivan walked to the old town
     e'. Ivan otide$_{pfvAor}$ v star-ija grad
        Ivan walked in old-the town

There is no lexical contrast in Bulgarian similar to the contrast in English between the prepositions *in* and *into*. Sentences like (163d) and (164d) are both translated through the preposition *v* which thus stands for '*to*, *in*, and *into*' – cf. the Bulgarian sentences (164e') above and (163d') and (164d') below in which aspectual reading is determined by the form of the verb:

(163) d. The boy rolled the barrel in the cellar
     d'. Momče-to tărkaljaše$_{impfvImp}$ varel-a v maza-ta
        Boy-the rolled barrel-the in cellar-the
(164) d. The boy rolled the barrel into the cellar
     d'. Momče-to vtărkoli$_{pfvAor}$ varel-a v maza-ta
        Boy-the rolled barrel-the in cellar-the

This shows that the general rules underlying the use of prepositions in a particular language, along with their semantics, can play a major role in the explication of aspect in compositional terms and can be an essential part of the overall system of aspect. It is also worth noting that in languages with a case system the use of prepositions in the compositional explication or in the direct (verbal) expression of aspect ties in with the choice of case. Compare the following two pairs of sentences in German (243) and Russian (244), where the prepositions equivalent to English *in* and *into* are the same (German *in*, Russian *v*) but the cases in the nouns (NPs) differ. The accusative is used in the perfective sentences (243a) and (244a) in both German and Russian, and in the imperfective sentences (243b) and (244b) the dative is used in German, the prepositional (locative) case in Russian:

(German)
(243) a. Die Kinder gingen in den Park$_{Acc}$
The children went in(to) the park
'The children went into/entered the park'
b. Die Kinder spielten in dem (im) Park$_{Dat}$
The children played in the park
'The children played in the park'

(Russian)
(244) a. Deti vošli v park$_{Acc}$
Children went in(to) park
'The children went into/entered the park'
b. Deti igrali v parke$_{Loc}$
Children played in park
'The children played in the park'

Unfortunately, but not surprisingly, the standard grammars of these two languages usually describe the phenomenon using concepts like direction, motion, destination, location, etc., and not in terms of the perfective/imperfective opposition which constitutes the actual contrast in the above examples. Recall that case plays a major role in the compositional explication of aspect in Finnish. However, since the description of the role of prepositions in the overall system of aspect in a language like English would require a separate large investigation, only the outlines of this problem are given in the present work.

ADVERBIALS OF MANNER

If adverbials of time and adverbials of place are, generally speaking, important for the explication of aspect in English, it is interesting to consider whether adverbials of manner would play a similar role. In his original theory of compositional aspect Verkuyl (1972: 109) maintained that instrumental adverbials fall outside that scope of the sentence in which aspect is composed. He gave the examples (245a) and (245b) below, arguing that the action in both sentences is perfective (non-durative, in his terminology), hence, in his judgement, these sentences are ungrammatical with a *for*-time adverbial:

(245) a. *Carla wrote that letter with a pencil for half an hour
b. *Carla wrote that letter with pencils for half an hour

More than two decades later, Tenny (1994) also claimed that instrumental adverbials do not take part in the explication of aspect at the level of the sentence, arguing that the action in her sentences (246) below is perfective (delimited, in her terminology), hence the possibility of adding an *in*-time adverbial, and the ungrammaticality after adding a *for*-time adverbial:

(246) a. John melted the ice cube with <u>a candle</u> in a minute/*for a minute
      b. John melted the ice cube with <u>hot coal</u> in a minute/*for a minute[6]

(Tenny 1994: 28). This observation gave Tenny further justification of her claim, previously discussed, that only direct objects, not even subjects, take part in the explication of aspect (Tenny 1994: 29). But if direct objects do take part in the explication of aspect, as both Verkuyl and Tenny have strongly insisted, consider sentence (247a) below with an instrumental adverbial. Sentence (247a), along with its (247b) correspondence, is a famous example that has been used frequently in linguistic studies to support the idea that instrumental adverbials can be transformed into direct objects. Compare the two sentences:

(247) a. Seymour sliced the salami with a knife
      b. Seymour used a knife to slice the salami

How can it be that instrumental adverbials, incapable of taking part in the explication of aspect, are at the same time capable of being transformed into direct objects – which, in turn, are capable of taking part in the explication of aspect?

No doubt, transformation into a direct object is also possible if the noun in the instrumental adverbial is pluralised and deprived of an article. Compare the sentences in (248):

(248) a. Seymour sliced the salami with knives
      b. Seymour used knives to slice the salami

Thus a sentence like (247b) can be said to explicate perfectivity, according to all accounts, including Verkuyl's perfective schema and Tenny's 'measuring out' the event by a count-noun object, in contrast to a sentence like (248b), which ought to explicate imperfectivity, for opposite reasons, already defined:

(247) b. Seymour used a knife to slice the salami
(248) b. Seymour used knives to slice the salami

But let us also check this conjecture against a description of the situation in real-life terms. Suppose *Seymour* is a shop-assistant at the meat department in a supermarket. He has various kinds of salami and various kinds of knives to slice them with. Sentence (247b) will then normally be used to describe a single occasion of his 'slicing the salami' as a bounded action, whereas sentence (248b) will be used to

---

[6] But, as Tenny (1994: 33) herself admitted, there are native speakers of English who have no trouble in accepting the phrase *melt the ice cube* with a *for*-time adverbial.

describe his permanent activities at the supermarket. And there is no reason not to treat the two sentences with the instrumental adverbials, (247a) and (248a), in a similar fashion, complementing the structural and semantico-syntactic analysis with the explanation given above in purely pragmatic terms. Cf. (247a) and (248a):

(247) a. Seymour sliced the salami with a knife
(248) a. Seymour sliced the salami with knives

Thus, contrary to Verkuyl's and Tenny's views, instrumental adverbials do play a role in the explication of aspect (see also Kabakčiev 1986), and this provides further support for the validity and significance of the compositional theory of aspect, including Verkuyl's own original version of it.

CONCLUDING REMARKS

Indeed, it can be argued that the contrast between perfectivity and imperfectivity is best explicated through the contrast between a quantified and an unquantified (syntactic) object in a simple sentence (of a certain kind already defined). Subjects, indirect objects and especially adverbials of manner, being less directly associated with the action, tend to explicate aspect distinctions less clearly, but, nevertheless, their role in the compositional explication of aspect cannot be denied. It has already been demonstrated that many other language entities of a grammatical or semantic nature are capable of influencing the expression of aspectual values. One such entity, negation, has not been considered yet. It will be dealt with in the following chapter (again in a polemical fashion, for negation has usually been considered a major factor for explicating imperfectivity).

CHAPTER 12

ON NEGATIVITY AND THE EXPLICATION OF PERFECTIVITY

ON THE GENERAL RELATIONSHIP BETWEEN NEGATIVITY AND PERFECTIVITY

The review of some major studies of aspect in English has shown that there is no agreement among aspectologists about the real scope in syntactic terms of the compositional mechanism for explicating the perfective/imperfective contrast. In spite of a number of proposals put forward by different authors concerning the degree of the alleged non-involvement of (syntactic) subjects, of certain kinds of adverbials, etc. in the explication of aspect, in other publications the aspectual interpretation of sentences has been shown to be influenced by the entities mentioned. Negation, however, depending on the point of view, has either been regarded as a basic factor interfering with the rules of the compositional explication of perfectivity or as an aspectual marker in itself, a marker of imperfectivity.

The literature on aspect, especially works analysing data from Germanic languages, abounds in assertions that there is a general incompatibility between perfectivity and negation. To quote but a few, according to Galton (1984: 27), an event, simply, cannot be negated. According to Bartsch, too, a negative event is a state (Bartsch 1995: 34). Among the few authors who, when dealing with aspect took into account the temporal (or, rather, the spatio-temporal) status of participants in situations, Cooper, trying to determine the status of his so-called located individuals finds that it is not clear what to do with them in negative sentences (Cooper 1985: 16). The reason is that the participants in situations denoted by negated sentences tend to "exist" in arbitrary locations. This means, for instance, that *John* and *Mary* in Cooper's sentence (249) are to be interpreted as different entities from the "located" referents of *John* and *Mary* in (112b):

(249)   John didn't kiss Mary
(112) b. John kissed Mary

As far as Slavic languages are concerned, indeed, a certain incompatibility between negation and perfectivity exists there, and it manifests itself mainly in the imperative. However, leaving aside semantic subtleties, in Russian, for example, there is no general rule restricting the negation of perfective verbs. Indeed, negated perfectives in the imperative have special uses. For instance, they can be warnings (*Ne zabud'*$_{pfv}$*!* 'Don't forget', *Ne opozdaj*$_{pfv}$*!* 'Don't be late'), see Russian Grammar (1982: 611), requests (*Ne pogubite*$_{pfv}$*!* 'Don't destroy/kill!'), apologies (*Ne obessud'te*$_{pfv}$*!* 'I am sorry'), polite forms of address, sometimes ironic (*Ne otkažite*$_{pfv}$ *v ljubeznosti!* 'Would you be so kind' [lit. 'Don't refuse in politeness']), see Russian Grammar (1982: 623). An all-round restriction for negated perfectives to appear in the imperative holds for Bulgarian. Sentences identical to the Russian ones above are simply impossible: **Ne zabravi*$_{pfv}$*!* 'Don't forget', **Ne zakăsnej*$_{pfv}$*!* 'Don't be late!', **Ne pogubi!* 'Don't destroy/kill', etc. The use of an imperfective verb here is obligatory: *Ne zabravjaj*$_{impfv}$*!*, Ne *zakăsnjavaj*$_{impfv}$*!* 'Don't be late', *Ne pogubvaj*$_{impfv}$*!* 'Don't destroy/kill'.

But there is absolutely no restriction with respect to the use of negation with past and future (tensed) perfective verb forms in both Russian and Bulgarian, cf.: *Ja ne zabyl*$_{Pastpfv}$ 'I didn't forget', *Ne zabudu*$_{pfvFut}$ 'I won't forget' (Russian); *Ne zabravih*$_{pfvAor}$ 'I didn't forget', *Njama da zabravja*$_{pfvFut}$ 'I won't forget' (Bulgarian). This means that negated actions in the past and in the future can freely be represented as perfective or imperfective. Of course, while the Present Tense of a perfective verb in Russian is used with a future meaning or with a meaning of present indefinite repetition, the Bulgarian Present Tense of a perfective verb is either ungrammatical (when it is used in isolation) or allows the meaning of present indefinite repetition – in special syntactic environments (see Chapter One, *On the essence of aspect*).

VERKUYL'S TREATMENT OF NEGATIVITY AND PERFECTIVITY

Verkuyl (1972) was probably the first linguist to point out a certain incompatibility between perfectivity and negation in English. And in his extended theory (Verkuyl 1993) he dealt extensively with the problem maintaining that all the negative English sentences below (and, supposedly, also their Dutch equivalents) are imperfective (durative, in his terms), despite the perfectivity (terminativity) of their positive counterparts (see Verkuyl 1993: 92):

(250) a. No child came in
 b. Nobody stumbled
 c. He lifted nothing
 d. Mary didn't mail a single letter/mailed no letter
 e. None of them came in

Imperfective (durative), according to Verkuyl, are also sentences like:

(251) a. No girl ate five sandwiches
 b. Two girls did not eat five sandwiches
 c. Nobody lifted four pianos
 d. The three men did not lift four pianos

From a general and categorical assertion like this, maintained by other authors as well, it ought to be inferred that there exists a general semantic rule in English to the effect that the introduction of negativity into a perfective sentence will automatically trigger imperfectivity in the resulting sentence. And a rule of this kind ought to be expected to have a large cross-language validity, too. However, if the originally denoted situation of the sentences in (251) is to be preserved, their translation into Slavic languages like Russian and Bulgarian yields perfective sentences (examples are given below). Verkuyl's suggestion that these sentences in English (and, obviously, in Dutch) can only be imperfective apparently rests on the assumption that negative NPs are [-SQA] simply by definition: if a negated verb expresses an action that did not happen, then nobody performed any action and there can be no 'specified quantity' associated with the agent of such an action. Or, as Verkuyl put it, trying to account for the action as well:

> "if no(ne of the) men in a model lifted pianos, why should one be interested in structuring the set of men? And, if two girls ate no sandwich, why should one be interested in the way they did not eat them?"

(Verkuyl 1993: 163-164).

But what are Verkuyl's other arguments for assigning durativity to negative sentences? Here they are:

> "These [negated] sentences are all durative. They allow for durational adverbials, they cannot be combined with *in an hour*, they express a state in conjoined temporal adverbials, and so on"

(Verkuyl 1993: 92).

Argumentation based on temporal adverbials is, again, strange. For even leaving aside cross-language data like the fact that all the negative English sentences above translate most naturally into Bulgarian and other Slavic languages with a perfective verb and that many of them are even ungrammatical or strange with an imperfective verb (see below), Verkuyl actually distanced himself from all problems concerning adverbial modification and declared that he would not deal with them:

> "The present study is crucially focused on the composition of inner aspect. It does not deal with the description of sentences [with *in/for* temporal adverbials], in the absence of a sufficiently articulated theory of adverbial modification."

(Verkuyl 1993: 14). A statement like this, if it does not exactly invalidate the thesis with respect to negation and imperfectivity (because the *in*-time/*for*-time test can generally be taken as valid in spite of the complexity of its employment), at least seriously undermines the argumentation (of the kind cited above), should it be based on temporal adverbials in the first place.

Another piece of reasoning in favour of the connection between negation and imperfectivity comes some 70 pages below in Verkuyl's book:

> "In all cases considered in the present section, it is intuitively clear why (regular) negation and terminative aspect cannot go together: there is no domain for a possible mapping between atemporal and temporal structure"

(Verkuyl 1993: 166). This argument might prove very revealing. For it links negation with the alleged lack of temporality in NPs, a point which has already been discussed and will again be considered below.

NEGATION AND THE TEMPORAL STATUS OF PARTICIPANTS: A CONTRASTIVE ANALYSIS

Now compare the most natural translation of Verkuyl's negative English sentences (250a) through (250e) into Bulgarian (250a') through (250e'):

(250)   a. *No child* came in
   a'. Nito   edno/ nikoe/ nikakvo   dete   ne   vleze$_{pfvAor}$
       Not   one/   no/   no kind of   child   not   entered
   b. *Nobody* stumbled
   b'. Nikoj   ne   se   spăna$_{pfvAor}$
       Nobody   not   *prt.*   stumbled
   c. He lifted *nothing*
   c'. Toj   ne   vdigna$_{pfvAor}$ ništo
       He   not   lifted   nothing
   d. Mary did*n't* mail *a single letter*/mailed *no letter*
   d'. Meri   ne   izprati$_{pfvAor}$ nito   edno/   nikakvo   pismo
       Mary   not   sent   not   one   no kind of   letter
   e. *None of them* came in
   e'. Nikoj   (ot tjah)/   Nito   edin   (ot tjah)   ne   vleze$_{pfvAor}$
       Noone   (of them)/   Not   one   (of them)   not   entered[1]

These most natural translations are rendered by using the prototypically perfective/bounded past tense verb form: the perfective Aorist. Conversely, if, for example, the English sentence (250a) is to be translated into Bulgarian with the prototypically imperfective/non-bounded past tense form, the imperfective Imperfect, the meaning becomes such that the Bulgarian sentence either lends itself into a translation with the Progressive (rather than the Simple Past) back into English or, in the act of describing a rather strange or rare kind of situation, a habitual reluctance to entering on the part of a child or children is referred to:

(250)   a''. Nito   edno/   nikoe/nikakvo   dete   ne   vlizaše$_{impfvImp}$
            Not   one/   no/no kind of   child   not   entered
            'No child was entering/would enter'

A similar case obtains with respect to the other sentences. Cf. for example (250b''), where everyone takes care not to stumble (hence 'Nobody would stumble' in the translation back into English), and (250c''), where the subject is habitually reluctant to lift anything:

---

[1] Double and even triple and quadruple negation is possible and normal in Bulgarian.

(250) b". Nikoj   ne   se   spăvaše$_{impfvImp}$
　　　 Nobody   not   prt.   stumbled
　　　 'Nobody was stumbling/would stumble'
　　c". Toj   ne   vdigaše$_{impfvImp}$ ništo
　　　 He   not   lifted   nothing
　　　 'He wasn't lifting/wouldn't lift anything'

Clearly, the Bulgarian sentences with the prototypical imperfective form impart special nuances to the action, while the simple non-occurrence of a single act of entering or stumbling or lifting is covered only by the perfective form.

In other words, the most natural translation of Verkuyl's negative sentences into Bulgarian yields perfective, not imperfective sentences. Hence, firstly, how could the possible perfectivity of the English negative sentences be accounted for? And, secondly, doesn't this possible perfectivity have something to do with the semantics of the NPs?

If the sentences with (English) *nobody* (or Bulgarian *nikoj* 'nobody') are considered, it could be argued that *nobody* is able to partake of the semantic status of *somebody*. What do we mean when we say *somebody* in (252a) or (252b)?

(252) a. Somebody has eaten John's breakfast
　　　b. Somebody told me it wasn't easy to catch a bus so early in the morning

What we refer to is a stage of a human agent which is thought to have performed the action, but its temporal location is unknown and its existence cannot definitely be asserted. Or, in ordinary language, by uttering sentences like (252), we are not entirely sure the action took place: maybe nobody ate from John's breakfast, maybe the speaker himself/herself ate it and then forgot. Maybe nobody told me it wasn't easy to catch a bus so early in the morning, I just jumped to the conclusion myself. But whether the temporal location of the participants (or whatever it is that a subject like *someone* stands for) in sentences like (252) is unknown or whether their existence can be asserted or not, the actions denoted by the verbs *has eaten* and *told* in them are perfective.

Thus a solution to the problem could present itself along the following lines. If the idea of the stages of individuals doing or not doing something is conceived of as a valid explanation of the semantics of such sentences, there remains no obstacle to viewing negative NPs not as [-SQA] (using Verkuyl's terminology) but as NPs that refer to stages of individuals that are in a certain sense empty (being negated) but can be either [-SQA] or [+SQA] (bounded or non-bounded) according to the contribution of other semantic or grammatical components in the sentence or context. 'Empty' here covers a particular non-temporal value of the information in the NP which pertains to the negation. No attempt will be made here to define it, but obviously it does not block the existence of a stage of an individual. This solution is a natural one, and it is in consistence with the major thesis about the temporal status of participants in situations developed in the previous chapters of the book.

An analysis of the temporal status of participants (or complements to the verb like *nothing* or *no letter*) in sentences like those in (250) is also possible in commonsense terms, identical or similar to the one made in Chapter Five, *Extension in time of subjects and objects from a "common-sense" point of view*. Consider again the following two sentences:

(250) c. He lifted *nothing*
       d. Mary did*n't* mail *a single letter*/mailed *no letter*

On the one hand, note that these two sentences can be answers to questions like *What did he do?* and *What did Mary do?* where *he* and *Mary* can be analysed as either single bounded stages of the corresponding individuals (in the primary, perfective interpretation of these questions) or as recurring non-bounded stages (in the secondary, imperfective interpretation – which would require contextual support). And if each question can be either perfective or imperfective, there is no reason for the answers to have only one of the values – that is, there is no reason for rejecting an interpretation in which the referents of the participants (or the verb complements) are single bounded stages and the action itself is a single bounded one. On the other hand, single bounded actions like *lift something* or *mail a letter* take place in particular circumstances on a particular time stretch. Therefore, consider a phrase like *on that particular occasion*. Complemented to the two questions (*What did he do on that particular occasion?*, *What did Mary do on that particular occasion?*) or to the two negative sentences, it yields sentences that are both perfective and perfectly grammatical:

(250) c'''. He lifted *nothing* on that particular occasion
       d''. Mary did*n't* mail *a single letter*/mailed *no letter* on that particular occasion

To be able to utter truthfully the sentences (250c''') or (250d'') or the questions eliciting them as answers the observer/speaker would have to have perceived (or imagined) the referents of the subjects and the (syntactic) objects as single bounded stages of the corresponding individuals or physical objects taking part in a single bounded action. Thus, clearly, both the question and the negative answer can be perfective sentences with an accomplishment situational value – though, of course, there is no accomplishment in real-world terms, for nothing is lifted, no letter is mailed. But the accomplishment situational value and the lack of an accomplishment in real-world terms should be kept apart.

Such an approach is a viable one, as the analysis of sentences with negative NPs and *in*-time and *for*-time adverbials below will again show. Negation does not simply erase the temporal configuration of a certain referent of the NP, although this is exactly what Verkuyl's and other aspectologists' theses lead us to assume. Verkuyl used the following negative sentences with temporal adverbials:

(253) a. For hours no child came in
 b. ?Nobody mailed a letter in an hour
 c. Mary let in none of the children on Monday and Tuesday

Now compare the following sentences in Bulgarian that constitute translations of these English sentences. Either prototypically perfective verbs, as in the (253э) sentences, or prototypically imperfective verbs, as in the (253ээ) sentences, are used in the Bulgarian versions[2]:

(253) a. For hours no child came in
 aэ. V prodălženie na časove/?S časove nito edno dete ne vleze_pfvAor
  In course of hours/With hours not one child not came-in
 aээ. V prodălženie na časove/S časove nito edno dete ne vlizaše_impfvImp
  In course of hours/With hours not one child not came-in
 b. ?Nobody mailed a letter in an hour
 bэ. Nikoj ne izprati_pfvAor pismo za edin čas
  Nobody not sent letter in [literally: *for*] one hour
 bээ. Nikoj ne izpraštaše_impfvImp pismo za edin čas
  Nobody not sent letter in [literally: *for*] one hour
 c. Mary let in none of the children on Monday and Tuesday
 cэ. Meri ne pusna_pfvAor vătre nikoe ot deca-ta v ponedelnik i vtornik
  Mary not let inside none of children-the on [literally: *in*] Monday and Tuesday
 cээ. Meri ne puskaše_impfvImp vătre nikoe ot deca-ta v ponedelnik i vtornik
  Mary not let inside none of children-the on [literally: *in*] Monday and Tuesday

In English, the otherwise "unnatural" combination of *for hours*, which is non-bounded in isolation, and the perfective *No child came in* which results in a grammatical sentence (253a) above should be viewed as a specific semantic feature of English that is relatively peripheral with respect to the general aspect mechanism –

---

[2] In Bulgarian, the adverbial *s časove* 'for hours [literally: *with hours*]', which is mainly used in the description of non-bounded situations and is the more usual equivalent of (English) *for hours*, makes the sentence (253aэ) partly unacceptable because of a clear incompatibility between *s časove* 'for hours' and a perfective verb form. But a perfective situation of this type is not at all impossible, as shown by the first version of sentence (253aэ), in which the adverbial *v prodălženie na časove* 'for hours [literally: in course of hours]' is not incompatible with a perfective (verb in the) Aorist.

but still worth taking into account. In any case, there is no reason for the aspectologist to be forced to interpret the action in a sentence like this as imperfective simply because a *for*-time adverbial (in this case of the special *for-hours* type) is present. Or at least the association with the adverbial is not a reason to rule out perfectivity. If the perfective reading of (253a) above remains opaque when interpreting this sentence through the metalanguage of Modern English itself, it becomes manifest in a contrastive analysis of the English sentence (253a) and its major Bulgarian equivalent – sentence (253aэ), with a perfective verb in the Aorist.

But whatever the implications of the contrastive analysis (they are many and require a separate study), the English data here leads to a conclusion that, actually, there are two different types of *for*-time adverbial phrases in English:

(i) a *for-an-hour* type which has a special bounded (terminated) situational meaning, and

(ii) a *for-hours* type which has a 'state' or 'process' (non-bounded, non-terminated) situational meaning.

This is a general conclusion. The following chapter will deal with the semantics of sentences with the *for-an-hour* type of adverbial phrase and future research ought to show the exact parameters of the difference between the *for-an-hour* type of adverbial phrase and the *for-hours* type of adverbial phrase, as well as the compatibility of the two types of adverbials with verbs, verb phrases or whole sentences with different situational meanings. For example, one problem is whether temporal adverbials like *for hours* (cf. also *for months, for years*, etc.) should be seen as exponents of a special situational meaning or as exponents of a simple 'state' reading. Judging from a sentence like (156a) at least (repeated below), in spite of its bare plural noun *hours*, the adverbial *for hours* seems to bound the non-bounded action of *John pushed trolleys into the supermarket* in a certain sense. Conversely, the phrase *for hours on end* seems to imperfectivise the action again by serialising it further. Note that the serialisation applies to an action which is iterative in itself (*pushed trolleys*). Compare sentence (156a) with the two types of adverbials allowed:

(156) a. John pushed trolleys into the supermarket ?*in an hour/for hours/for hours on end [this was his job]

The adverbial *for hours* will be dealt with again later on in this chapter, and it will be seen that it can even allow, in a somewhat specific case (of negation), a perfective interpretation in the rest of a sentence.

The contrastive analysis also shows that negative Bulgarian sentences like (253b') and (253b''), repeated below, in which there is a temporal adverbial of the *in*-time type (*za edin čas* 'in an hour') and a prototypically perfective or an imperfective verb form are equally grammatical, although they differ semantically. Sentence (253b') describes a failure on the part of an agent, probably within a group of possible agents, to send a letter in an hour. Sentence (253b'') describes the same failure realised habitually, as an extended process or a state, observed by the speaker.

(253) b. ?Nobody mailed a letter in an hour
    b'. Nikoj   ne izprati$_{pfvAor}$ pismo za   edin   čas
       Nobody   not sent   letter in [literally: *for*] one   hour
    b". Nikoj   ne izprataše$_{impfvImp}$ pismo za   edin čas
       Nobody   not sent   letter in [literally: *for*] one hour[3]

There is no doubt that many other fully grammatical negative sentences of type (253b') with a prototypically perfective past tense verb form in Bulgarian can be constructed. Thus the availability of such a large amount of data refutes the thesis according to which there is a general incompatibility between negation and perfectivity. Or, at least, the applicability of such a thesis to certain languages different from Dutch and English is rejected.

But is this thesis really valid with respect to English? Compare some other English examples constructed by Verkuyl with their Bulgarian equivalents. Sentence (254a) below translates naturally with a perfective Aorist (254b). Translations in which an imperfective verb (primary or secondary) in the Imperfect is used in Bulgarian do not actually cover the meaning of the English sentence (254a). Instead, they refer to an activity (254c) or an extended (possibly habitual) situation (254d):

(254) a. Nobody wrote a letter in an hour
    b. Nikoj   ne napisa$_{pfvAor}$ pismo za   edin   čas
      Nobody   not wrote   letter in [literally: *for*] one   hour
    c. Nikoj   ne pišeše$_{impfv1Imp}$ pismo za   edin   čas
      Nobody   not wrote   letter in [literally: *for*] one   hour
    d. Nikoj   ne napisvaše$_{impfv2Imp}$ pismo za   edin   čas
      Nobody   not wrote   letter in [literally: *for*] one   hour

To double-check these conclusions, the direction of the translation can be reversed. In that case the prototypically perfective Bulgarian sentence (254b) would naturally be translated through (254a), and the prototypically imperfective Bulgarian sentence

---

[3] Of course, as noted by an anonymous reviewer, negativity could involve various complications. To quote him/her, a sentence like *Nobody left for an hour* could have two readings, depending on the scope of the negative element: "If it means 'It is not the case that somebody left for an hour' (where *for an hour* specifies the amount of time a person who left would have been gone for), it is unbounded (unless bounded contextually); but if it means 'For an hour it was the case that nobody left' then it has a bounded interpretation." Note, however, on the one hand, that *Nobody left for an hour* could be regarded as a special case, similar to a sentence like *The patient left the hospital for an hour* (dealt with in the previous chapter), which is perfective in spite of the *for*-time adverbial – recall Dowty's (1979: 251) example *John awakened for an hour*. Cf. also *Somebody left for an hour*, which is perfective, and the imperfective reading would only be possible in an iterativising context. On the other hand, it is true that *Nobody left for an hour* could be non-bounded, just like *Some people left for an hour*, where no iterativising context is needed for the imperfective reading and it seems to be the plural in the subject that allows it. In any case, the issue of how the scope of a negative element can influence the aspectual reading will not be addressed here – because of its complexity – and will be left for future research.

(254c) with a progressive-like meaning would be rendered in English through the Progressive, as in (254c') below – not through the sentence in (254a) with a Past Simple Tense form of the verb. Similarly, the Bulgarian sentence (254d) with a secondary imperfective in the Imperfect and a habitual meaning would naturally be rendered in English through a *used to* habitual verb form, as in (254d') below, not through (254a) with a Past Simple Tense form of the verb.

(254) b. Nikoj ne napisa$_{pfvAor}$ pismo za edin čas
↓
a. Nobody wrote a letter in an hour

c. Nikoj ne pišeše$_{impfvImp}$ pismo za edin čas
↓
c'. Nobody was writing a letter in an hour

d. Nikoj ne napisvaše$_{impfv2Imp}$ pismo za edin čas
↓
d'. Nobody used to write a letter in an hour

Or, in other words, while the Bulgarian perfective Aorist sentence (254b) naturally translates into the sentence with the Past Simple Tense (254a), the imperfective Imperfect sentences (254c) and (254d) are conveyed more felicitously through the overtly imperfective English sentences (254c') or (254d') with a Progressive or a *used to* habitual form. Thus the contrastive analysis demonstrates that an English negative sentence with an *in-an-hour* type of adverbial and a basically perfective verb phrase (in this case *wrote a letter*) like (254b) ought to be considered perfective rather than imperfective. And there is no doubt that the conclusion concerning this sentence can be extended to an enormous number of other negative sentences in English with a similar structure.

Along these lines, another piece of argumentation can be put forward in favour of viewing the referents of negative NPs as temporal. There are sentences in which the action denoted is not simply one that has not taken place, but is one that was supposed to take place in a particular fashion. In an often quoted example (255a) below, constructed by Partee (1973), it is clear, first, that the action that was not realised was supposed to be realised, at least in the most natural reading of the sentence. Second, the unrealised action was to be carried out as an accomplishment, that is, as a perfective one. Hence, there is no reason for the referents of *I* and *the stove* in a negative sentence like (255a) to be considered different, both as ordinary individuals and as stages, from the referents of *I* and *the stove* in the corresponding positive sentence (255b):

(255) a. I didn't turn off the stove
b. I turned off the stove

Both sentences assert the existence of a stage of the individual *I* which did or did not turn off the stove; both sentences assert the existence of a stage of the (ordinary) object *the stove* which did or did not take part in the action. No doubt, many negative sentences in English (and in other languages) are of this type precisely: denoting actions that did not take place but were planned to be realised as a particular situational type – not actions that just did not happen to take place. And the existence of the stages of the participants in these situations is asserted – although the (real-life) situations do not take place and remain hypothetical (imaginary, planned, expected, etc.).

Therefore, the idea of viewing negative sentences in English as necessarily imperfective ought to take into account not only Simple Past Tense sentences where it is difficult to see the actions as imaginary, planned, expected, etc. but also, for example, sentences in the Indefinite Future Tense – where actions are expected to take place or are not expected to take place. In both positive and negative expectations with respect to actions, these actions can be regarded as either perfective or imperfective. Consider sentences like the following:

(74')   The boy will throw the stone
(74")   The boy will not throw the stone
(100) a'.   The boy will carry the stone
(100) a".   The boy will not carry the stone

Sentences like (74') and (74") can easily be defined as perfective, conversely, sentences like (100a') and (100a") can easily be defined as imperfective – and in both cases negation can be said to play no role in determining the aspectual value. More importantly, the negation of the action in (74'), resulting in (74"), cannot be said to imperfectivise the action of throwing.

But, to return to the contrastive analysis once again, a very interesting phenomenon related to the problem of determining the particular temporal or atemporal status of NPs in negative sentences can be observed in Bulgarian. In a special case of emphatic negation, the temporal feature of certain NPs primarily denoting physical objects springs to the surface. Consider the following sentences:

(256) a. Včera   ne săm   vključval$_{impfv}$ v kăšti nikakăv televizor
         Yesterday not have-I [literally: *am*] switched-on   at home no TV set[4]
         [literally] 'I have switched no TV set at home yesterday'
      b. V taja   staja njama   da vključvam$_{impfv}$ nikakva pečka
         In this   room   won't-I to switch-on   no   heater
         'I am not going to switch on any heater in this room'

---

[4] The (only) Present Perfect auxiliary in Bulgarian is *săm* 'be' and, unlike in English, past-time adverbials like *včera* 'yesterday' are compatible with the Present Perfect (usually called 'Past Indefinite').

Since many people have only one TV set in their home and, normally, only one heater in a room, we should take it that in sentences like (256a) and (256b) only one physical electrical appliance is referred to, not a choice made in the presence of several appliances. At least this is the usual sense which the Bulgarian native speaker makes out of sentences like (256a) and (256b). Therefore, obviously, what the seeming plurality of 'heaters' in the negative NP actually signifies is not a plurality of appliances but the possibility to switch on a single appliance several times. By using *nikakăv televizor* 'no TV set' and *nikakva pečka* 'no heater' reference to a stage of the corresponding (ordinary) object, or even to an event, is made – the switching-on of a TV set or a heater. Or, in other words, *nikakăv televizor* 'no TV set' and *nikakva pečka* 'no heater' acquire a temporal meaning of a kind that is even visible to the ordinary speaker, perhaps with some mental effort. This slightly colloquial Bulgarian syntactic pattern is actually a very productive one and negation and perfectivity in it make a perfect match! A similar phenomenon can be found in the English sentence (257a) and (257b) below, directly (literally) translatable into Bulgarian, cf. (257c) and (257d):

(257) a. Last week we had no school
b. Next week we are going to/we'll have no school
c. Minala-ta sedmica njamahme$_{impfvImp}$ nikakvo učilište
Last-the week not-had-we no school
'Last week we had no school'
d. Sledvašta-ta sedmica njama da imame$_{impfvFut}$ nikakvo učilište
Next-the week will-not to have-we no school

Although, nominally, the (syntactic) objects in the four sentences, *no school* in (257a) and (257b), and *nikakvo učilište* 'no school' in (257c) and (257d), ought to refer to a choice of school buildings, this reading is entirely suppressed. Instead, the sentences may be said to have (syntactic) object referents that are overtly temporal for the ordinary speaker who definitely conceives of *school* in (257a) and (257b) and *učilište* 'school' in (257c) and (257d) as 'classes', not as 'a school building'. Note that the latter interpretation ('school' conceived of as 'a school building') is not at all impossible: consider sentences like (257b) or (257d) produced in the unfortunate circumstances of a war.

What is especially noteworthy for the sentences in (256) above is that the verbs in them are normally imperfective. (The perfective is possible but less common, produces specific implications and conceals the temporality of the referents of the NPs denoting the appliances.) The negative NPs *nikakăv televizor* 'no TV set' and *nikakva pečka* 'no heater', according to the mechanism of mapping already described (no doubt, valid entirely for Bulgarian as well), receive the following temporal status: they constitute a non-bounded series of a stage of a TV-set and a heater. The effect is similar to overt pluralisation but there is also a difference. If *nikakăv televizor* 'no

TV set' and *nikakva pečka* 'no heater' in these two examples refer to one (physical) electrical appliance and, simultaneously, to a temporal role involving an unbounded series of TV-set- and heater-switchings on, in the case of overt pluralisation reference would be made to a plurality of (physical) TV-sets and heaters and the temporal role would be less visible. The (here so-called) temporal role has not received much attention in the literature. Glasbey (1994: 214-231) voiced the necessity for her TIME-OF thematic role to be studied alongside major (generalised) roles like (Proto-)Agent and (Proto-)Patient. Proto-Agent and Proto-Patient have been put forward as terms and semantic notions by Dowty (1991); largely the same phenomenon is explored in Fillmore's (1968) case theory. However, if the temporal (TIME-OF) role in Glasbey's thesis does not purport to be universally present among the major arguments of the verb, the present study has shown that subjects and objects should always be regarded as having a fully identifiable temporal status.

Now, to return to Verkuyl's (1993) extended compositional theory, Verkuyl, along with other aspectologists working within a Montague-type approach, often used sentences with severely quantified subjects (*two girls, three men*) and objects (*five sandwiches, four pianos*) to test aspectual meanings. It can be argued that the complicated possibilities for interpreting the action in such sentences does not influence the aspectual interpretation in a significant way – as long as the subjects and the objects are quantified. That is, as long as they are bounded, and, hence, map their boundedness onto the referent of the verb. (The problem of whether the collective/distributive distinction might be relevant or not to the explication of aspect in the sentence is not dealt with here – or elsewhere in this work.) Note also that negative sentences with a complex quantification of the participants and an even more complex pattern of the action like (258a) and (258b) below, analysed as they are, out of context, refer to actions that are strange, uncommon in real-world terms.

(258) a. Two girls did not eat five sandwiches
b. Three men did not lift four pianos

And if we apply the contrastive linguistic test again, the strangeness of the action denoted is probably the reason why none of the two major aspectual possibilities in Bulgarian would be favoured – a perfective (verb in the) Aorist or an imperfective (verb in the) Imperfect. The imperfective Imperfect can in certain cases like these be either primary or secondary, as shown in (259aɜ):

(259) a. Two girls did not eat five sandwiches
aɜ. Dve momičeta   ne   izjadoha$_{pfvAor}$ pet   sandviča
    Two girls   not   ate   five   sandwiches
aɜɜ. Dve momičeta   ne   jadjaha$_{impfv1Imp}$/izjaždaha$_{impfv2Imp}$ pet sandviča
    Two girls   not   ate   five sandwiches
b. Three men did not lift four pianos

b'.	Trima măže	ne	vdignaha$_{pfvAor}$		četiri	piana
	Three men	not	lifted		four	pianos
b''.	Trima măže	ne	vdigaha$_{impfvImp/impfvAor}$[5]		četiri	piana
	Three men	not	lifted		four	pianos

Thus two separate sets of sentences are formed which refer to two different kinds of actions (situations), bounded and non-bounded, and there is no reason to insist that the same aspectual readings do not exist for the two English sentences (259a) and (259b). That is, negated sentences with severely quantified participants do not allow an imperfective interpretation only.

It seems, however, that Verkuyl's decision to treat negative NPs as simply [-SQA] has to do with the specificity of the English and Dutch data or, in the long run, with the specificity of the grammatical structure of English and Dutch. Thus sentences like (260a) and (260b) below tend to foster a straightforward and natural interpretation in which a child such that did not enter is simply taken to be non-existent. However, as already argued, any sentence of this kind potentially carries another reading, which is, perhaps, a secondary one, and which in ordinary-language terms implies the following: for hours there was a permanent expectation such that a child might come in any hour or minute of these hours, but the expectation remained unfulfilled. The difference between the simple-erasure-of-the-child reading and the any-minute-expectation-of-the-child reading is now clear. But while it is fully transparent in Bulgarian through the tense-aspect perfective/imperfective contrast in the verb, it appears to be harder to perceive on English or Dutch data. In English, the difference in question becomes quite transparent if sentences like (260a) and (260b) are compared:

(260) a. For hours no child was coming in
b. For hours no child came in
c. For hours a child came in
d. For hours children came in

What the use of the *for*-time adverbial in these cases brings about is the following. While in sentences like (260a) and (260d) it is naturally compatible with the non-boundedness of the referent of the verb and the referent of the subject, respectively, and in sentences like (260c) it either disallows a perfective reading or imposes an iterative imperfective reading, in a sentence like (260b) it actually **allows** a perfective interpretation **due to the negation effect**. The explanation of the relationship between negation and perfectivity that Verkuyl and others offer is in a rather different direction, and it is that the *for*-time adverbial complementation is a test simply confirming the imperfectivity of a sentence.

---

[5] The verb *vdigaha* 'lifted' in (259b'') is imperfective, but this particular tense form for the 1st pers. pl., is unmarked with respect to the Aorist or the Imperfect. That is, this is a case of grammatical homonymy.

According to the analysis in this book and in this chapter in particular, a rather different solution arises, namely, that *in*-time and *for*-time adverbials should not be seen first and foremost (or solely) as language tests for aspectual values. *In*-time and *for*-time adverbials are simply natural language expressions that are added to verb phrases and sentences denoting states or actions for the sake of communicating certain temporal meanings, and these meanings are not necessarily dependent on the aspectual values of the verb phrases or sentences the temporal adverbials in question are added to.

CONCLUSION

With the help of a contrastive analysis it has been shown in this chapter that the relations between negativity and aspect are much too complex for a one-to-one correspondence between negativity and imperfectivity to be argued for. Claims about a general incompatibility between perfectivity and negation fail to meet the cross-language test and provide an inadequate picture of the semantics of English negative sentences. Although this problem sphere clearly requires further research, perfectivity should by no means be regarded as simply precluded by negation.

CHAPTER 13

ON ASPECTUAL CLASSES IN ENGLISH

HOW TO CLASSIFY TERMINATED STATES AND ACTIVITIES?

The main purpose of this work has so far been to describe aspect in English in terms of a contrast between perfectivity (boundedness) and imperfectivity (non-boundedness), understood as a universal distinction that can also be found in other languages or even, most probably, in all natural languages. The idea of viewing aspect as a perfective/imperfective contrast expressed in various overt or covert ways has been prevalent in many studies of aspect. However, the notions of perfectivity and imperfectivity (boundedness and non-boundedness), if they can serve as basic tools for the analysis of aspect in most general terms and for a broad description of the aspect mechanisms found across languages, prove insufficient in an attempt at a more comprehensive and precise analysis of the semantics of all kinds of sentences and situations denoted by them. According to Vendler's classification and similar descriptions, which establish four different situations, not a single distinction, imperfectivity/non-boundedness is conceptualised as two major kinds: activities and states. These two situations are widely recognised as necessary and valid separate characterisations of the semantics of sentences. But, on the one hand, the need for making a distinction between accomplishments and achievements as perfective actions/situations has often been challenged by aspectologists: as already shown earlier, it is often difficult to tell whether a perfective action takes place as a more or less momentary transition from one state into another or as a time-consuming event. And, on the other hand, many investigators have pointed out that there is a certain feature in the essence of the accomplishment situation that has to do with the way the action terminates. Thus, if an action can normally terminate in a way that was anticipated from the very beginning it started to take place, in some cases it can terminate before having reached the anticipated point.

To take an archetypal example with the phrase *build a house*, houses usually end up built, and when finally built they are such that they can be lived in. Could this implication of completion in the phrase *build a house* somehow be avoided? Compare the discourse sequence in (261c) below, in which the implication of a result of the action described in (261a) and (261b) ought to be cancelled. But, actually, in (261c) this cancellation does not seem to be possible – native speakers invariably find this sentence ungrammatical:

(261) a. John built the house
b. John built the house from 1990 to 1992
c. *John built the house from 1990 to 1992. But it was not ready until 1996. He had financial problems which his brother had to help him solve and he resumed the construction after it was stopped for several months

Obviously, the implication that the house John built is ready to be lived in is much too strong in (261a) and (261b) for the accomplishment value to be cancelled, although, as Tenny (1994: 33) points out, phrases like *build a house* **are** used imperfectively by some speakers – probably in sentences and contexts different from those in (261c).

Consider, however, the phrase *paint the table* once again. Palmer's (1965: 79) judgement that a sentence like (16a) below does not necessarily refer to a completed action has already been discussed:

(16) a. I painted the table this morning

Verkuyl (1993: 330) even argues that *paint* is a *push*-verb, i.e., a verb with an ambiguous aspectual potential (according to the terminology employed here), and gave sentence (170c) as an example:

(170) c. Roland painted the door

Note also that a paraphrase of *paint the table* that describes the endpoint or the result of the action is difficult to find. Hence, the possible implication that the table was completely painted, as in (262a) below, or that it was completely painted before noon, as in (262b), ought to be easy to cancel, and this is done in the discourse sequence in (262c). However, although a sequence like (262c) below is generally found to be much more acceptable than (261c) above, native speakers' judgements seem to vary again. A slightly different sequence, like (263d) below, appears to serve as a better illustration of a cancellation of the accomplishment implication[1]:

(262) a. John painted the table
b. John painted the table that morning
c. John painted the table that morning. But he finished it the evening because he had to stop painting in the afternoon
d. John painted the fence that morning. But he finished it in the evening because he had to stop painting in the afternoon

---

[1] It was Sheila Glasbey (personal communication) who found sentence (262c) odd and suggested the change from (262c) to (262d) for the purposes of the discussion. In her opinion, a sentence like (262d) is perfectly acceptable for the following reason: a fence is bigger than a table and can easily be thought of as taking more time to paint.

Consider, however, a phrase like *climb the mountain*. 'To climb the mountain' means to reach a particular place in the mountain after climbing it. That is, a result associated with the action can be formulated. Indeed, the implication that John reached a particular place in the mountain other than the peak in sentences like (263a) and (263b) below cannot be said to be directly cancelled in (263c). But if John did not reach the peak of the mountain – which was his aim (not reaching some other place in the mountain) – then the preliminary accomplishment implication in (262a) or (262b) could be said to be cancelled in (263c):

(263) a. John climbed the mountain
b. John climbed the mountain that morning
c. John climbed the mountain that morning. But he could not reach the peak until the evening because of the fog

Note also that, unlike (261c) and even (262c), sentence (263c) is fully acceptable.

Now, to return to the examples in (262) above, if sequence (262d) is acceptable, then, clearly, the first sentence in it, *John painted the fence that morning*, does not report that the fence was completely painted. It means that the fence was painted in the morning only to a certain degree. Similarly, if in the morning John did not reach the peak of the mountain, which was his aim, then his climbing the mountain in (263c) does not involve an accomplishment. Hence, an important question arises. Taking into account that the action of painting the fence was terminated in the afternoon and reached its 'natural endpoint' in the evening, what does *John painted the fence that morning* in (262d) mean then? Similar questions can be asked with respect to *John painted the table that morning* in (262c) in the idiolect of those speakers who find sequences of this kind acceptable, and with respect to *John climbed the mountain that morning* in (263c). Was the table completely painted in (262c)? Did John reach an accomplishment in (263c) by climbing the mountain? The answer is definitely negative. But if an attempt is made to classify the type of event present in the first sentences of the sequences in (262c), (262d) or (263c) according to Vendler's schemata, no place for a situation of this kind will be found there. The action is not an accomplishment because it is not brought to its natural endpoint. And it is not a process/an activity either, because it is terminated, i.e., it is not non-bounded.

Perhaps, we could take it that, e.g., *John painted the fence that morning* is an accomplishment in isolation as well as in the context of (263d) but that in the former, regular, case (in isolation) the accomplishment displays in a more marked way some special semantic feature, besides boundedness, setting accomplishments apart from activities. Among the authors who discerned this special feature of accomplishments in question, Moens (1987) called it a *consequence*. Moens proposed a classification of situations (called 'states of affairs') based on Vendler's in which, basically, events and states are distinguished. Events can be atomic and extended; atomic events can be culminations (*recognise, spot, win the race*) and points (*hiccough, tap, wink*). Extended events can be culminated processes (*build a house, eat a sandwich*) and processes (*run, swim, walk, play the piano*). Culminations and culminated processes have consequences, while points and processes have no consequences (see Moens 1987: 42-43). Similarly, in Smith's classification (discussed earlier), events like *tap* and *knock* are analysed as 'dynamic', 'atelic' and 'instantaneous', they are called semelfactives and form a separate situation (see Smith's 1991: 6).

So far so good. Intuitively, actions like *hiccough, tap, wink* and *knock* besides being, in contrast to accomplishments, momentary, could be said to have no consequences. There is no pragmatic result like, for instance, a house ready to be lived in, as in (261a) above, and no table or fence completely painted, as in (15a) or (262). No special 'change of state' in the subject or object to a verb of this kind can be traced. But, on the one hand, there is a problem with the notion of consequence. Any semantic analysis can show that its essence is extremely elusive. For example, it is difficult to answer a question like: what exactly is the consequence for the tourist and the peak if the tourist climbed to the peak? And, on the other hand, as a rule, no place is provided in descriptions of situations of the Vendlerian type for a distinction between, to use Moens's terms, non-culminated processes that are terminated and non-culminated processes that are non-terminated.

Galton (1984), another aspectologist who was aware of the semantic complexity of bounded actions, actually proposed a special schema for actions terminated without having reached their 'natural endpoint'. He called the category representing the schema *the pofective*, after the class of Russian delimitative perfective verbs with a prefix *po-*. Here is Galton's explanation for his choice of the term pofective and the motivation for employing it:

> "The designation *Po* comes from the Russian perfective prefix *po-*, one of whose functions is essentially the same as this operator's. Thus from *p'et'* (to sing), *plakat'* (to weep) and *stojat'* (to stand), we get *pop'et'* (to sing for a while), *poplakat'* (to weep for a while), and *postojat'* (to stand for a while) [...] *Po* is an operator which, like *Ingr*, forms radicals out of propositions; it is thus a perfective aspect operator, and I cannot resist the temptation of calling it the *pofective operator*"

(Galton 1984: 81-82). Clearly, according to Galton, the essence of the pofective in English is covered by the phrase *for a while* which, no doubt, is a *for-*time adverbial phrase.

But Galton's conceptual framework and terminology are somewhat different from those employed here in reference to types of situations. Furthermore, some of the points Galton made appear to be rather incompatible with the basic tenets of this work. For instance, in Galton's model sentences like (264a) and (264b) below with progressive verb forms report states (see Galton 1984: 68), not activities or processes:

(264) a. Jane is swimming
b. Jane is swimming a length

Also, to quote Galton again:

> "an atelic durative event consists of some state's obtaining for an unspecified but bounded period of time, and we have made use of locutions such as *have a ...* and *... for a while* and *spend a while ...-ing* to express them. Thus to say that the state reported by the sentence *Jane is swimming* obtained for an unspecified duration we may say any of *Jane had a swim, Jane swam for a while,* and *Jane spent a while swimming*; and in many contexts exactly the same meaning will be conveyed by *Jane swam* (for example, in response to the question *What did Jane do this morning?*). [...]
>
> Now a necessary and sufficient condition for Jane to have spent a while swimming is that Jane started swimming and later stopped swimming"

(Galton 1984: 80).

Obviously, Galton was aware of the necessity to deal with terminated and non-terminated states or activities. But the problem is that if phrases like *had a swim* (that is, phrases of the *have a look* type already analysed earlier) are classified as atelic, this would interfere with the interpretation of the meaning of the homonymous verb when it is to be classified as an accomplishment or achievement (in Vendler's terms). Compare the sentences in (265) and (266) below, where, if the verbs *look* and *met* in (265a) and (266a) represent accomplishments, then there is no reason for their correspondences *have a look* and *had a meeting* in (265b) and (266b) not to be classified as accomplishments as well:

(265) a. Look at this
      b. Have a look at this
(266) a. The President met with some opposition members last week
      b. The President had a meeting with some opposition members last week

It could be maintained that the syntactic objects in (265a) and (266a) are prepositional phrases rendering the objects indirect and less susceptible to a standard aspectual interpretation. Recall Tenny's argument about the direct object being the only syntactic component capable of changing the aspectual interpretation through its own (spatial) boundedness or non-boundedness. But then note that *meet* can also be made intransitive, as in the sentence (267a) below, with a very clear accomplishment meaning equivalent to that of (266a). Therefore, it seems totally unreasonable to assign a different situational meaning like Galton's pofective to the equivalent sentence (267b) with the phrase *have a meeting*:

(267) a. The President and some opposition members met last week
      b. The President and some opposition members had a meeting last week

It could even be argued that the phrase *have a meeting* is such a strong exponent of perfectivity that, in certain cases at least, it does not allow the bare plural of the indirect object to explicate imperfectivity. This can be illustrated by a sentence like (268b) below. It clearly reports a perfective action in spite of the bare plural of the indirect object – so much so that even the corresponding sentence with a simple verb in (268a) cannot be said to explicate perfectivity more markedly[2]:

(268) a. The President met with opposition members
b. The President had a meeting with opposition members

Galton's work set apart, the difference between accomplishments proper and terminated activities, or between (non-bounded) activities proper and terminated activities (that is, bounded activities that have not yet turned into accomplishments), generally either remains unnoticed in the aspectological literature or only some of the relevant features are discussed there. Binnick, too, made an important observation, namely, that in a sentence like (269) below a phrase like *finish walking* sounds odd:

> "*Finished walking* in its normal, activity sense is odd, because *finish* presupposes a delimited goal, whereas walking is normally an activity without a delimited goal"

(Binnick 1991: 178).

(269) John finished walking

Similarly, in his description of states Mellor (1995: 11) maintained that states "obtain over time, holding regardless of surrounding events" but they can also start and stop.

But how should a state that has stopped be referred to?

Starting and stopping of states can be exemplified through standard sentences like (270a) or (270b) below in which starting and stopping are achievements and *loving* and *hating* can be defined as states that are bounded at one end only:

(270) a. John started loving/hating Mary
b. John stopped loving/hating Mary

According to Galton's thesis, adding a *for-a-while* adverbial to a state-denoting sentence ought to produce a sentence which denotes a state that has started and then stopped. For instance:

(271) a. John loved Mary for a while
b. John hated Mary for a while

---

[2] On the contrary, sentence (268b) is more perfective than (268a) – probably because of the singular form *a meeting* which emphasises the singularity of the event. But, on the other hand, both sentences (268a) and (268b) explicate perfectivity in contradiction with Verkuyl's perfective schema. The reason for this can be explained in pragmatic terms. See Chapter Fourteen. *On 'knowledge of the world' in the explication of aspect in English.*

Earlier in this book, in Chapter Ten, *Meanings of nouns and noun phrases, and aspect in English*, Bache's (1983) sentence (182b) was discussed and it was argued there that although *peace* can be regarded as non-bounded in isolation, in this particular case the referent of the otherwise state-designating noun *peace* is actually bounded in time – through the adverbial *only a couple of months*:

(182) b. Peace lasted only a couple of months

It is worth noting also that, according to the mechanism of mapping described in some of the previous chapters, both the referent of the verb *lasted* and the referent of the subject *peace* can be transformed from a single bounded instance, as in (182b) above, to a non-bounded series of separate bounded instances, as in (272):

(272) Peace lasted only a couple of months each time it was restored

Thus, excepting some occasional observations of different authors, and despite a certain incompatibility with the present approach, Galton's proposal concerning the so-called pofective turns out to be radically different from the standard assumptions of aspectologists studying the subtleties of situation classes. It is strange why a separate class of situations similar to Galton's pofective has not generally been identified, at least in the majority of aspectological studies. Not that Galton's own thesis is, as already argued, without problems. He justifiably assigns the pofective to sentences like (273b) below when they are conceived of as a response to a question like (273a):

(273) a. What did Jane do?
b. Jane swam

But Galton considers pofective not only phrases like *have a swim* – which in the present framework have already been analysed as exponents of perfectivity proper (see the discussion of phrases of the *have a look* type in Chapter Ten, *Meanings of nouns and noun phrases, and aspect in English*) – and phrases like *swim for a while*, but also phrases like *spend a while swimming*. It can be argued that in a phrase like this the 'spending' reached its natural endpoint – signified by the whole phrase *spend a while*.

On the one hand, the sentences in the discourse sequence (273a) – (273b) above have already been dealt with in the description of English sentences falling within a semantic pattern similar to the semantics of the Bulgarian imperfective Aorist. On the other hand, the fact that a category like Galton's pofective appears as an exotic proposal in the aspectological literature seems to rest on an assumption that the exponents of a category like this could only be found in the domain of specific verb-noun collocability. Compare the examples of the pofective given above. The pofective, according to Galton's thesis, is restricted to the *spend a while ...-ing* expression, to phrases containing the adverbial *for a while*, and to phrases of the *have a look* type – all of which are rather specific expressions.

EPISODES: A NEW CLASS OF SITUATION

One need not, however, delve deep into the lexical and phraseological resources of English in search of special collocations like the *have a look* or the *for a while* type of phrases to be able to find examples of a situational category like Galton's pofective. The English language offers a much better exponent of the situational schema in question, and it is precisely the *for*-time adverbial phrase – discussed at length in the previous chapter. Notorious for its semantico-syntactic complexity, rather messy in its applicability to phrases and sentences as a test for imperfectivity, the *for*-time adverbial can be seen as a perfect representative of what will here be called the situational class of episodes.[3]

What are here called episodes can best be defined as Vendlerian 'states' or 'activities' that have terminated. Or, in other words, episodes are states and activities brought to an end without having reached some inherent endpoint. In the classification of situations that will be proposed below Vendler's activities are called processes, accomplishments and achievements are merged into the class of events. States and processes are imperfective, non-bounded, situations; episodes and events are perfective, bounded, situations. However, while there can be no doubt that events (that is accomplishments and achievements) are perfectives, and that episodes are perfectives in so far as they depict situations (originally states or processes) that have terminated, episodes differ from events in that they do not contain a certain pragmatic result or consequence inherent in events (that is, in both accomplishments and achievements).

To give an example, there is a concrete result of the action in sentences like (71a), (43b), (274a) or (274b) below, pragmatically identifiable. The apple described in (71a) is no longer in existence. There is a book written in (43b). John has acquired a mental picture of a bird in his memory in (274a). John has changed his mind in a certain way in (274b).

(71) a. John ate an apple
(43) b. John wrote a book
(274) a. John spotted the bird
b. John realised the truth

Conversely, episodes are not associated with a similar, pragmatically identifiable, result of a given action, and no inherent endpoint of the action is reached. As argued in the previous chapter, sentences like those in (222c), repeated below, with

---

[3] Galton does not expressly assign the pofective to time adverbials of the *for an hour* type – which, as already argued extensively in this book, are of extreme importance for the description of the overall system of aspect in English.

accomplishment phrases and a *for*-time adverbial are not necessarily ungrammatical for all native speakers of English:

(222) c. (?)She played a game of tennis/played the sonata/sang a song/swam to the other bank/knitted three sweaters/painted the wall for half an hour

Hence, in a sentence like (275a) below the sonata is not finished, the three sweaters are not yet ready in (275b), the wall is not yet painted in (275c), but, nonetheless, all the actions described are terminated:

(275) a. John played the sonata for half an hour
b. Katinka knitted three sweaters for half an hour
c. John painted the wall for half an hour

Terminated situations that are initially states have not been excluded here as candidates for the class of episodes but such a proposal would not seem to be universally accepted: there is unwillingness on the part of many linguists to analyse states in temporal terms. Recall Carlson's (1980) assignment of an atemporal 'individual' status to referents of subjects and objects in state-denoting sentences like *X knew Y* or *X loved Y*. Smith (1999) actually subscribes to Taylor's (1977: 206) view that states do not take time – but are **in** time. Yet she abstains from assigning the 'event' feature to sentences like *Mary was here for 2 hours* containing 'state' phrases like *Mary be here*. Among those scholars who dealt with the Vendlerian distinctions, Pustejovsky (1992) also noted the possibility for both processes and states to be complemented by *for*-time adverbials but paid more attention to processes than to states. Pustejovsky (1992: 49), among others, referred to processes complemented by *for*-time adverbials as *bounded processes*. On the one hand, this term is not felicitous, for processes are inherently non-bounded situations. On the other, it shows the need for establishing a different situation. Following Parsons' (1990) analysis of events, Larson and Segal (1995) did point out, however, certain similarities between non-bounded physical entities (masses) and non-bounded situations (e.g. states). Just like masses can often be presented as bounded entities, states can be coerced into bounded (object-like) pieces of time:

> "States appear to be like masses, and events like individuals. Thus we can count arrivals or departures, these being events, but we can't count knowledges or latenesses, these being states. States can also be divided up into objects. Water can be divided into glasses, seas, and so on. Analogously, happiness can be divided up into particular states of individuals' being happy. If Fraser is happy between 8 P.M. and 11 P.M. on Wednesday evening, then there is a particular instance of happiness, a particular chunk of the larger state that is happiness in general."

(Larson and Segal 1995: 503-504). Arguments of this kind show that there is no reason why states should be excluded from the situations capable of giving rise to episodes. An all-round characterisation of the class of 'episodes' will be given below – along with the essential features of the other situational classes that will be proposed for English in this chapter.

The employment of 'episode' as an aspectological notion here is actually in full consistence with the general terminology of science. For instance, it is similar, or even analogous, to the use of 'episode' as a medical term. Thus in the professional jargon of cardiology or, even more generally, in the language of medicine, a temporal stretch of certain disease symptoms is, as a rule, referred to as an 'episode'. For instance, the time stretch during which a patient has breathing problems is called *an episode of dyspnea*, the time stretch during which a patient coughs is called *an episode of coughing*, the time stretch during which a patient has pain is called *an episode of pain*. Note that the semantic content of 'episode' in this medical sense of the word differs substantially from other temporal stretches referred to by nouns describing certain specific medical phenomena like *fit, faint, stroke, impairment* or more general phenomena like, e.g., *increase, drop, aberration*, etc. Because temporal notions like *fit, faint, stroke, impairment, increase, drop* or *aberration* can easily be associated with a pragmatically identifiable consequence or result – either in the patient's health condition (*fit, faint, stroke, impairment*) or in the general state of affairs (*increase, drop, aberration*). In other words, if the referents of these lexical items involve temporal stretches that change the status quo (i.e., that lead to an essentially new state), episodes are not seen as temporal stretches bringing about a new state. An episode of dyspnea or coughing or pain is a temporal interval during which a patient is in a state (an abnormal one) different from the preceding (normal) state. However, after the termination of the abnormal state the patient goes back to the preceding normal state without having sustained any substantial negative changes in his/her health. Furthermore, an episode of coughing or dyspnea or pain is, as a rule, associated with a patient who has already shown relevant complaints or has been diagnosed as suffering from a disease. Whereas fits, faints, strokes etc. normally refer to occurrences that are either associated with a sudden transition or are seen as after-effects of different complaints, and are taken to be indicative of a change in the health condition of a patient immediately after their onset and also after their termination. Therefore, this borrowing of the notion of episode from medical terminology into linguistics can be judged as legitimate – in view of the necessity to refer to the new kind of situation in question.

Episodes have an outward expression that has generally escaped the attention of aspectologists so far, with certain exceptions[4], but their foremost language exponent, the *for*-time adverbial phrase, has received a lot of attention. The importance of the *for*-time test for checking the perfectivity or imperfectivity of phrases and sentences has long been established. However, the fact that there is a substantial difference of meaning between sentences with and without the *for*-time phrase has been either

---

[4] As already mentioned, apart from Galton (1984), whose position has already been considered, other authors, like Mellor (1995) and Binnick (1991), have discussed certain features of what is here referred to as an episode, without establishing a separate situational class. Langacker (1987/1991) actually uses the term 'episode' in an aspectological framework, but with a rather different meaning. He assumes that sentences like *A statue of George Lakoff is standing in the plaza* or *This machine is lacking a control lever* portray the situation as "constituting a bounded episode" (Langacker (1991: 94) – a view which is incompatible with the present approach.

fully ignored or greatly underscored. Compare, for instance, the sentences in (276) and (277):

(276) a. John walked
      b. John walked for an hour
(277) a. John wrote the novel
      b. John wrote the novel for an hour

If we take one of the possible readings of a sentence like (276a), namely, that this sentence reports a non-bounded action – which can be either a state (a characteristic of the subject) or an ongoing activity – then this action is clearly different from the action in a sentence like (276b) which definitely reports a terminated (bounded) activity, i.e., an episode. Conversely, if a sentence like (277a) reports an accomplishment, which is a bounded action having reached its inherent endpoint with a pragmatically identifiable result, it is clearly different from a sentence like (277b) which reports an interrupted (unfinished) accomplishment – that is, again, an episode. The type of boundedness in (276b) and (277b) is different from the type of boundedness in (277a). While the action in (277a) has reached a natural endpoint with a pragmatically identifiable result (the book is completely read), the action in (276b) and (277b) has a definite beginning and a definite end, and, hence, it is bounded. But no natural endpoint is reached with a pragmatically identifiable result.

Of course, whether sentences like (276a) should be regarded as denoting activities or as states proper is a different question but it seems to be relevant to the current discussion. Consider the similar sentences in (278) below which are certainly good sentences of English, but are somewhat incomplete from a semantic point of view (as descriptions of real-world situations) – perhaps, in different degrees:

(278) a. John slept
      b. John worked
      c. The mechanic repaired

Their meanings are not easily analysable, unless the sentences are provided with a context. Conversely, other similar sentences, like (279a) and (279b) below, sound better even without any context:

(279) a. The secretary typed
      b. The actor rehearsed

From an aspectological point of view, on the one hand, the action in sentences like (278a) through (278c) above, viewed without context, seems to lack bounds. But, on the other hand, actions like sleeping, working and repairing, and also typing and rehearsing, as in (279), cannot easily be conceived of as habitual when associated with a single human performer. Hence, they could be seen as denoting episodes.

In some recent work Smith (1999) paid attention to the special features of sentences consisting of 'activity' and 'state' phrases complemented by *for*-time adverbials. She calls sentences containing activities and *for*-time phrases "giving the explicit bounds of the activity events" (Smith 1999: 484) but, as already mentioned, abstains from assigning her 'event' feature to sentences like *Mary was here for 2 hours* containing 'state' phrases like *Mary be here*. Smith (1999: 485) also noted the essential difference between the boundedness of accomplishments proper and the boundedness of sentences containing activity phrases and *for*-time adverbials:

> "while telic events [i.e., e.g., accomplishments] have intrinsic bounds, temporally bounded situations have bounds which are explicit and independent [...]; telic events are intrinsically bounded; other events are independently bounded."

Using sentences in narrative as examples, Smith (1999: 491-494) shows how verbs and verb phrases that in isolation ought to be considered as activities contribute to the advancement of the narrative. Thus, without radically changing her model of aspect, Smith introduced a certain revision of her system (criticized earlier here, in Chapter 2), specifically with respect to the so-called perfective viewpoint:

> "In earlier work I proposed that the perfective viewpoint presents sentences of all situation types with their characteristic endpoint features (Smith 1991), but the investigation here shows that this is incorrect. The Activity concept has potential endpoints only. In Activity sentences the perfective viewpoint actually adds information, conveying a temporally bounded unit [...]; the temporal bound may or may not coincide with the endpoints of the activity."

(Smith 1999: 503). It is obvious, however, that what Smith regards as a perfective viewpoint imposed onto activities may in many cases also be seen simply as an accomplishment. For instance, Smith's sentences *I [pushed the button and] waited*, *Clinton spoke to Hillary* and *Clinton laughed* could actually be seen in the particular context as accomplishments, although verbs like *wait*, *speak* and *laugh* are normally thought of as activities in isolation. Smith labels these cases 'terminative readings' and it is worth noting that all the three sentences would naturally be rendered in Slavic through perfective verb forms. The problem is with the explanation that it is the simple past (the perfective viewpoint) that imposes a bounded interpretation. It appears insufficient, for it is not so much the simple past itself as the quantificational status of the three subjects that is responsible for the explication of boundedness. Compare the perfectives *waited*, *spoke* and *laughed* in *I [pushed the button and] waited*, *Clinton spoke to Hillary* and *Clinton laughed* to the imperfectives (states or activities) *waited*, *spoke* and *laughed* in sentences like *Visitors [pushed the button and] waited*, *People spoke to Hillary* and *People laughed*. The comparison once again lends support to one of the major theses in this work, viz., that an analysis of the perfectivity/imperfectivity (boundedness/non-boundedness) of sentences within or without a larger context must be more participant-oriented than verb-oriented and must especially take into account (among other things) the quantificational structure of the participant(s) in order to be able to offer a proper assessment of the aspectual values of sentences, clauses or verb phrases.

Many examples in this book have already shown that the Simple Past Tense in English should be considered neutral with respect to whether a situation denoted through it is a state, an activity, an accomplishment or an achievement. Therefore, if we must admit that past activities are most properly represented by the Progressive, an assumption to the effect that activities fall beyond the semantics of the Simple Past would, of course, be incorrect. Consider, for example, sentences like (16c), (100a), (165b), (165e) and (197a), used earlier and repeated below:

(16) c. While he wrote the letters, I checked the addresses
(100) a. The boy carried a stone
(165) b. A journal lay open on the desktop
    e. Mary wore a nice shawl
(197) a. The animal lay in the grass without movement

It is interesting to note here that if the 'activity' situational value is, indeed, most typically represented by the Progressive, sentences like (165b) (165e) above (with the Simple Past) do not at all need the progressive form of the verb to denote an 'activity' meaning. The activity meaning in (100a), (165b), (165e) and (197a) is explicated mainly through the use of a verb with an atelic aspectual potential.

But sentences with a telic verb like (57d), (57e) or (58a) below are also capable of referring to activities taking place at a particular moment or period of time in the past, due to the non-boundedness of the referent of the subject or the (syntactic) object:

(57) d. A/The mechanic repaired cars
    e. A/The secretary typed reports
(58) a. Soldiers crossed the street

However, if sentences like (58a) could peripherally refer to current activities (they basically seem to denote habitual actions), sentences like (59c), (59d) and (59e) in which the referents of both the subject and the object are non-bounded can more easily be conceived of as denoting activities taking place at the reference point:

(59) c. Mechanics repaired cars
    d. Passers-by signed appeals
    e. Secretaries typed reports

Compare also examples like (280) below, given here for the first time, in which an 'activity' situational value is explicated through the description of the settings in pragmatic terms (knowledge of the world), in some cases with the help of adverbials (*impassionately, in the sunshine*) focusing on the currency of the situation:

(280) a. John watched the quarrel impassionately
    b. The engine purred under the hood

    c. The holiday-makers bathed in the sunshine
    d. The horse's ears twitched

Knowledge of the world is important in that it brings to the fore the 'activity' meaning – by contrasting the situation denoted to an entirely trivial, hence improbable, generic meaning. Holiday makers typically bathe in the sunshine, horses typically twitch their ears, hence, reference to a habitual, or a generic-like situation is very unlikely in this case. Consequently, a current activity is denoted. Compare also sentence (280a) above to (281a) below. Human beings often happen to watch something, engines typically purr, so sentences like (281a) and (281b) outside any further context would be almost meaningless in a non-activity reading (besides a possible inchoative perfective reading – which would, however, also require an additional supporting context):

(281)   a. John watched
        b. The engine purred

From the grammatical point of view, clearly, the definite article accompanying the nouns in (280) above also contributes to the grounding of the situation to some current moment/interval of time in the past and to the exclusion of the habitual (generic-like) meaning.

The English Simple Past Tense itself is unable to signify whether an action is generic or habitual or merely repetitive through a shorter or longer period, or whether it is a bounded action with or without a natural endpoint reached. It seems that the lesser probability for a habitual reading of sentences like (282) below (with verbs that can otherwise be complemented with nouns accompanied by an article as objects) – in comparison to sentences like (283) – is due to the lack of a lexical marker of habituality in the meaning of the verb as a lexical entry. Compare the sentences in (282), which allow a habitual interpretation (without imposing it, however), with the sentences in (283) in which the lexical meanings of the verbs tend to impart a habitual or state-like interpretation only, hence imperfectivity/non-boundedness proper:

(282)   a. John smoked
        b. John drank
(283)   a. John taught/lectured
        b. John bossed/bullied

Thus because verbs like *teach, lecture, boss, bully*, imparting a habitual or state-like action in sentences like (283) above are rare, most verbs in the Simple Past Tense in English would normally require markers of habituality for a situation to be conceived of as a state. But if the action in sentences like (283) above is state-like or habitual, and the same is true to a lesser degree of the action in (282), the action in sentences like (284a) and (284b) below cannot be conceived of in the same fashion. Sleeping and working are so natural as habits that, if predicated of John, as in (284), they can hardly be seen as anything else but isolated instances. Sentences (284a) and (284b) will thus receive the interpretation that the events described occurred recently:

(284) a. John slept
b. John worked

Hence, the situational meaning here ought to be seen as oscillating between an activity and an episode. The episode meaning would be explicit especially if sentences like (284a) and (284b) are answers to questions like (285a) and (285b) – for the questions themselves very clearly explicate an episode meaning. To corroborate this thesis, compare the episode meaning explicated in (285a) and (285b) to the activity meaning explicated in (285c) and (285d) through the difference between the Simple Past and the Progressive:

(285) a. Who slept this afternoon?
b. Who worked this afternoon?
c. Who was sleeping this afternoon?
d. Who was working this afternoon?

As already established, the Simple Past is neutral with respect to the aspectual value of the action in the sentence and the Progressive denotes imperfectivity by definition. But it should not be forgotten, therefore, that if an action is to be presented as bounded in one way or another, e.g. as an accomplishment, an achievement or an episode, the Simple Past is to be used.

Thus a difference arises in the way the meaning of 'episode' may occur. In sentences like (284a) and (284b), where the meaning of 'episode' is less explicit, and in sentences like (285a) and (285b), where it is more explicit, it may be said to arise, generally, as a result of an interpretation in terms of knowledge of the world, i.e., in pragmatic terms. The episode meaning is also possible in the sentences in (57d), (57e), (58a), (59c), (59d), (59e), (278), (279), (282) and (283) given above in this chapter. Compare also the examples (286) through (289) further below, and see the following Chapter Fourteen, *On 'knowledge of the world' in the explication of aspect in English*.

However, in each of the sentences in (275), and also in (276b) and (277b), all given below, the episode meaning is **imposed** by the *for*-time adverbial phrase. Whether the situational meaning of the rest of the sentence is non-bounded, as in (276b), or bounded, as in all the other sentences, the *for*-time adverbial phrase forces the episode meaning onto each separate sentence as a whole:

(275) a. John played the sonata for half an hour
b. Katinka knitted three sweaters for half an hour
c. John painted the wall for half an hour
(276) b. John walked for an hour
(277) b. John wrote the novel for an hour

It will be shown later that the episode meaning is also mapped onto the referents of the other major syntactic components.

Now recall Galton's proposal concerning the use of the phrase *for a while*. It is precisely this phrase that is most generally needed for the action in sentences like (284) above to sound meaningful, as in (286):

(286) a. John slept for a while
 b. John worked for a while

But it is not only a phrase like *for a while* that can make sentences like (284) meaningful. For example, sentences like (287a) and (287b) below are also meaningful and, again, denote episodes. On the other hand, a sentence like (287c) has been considered by Smith (1991: 221) and other aspectologists to denote an activity. There is no doubt, however, that if a sentence like (287c) is viewed as a current, not a habitual activity, its more natural interpretation would be one similar to (287d) – in which the activity has come to an end, due to 'natural limitations'. Hence, episodes are denoted not only in sentences like (287a) or (287b) but also in sentences like (287c) or (287d) – that have often been considered to denote activities:

(287) a. John slept that night
 b. John worked in the garden this morning
 c. Lily swam in the pond
 d. Lily swam in the pond this morning

It follows that the episode meaning will not be restricted to *for-a-while phrases* or, generally, to the *for*-time adverbial, although this adverbial is the best exponent of the episode.[5] Many other adverbials implying (not denoting) the temporal bounds of an action or a state will also contribute to the explication of an episode meaning. Compare the sentences in (288) below, in each of which the past activity is to be conceived of in its entirety, from beginning to end – in spite of the fact that there is no report or indication of some 'natural endpoint' reached. In other words, sentences like (288) basically refer to episodes, not to activities:

(288) a. The opposition candidate performed brilliantly in the television debate last night
 b. Did your guests sleep well?
 c. The former champion ran perfectly in the 200 meters event
 d. Manuela played against Steffi in the final match of the tournament

---

[5] Although, as already argued, *for*-time adverbials are different (e.g. the *for-an-hour* type is different from the *for-hours* type), by a *for*-time adverbial here a *for-an-hour* type is meant, unless stated otherwise.

Some sentences will be able to explicate an episode meaning even without the help of adverbials. Sentences like (289) below clearly refer to recent episodes, not to activities or accomplishments (there are no explicit end points or consequences):

(289) a. Have you eaten?
b. John's been to the pub

However, examples like those in (289) raise the following question. Does the episode meaning there somehow arise in the interpretation of each separate sentence as a whole, or should it, rather, be considered to be conveyed by the semantics of the Present Perfect? On the one hand, it seems reasonable to assume that the Perfect is incapable of inducing an episode meaning by itself, as shown by sentences like (290a), (290b) or (290c):

(290) a. John has eaten his sandwich
b. John has eaten sandwiches
c. John has taught English

While sentence (290a) is perfective, sentence like (290b) and (290c) are imperfective, and here aspect can be said to be explicated, generally, in compositional terms. But, on the other hand, it makes certain sense to argue that the meaning of the Perfect is always associated with two points on the time axis between which the action is located – the event point and the reference point. These two points could be seen as instrumental in bringing about the episode meaning when imperfective expressions are used, as in (289) above. Such a possibility will not be explored here, however, because, first, the semantics of the Perfect falls beyond the scope of this work and, second, because the solution of the problem needs further investigation on the basis of a much more adequate explanation of the Perfect than has been proposed so far in linguistics.

A CLASSIFICATION OF SITUATIONS

The classification of situations that will be proposed here takes as its point of departure Vendler's classification – and thus pays tribute to Vendler's remarkable insight into the problem. It claims to offer, however, a better picture of possibly identifiable situations by taking into account the impact of *for*-time adverbials on the composition of aspect in the sentence. The table below outlines the similarities and differences between the classification of situations proposed here and Vendler's classification (and some similar descriptions). The differences amount, broadly, to the following. Vendler's activities are substituted by processes. Vendler's accomplishments and achievements are merged into the class of events. A class of semelfactives (as in Smith's 1991 model) and a new class of episodes (similar to, but not identical with, Galton's pofective) are introduced.

Table 6

Situations in Vendler's classification and some other descriptions		Situations in the present approach
States	=	States
Activities	≅	Processes
Terminated states and activities, interrupted accomplishments	=	Episodes
Accomplishments + Achievements + Semelfactives	=	Events

States are identical in both classifications. It is to be noted that activities in Vendler's classification tend to be restricted to ongoing actions like those expressed by the English Progressive. However, an association between activities and the Progressive would be too language-specific for a classification aimed to be of a more universal nature. Therefore, the 'process' situation introduced here is meant to include also non-bounded actions taking place at extended stretches of time that are not covered by the Progressive. Of course, processes have already been proposed as types of situations in a large number of aspectological studies (e.g., Chung and Timberlake 1985: 214-220; Bach 1981; 1986; Hinrichs 1985; Moens 1987; Caenepeel 1989; Bartsch 1995). States and processes are non-bounded situations, episodes and events are bounded situations. Episodes, in contrast to events, typically constitute either states or processes that have terminated or accomplishments that have been interrupted. Semelfactives can be regarded as involving an inherent endpoint: although the action is momentary, it may be said to start at an initial point and then almost immediately to exhaust itself at an endpoint[6]. Events consist of accomplishments, achievements

---

[6] The inherent endpoint of an action has so far been associated with a pragmatically identifiable result of the action. Though the latter is a rather vague notion, it seems to be relevant to the description of situations. However, a pragmatically identifiable result of the action could be found in episodes as well. Compare the episode *I ate well* and the accomplishment *I ate myself full*. At first sight, it can be maintained that the result of my being not hungry any more is identifiable in the meaning of both sentences. Compare also the two Bulgarian sentences below which are conceived of as entirely equivalent semantically. An imperfective Aorist verb form (i.e., an episode) is used in the first, a perfective Aorist (i.e., an accomplishment) in the second:

and semelfactives. The table below represents the classification of situations proposed according to the general approach assumed in this work.

Table 7

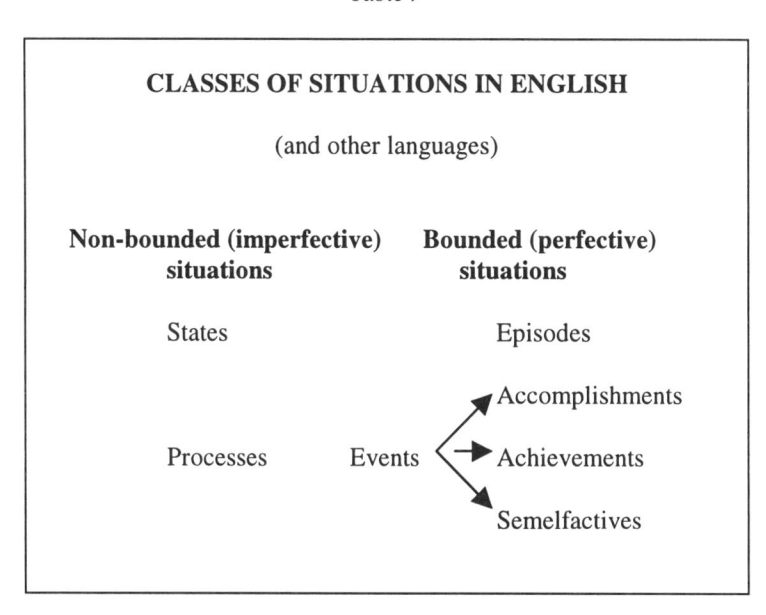

```
┌─────────────────────────────────────────────────────────┐
│            CLASSES OF SITUATIONS IN ENGLISH             │
│                                                         │
│                  (and other languages)                  │
│                                                         │
│     Non-bounded (imperfective)    Bounded (perfective)  │
│              situations                situations       │
│                                                         │
│               States                    Episodes        │
│                                                         │
│                                       ↗ Accomplishments │
│             Processes      Events  ←→   Achievements    │
│                                       ↘ Semelfactives   │
│                                                         │
└─────────────────────────────────────────────────────────┘
```

It can be maintained that the above classification is valid not only for English. It can be regarded as an adequate description for many other European languages, including all the Slavic languages – and, in particular, Bulgarian, with its extremely complex tense-aspect system capable of expressing most of the situations grammatically, through aspect and tense-aspect distinctions in the verb paradigm.

Now, if we go back to the Progressive, typically, as in the case of (291a) vs. (291b) below, it may be said to constitute a partial transformation of an accomplishment (recall Chapter Eight, *The Progressive in English*):

Dobre   jadoh$_{impfvAor}$
Well   ate-I
'I ate well'
Dobre   se   najadoh$_{pfvAor}$
Well   prt.refl. ate-I
'I ate myself full'

Again, it appears that the result of my being not hungry any more is identifiable in the meaning of both sentences. Nevertheless, it can be argued either that the pragmatically identifiable result is explicit in the latter and only implicit in the former or that the meaning of these sentences should be analysed in somewhat different (and more complex) terms. Compare the cancelable inference that I am not hungry any more in *I ate well but I am still hungry* and the non-cancelable inference in **I ate myself full but I am still hungry*. The same in Bulgarian: *Dobre jadoh$_{impfvAor}$, no săm ošte gladen* 'I ate well but I am still hungry' and **Dobre se najadoh$_{pfvAor}$, no săm ošte gladen* 'I ate myself full but I am still hungry'.

(291) a. John was singing a song
      b. John sang a song

In cases where the Progressive does not constitute a partial transformation of an accomplishment, it is precisely episodes that should be seen as corresponding to the 'whole' of such Progressives. Consider Progressives like (292a) below. If the situation in (291a) is a partial non-bounded stretch of the situation in (291b), then (292a) must (or at least could) also be a partial non-bounded stretch of something. This something is the episode (292b). The situation in (292b) is bounded, though the boundedness here differs from the boundedness of (291b) – there is no inherent endpoint of the action reached:

(292) a. John was singing
      b. John sang

In English, the two different types of boundedness, between events and episodes, will be distinguished primarily in pragmatic terms (i.e., in terms of knowledge of the world), rather than in grammatical terms when there is no temporal adverbial in the sentence. However, the fact that the distinction between episodes and events can sometimes in English be made explicit through the use of tense-aspect forms (as in Bulgarian, where it is directly expressed by the contrast between the perfective Aorist and the imperfective Aorist), lends support to the idea that it is analysable also at the grammatical (morphological or semantico-syntactic) level. This idea is also supported by the finding that the *for*-time adverbial phrase in its prototypical use (or, rather the *for-an-hour* type of adverbial phrase) can be regarded as an exponent of the episode meaning in English.

MAPPING OF TEMPORAL VALUES IN EPISODE SENTENCES

Some of the previous chapters of this book addressed the important problem of mapping temporal values between verbal and nominal sentence components – or, rather, between their referents. And after the establishment of a new class of situation, the episode, it would be natural to propose a similar mechanism for mapping temporal values within episode sentences. A model describing a mapping mechanism within a sentence comprising an episode meaning was actually developed a long time ago in Kabakčiev (1984b), on Bulgarian data. It employed a diagrammatic representation of the meanings displayed by the four morphologically distinguished forms, the perfective Aorist, the imperfective Aorist, the perfective Imperfect and the imperfective Imperfect and their effect, the mapping of their temporal values, on the participants. However, five aspectual meanings were differentiated, not four, because the imperfective Imperfect can be read in two separate ways – as representing a progressive-like meaning or a state-like meaning.

The diagrammatic representation in Kabakčiev (1984b) is given below in broad terms as (294), and it is made here on the basis of the sentences in (293).[7] The combination between either the perfective verb *pročeta* 'read' or the imperfective verb *četa* 'read' with either the Aorist or the Imperfect (with *momčeto* 'the boy' and *pismoto* 'the letter' as subject and object) yields four sentences with five clearly identifiable situational meanings including the episode: viz. the perfective Aorist, an accomplishment (*pročete*); the imperfective Aorist (*čete*), an episode; the perfective Imperfect, an accomplishment which has been indefinitely repeated (*pročeteše*); and the imperfective Imperfect, with two possible readings – state-like (*četeše*$_{\text{impfvImp1}}$) and progressive-like (*četeše*$_{\text{impfvImp2}}$).

(293) a. Momče-to pročete$_{\text{pfvAor}}$ pismo-to
Boy-the read letter-the
'The boy read the letter'
b. Momčeto čete$_{\text{impfvAor}}$ pismo-to
Boy-the read letter-the
'The boy read the letter [as if continued with adverbials like *for three minutes*]'
c. Štom momče-to pročeteše$_{\text{pfvImp}}$ pismo-to, go skăswaše
Whenever boy-the read-he letter-the it tore-to-pieces
'Whenever the boy read the letter, he tore it to pieces'
d. Momče-to četeše$_{\text{impfvImp1}}$ pismo-to
Boy-the read letter-the
'The boy was reading the letter'
e. Momče-to četeše$_{\text{impfvImp2}}$ pismo-to
Boy-the read letter-the
'The boy read the letter [in a state-like reading of an indefinite repetition]'

Below is the representation of the temporal status of the referents of the verb and the subject and the object after the mapping of values from the referent of the verb onto the referents of the subject and the object has taken place:

---

[7] The difference is that in Kabakčiev (1984b) the examples contained the NPs *momčeto* 'the boy' and *kamăka* 'the stone' as participants, and the verb *hvărlja*$_{\text{pfv}}$/*hvărljam*$_{\text{impfv}}$ 'throw'. The examples (293) given here with *momčeto* 'the boy' and *pismoto* 'the letter' as participants, and the verb *pročeta*$_{\text{pfv}}$/*četa*$_{\text{impfv}}$ 'read', have been chosen as a better illustration that can more easily be rendered into English.

300   CHAPTER 13

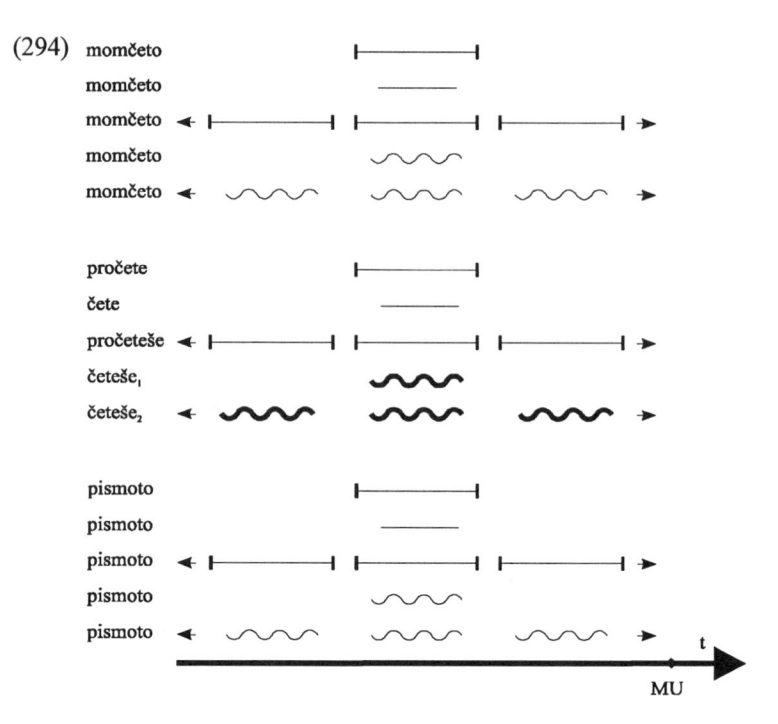

(294) momčeto
       momčeto
       momčeto
       momčeto
       momčeto

       pročete
       čete
       pročeteše
       četeše₁
       četeše₂

       pismoto
       pismoto
       pismoto
       pismoto
       pismoto
                                                                        t
                                                                       MU

As mentioned above, the diagrammatic representation of the temporal status of the referents of the NPs and the referent of the verb in the sentences in (293) broadly follows the one given in Kabakčiev (1984b: 669). As earlier, a wavy line signifies non-boundedness, a straight line signifies boundedness. Boundedness/perfectivity proper (i.e., when there is an inherent endpoint of an action reached) is signified by a stretch (a restricted line); the episode meaning, representing a bounded/perfective action lacking an inherent endpoint, is signified by a straight but non-restricted line. The formal markedness of the Bulgarian verb for imperfective aspect (as in the English Progressive and in contrast to the aspectual non-markedness of the Simple Past Tense verb in English and in similar languages) is signified by a thick wavy line. The mapping mechanism is such that the verb maps its own temporal value (overtly, grammatically marked) onto the participants. Note again that the temporal values inherent in the verb forms are represented in (294) as already mapped on the referents of the subject and the object. The problem of how the definiteness, hence boundedness, of NPs like *momčeto* 'the boy' and *pismoto* 'the letter' in Bulgarian should be interpreted in temporal terms is here ignored – for being irrelevant to the present discussion (a solution is proposed in Kabakčiev 1984b).

However, in adapting the Bulgarian model of the mapping mechanism for English data, as will be done here, the fact that the situational value in English is explicated compositionally, while in Bulgarian it is directly expressed in the verb, ought to be taken into account. Compare sentences like (295a) and (295b) below. The semantic feature 'arrival at the inherent endpoint of the action' (i.e., reading the story to the end), present in the normal, accomplishment, reading of the English sentence (295a), is absent in the episode meaning of (295b):

(295) a. The boy read the letter
b. The boy read the letter for two minutes

Recall that, according to the model for explaining the Progressive in Chapter Eight, the referent of *was throwing* in a sentence like (134) is to be regarded as a partial and non-bounded stretch with respect to the referent of *threw* in a sentence like (74). Hence, the referents of the subject-NP and the object-NP *the boy* and *a stone* in (134) have to be represented as partial temporal stretches with respect to *the boy* and *a stone* in (74):

(134)   The boy was throwing a stone

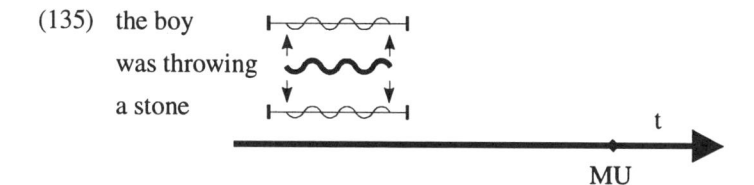

(135)   the boy
        was throwing
        a stone

                                    MU

(74)   The boy threw a stone

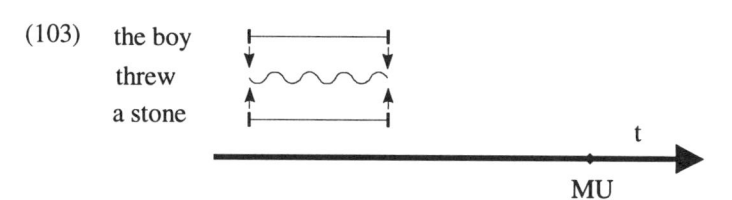

(103)   the boy
        threw
        a stone

                                    MU

Similarly, in Kabakčiev (1984b), the mapping of temporal values was exemplified by representing the Bulgarian imperfective Aorist as a partitive transformation of the perfective Aorist – see (294) above. But this partitive transformation is a bounded one, in contrast to the change from (103) into (135) above, which is a transformation from boundedness into non-boundedness. Compare again (293a) and (293b) above and their diagrammatic representations in (294). The imperfective Aorist form *čete* 'read [for some time]' is a partial bounded stretch of time with respect to the perfective Aorist *pročete* 'read [to the end]'. The semantic feature of reaching the inherent endpoint of the action, present in the accomplishment sentence (293a), is cancelled in the episode meaning of (293b). The cancellation through the imperfective Aorist is effected directly, through the verb form itself in Bulgarian, and is available for most perfective Aorists, that is, accomplishments, unless certain

302   CHAPTER 13

morphological restrictions occur (these restrictions, however, constitute a negligible exception).

Hence, analogously, the referent of *read* in an English sentence like (295b), repeated below, will be a partial bounded temporal stretch with respect to the referent of *read* in a sentence like (295a):

(295) a. The boy read the letter
      b. The boy read the letter for two minutes

But there is a difference between Bulgarian and English, and it is in the direction of mapping the temporal values. Since in (295b) above it is the adverbial *for two minutes* that brings about the episode meaning and imposes it onto the rest of the sentence, the mapping may be said to be effected from the referent of the adverbial onto the referent of the verb first, and then from the referent of the verb onto the referents of the subject and the object. Note that after the mapping takes place from the nominal components onto the verbal one in the structurally identical sentence (74) above, the referent of the verb acquires the temporal boundedness initially associated with the referents of the subject and the object (though this association is inaccessible to the ordinary speaker). Hence, ultimately, the values of the three major sentence components in (295a) become identical – and would be best represented as in diagram (296) below.

(295) a. The boy read the letter

(296) the boy   ├──────────┤
       read   ├──────────┤
       the letter   ├──────────┤
       ────────────────────────────────▶ t
                                MU

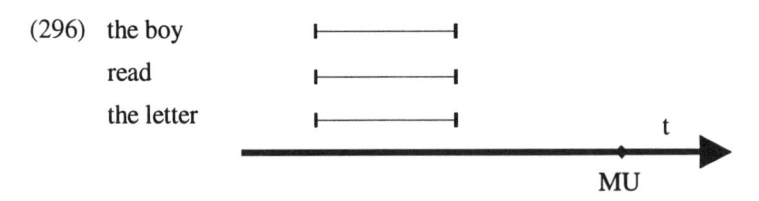

We, naturally, also take it that the temporal values of the referents of the subject, the verb and the object are the same in (295b) and (295a) before the mapping of the temporal value from the adverbial onto the rest of the sentence takes place in (295b). The temporal value of the adverbial *for two minutes* applied to a sentence like (295a) then ought to be a partial bounded stretch with respect to the bounded stretch representing *read* in (295a). Or, in common-sense terms, if you have read a letter **for** some time, you have not finished the letter. Compare the diagrammatic representation for the accomplishment meaning of *The boy read the letter* in (296) and the diagrammatic representation for the episode meaning of *The boy read the letter* in (295b) in (297) below. The episode meaning is, of course, induced by the *for*-time adverbial – which maps its own value onto the verb and the participants:

(295) b. The boy read the letter for two minutes

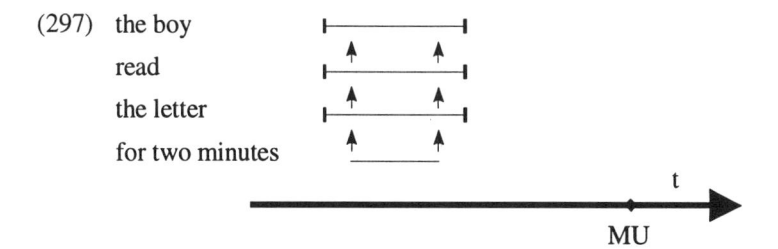

(297) the boy
       read
       the letter
       for two minutes

                                              t
                                          MU

As already argued, the episode value is mapped from the *for*-time phrase onto the referent of the verb first, and then onto the referents of the participants, but this order of the mapping stages is not covered in the diagram.

The diagrammatic representation of the resulting meaning in episode sentences in English derived from accomplishment sentences is given in (298) below. It follows the representation employed for the Bulgarian imperfective Aorist, i.e., sentence (293b), as in (294) above (and also in Kabakčiev 1984b: 669)[8]. After the application of the mapping mechanism from the referent of the adverbial onto the referents of the verb and onto the referents of the two NPs, the following picture obtains for the episode meaning versus the accomplishment meaning in which the temporal values of all the separate major syntactic components are also contrasted:

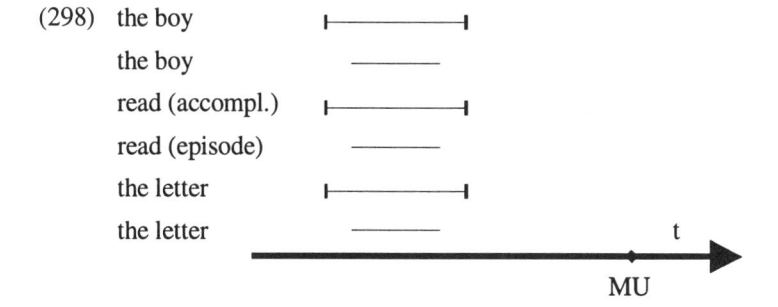

(298) the boy
       the boy
       read (accompl.)
       read (episode)
       the letter
       the letter
                                              t
                                          MU

Recall that the temporal value of the *for*-time (*for-an-hour*) type of adverbial has always (or almost always) been described as compatible with non-boundedness and employed as a test for imperfectivity in the verb phrase or in the rest of the sentence.

---

[8] In the classification of situations in English proposed in this chapter there is no correspondence for the situational meaning denoted by the perfective Imperfect in Bulgarian. This is because Vendler's classification and similar descriptions, including the classification proposed here, cover the major possible situational meanings only. Out of the combination between, e.g., a state or an activity or an accomplishment, etc., on the one hand, and another aspectual value, like, e.g. bounded repetition or non-bounded repetition, etc., on the other hand, some other, secondary, aspectual (situational) values are derived. The present work needs to focus on the major situational values. Further research will be needed for an exhaustive description of all possible aspectual (situational) values valid and appropriate for a particular language like English or for language in general.

But its effect on the rest of the sentence is two-fold. Let us conceive of situational values as a scale from prototypical non-boundedness (e.g., an activity) to prototypical boundedness (e.g., an accomplishment). An episode is a bounded situation, unlike an activity, but it is, broadly speaking, less bounded than an accomplishment, for it describes an action lacking its inherent endpoint, i.e. an action without a clearly (pragmatically) identifiable result. When a *for*-time (*for-an-hour*) phrase is applied to a perfective sentence, as in (295b) vs. (295a) above, the *for-an-hour* phrase precludes the arrival at the inherent endpoint and forces the accomplishment into a situation which is bounded to a lower degree, an episode. In other words, the effect is of partial imperfectivisation.

However, conversely, when the *for*-time phrase is applied to an imperfective sentence, as in (299b) vs. (299a) below, the effect is that of partial perfectivisation, in contrast to the full perfectivisation (involving an inherent endpoint) in (299c) or (299d):

(299) a. The boy walked
b. The boy walked for an hour
c. The boy walked the distance
d. The boy walked from the centre to the station

If sentence (299a) is taken in its non-episode reading, that is, for example, in a progressive-like reading, the effect of the *for*-time phrase is to impose its boundedness onto the non-boundedness of the rest of the sentence – but without involving an inherent endpoint. Or, diagrammatically, see (300) below, if *walked* is non-bounded, *for an hour* bounds it partially. That is, *for an hour* maps its boundedness onto *walked*, without establishing an inherent endpoint of the action as in (299c) or (299d) above:

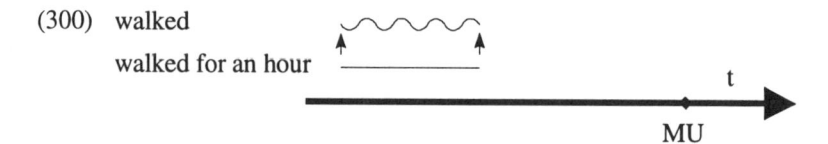

(300) walked
walked for an hour

MU

However, in order to evaluate the temporal status of *walked* and *walked for an hour* one ought to judge these relative to an action with an inherent endpoint as, e.g., the one in sentence (299c). Or, if (299a) is contrasted to a sentence like (299b), on the one hand, and to (299c), on the other, (301) would be an adequate diagrammatic representation:

(301)   the boy   ∿∿∿

      the boy   ─────

      the boy   ├────────┤

      walked   ∿∿∿

      walked for an hour   ─────

      walked the distance   ├──────┤

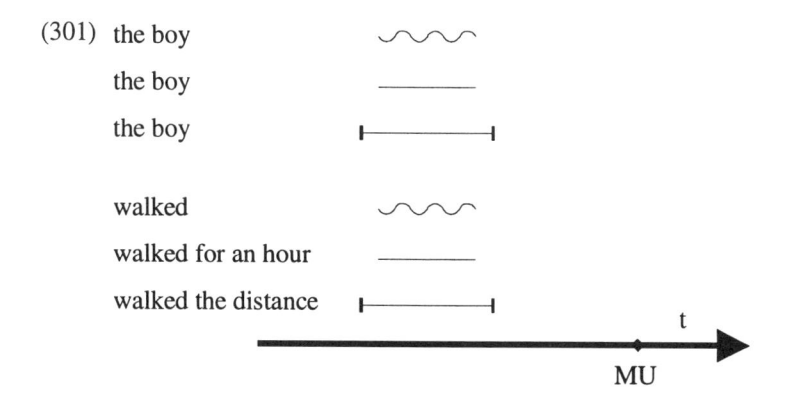

⟶ t

MU

Diagram (301) shows the temporal values of the VPs *walked*, *walked for an hour* and *walked the distance* and the temporal values of *the boy* in (299a), (299b) and (299c), respectively, after the mapping in its two versions has taken place: (i) non-boundedness resulting from the non-bounded nature of *walk* which is mapped onto *the boy*; (ii) boundedness without an inherent endpoint mapped from the referent of the adverbial *for an hour* onto the referent of the verb and then onto the referents of the subject and the object in (299b); (iii) boundedness marked by the article mapped from the referents of the subject-NP and the object-NP onto the referent of the verb in (299c) – if necessary, see again Chapter Six, *The mechanism for mapping the temporal values of subjects*, about the latter case.

Finally, the representation, already made, of the temporal status of the referents of the three major components (subject, verb and object) in a sentence with an episode meaning versus the representation of the referents of the three major components in a sentence with an accomplishment meaning allows the ultimate diagrammatic representation of the four major situational meanings proposed in this chapter for English to be completed. After the mapping of temporal values between the major sentence components takes place, roughly, the following picture obtains, covering the state, the process, the episode and the accomplishment meaning found in sentences with 'the boy' and 'the letter' as participants and 'read' (in the Simple Past Tense) as an action:[9]

---

[9] Note that the state meaning is represented as a non-bounded iterative, because the nature of *read the letter* is such that it requires non-bounded iterativity in order to be understood as a state. Also, the separate actions of reading the letter are represented as non-bounded, but they could be bounded as well (for detail, see Chapter Five, *Extension in time of subjects and objects from a "common-sense" point of view* or Chapter Eleven, *The impact of adverbials in the sentence, and aspect in English*).

(302) the boy

        the boy

        the boy

        the boy

        read (accompl.)

        read (episode)

        read (process)

        read (state)

        the letter

        the letter

        the letter

        the letter

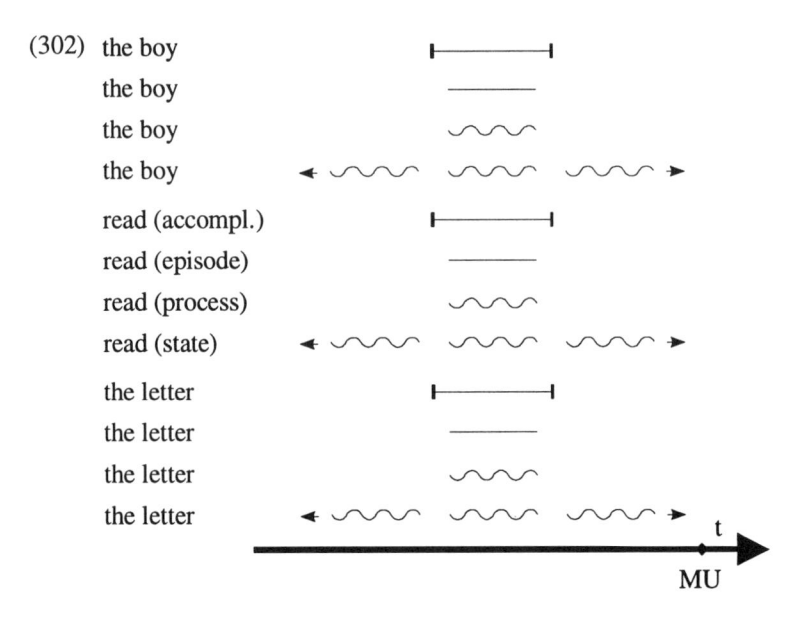

MU

ASPECTUAL CLASSES IN ENGLISH: A SUMMARY

In this chapter, four situational classes, viz. states, processes, episodes and events, have been proposed as an adequate description of the types of aspectual values that can mainly be denoted by phrases and sentences in English. The description offered could also be regarded as a universal natural-language characterisation of situations. Furthermore, if in English, and in other languages too, the distinction between Progressive and Non-Progressive is ignored, there can be no strict borderline between states and processes. This can happen at such a level of analysis at which the Progressive/Non-Progressive contrast is not yet applicable. Similarly, at the level of isolated verbs or verb phrases in English situational meanings cannot easily be explicated, and the episode meaning will be distinguishable mainly at the level of the sentence – through the impact of adverbials of time, especially *for*-time (*for-an-hour* type of) adverbials.

For-time adverbials make episodes a special class of situations – because episodes can, generally, be composed out of all other kinds of situations through the complementation of a *for*-time (*for-an-hour* type of) phrase. In contrast, the *in*-time adverbial phrase cannot easily turn states or activities into perfectives since, if complemented to verbs or verb phrases denoting states or activities, it yields non-grammatical expressions much more often than does the *for*-time phrase complemented to perfectives.

Finally, the notion of event holds together three types of truly perfective actions/ situations: accomplishments, achievements and semelfactives. Thus, a three-way division between imperfectives (states and processes), episodes and events (consisting of accomplishments, achievements and semelfactives) arises in which states and processes are true imperfectives, accomplishments, achievements and semelfactives are true perfectives, while episodes form a borderline area between true imperfectives and true perfectives.

CHAPTER 14

ON 'KNOWLEDGE OF THE WORLD' IN THE EXPLICATION OF ASPECT IN ENGLISH

WHY DOES THE COMPOSITIONAL MECHANISM FAIL TO WORK OCCASIONALLY?

In previous chapters of this book many cases were dealt with in which the compositional mechanism for explicating aspectual distinctions did not seem to work or did not work. A sentence like (241b), for example, constructed by Tenny (1994: 28), was shown to explicate imperfectivity. Tenny argued that the verb *surround* in this sentence is stative and that the boundedness of the entire expression will be unaffected whether the verb is accompanied by a bare mass noun subject, as in (241b), or by a mass noun subject with an article, as in (303a). As already discussed earlier, an argumentation of this kind appears to undermine the compositional mechanism. The failure on Tenny's part to notice that in a slightly different sentence like (242b) the compositional mechanism does work does not, however, remove the problem stemming from the fact that in a sentence with a bare singular noun subject like (303b), again, there is something that prevents the compositional mechanism to work, at least in so far as the sentence is perfective, fully grammatical and acceptable with the adverbial *in two hours*.

(241) b. Snow surrounded the house for one winter/*in one winter
(242) b. The snow surrounded the house in two hours/for two hours
(303) a. The snow surrounded the house for one winter/*in one winter
       b. Snow surrounded the house in two hours/for two hours

Previous chapters in this book also focused on the subtle interplay between various grammatical and semantic factors intertwined with the conceptualisation of reality and showed that it is this interplay that the aspectual interpretation of sentences in English basically depends on. It has already become obvious, however, that the aspectual values of some sentences can be properly explicated not only on the basis of their semantico-syntactic structure, but also, sometimes, on the basis of information contained in such sentences that goes beyond the grammatical and purely semantic domains. In the original version of Verkuyl's theory (1972) the role of 'knowledge of the world' as a factor for explicating aspect compositionally (as in

English) was not taken into account. In his extended theory, Verkuyl (1993: 133-135) argued that this pragmatic factor is important for discerning aspectual distinctions but offered no special discussion of the problem.

Some years earlier Moens (1987: 111, 135) had emphasised the need for "general and specific world knowledge available" to identify the aspect of a particular language expression, without fully accepting the idea that aspect can be accommodated in grammatical terms:

> "determining the aspectual class of an expression cannot be carried out at the level of syntax, but belongs at the level of model theoretic interpretation. It does remain possible to have rules in the grammar that specify what aspectual type a particular expression should belong to for the sentence to be true. But no attempt should be made at that level to determine whether the expression is of the right type, and – if not – how its aspectual type can be changed."

Moens (1987: 111).

It could be argued that a pragmatic component, that is, generally, 'knowledge of the world', is permanently present in one way or another in most if not all rules of grammar. To give an example from another grammatical sector, in a language with a relatively free word order like Bulgarian the determination of which is the subject and which is the object in a given sentence in many cases relies solely on 'knowledge of the world'. Otherwise subjects and objects could by no means be identified on the basis of their positions in the sentence. This phenomenon is less explicit in a language like English with its rather fixed word order. And to the extent that, for example, third person singular personal pronouns are marked for the animate/non-animate distinction or that the Progressive is not used with certain verbs, many rules of English grammar can, of course, also be said to depend crucially on 'knowledge of the world'. Thus there seems to be no serious argument against including knowledge of the world as a shortcut 'pragmatic component' in the grammatical description of aspect.

In some of the previous chapters of the book, the following sentences were used as an illustration of the expression of perfectivity:

(46) b. A tourist climbed the mountain
(56) a. A/The boy threw a/the stone
   b. A/The child ate an/the apple
   c. A/The soldier crossed a/the street
   d. A/The girl ironed a/the skirt
   e. A/The woman cleaned a/the room
   f. A/The mechanic repaired a/the car
   g. A/The housewife prepared a/the lunch
   h. A/The passer-by signed a/the appeal
   i. A/The secretary typed a/the report
   j. A/The journalist read a/the newspaper

All the sentences in (46b) and (56) above represent an accomplishment situation, and sentences like those in (304) below represent an achievement situation:

(304) a. A/The child found a/the bird
b. A/The girl lost a/the pencil
c. A/The bystander spotted a/the plane

Both accomplishments and achievements denote perfective actions, in contrast to sentences like (47), (57e), (58a) or (59e) below, in which either the referent of the subject is non-bounded or the referent of the object is non-bounded, or both the (referents of the) subject and the object are non-bounded, thus making each separate sentence non-bounded/imperfective:

(47)   Tourists climbed the mountain
(57) e. The secretary typed reports
(58) a. Soldiers crossed the street
(59) e. Secretaries typed reports

The possibility to regard many sentences as clearly agentive to the exclusion of others has been noted in the literature (see, e.g., Miller and Johnson-Laird 1976: 482; Chung and Timberlake 1985: 215). The examples in (46b) and (56) are especially important in that they describe situations in which a human agent performs a kind of action directed towards an object and some kind of pragmatically identifiable result is achieved after the completion of the action. As already mentioned, they form a major semantico-syntactic pattern in English – sentences of this kind are constantly received and produced in actual discourse. According to Chung and Timberlake (1985: 215), the difference between agentivity and non-agentivity has something to do with the distinction between stativity and dynamicity and, hence, with the perfective/imperfective contrast, as in a sentence like (305a), Chung and Timberlake's, compared to (305b):

(305) a. The window opened onto the garden
b. The window opened

Of course, in so far as non-agentivity is not incompatible with the expression of perfectivity, as this is observed in the perfective sentence (305b), the association between agentivity and perfectivity and non-agentivity and imperfectivity (stativity) is only typical, not mandatory.

Thus, although a number of arguments have already been given to support the thesis, that, for example, the primary interpretation of sentences like (46b), (56a) through (56j) and (304a) through (304c) above is a perfective one, and that the primary interpretation of sentences like (47), (57e), (58a) or (59e) is an imperfective one (see above, cf. also Kabakčiev 1993a; 1993b), obviously an analysis in pragmatic terms would still be needed to check if, when, and why such sentences are perfective or imperfective. The relevance of pragmatic factors in general, including general knowledge of the world, for interpreting certain sentences as generic has also been stressed by other authors. For example, Declerck (1986) gives the following reasons why a sentence with a definite object-NP like *John drank the milk* should be considered non-generic and perfective:

> "boundedness of the referent of the NP may entail boundedness of the number of occasions. Since the same milk can only be drunk once, the bounded interpretation of the *milk* [...] renders the number of occasions bounded as well"

(Declerck 1986: 175). Conversely, Harlig argues that a sentence with a bare object-NP like *John drank water* should be considered bounded because:

> "our knowledge of the world tells us that most actions and events are finite"

(Harlig 1983: 167). Leaving aside the apparent contradiction – because the problem has already been discussed at length and can be considered resolved – observations like these about the influence of 'knowledge of the world' are frequent, but they lack the systematicity needed to describe fully the role played by pragmatic factors in the explication of aspectual distinctions. Therefore, in the following two sections of this chapter an attempt will be made to test a particular pragmatic theory of agentivity against the rules of compositional aspect.

ALLWOOD'S PRINCIPLES

Bearing in mind the complexity of the grammatical and the semantic structure of perfective sentences and of the varying influence of pragmatic factors, it would be useful to give a more detailed account of the possible influence of 'knowledge of the world' upon the sentences of type (46b) and (56). With this purpose in mind, Jens Allwood's seven principles of normal rational agenthood will be exploited. Allwood's principles are listed in Table 11 below. They include assumptions about agenthood, a basic feature of sentences like (46b) and (56).

Table 11

ALLWOOD'S SEVEN PRINCIPLES
OF NORMAL RATIONAL AGENTHOOD

(1) Allwood's first (general) principle is the principle of normal rational agenthood: typical human beings are normal rational agents. Associated with it is the assumption that other human beings are normal rational agents. The other principles and the assumptions associated with them are the following:

(2) The principle of intentional and purposeful behaviour. Assume the behaviour of other agents to be intentional and purposeful.

(3) The principle of voluntary action. Assume the actions of other agents not to be against their own will.

(4) The principle of motivated action. Assume that other agents have motives for their actions.

(5) The principle of pleasure and pain. Assume that other agents are not intending to decrease their pleasure or increase their pain by their actions.

(6) The principle of adequacy. Assume that other agents in their actions intend to achieve their purposes as adequately and efficiently as possible.

(7) The principle of competence. Assume that other agents act only when they believe that it is possible to achieve the purpose of their actions.

It should be specifically noted that all the assumptions belonging to the principles hold unless there is clear indication to the contrary. For more detail, see Allwood (1976: 46-50).

It has already been argued that sentences like (46b) and (56a) through (56j) above are in many ways more important than those of type (304):

(304) a. A/The child found a/the bird
   b. A/The girl lost a/the pencil
   c. A/The bystander spotted a/the plane

The achievement sentences in (304) will not be included in the analysis because they do not clearly represent an action in Allwood's sense: in his theory action is always connected with intention (Allwood 1976: 6). Although the referents of the subjects in (304) can be regarded as potential agents, these sentences denote situations in which the referents of the subjects only take an indirect part in the event, without actively trying to change the state of affairs, at least in the normal interpretations of the sentences. Therefore, the object of enquiry in this chapter will be restricted to the sentences in (46b) and (56c) through (56j), given again below, since they, according to a preliminary judgement, contain normal rational agents in common real-life circumstances. Excluded from the analysis will be sentences of type (47), (57e), (58a) or (59e) as well, for imperfective sentences do not seem to be analysable in the way perfective sentences are (see also below). Furthermore, first, perfectivity should be seen as more important than imperfectivity for the understanding of the overall mechanism of aspect: recall this thesis of Verkuyl's (1993: 21), considered in detail in Chapter Ten, *Meanings of nouns and noun phrases, and aspect in English.* Second, cross-linguistic analysis shows that perfectivity is more difficult to explicate or express: in contrast to imperfectivity, special devices (markers of boundedness – either in verbs or in nouns) are needed for its ultimate systematic effectuation in a given language. Finally, excluded from the analysis will also be the first two sentences in (56), because they have already been extensively analysed and because there is some doubt whether their subjects really denote typical (adult) agents.

(56) a. A/The boy threw a/the stone
b. A/The child ate an/the apple

Children, or at least younger children, can be said to conform to somewhat different, specific, rules of agenthood.

Taken in their perfective interpretation, which has been regarded as primary or prototypical, the sentences in (46b) and (56c) through (56j) do not contradict Allwood's principles. We can assume that the action in each of the sentences is intentional, purposeful, voluntary and motivated, that it is carried out adequately and efficiently, that the agents conform to the principles of pleasure and pain and that they believe that it is possible to achieve their purposes:

(46) b. A tourist climbed the mountain
(56) c. A/The soldier crossed a/the street
d. A/The girl ironed a/the skirt
e. A/The woman cleaned a/the room
f. A/The mechanic repaired a/the car
g. A/The housewife prepared a/the lunch
h. A/The passer-by signed a/the appeal
i. A/The secretary typed a/the report
j. A/The journalist read a/the newspaper

There is no indication to the contrary in these sentences – as they are observed in isolation from context. Of course, it should be borne in mind that the principle of immediate pleasure may be temporarily suspended in view of some long-term pleasure (see also below)[1].

---

[1] For example, as Allwood (1976: 43) argued, digging in the garden may suspend immediate pleasure but increase a long-term one.

ALLWOOD'S PRINCIPLES IN ACTION

However, the fact that the sentences in (46b) and (56c) through (56j) do conform to the principles of normal rational agenthood in their perfective interpretation does not yet provide sufficient grounds to conclude that their perfectivity is pragmatically sanctioned. Therefore, let us assume the opposite, viz., that the actions in (46b) and (56c) through (56j) are imperfective, non-bounded, and see if imperfectivity can be associated with the cancellation of some pragmatic principle or principles. The imperfective reading is a possible one, for, as already established, the action in sentences of type (46b) or (56c) through (56j) could be interpreted either as a non-bounded iterative one or as a current activity – that has also been referred to as a progressive-like reading. Let us consider the principles and check whether and how the sentences could conform or fail to conform to them in their imperfective readings.

First principle. The first principle will not be taken into account since it is the general one and the other principles constitute its basis. Compare each of the sentences against the relevant pragmatic principle(s).

Second principle. In the imperfective reading of many of the sentences in (46b) and (56c) through (56j) the action referred to could be non-intentional and non-purposeful. This is especially possible, for example, in (56e) and (56j), where room-cleaning and newspaper reading could be done by sheer force of habit or obligation, without any immediate purpose in mind.

(56) e. A/The woman cleaned a/the room
j. A/The journalist read a/the newspaper

However, since there is no clear indication of a lack of intention and purpose implied in any way in these sentences considered in isolation, it should be assumed that the actions described will normally be conceived of as intentional and purposeful.

Third principle. Some of the actions in (46b) and (56c) through (56j) could, in their imperfective reading, be non-voluntary, i.e., done under command, and hence (perhaps) purposefully ineffective. This is possible, for example, in sentences (56c) and (56i), where the actions denoted are often done on other people's orders.

(56) c. A/The soldier crossed a/the street
i. A/The secretary typed a/the report

However, different types and degrees of voluntariness ought to be distinguished. Orders obeyed by soldiers and employees can be obeyed voluntarily (when orders are accepted) and, in fact, usually are. Hence, these two sentences in isolation should not be taken to contain or imply any indication to the contrary.

Fourth principle. Non-motivated action, that is, lack of desire, want or need (in Allwood's sense – Allwood 1976: 48), could perhaps be traced in (56d) through (56f):

(56) d. A/The girl ironed a/the skirt
 e. A/The woman cleaned a/the room
 f. A/The mechanic repaired a/the car

This principle is similar to the second principle, and the actions could again be done by sheer force of habit or obligation, or, simply, by accident. But since no explicit or implicit evidence for this can be provided in the sentences in isolation, it ought to be assumed that in the normal readings of these sentences the actions described are motivated.

Fifth principle. This principle is especially relevant in (46b), and also in (56e), (56f) or (56i), where the actions may require considerable effort:

(46) b. A tourist climbed the mountain
(56) e. A/The woman cleaned a/the room
 f. A/The mechanic repaired a/the car
 i. A/The secretary typed a/the report

In their imperfective interpretation these sentences are likely to bear a meaning violating the fifth principle. The fifth principle should be considered in its 'long-term' sense. That is, one may temporarily decrease one's pleasure and increase one's pain in climbing a mountain, cleaning a room, repairing a car or typing a report in view of the fulfillment of some long-term goal – which would, hence, be in conformity with the principle (see Allwood 1976: 43). Viewed in this way, sentences (46b), (56e), (56f) and (56i) offer no clear indication or implication that the agents act so as to decrease their pleasure or increase their pain.

Sixth principle. The principle concerning the agent's intention to achieve his/her purposes adequately and efficiently is especially relevant in e.g. (56f), where the task is more complicated and could, for example, be beyond the agent's competence.

(56) f. A/The mechanic repaired a/the car

The mechanic could, furthermore, be acting ostentatiously in an attempt to exaggerate the severity of the damage. Thus an utterance like (56f) could be made in violation of some other pragmatic principles as well, like, e.g., some of Grice's (1975) well-known maxims of communication.
 Two of Grice's maxims are:

"1. Do not say what you believe to be false.
2. Do not say that for which you lack adequate evidence."

(Grice 1975: 46). It can be argued, for instance, that if a speaker says "The mechanic repaired the car" when it is clear that the vehicle won't start, he is either:

(i) breaking Grice's maxims, or,
(ii) is conforming to them but is using sentence (56f) in a secondary, non-accomplishment (episode) reading.

In this possible (secondary) reading of the sentence the action denoted has taken place but was terminated before reaching its inherent endpoint – and, hence, no pragmatically identifiable result of the action is accomplished. But, on the basis of information contained or implied in sentence (56f) only (as given here, without any specifying context), we do not have to assume that the car was not repaired – and that there is a violation of Allwood's sixth principle or of Grice's supermaxim 'Try to make your contribution one that is true', under which the two specific maxims above are subsumed.

Seventh principle. Failure to conform to this principle could be critical for the aspectual interpretation of a sentence like (46b), where the tourist may, as sometimes happens in practice, disregard, or be unaware of, the impossibility of climbing to a particular place in the mountain along a particular route or under certain conditions.

(46) b. A tourist climbed the mountain

This additional information, however, cannot be supplied or implied by sentence (46b) alone. We ought to assume, therefore, that its overall meaning is in conformity with the seventh principle.

To sum up, if we have to interpret the sentences in (46b) and (56c) through (56j) either imperfectively or in some other non-accomplishment sense, there should be some information/implication available somewhere that for some reason the action is being fulfilled non-intentionally or non-purposefully, or ineffectively or non-voluntarily, or inadequately or that the actor lacks motives/competence to carry it out to the end. Sentences (46b) and (56c) through (56j) as they are, given out of context, contain no information or implication as to the presence of a deviation of this kind from the assumptions of normal rational agenthood. Hence, these sentences have to be regarded as referring to perfective, bounded, accomplishment situations in their prototypical, primary reading. If in their secondary aspectual interpretation they start to refer to imperfective, non-bounded actions or to some other non-accomplishment situations, the information/implication related to the violation of one or some of the principles above would have to be supplied by the context.

As already noted, the secondary interpretation should not necessarily be non-bounded/imperfective. The aspectual value of 'episode', as defined in the previous chapter, could be explicated. Compare the discourse sequences in (306) below, where the implication of an accomplishment (also in the everyday sense of the word, not from the Vendlerian 'situational' point of view), already assumed to be present in isolated sentences like (46b), (56f), (56i) and (56j), is cancelled:

(306) a. The weather was nasty. The mountaineer climbed the mountain. He had almost reached the peak when it turned out to be impossible
    b. The mechanic repaired the car. But driving on my way home later I realised he only cheated me
    c. The secretary typed the report. Later, when I read it, I saw that whole passages were missing and it was also full of mistakes
    d. The journalist read the newspaper. Later, however, when asked why he did not comment on the editorial, he gave no explanation[2]

Or, to put it in more general terms, in the imperfective, the episode, or, simply, in the non-prototypical (i.e. non-accomplishment) interpretation of any of the sentences in (46b) or (56c) through (56j) its pragmatic interpretation could be expected to violate one or some of the principles of normal rational agenthood. Any information or implication indicating a violation of this kind is to be supplied by the preceding and/or following sentence/sentences or, alternatively, by the sentence itself – that is, if the sentence in question is viewed as an expression complemented by adverbials, adjectives, etc. bearing upon its aspectual interpretation. Compare examples like (307a) and (307b):

(307) a. Stubbornly, the mountaineer climbed the mountain
    b. The poor secretary typed the third report in succession

These sentences can be regarded as imperfectivised through the complementation of manner adverbials to a sentence or expression which was originally perfective.

RELATED PHENOMENA

Glasbey (1994) analysed sentences like (308) and (309) below and came to the following conclusions. If (308a) and (308b) are part of a discourse sequence like the one in (308c), the adverbial *then* in (308b), called sentence-final *then*, is necessarily cotemporal with *July* in (308a), and the two actions, in (308a) and (308b), are, generally, simultaneous:

(308) a. Daniel climbed Ben Nevis in July
    b. Gareth climbed Snowdon then
    c. Daniel climbed Ben Nevis in July. Gareth climbed Snowdon then

---

[2] The translation of these sequences into the Bulgarian metalanguage easily confirms the thesis: both the perfective and the imperfective Aorist (the former representing an accomplishment, the latter an episode) will be possible in the translation equivalents of (306) but the imperfective Aorist would be more appropriate and natural.

Conversely, in the case of a sentence-initial *then*, if sentences like (309a) and (309b) below are part of a discourse sequence like the one in (309c), the adverbial *then* in (309b) falls outside the scope of the action in (309a), and the action in (309a) precedes the one in (309b):

(309) a. Daniel climbed Ben Nevis in July
  b. Then Gareth climbed Snowdon
  c. Daniel climbed Ben Nevis in July. Then Gareth climbed Snowdon

(see Glasbey 1994: 12-14). This means that while sentence-initial *then* would generally trigger off perfectivity, sentence-final *then* could more easily be associated with an imperfective or a non-accomplishment situation, e.g. an episode. A sentence like (309a) asserts that Daniel actually managed to climb Ben Nevis (once) and reached the intended place. However, since Gareth's climb in (308b) is cotemporal with Daniel's, sentence (308b) allows the interpretation that Gareth was involved in climbing Snowdon in the sequence in (308c) and did not necessarily reach the intended place. That is, we cannot be sure that in (308b) or, rather, in the identical sentence in (308c) Gareth managed to reach the intended place in the mountain. He could have just tried to reach it, or he could have climbed the mountain several times without fulfilling a particular purpose – and all these possibilities could be subsumed under the meaning of (308b) and (308c).

These examples with the two types of the adverbial *then* show again that the role of the temporal adverbial is essential in the explication of aspectual meanings. Clearly, different temporal adverbials contribute in various ways to the composition of aspect at the level of the sentence. They can also intertwine in a very subtle manner with pragmatic principles (and, generally, 'knowledge of the world') to produce the ultimate primary, secondary, or any other possible aspectual reading of a particular sentence.

Of course, pragmatic principles (like e.g. Allwood's described above) need not **always** be violated for the action in certain types of sentences, like those in (46b) or (56c) through (56j), to be interpreted as imperfective. To illustrate this point, consider, for example, sentence (46b) in the following real-life circumstances. A mountain peak in a certain country is only several meters shorter than another mountain peak in a neighbouring country. For reasons of patriotism, every mountaineer climbing to the shorter peak brings a stone and leaves it on the peak, so that the shorter peak should one day become higher than the one in the neighbouring country. The following discourse sequence could denote the indefinitely repeatable act of a tourist or a mountaineer climbing the mountain and leaving a stone on the peak with the intention already described:

(310) A tourist climbed the mountain. Then he or she left the stone on the peak

In the discourse sequence (310), the first sentence, which is the same as (46b) above, describes an imperfective action, an indefinitely repeated act, but a violation of a pragmatic principle like one of those listed above could hardly be traced. Note, first, that sentence-initial *then* fails to take effect in this case, due to the influence of the context which informs us of an indefinite repetition of the act. Second, it is the subject *he or she* in the second sentence of (310) that reflects the repetitive non-boundedness imposed by the context. Recall also Verkuyl's rule about perfectivity being more well behaved – which seems to be associated with the tendency for sentences with imperfective readings, not with perfective ones, to violate pragmatic principles – if they are violated.

The kind of solution to the problem of interpreting aspectual values of sentences in terms of pragmatic principles described above is, hence, compatible with the thesis according to which sentences like (46b) or (56c) through (56j) can explicate imperfectivity only if additional aspectual markers are present in preceding and/or following sentences or in the sentence itself (see Kabakčiev 1984: 647). Exponents of imperfectivity can be grammatical entities like the Progressive, the auxiliaries *would* and *used to*, overt lexical indicators of non-bounded repetition (*seldom, always, often, repeatedly, regularly, occasionally*, etc.), various other adverbials, or other words and phrases serving as markers of imperfectivity – like *he or she* in the example (310) above. This thesis has been complemented here with an outline of a possible pragmatic component for a general aspectual theory – allowing different aspectual interpretations of a sentence according to the effect of principles underlying social behaviour (like Allwood's principles of normal rational agenthood or Grice's maxims of communication).

Clearly, the discussion of 'knowledge of the world' as a factor for explicating aspectual values ties in with the problem of the proper identification and formulation of basic grammatical rules of aspect construal. Recall that in English a relatively large number of phrases constitute exceptions to the rule to have an article where boundedness is explicated in the whole expression and to have no article where non-boundedness is explicated. Compare once again those listed in (180) and (181), already discussed from a somewhat different viewpoint.

VERB-NOUN PHRASES WITH NO ARTICLE, WITH A BOUNDED MEANING

(180)

IN THE SINGULAR	IN THE PLURAL
make use of	shake hands
give rise to	exchange glances
take part in	take measures
express concern	express thanks
take/gain advantage	offer condolences
set foot on something	settle matters
restore order	hold talks
have breakfast, lunch, etc.	carry out negotiations

show/have mercy
provoke laughter
cause destruction

VERB-NOUN PHRASES, WITH AN ARTICLE, WITH A
NON-BOUNDED MEANING
(181)   have a desire
have a sense of humour (etc.)
serve a purpose
owe an excuse

Could the deviant behaviour of these phrases be accounted for simply as an exception in grammatical terms? It seems that it is mainly our knowledge of the world that tells us how to interpret sentences in which phrases like those in (180) and (181) are used.

Consider the following three sentences with the phrases *take part, restore order* and *gain advantage*:

(311)   a. John took part in the conference on family planning
b. The police were called on to restore order
c. Peter gained little advantage from the postgraduate courses

Though a conference could, in principle, acquire a status of indefinite repetition, cf. (312a) below, we normally conceive of *the conference* in (311a) as a unique event. Hence, a sentence like (311a) above is, in spite of the bare singular noun *part*, a perfective one, unless an adverbial like *each year* is added, as in (312a) below. Similarly, although *order* in *restore order* in (311b) is a bare singular noun, and, furthermore, is primarily non-bounded as a lexical entry (in contrast to *part*, which is primarily bounded), sentence (311b) is perfective and can be made imperfective through the complementation of an adverbial of indefinite repetition like *every other night*, as in (312b). The (referent of the) noun *advantage* is primarily non-bounded and atemporal but in (311c) its temporalisation (effected in a complex fashion within the sentence as a whole) makes it bounded despite the lack of quantification. Conversely, in (312c) the non-boundedness (understood as an indefinite series) of the indirect object *postgraduate courses* can be said to be mapped onto the meaning of *advantage* rendering its referent indefinitely recurrent and, hence, again non-bounded (at least in the most typical reading of the sentence).

(312)   a. John took part in the conference on family planning each year
b. The police were called on to restore order every other night
c. Peter gained little advantage from postgraduate courses

But, whatever the result of the semantic and grammatical analysis of the sentences in (311), it can be asserted that, simply, we **know** that *take part, restore order* and *gain* *advantage* in sentences like (311), or even in isolation, are normally bounded. Hence, at the level of lexical analysis, it could be justified to claim that verb-noun phrases like these behave like separate verbs and could be analysed as special syntactic (phraseological) entities with a function different from the one normally assigned by the rules of compositional aspect. Note also that a phrase like *restore order* in its bounded interpretation (the normal one) seems to be derived from the ordinary phrase *restore the order* in which the definite article exercises its function of delimiting the scope of the action.

It is also worth noting that in certain cases some of the phrases of the aspectually deviant type in (180), actually, must be used with either an article or with another determiner, for example, when an adjective is present:

(313)   take part in   take **an** *active* part in
        have breakfast   but have **an** *early* breakfast
        express concern   express **one's** *serious* concern

This simple and basic grammatical rule – which is, nonetheless, generally neglected in the grammars of English – corroborates the idea of viewing the perfective phrases in (180) as a special group semantically similar to, or even derived from, similar phrases with articles, determiners or (other) quantifiers. What makes the omission of the determiner or quantifier from the initial phrase possible and guarantees the correct interpretation in conflict with the rule of grammar is, in the long run, 'knowledge of the world'. Of course, 'knowledge of the world' is a notion similar to 'context'. It is too broad to be able to serve as an adequate description of the interplay between the compositional explication of aspect and the pragmatic influences within discourse. Future studies in aspectology ought to develop a more appropriate framework for the adequate description of the phenomenon.

Thus in the grammar of English the special phrases in (180) and (181) ought to be subsumed under the heading of 'exception' or, alternatively, under some specific subrules of aspectual composition. However, there are some other cases that resist even an explanation along these lines and render the general picture of compositional aspect (which, as already shown, is a complex phenomenon) even more complicated. It was established above that sentences like (46b) and (56), on the one hand, and sentences like (47), (57e), (58a) and (59e), on the other, represent two clearly distinguishable types in terms of their outward characteristics and their aspectual values. Sentences like (46b) and (56) normally explicate perfectivity of the action, and when in their secondary interpretation they denote a non-bounded or a non-accomplishment situation, certain pragmatic principles (for example, of agenthood) may be violated. Conversely, sentences like (47), (57e), (58a) and (59e), repeated below, with either a non-bounded subject or a non-bounded syntactic object (or a non-bounded subject **and** a non-bounded syntactic object) normally explicate imperfectivity of the action – for reasons extensively analysed and defined in the previous chapters:

(47)   Tourists climbed the mountain
(58) a. Soldiers crossed the street
(57) e. The secretary typed reports
(59) e. Secretaries typed reports

It has been established here (as well as in other publications, discussed at length), however, that it is the non-boundedness of the object in a certain type of simple sentences that most clearly contributes to the imperfectivisation of an action, as in sentences like (1c), (13a), (21a), (40a):

(1) c. John drank beer
(13) a. Peter sang songs
(21) a. He gave orders
(40) a. Katinka knitted Norwegian sweaters

And even if some of these sentences explicated a non-bounded situation less markedly than others, cf. (1c) and (21a), the analysis showed that the imperfective meaning in this type of sentences is to be regarded as the prototypical one, and the perfective one is possible, constituting a non-prototypical (less typical), secondary, aspectual value that can be explicated, broadly speaking, through the influence of context.

However, it will be shown now that in English a different, special type of simple sentences also exists. It is a relatively rare case of sentences which describe typical everyday events very similar to those in (57e), (1c), (13a), (21a) and (40a) above; the sentences unmistakably fall into the same pattern according to their outward characteristics but they totally fail to behave like the sentences in (57e), (1c), (13a), (21a) and (40a) from an aspectological point of view. Recall, in this vein, the discussion about sentences like (203a) and (203b), given below, which follow the same (outwardly identical) agentive pattern. Both ought to be perfective but, actually, they differ aspectually, and the difference was defined as due to 'knowledge of the world'. Sentence (203a) is perfective, (203b) is imperfective:

(203) a. John preached the sermon
      b. John preached the Gospel

Now compare a similar case of a deviant aspectual reading in the following three sentences, in which the verb *buy* is used:

(314) a. John bought tickets
      b. John bought flowers
      c. John bought beer

Structurally, the examples in (314) belong to the group of sentences with a bounded subject, a verb with a telic aspectual potential, and a non-bounded (bare) object-NP, representing the so-called (by Verkuyl) object leakage. Clearly, however, they are not normally used to denote a non-bounded action. On the contrary, uttered in a neutral context or considered in isolation, each of them would normally be read as a single act, i.e., as an accomplishment. Thus, if a rule for sentences with an object-NP unaccompanied by an article has already been posited to the effect that such sentences express non-bounded actions, and if some specific subrules can be posited dealing with cases like (180) and (181) above, the rule and the subrules will have to allow for certain additional (though perhaps statistically minor) exceptions conditioned exclusively by 'general knowledge of the world'. In the case of (314), it is typical of *tickets, flowers* and *beer* to be bought by a particular person on a particular occasion.

Conversely, compare the examples in (315) below, where the sentences have absolutely identical outward grammatical characteristics, only the lexical entry for the verb is different – unlike the contrast between (203a) and (203b) above, where the verbs are the same but the object-NPs differ (and in their semantic content only, not in their grammatical characteristics). The sentences in (315) are normally used to refer to a non-bounded, usually habitual, action:

(315) a. John sold tickets
  b. John sold flowers
  c. John sold beer

It may also be argued that the abnormal behaviour of (314), triggering off a perfective interpretation, could hardly be explained in terms of a violation of some special pragmatic principle like Allwood's or Grice's discussed above. Simply, **we know** that sentences like those in (314) are perfective, despite their structure.

The lexical parameters of the *buy-sell* distinction have frequently been exploited in the literature in analyses of various semantic and grammatical problems. The verb *sell* has also been extensively dealt with in the analyses in Verkuyl (1993: 135-140). But the fact that in his two major works Verkuyl (1972; 1993) did not make the observation above concerning the perfective reading of sentences with object-NPs unaccompanied by an article like (314) is somewhat strange. It could be explained either through his desire to present a theory as streamlined as possible, ignoring the flexibility of language, or through his preoccupation with the complexities of nominal quantification at the expense of the subtleties of the interaction between verbal and nominal referents.

It was probably the preoccupation with nominal quantification that made Verkuyl prone to certain overgeneralisations – rather superfluous for a theory which is general enough. Consider Verkuyl's interpretation of the discourse sequence in (316a) below. He insists that in (316a)

"*Judith ate sandwiches* is durative and remains so even if later information makes it clear that Judith ate a finite amount of sandwiches"

(Verkuyl 1993: 182). This overgeneralisation was dealt with earlier in terms of a different context. If we now substitute *ate* with *bought*, as in (316b) below, the regularity proposed can again easily be shown to be invalid. Compare the two discourse sequences, in which only the verbs differ:

(316) a. Judith **ate** sandwiches. She had all five of them in her box
b. Judith **bought** sandwiches. She had all five of them in her box

The first sentence in (316b), *Judith bought sandwiches*, is perfective, just as Verkuyl's sentence *Judith ate sandwiches* in (316a) is. But (316a) clearly displays the situational meaning of an episode, not of an accomplishment. Note that in (316b) the anaphoric relation of the preposition *them* runs counter to the expectations for preserving genericity, near-genericity or at least non-specificity of a noun unaccompanied by an article (in this case *sandwiches*) – due to the perfectivity of the first sentence (*Judith bought sandwiches*) in the sequence. The boundedness of the referent of *bought* in *Judith bought sandwiches* corresponds to the boundedness of the referent of the bare plural object-NP *sandwiches*, and this boundedness automatically induces specificity to the pronoun *them* in the second sentence. Cases like this may not be very common, but they are not so rare either, and this thesis can be corroborated by the large number of exceptions to the rule of having an article in the explication of boundedness in phrases like those in (180) – see the discussion above. But whatever the implications of the distribution in actual discourse of sequences like (316b), the analysis here shows, firstly, that, generally speaking, NPs that are superficially [-SQA]-NPs **are** actually able to receive a [+SQA]-interpretation under certain conditions (the problem of temporality vs. atemporality of NPs is here ignored). Secondly, there is a higher degree of language flexibility than the general rules usually predict. And, thirdly, since purely grammatical features become inoperative in cases like these, context and 'knowledge of the world' once again prove to be factors of considerable importance that are to be adequately accounted for in any theory of aspect.

ASPECTUAL INTERPRETATION BASED ON PRAGMATIC PRINCIPLES ONLY?

To conclude this chapter, let us discuss the question that arises here – whether aspectual interpretation could not possibly be regarded as always based on pragmatic factors only. If the line of argumentation adopted above is followed further on, it will inevitably turn out that the aspectual interpretation of a sentence with a Simple Past Tense in English (and in other languages with a similar tense-aspect structure) will always be analysable in terms of pragmatic factors like 'general knowledge of the world' and in terms of certain concrete principles underlying social communication developed intuitively by the participants in it. A solution of this kind appears more than natural. But could it really be the case that it is pragmatic principles only that determine aspectual interpretation? For example, if we wish to verify the imperfectivity of sentences like (47), (57e), (58a) or (59e) through their compatibility to Allwood's principles of normal rational agenthood, it may turn out that these sentences do not differ in any essential way from the sentences in (46b) and (56c) through (56j). Viewed in their primary imperfective interpretation or in their secondary perfective interpretation, the actions described in these sentences could correspond to the assumptions of voluntary, motivated and purposeful action, etc., as already argued above. The imperfectivity of sentences of this kind should, therefore, be taken to originate mainly in the choice of the speaker to use a particular grammatical structure, and should not be considered as due to a violation of some pragmatic principle or principles. Or, in other words, sentences like (47), (57e), (58a) or (59e) are imperfective because the speaker has not availed himself of the opportunity to use any device present in the language (e.g. a quantifier, an article, etc.) for making the NP/NPs, and hence the action, bounded, and the hearer interprets these sentences accordingly.

Thus both perfectivity in sentences like (46b) and (56c) through (56j) and imperfectivity in sentences like (47), (57e), (58a) or (59e) are marked by formal language means (determiner/quantifier vs. zero determiner/quantifier) but whereas perfectivity is generally analysable in terms of pragmatic principles, imperfectivity does not seem to be easily analysable in that way. The imperfectivity of sentences like (47), (57e), (58a) or (59e) seems to be more easily interpreted through cognitive structures, that is, in terms of the way a happening is normally perceived or conceived of by a speaker/observer and communicated to a hearer/receiver. However, this problem is clearly in need of further research outside the scope of the present study and, therefore, it will not be addressed here.

CONCLUSION

Although as early as two decades ago a relative consensus was reached among linguists to view the perfective/imperfective aspectual opposition in languages like English in compositional terms[1], since then the real foundations of aspect have nevertheless remained unclear in most studies of this notoriously difficult linguistic category. What is more, the compositional mechanism, which, according to one of the main assumptions in the present work, constitutes the basis for the proper understanding of aspect, has been incorrectly challenged in the literature (either directly or, in most cases, indirectly). As an unfortunate consequence, both its scientific importance and its true parameters remained, prior to the present work, virtually unrecognised.

The results of the analyses undertaken here have confirmed once again (cf. Kabakčiev 1984a) the idea that:

(i) aspect in a language like English should be explored primarily along the lines of the compositional mechanism;

(ii) there are two major ways in cross-language terms for explicating aspectual distinctions – compositional and verbal;

(iii) compositional aspect is a mirror image of verbal aspect.

This book has broadened the outlines of an aspectual theory presented a long time ago (in Kabakčiev 1984b) – by widening the possibilities for locating the parameters of aspect not only in the grammar and the semantics of sentences but also in man's cognitive organisation and pragmatic assumptions.

Of course, from the point of view of language structure, aspect is a result not only of the way reality is conceptualised but also of a particular historical development in a certain language or in a group of languages. And, as far as compositional aspect is concerned, it should be borne in mind that the aspectual value of a sentence in a language like English is also greatly dependent on the consequences imposed by the already acquired knowledge of the world – in contrast to verbal aspect which imposes certain values on the sentence and these values become, or at least seem to become, less interpretable through pragmatic principles. Diversity of historically determined form (verbal and compositional aspect in their varieties) should not, however, misguide the efforts to define the essence of one of the most complex and difficult (but fascinating) language phenomena mainly in terms of the mechanisms of cognition.

---

[1] Besides Verkuyl (1972), among earlier publications see also, e.g., Zydatiß (1976); Heinämäki (1978); Dowty (1979); Markkanen (1979); most of the contributions in Tedeschi and Zaenen (1981); Lindstedt (1984).

In the long run, determining the aspectual reading of a particular sentence in English in which it is construed compositionally is not a difficult task at all, provided a good understanding of the global mechanism of explicating aspect has already been acquired. What is especially interesting is that English native speakers determine the aspectual value, however complex, of a sentence automatically, without any effort, and never, or almost never, asking questions about the type of situational meaning involved. The linguist can only marvel at the capacity of man to receive, process and interpret the enormous quantity of information contained in a simple sentence at a fraction of a second.

APPENDIX

THE MAJOR CHARACTERISTICS OF THE BULGARIAN TENSE-ASPECT SYSTEM

The Bulgarian system of verbal aspect may be said to consist of two basic distinctions: the perfective/imperfective distinction, a purely aspectual one, and the Aorist/Imperfect (Past Tense) distinction, which is a tense-aspect distinction.

THE TENSE SYSTEM

Bulgarian features a system of nine tenses. Examples are given below (in the 1st, 2nd and 3rd pers.sing., active voice) for the first five tenses – which are more relevant to the present study.

1) The Present Tense.
With an imperfective verb, *piša*$_{impfv}$ 'write':

(az) piša 'I write/am writing'
(ti) pišeš 'you write/are writing'
(toj) piše 'he writes/is writing'

With a perfective verb, *napiša*$_{pfv}$ 'write':

(az) napiša 'I write'
(ti) napišeš 'you write'
(toj) napiše 'he writes'

Perfective Present verb forms are allowed only in special syntactic environments – denoting non-bounded repetition (disallowing single acts), conditional or futurate meanings.

2) The Aorist Tense (Bulgarian *minalo svăršeno vreme*, 'past completed tense').
With an imperfective verb, *piša*$_{impfv}$ 'write':

(az) pisah 'I wrote [for some time]'
(ti) pisa 'you wrote [for some time]'
(toj) pisa 'he wrote [for some time]'

With a perfective verb, *napiša*$_{pfv}$ 'write':

(az) napisah 'I wrote [to the end/completely]'
(ti) napisa 'you wrote [to the end/completely]'
(toj) napisa 'he wrote [to the end/completely]'

3) The Imperfect Tense (Bulgarian *minalo nesvărseno vreme* 'past non-completed tense').
With an imperfective verb, *piša*$_{impfv}$ 'write':

(az) pišeh 'I was writing/wrote [habitually]'
(ti) pišeše 'you were writing/wrote [habitually]'
(toj) pišeše 'he was writing/wrote [habitually]'

With a perfective verb, *napiša*$_{pfv}$ 'write':

(az) napišeh 'I wrote [to the end, habitually]'
(ti) napišeše 'you wrote [to the end, habitually]'
(toj) napišeše 'he wrote [to the end, habitually]'

The most frequent and natural verb forms within the Aorist/Imperfect distinction are the perfective Aorist (*toj napisa* 'he wrote [to the end/completely]') and the imperfective Imperfect (*toj pišeše* 'he was writing/wrote [habitually]'); they denote the two prototypical aspectual values – of perfectivity and imperfectivity. Less common than the previous two, imperfective Aorist forms (*toj pisa* 'he wrote [for some time]') denote actions that are not completed with a particular, pragmatically identifiable result, but are terminated. Even more rare, perfective Imperfect forms (*toj napišeše* 'he wrote [to the end, habitually]') have a specific meaning. If their homonymous use to denote Future-in-the-Past actions is ignored, they refer to a non-bounded series of actions in which every separate action is a completed one. The contrast between the Imperfect and the Aorist with imperfective verbs very often finds no morphological expression: a relatively large number of verb forms outside the second and third person singular, where the distinction is made always, are homonymous for the two tenses.

4) The Perfect Tense (Bulgarian *minalo neopredeleno vreme* 'past indefinite tense'), broadly similar to the Present Perfect Tense in English but allowing adverbials of past time like *včera* 'yesterday', *predi tri dni* 'three days ago', etc. The auxiliary is *săm* 'be'.

With an imperfective verb, *piša*_{impfv} 'write':

(az) săm pisal 'I have written'
(ti) si pisal 'you have written'
(toj) e pisal 'he has written'

With a perfective verb, *napiša*_{pfv} 'write':

(az) săm napisal 'I have written'
(ti) si napisal 'you have written'
(toj) e napisal 'he has written'.

5) The Past Perfect Tense, broadly similar to the Past Perfect Tense in English:
With an imperfective verb, *piša*_{impfv} 'write':

(az) bjah pisal 'I had written'
(ti) beše pisal 'you had written'
(toj) beše pisal 'he had written'

With a perfective verb, *napiša*_{pfv} 'write':

(az) bjah napisal 'I had written'
(ti) beše napisal 'you had written'
(toj) beše napisal 'he had written'.

6. The Future Tense. Future auxilary *šte* 'will' (negative: *njama* 'won't' + *da* 'to').

7. The Future-in-the-Past Tense. Future-in-the-past auxilary *štjah* 'would' + *da* 'to' (negative: *njamaše* 'wouldn't' + *da* 'to').

8. The Future Perfect Tense. Future auxilary *šte* 'will' + *săm/băda* 'be' + past active participle (negative: *njama* 'won't' + *da* 'to' + *săm/băda* 'be' + past active participle).

9. The Future-in-the-Past Perfect Tense. Future-in-the-past auxilary *štjah* 'would' + *da* 'to' + *săm/băda* 'be' + past active participle (negative: *njamaše* 'wouldn't' + *da* 'to' + *săm/băda* 'be' + past active participle).

THE ASPECT SYSTEM

The great majority of Bulgarian verbs are either perfective or imperfective, like *napiša*$_{pfv}$ 'write [complete an act of writing]' and *piša*$_{impfv}$ 'write [generally or be in the process of writing]', already used above, in the description of the tense system.

The perfective/imperfective distinction is of a mixed type. It can be regarded as partly morphological and partly lexical. Perfective verbs are formed by affixation, usually through prefixes. But very often the particular prefix signals other meanings as well, e.g. transitivity, or a certain change in the lexical meaning. Taken in isolation, any prefix used to make a given perfective verb out of an imperfective one, can be found to serve other functions when complemented to a different verb. The great majority of unprefixed verbs are imperfectives, out of which their perfective partners are formed. For example, *piša*$_{impfv}$ 'write [generally or be in the process of writing]' – *napiša*$_{pfv}$ 'write [complete an act of writing]'. There are few primary perfectives, e.g. *dam*$_{pfv}$ 'give'.

There is a special group of so-called secondary imperfective verbs (*napisvam*$_{impfv}$ 'write') which denote a bounded action – the same as the one denoted by the perfective verb (*napiša*$_{pfv}$ 'write [complete an act of writing]') but which is repeated an indefinite number of times. These verbs are regularly formed in Bulgarian (in contrast to other Slavic languages where the phenomenon, called secondary imperfectivisation, is less widespread) by adding the suffix *-vam* to the perfective verb. Certain minor additional morphophonetic changes may occur. Some secondary imperfectives are used less often – when the primary imperfective is found to be capable of expressing the boundedness of the individual action, presented as indefinitely serialised.

There are also several hundred biaspectual verbs in Bulgarian that may be said to fall outside the system of aspect. They function in a way similar to the functioning of verbs in English and, according to traditional descriptions, their aspectual value is explicated on the basis of their use in particular contexts.

A detailed description in English of the Bulgarian tense-aspect system can be found in Lindstedt (1985).

REFERENCES

Allen 1966: W.R.Allen. *The verb system of present-day American English*. The Hague: Mouton.
Allwood 1976: J.Allwood. *Linguistic communication as action and cooperation. A Study in pragmatics.* (*Gothenburg Monographs in Linguistics 2*). Dept. of Linguistics. University of Göteborg.
Andersson 1973: J.Anderson. *An essay concerning aspect. Some considerations of a general character arising from the Abbe Darrigol's analysis of the Basque verb.* The Hague/Paris: Mouton.
Atanassova et al 1988a: T.Atanassova, M.Rankova, R.Roussev, D.Spassov, V.Phillipov, G.Chakalov. *Bulgarian-English dictionary, Vol. I, A – N* (3rd edition). Sofia: Naouka i izkoustvo.
– 1988b: T.Atanassova, M.Rankova, R.Roussev, D.Spassov, V.Phillipov, G.Chakalov. *Bulgarian-English dictionary, Vol. II, O – JA* (3rd edition). Sofia: Naouka i izkoustvo.
Bach 1981: E.Bach. On time, tense and aspect. An essay in English metaphysics. In P.Cole (ed.). *Radical pragmatics*, 63-81. New York: Academic Press.
– 1986: E.Bach. The algebra of events. *Linguistics and Philosophy* 9, 5-16.
Bache 1983: C.Bache. *Verbal aspect. A general theory and its application to present-day English.* Odense: Odense University Press.
Bartsch 1995: R.Bartsch. *Situations, tense, and aspect. Dynamic discourse ontology and the semantic flexibility of temporal system in German and English* (*Groningen-Amsterdam Studies in Semantics; 13*). Berlin, New York: Mouton de Gruyter.
Binnick 1991: R.I.Binnick. *Time and the verb. A guide to tense and aspect.* New York, Oxford: Oxford University Press.
Brinton 1988: L.J.Brinton. *The development of English aspectual systems. Aspectualizers and postverbal particles.* Cambridge, etc.: Cambridge University Press.
– 1998: L.J.Brinton. Aspectuality and countability: a cross-categorial analogy. *English Language and Linguistics* 2, 37-63.
Bulygina 1982: T.V.Bulygina. K postroeniju tipologii predikatov v russkom jazyke. In Seliverstova 1982a, 7-85.
Bybee 1985: J.L.Bybee. *Morphology. A study of the relation between meaning and form.* Amsterdam/Philadelphia: John Benjamins.
– et al 1994: J.Bybee, R.Perkins, W.Pagliuca. *The evolution of grammar. Tense, aspect, and modality in the languages of the world.* Chicago and London: The University of Chicago Press.
Caenepeel 1989: M.Caenepeel. *Aspect, temporal ordering and perspective in narrative fiction.* Edinburgh (Ph.D. dissertation, the University of Edinburgh).
Carlson 1977/1980: G.N.Carlson. *Reference to kinds in English.* New York, 1980 (=Ph.D. dissertation, University of Massachusetts, 1977): Garland Publishing.
– 1982: G.N.Carlson. Generic terms and generic sentences. *Journal of Philosophical Logic*, 11, 145-181.
– and Tanenhaus 1984: G.Carlson, M.K.Tanenhaus. Lexical meanings, structural meanings, and concepts. In *Papers from the Parasession on Lexical Semantics, Chicago, 27-28 April, 1984*, 39-52. Chicago Linguistic Society.
Carlson 1981: L.Carlson. Aspect and quantification. In Tedeschi and Zaenen 1981, 31-64.
Cavedon and Glasbey 1996: L.Cavedon, S.Glasbey. The role of context in the interpretation of generic sentences. In P.Dekker, M.Stokhof (eds.). *Proceedings of the 10th Amsterdam Colloquim, March, 1996*, 143-162. ILLC/Department of Philosophy, University of Amsterdam.
Chung and Timberlake 1985: S.Chung, A.Timberlake. Tense, aspect and mood. In T.Shopen (ed.). *Language typology and syntactic description. Volume III. Grammatical categories and the lexicon*, 202-258. Cambridge, etc.: Cambridge University Press.
Comrie 1976: B.Comrie. *Aspect. An introduction to the study of verbal aspect and related problems.* Cambridge: Cambridge University Press.
– 1985: B.Comrie. *Tense.* Cambridge: Cambridge University Press.

References

Cooper 1985: R.Cooper. *Aspectual classes in situation semantics*. Centre for the Study of Language and Information. Stanford University, Report No CLSI 84-14-C: Ventura Hall, Stanford University.
Dahl 1981: Ö.Dahl. On the definition of the telic-atelic (bounded-nonbounded) distinction. In Tedeschi and Zaenen 1981, 79-90.
– 1985: Ö.Dahl. *Tense and aspect systems*. Oxford: Blackwell.
Danchev 1974: A.Danchev. A Slavic/Bulgarian view of the modern English de-adjectival *-en* verbs. *Linguistics* 127, 5-25.
– 1976: A.Danchev. Za njakoi strani na săpostavitelnite izsledvanija. *Bjuletin za săpostavitelno izsledvane na bălgarskija ezik s drugi ezici* 1, 7-26.
– 1992: A.Danchev. An outline of aspectuality in English within a compromise linguistic model. In M.Stamenov (ed.). *Current advances in semantic theory*, 321-337. Amsterdam: John Benjamins.
– and Alexieva 1974: A.Danchev, B.Aleksieva. Izborăt meždu minalo svăršeno i minalo nesvăršeno vreme pri prevoda na *past simple tense* ot anglijski na bălgarski ezik. *Godišnik na SU. FZF*. Tom LXVII, 1, 249-329.
Declerck 1986: R.Declerck. The manifold interpretations of generic sentences. *Lingua* 68, 149-188.
Derzhanski 1995: I.A.Derzhanski. *Groups and eventualities: a theory of aspectuality*. Edinburgh (Ph.D. dissertation, the University of Edinburgh).
Dowty 1979: D.R.Dowty. *Word meaning and Montague grammar: the semantics of verbs and times in generative semantics and in Montague's PTQ*. Dordrecht: Reidel.
– 1991: D.R.Dowty. Thematic proto-roles and argument selection. *Language* 67, 547-619.
Dušková 1983: L.Dušková. Has the English verb system the category of aspect? *Philologica pragensia* 1, 14-23.
Enç 1981: M.Enç. *Tense without scope: an analysis of nouns as indexicals*. Ph.D. dissertation, University of Wisconsin, Madison.
Fenn 1987: P.Fenn. *A semantic and pragmatic examination of the English perfect* (= *Tübinger Beiträge zur Linguistik, 312*). Tübingen: Gunter Narr Verlag.
Filip 1993: H.Filip. Aspect and interpretation of nominal arguments. *Chicago Linguistic Society* 28, 139-158.
Fillmore 1968: C.J.Fillmore. The case for case. In E.Bach, R.T.Harms (eds.). *Universals in linguistic theory*, 1-88. New York: Rinehart and Winston.
Fodor, Fodor and Garret 1975: J.Fodor, J.D.Fodor, M.Garret. The psychological unreality of semantic representations. *Linguistic Inquiry* 4, 515-531.
Forsyth 1970: J. Forsyth. *A grammar of aspect. Usage and meaning in the Russian verb*. Cambridge.
Friedrich 1974: P.Friedrich. On aspect theory and Homeric aspect. *International Journal of American Linguistics*. Memoirs 28 and 29. Vol. 40, No 4, Part 2, 1-44.
Galton 1984: A.Galton. *The logic of aspect. An axiomatic approach*. Oxford: Clarendon Press.
Garey 1957: H.B.Garey. Verbal aspect in French. *Language* 33, 91-100.
Geis 1975a: J.E.Geis. English time and place adverbials. *Working Papers in Linguistics*. No. 18. Department of Linguistics, The Ohio State University, Columbus, 1-11.
– 1975b: J.E.Geis. Two theories about action sentences. *Working Papers in Linguistics*. No. 18. Department of Linguistics, The Ohio State University, Columbus, 12-24.
Glasbey 1994: S.R.Glasbey. *Event structure in natural language discourse*. Edinburgh (Ph.D. dissertation, the University of Edinburgh).
Goldschmidt and Woisetschlaeger 1982: J.Goldschmidt, E.Woisetschlaeger. The logic of the English progressive. *Linguistics and Philosophy* 13, 79-89.
Grice 1975: H.P.Grice. Logic and conversation. In P.Cole, J.L.Morgan (eds.). *Syntax and semantics 3: Speech acts*, 41-58. New York, etc.: Academic Press.
Harlig 1983: J.Harlig. An appeal to the masses (?). In A.Chukerman, M.Marks, and J.F.Richardson (eds.). *Papers from the Nineteenth Regional Meeting of the Chicago Linguistics Society, Chicago, April 21-22, 1983*, 158-170.
Hatav 1993: G.Hatav. The aspect system in English: an attempt at a unified analysis. *Linguistics* 31, 209-237.
Heinämäki 1974/1978: O.Heinämäki. *Semantics of English temporal connectives*. Indiana University Linguistics Club.
Heller 1962: J.Heller. *Catch 22*. London: Jonathan Cape.

Heller 1990: Dž.Helăr. *Paragraf 22* [*Catch 22*, transl. into Bulgarian by B.Atanasov]. Sofia: Atlantis.
Hinrichs 1983: E.Hinrichs. The semantics of the English progressive. A study in situation semantics. In A.Chukerman, M.Marks and J.F.Richardson (eds.). *Papers from the Nineteenth Regional Meeting of the Chicago Linguistics Society, Chicago, April 21-22, 1983*, 171-182.
- 1985: E.Hinrichs. *A compositional semantics for Aktionsarten and NP reference*. Ohio (Ph.D. Dissertation, Ohio State University).
- 1986: E.Hinrichs. Temporal anaphora in discourses of English. *Linguistics and Philosophy* 9, 63-82.
- 1988: E.Hinrichs. Tense, quantifiers and contexts. *Computational Linguistics* 14, 3-14.
Hirtle 1967: W.H.Hirtle. *The simple and the progressive forms. An analytical approach*. Quebec.
Hoepelman 1981: J.Hoepelman. *Verb classification and the Russian verbal aspect*. Tübingen: Gunter Narr Verlag.
Hopper and Thompson 1980: P.J.Hopper, S.A.Thompson. Transitivity in grammar and discourse. *Language* 56, 251-299.
Hornby 1949: A.S.Hornby. Non-conclusive verbs. Some notes on the progressive tenses. *English Language Teaching* 3, 7, 172-177.
- 1974: A.S.Hornby. *The Oxford advanced learner's dictionary of current English*. Oxford: Oxford University Press.
Issatschenko 1974: A.V.Issatschenko. Review of T.Pettersson, *On Russian predicates. A theory of case and aspect*. *Foundations of Language* 11, 141-147.
Ivanova 1961: I.P.Ivanova. *Vid i vremja v sovremennom anglijskom jazyke*. Leningrad.
Jackendoff 1983: R.Jackendoff. *Semantics and cognition*. Cambridge, Mass.: MIT Press.
- 1992: R.Jackendoff. Parts and boundaries. In B.Levin, S.Pinker. *Lexical and conceptual semantics*, 9-45. Cambridge (MA)/Oxford, 1992: Blackwell.
Jakobson 1957: R.Jakobson. Shifters, verbal categories and the Russian verb. In *Roman Jakobson. Selected writings*, III. The Hague: Mouton.
James 1969: C.James. Deeper contrastive study. *International Review of Applied Linguistics in Language Teaching (IRAL)* 7, 83-95.
Jespersen 1924: O.Jespersen. *The philosophy of grammar*. London: George Allen & Unwin.
Joos 1964: M.Joos. *The English verb. Form and meanings*. Madison and Milwaukee: The University of Wisconsin Press.
Kabakčiev 1984a: K.Kabakčiev. Verkuyl's compositional aspects and aspect in the Slavonic languages. *Balkansko ezikoznanie/Linguistique balkanique* 27, 78-83.
- 1984b: K.Kabakčiev. The article and the aorist/imperfect distinction in Bulgarian: an analysis based on cross-language 'aspect' parallelisms. *Linguistics* 22, 643-672.
- 1986: K.Kabakčiev. Opozijata perfektivnost/imperfektivnost, instrumentalnite adverbiali i temporalnata im specifikacija (vărhu material ot anglijskija i bălgarskija ezik). *Săpostavitelno ezikoznanie/Contrastive Linguistics*, XI, 4, 48-55.
- 1987: K.Kabakčiev. Za dvuvidovostta na glagolite i estestvenija vid na dejstvijata. In *Vtori meždunaroden kongres po bălgaristika. 3. Săvremenen bălgarski ezik*, 543-557. Sofia: Izdatelstvo na BAN.
- 1989: K.Kabakčiev. On telicity and related problems. In Lars-Gunnar Larsson (ed.). *Proceedings of the Second Scandinavian Symposium on Aspectology* (=Acta universitatis upsaliensis. Studia uralica et altaica upsaliensia 19), 13-32. Uppsala.
- 1993a: K.Kabakčiev. On the semantic basis of aspect (with special reference to nominal aspect). *Săpostavitelno ezikoznanie/Contrastive linguistics*, XVIII, 1, 37-45.
- 1993b: K.Kabakčiev. On the cognitive basis of aspect. *Săpostavitelno ezikoznanie/Contrastive linguistics*, XVIII, 2, 23-30.
- 1993c: K.Kabakčiev. On the pragmatic basis of aspect. *Săpostavitelno ezikoznanie/Contrastive linguistics*, XVIII, 6, 40-46.
- 1994: K.Kabakčiev. *An English-Bulgarian learner's dictionary (English for everyone. Easy acquisition textbook series. I)*. Sofia: Albo.
- 1996: K.Kabakčiev. Time adverbials and aspect marking: a long-neglected problem revisited. In M.Milapides (ed.). *Proceedings of the 9th International Symposium on Theoretical and Applied Linguistics. Thessaloniki, Greece, 3-5 April 1995*, 51-60. Thessaloniki: School of English, Aristotle University of Thessaloniki.

References

Kabakčiev 1998: K.Kabakčiev. *Anglijska gramatika. Osnovni problemi za bălgarite, izučavašti anglijskija ezik.* Sofia: Akademično izdatelstvo Profesor Marin Drinov.
– 1999: K.Kabakčiev. *Situacionna semantika na terminologičnite izrazi v săvremennija bălgarski knižoven ezik.* Sofia: Akademično izdatelstvo Profesor Marin Drinov.
Kenny 1963: A.Kenny. *Action, emotion and will.* London, New York: Routledge and Kegan Paul.
Kintsch 1974: W.Kintsch. *The representation of meaning in memory.* Hillsdale (N.J.): Lawrence Erlbaum Associates.
Klein 1995: W.Klein. A time-relational analysis of Russian aspect. *Language,* 71, 669-695.
Koenig 1980: E.Koenig. On the context-dependence of the progressive in English. In C.Rohrer (ed.). *Time, tense and quantifier.* Tübingen: Niemeyer.
Koffka 1935: K.Koffka. *Principles of Gestalt psychology.* New York: Longman.
Krifka 1989: M.Krifka. *Nominalreferenz und Zeitkonstitution. Zur Semantik von Massentermen, Pluraltermen und Aspektklassen.* München: Wilhelm Fink.
– 1992: M.Krifka. Thematic relations as links between nominal reference and temporal constitution. In I.A.Sag and A.Szabolcsi (eds.). *Lexical matters.* Stanford, CA: Center for the Study of Language and Information.
Langacker 1987/1991: R.W.Langacker. Nouns and verbs. *Language,* 63, 53-95. Also (revised) in R.W.Langacker. *Concept, image, and symbol. The cognitive basis of grammar,* 59-100. Berlin/New York, 1991: Mouton de Gruyter.
Larson and Segal 1995: R.Larson, G.Segal. *Knowledge of meaning. An introduction to semantic theory.* Cambridge (MA)/London, 1995: MIT.
Lascarides 1988: A.Lascarides. *A formal semantic analysis of the progressive.* Edinburgh (Ph.D. dissertation, the University of Edinburgh).
Leech 1971: G.N.Leech. *Meaning and the English verb.* London: Longman.
Leinonen 1982: M.Leinonen. *Russian aspect, "temporal'naja lokalizacija", and definiteness/indefiniteness.* Helsinki.
Lindstedt 1984: J.Lindstedt. Nested aspects. In C. de Groot, H.Tommola (eds.), *Aspect bound. A voyage into the realm of Slavic, Germanic and Finno-Ugrian aspectology,* 22-38. Dordrecht: Foris.
– 1985: J.Lindstedt. *On the semantics of tense and aspect in Bulgarian.* Helsinki: Helsinki University Press.
Live 1965: A.H.Live. The discontinuous verb in English. *Word* 21, 428-445.
Lloyd 1979: A.L.Lloyd. *Anatomy of the verb. The Gothic verb as a model for a unified theory of aspect, actional types and verbal velocity.* Amsterdam.
Lyons 1977: J.Lyons. *Semantics.* Vol. I-II. London/New York/Melbourne: Cambridge University Press.
Markkanen 1979: R.Markkanen. *Tense and aspect in English and Finnish. A Contrastive Study.* Yväskylä.
McCoard 1978: R.W.McCoard. *The English perfect (North Holland Linguistics Series, 38).* Amsterdam: North Holland.
Mellor 1995: M.D.Mellor. *Aspects of aspectual verbs in English and Russian.* Edinburgh (Ph.D. dissertation, the University of Edinburgh).
Miller 1970: J.E.Miller. Stative verbs in Russian. *Foundations of Language* 6, 488-504.
Miller and Johnson-Laird 1976: G.A.Miller, P.N.Johnson-Laird. *Language and perception.* Cambridge/London/Melbourne: Cambridge University Press.
Mincoff 1958: M.Mincoff. *An English grammar.* Sofia: Naouka i izkoustvo.
Mittwoch 1971: A.Mittwoch. Idioms and unspecified NP deletion. *Linguistic Inquiry* 2, 255-259.
Moens 1987: M.Moens. *Tense, aspect and temporal reference.* Edinburgh (Ph.D. dissertation, the University of Edinburgh).
Mourelatos 1981: A.P.D.Mourelatos. Events, processes and states. In Tedeschi and Zaenen 1981, 191-212.
Musan 1995: R.Musan. *On the temporal interpretation of noun phrases.* Ph.D.Dissertation, MIT.
– 1999: R.Musan. Temporal interpretation and information-status of noun phrases. *Linguistics and Philosophy* 22, 621-661.
Norreklit 1973: L.Norreklit. *Concepts.* Odense: Odense Unversity Press.
Olsson 1961: Y.Olsson. *On the syntax of the English verb. With special reference to* have a look *and similar complex structures.* Göteborg: Elanders Boktryckeri Aktiebolag.

REFERENCES

Palmer 1965: F.R.Palmer. *A linguistic study of the English verb.* London: Longmans.
Parsons 1989. T.Parsons. The progressive in English: events, states and processes. *Linguistics and Philosophy* 12, 213-241.
– 1990. T.Parsons. *Events in the semantics of English. A study in subatomic semantics.* Cambridge (Mass.): MIT Press.
Partee 1973: B.H.Partee. Some structural analysis between tenses and pronouns. *The Journal of Philosophy* 70, 18, 601-609.
Psaltou-Joycey 1991: A.Psaltou-Joycey. *The temporal, aspectual, and pragmatic functions of the perfect in Modern Greek.* Thessaloniki (Ph.D. dissertation, Aristotle University of Thessaloniki).
Pustejovsky 1992. J.Pustejovsky. The syntax of event structure. In B.Levin, S.Pinker. *Lexical and conceptual semantics*, 47-81. Cambridge (MA)/Oxford: Blackwell.
Quine 1960: W.Quine. *Word and object.* Cambridge (Mass.): MIT Press.
Quirk et al 1985: R.Quirk, S.Greenbaum, G.Leech, J.Svartvik. *A comprehensive grammar of the English language.* London and New York: Longman.
Rankova et al 1987: M.Rankova, T.Atanassova, I.Harlakova. *English-Bulgarian dictionary, Vol. II, M – Z.* Sofia: Naouka i izkoustvo.
Reichenbach 1947: H.Reichenbach. *Elements of symbolic logic.* New York: New York, The Free Press & London, Collier-McMillan.
Ridjanović 1969/1976: M.Ridjanović. *A synchronic study of verbal aspect in English and Serbo-Croatian* (1969 Dissertation). Cambridge (Mass.): Slavica.
Russian Grammar 1982: *Russkaja grammatika. Vol. I.* Moscow: Nauka.
Ryle 1949: G.Ryle. *The concept of mind.* London.
Sapir 1921: E.Sapir. *Language.* New York.
Saurer 1984: W.Saurer. *A formal semantics of tense, aspect and Aktionsarten.* Indiana: Indiana University Linguistics Club.
Scheffer 1975: J.Scheffer. *The progressive in English.* Amsterdam: North Holland.
Schopf 1974: A.Schopf (ed.). *Der englische Aspekt.* Darmstadt: Wissenschaftliche Buchgesellschaft.
Seliverstova 1982a: O.N.Seliverstova (ed.) *Semantičeskie tipy predikatov.* Moskva: Nauka.
– 1982b: O.N.Seliverstova. Vtoroj variant klasifikacionnoj setki i opisanie nekotoryh predikatnyh tipov russkogo jazyka. In Seliverstova 1982a, 86-157.
Shi 1990: Z.Shi. On the inherent aspectual properties of NPs, verbs, sentences and the decomposition of perfectivity and inchoativity. *Word* 41, 47-67.
Slabakova 1997: R.Slabakova. Bulgarian preverbs: aspect in phrase structure. *Linguistics*, 35, 673-704.
– 1998: R.Slabakova. L2 Acquisition of an aspect parameter. *Journal of Slavic Linguistics* 6, 71-105.
Smith 1991: C.S.Smith. *The parameter of aspect.* (*Studies in Linguistics and Philosophy; 43*). Dordrecht/Boston/London: Kluwer.
– 1999: C.S.Smith. Activities: states or events? *Linguistics and Philosophy* 22, 479-508.
Smith and Medin 1981: E.E.Smith, D.L.Medin. *Categories and concepts.* Cambridge (Mass.), London: Harvard University Press.
Stephanides-Diósy 1982: E.Stephanides-Diósy. The generic use of the article in English and in Hungarian. In L.Dezső (ed.). *Contrastive studies Hungarian – English,* 89-111. Budapest: Akadémiai Kiadó.
Taylor 1977: B.Taylor. Tense and continuity. *Linguistics and Philosophy* 1, 199-220.
Tedeschi and Zaenen 1981: P.Tedeschi, A.Zaenen (eds.). *Aspect and quantification. Syntax and semantics. Vol. 14. Tense and Aspect.* New York: Academic Press.
Tenny 1994: C.L.Tenny. *Aspectual roles and the syntax-semantics interface* (*Studies in Linguistics and Philosophy; 52*). Dordrecht/Boston/London: Kluwer.
– 1996: C.L.Tenny. Review of H.J.Verkuyl (1993). *Language* 72, 121-126.
Tobin 1993: Y.Tobin. *Aspect in the English verb: process and result in language.* London and New York: Longman.
Vendler 1957: Z.Vendler. Verbs and times. *The Philosophical Review* 66, 143-160.
Verkuyl 1971/1972: H.J.Verkuyl. *On the compositional nature of the aspects* (= Ph.D. dissertation, Amsterdam, 1971): Dordrecht: Reidel.
– 1993: H.J.Verkuyl. *A theory of aspectuality. The interaction between temporal and atemporal structure.* Cambridge: Cambridge University Press.

Verkuyl 1998: H.J.Verkuyl. *Tense, aspect and aspectual composition*. Utrecht Institute of Linguistics OTS.
Vinogradov 1947: V.V.Vinogradov. *Russkij jazyk*. Moscow: Nauka.
Vlach 1981a: F.Vlach. The semantics of the progressive. In: Tedeschi and Zaenen 1981, 271-292.
– 1981b: F.Vlach. La semantique du temps et de l'aspect en anglais. *Langage* 64, 65-79.
– 1993: F.Vlach. Temporal adverbials, tenses and the perfect. *Linguistics and Philosophy* 16, 231-283.
Voroncova 1948: G.N.Voroncova. O leksičeskom haraktere glagola v anglijskom jazyke. *Inostrannye jazyki v škole*, 1, 19-31.
Wallace 1982: S.Wallace. Figure and ground: the interrelationships of linguistic categories. In P.J.Hopper (ed.). *Typological studies in language. Vol. 1. Tense-aspect: between semantics & pragmatics*, 201-223. Amsterdam: John Benjamins.
Zandvoort 1962: R.W.Zandvoort. Is 'aspect' an English verbal category? In F.Behre (ed.). *Contributions to English syntax and philology*.
Zucchi 1993: A.Zucchi. *The language of propositions and events: issues in the syntax and the semantics of nominalization (Studies in Linguistics and Philosophy; 51)*. Dordrecht/Boston/London: Kluwer.
Zydatiß 1976: Z.Zydatiß. *Tempus und Aspekt im Englischunterricht*. Kronenberg: Scriptor.

INDEX OF TERMS

Abstract (noun, entity) 16, 62-63, 70-72, 77-79, 96, 173, 179, 187-189, 207, 215-220, 224-228
Accomplishment 34-45, 48-51, 53, 60, 79, 102. 114, 120, 163, 174, 177-178, 182-183, 190, 222, 226, 252, 257, 268, 272, 279-307, 310-311, 317-319, 322-325
Achievement 34-42, 45, 48-53, 79, 93, 114, 120, 149, 163, 174, 182-183, 199-201, 252, 254, 257, 279, 283-284, 286, 291, 293, 295-297, 306-307, 310-313
Act 1-2, 46, 52, 65, 111-112, 136, 148, 163, 174, 187, 190, 200-201, 211-212, 220, 222, 224, 267, 319-320, 324, 329, 332
Action xiv-xv, xix-xxi, Chapter 1, 31, 32, 34, 36, 42-46, 49, 57-61, 63-65, 77-84, 88-89, 91, 93-95, 97-101, 103-104, 107-121, 124-143, 147-151, 153-156, 159-160, 163-167, 169-179, 182-204, 208, 211-221, 228-230, 242-246, 250-253, 256-258, 260-262, 264-265, 267-268, 270-277, 279-283, 286-301, 304-306, 311-326, 330, 332
Activity 31-45, 48-53, 93, 102, 114, 120, 139-141, 145, 150, 170, 181-184, 190, 218, 226, 231, 249, 257, 262, 271, 279, 281-284, 286, 289-296, 303-304, 306, 315
Adverb, adverbial 7, 9, 19, 21-22, 26-28, 31, 46, 62, 65, 75, 82, 113-115, 124, 129-131, 137-140, 158, 164, 167, 183, 194-195, 202-204, 206, 215, 221, 226, 236, 238, Chapter 11, 263, 265, 268-273, 276-277, 282, 284-288, 290-291, 293-295, 298-299, 302-303, 305-306, 309, 318-321, 330
Affix (affixal, affixation) xv, 5, 332
Agent 6, 9, 20, 47, 58, 79-81, 88, 91, 97-103, 107-108, 124, 126, 172, 179, 184, 186-187, 189, 194, 199-200, 207, 216, 265, 267, 270, 275, 311, 313-316
Agenthood (Allwood's principles of) 312-326
Agentive (agentivity) xxi, 196, 207, 212-213, 216, 224, 311-312, 323
Anaphoricity 105-106, 233, 325
Animate 6, 27, 99, 138, 200, 220, 310
Antecedent 85-86
Aorist 6, 8, 14, 16, 27, 29, 46, 48-50, 78, 159, 186, 191, 198, 243, 245, 253, 259, 266, 269-272, 275-276, 285, 296, 298-299, 301, 303, 318, 329-330
Article xxi, 22-23, 26-29, 42-43, 52, 56-62, 65, Chapter 4, 92, 95, 97, 112-113, 123, 125-133, 139-140, 142, 144, 146, 154-157, 159, 171-172, 178-179, 188-189, 191, 196-198, 202, 207, Chapter 10, 244, 247, 261, 292, 305, 309, 320-322, 324-326
Asymmetric aspect construal (Verkuyl's term) 228, 235-238
Atelic (atelicity) xx-xxi, 19-23, 47, 60, 111, 123, 130, 139, 145, 185, 188-189, 197, 201-202, 204-208, 212-213, 222-226, 231, 233, 235, 244, 258-259, 282-283, 291
Atemporal (atemporality) xvi, 66, 92, 94, 99, 115, 120, 149, 208, 228-230, 234-235, 265, 273, 287, 321, 325
Atypical xviii, 50, 77-78, 80-81, 140, 185

Bare (noun) xxi, 52, 57, 65, 71, 75, 81-84, 110, 142, 195, 198, 241, 255-256, 270, 283, 309, 312, 321, 323, 325

Biaspectual (biaspectuality) 4, 16, 35, 332

Bound 2, 57, 61-62, 65-66, 71, 77, 94, 154, 201-202, 230, 241, 289-290, 294

Bounded (boundedness) xv-xvi, xix-xxi, 2-4, 10-12, 16, 19, 22-24, 26, 32-35, 40-41, 43, 45, 47, 50, 55, 58, 60-66, 69-72, 76-79, 81-90, 94-96, 98-100, 102, 106-108, 110-114, 117-120, 123-136, 138-150, Chapter 7, 164, 168-180, 187-194, 197-204, 207, 212-227, 230, 233-234, 237-238, 244-247, 249, 252-258, 261, 266-271, 275-276, Chapter 13, 309, 312, 314, 317, 320-326, 332

Bulgarian ix-x, 2-3, 5-21, 25-27, 29, 32-38, 46-50, 63, 69, 72-75, 83, 85-87, 89, 93, 108-109, 112, 114, 116, 127-128, 147, 150-151, 153, 159, 165, 185-186, 191, 196-197, 221, 230, 236, 238, 242-243, 245-246, 253, 259, 264-267, 269-276, 285, 297-298, 300-303, 310, Appendix

Case 1, 5, 157, 207, 216, 259-260, 275

Cognitive (cognition) x, xvi, xix, 100, 116-121, 124, 167, 172, 326-328

Common-sense xviii, xx, 64, 66, 89-90, Chapter 5, 131, 133, 138, 141, 146, 148, 150, 154, 159, 169, 172-174, 177, 187-188, 199-200, 229, 235, 268, 302, 305

Compensatory function of aspect markers xvi-xvii, Chapters 7, 8

Complement (complementation) 22, 26, 36-37, 45, 51-52, 149, 202, 204, 206, 244, 251, 253, 257, 268, 276, 287, 290, 292, 306, 318, 321, 332

Completed (completedness) xiv, xix, xxi, 2, 4, 6, 16, 22, 24, 42, 44, 46, 57, 59, 65, 91, 99, 120, 126-129, 135, 148, 174, 194, 206, 222, 242-244, 256-257, 280, 329-330

Completion xiv, 1-5, 9-10, 19, 28, 91, 99, 149, 163, 242, 279, 311

Composition (aspectual), compositional (aspect, etc.), compositionality ix, xi, xvi-xix, 10, 42, 45, Chapter 3, 70, 82, 105, 112, 126-128, 133, 142, 145, 151, 158-161, 178, 180-184, 187-188, 191, 208-209, 218, 224, 226-227, 232-233, 236, 238-239, 242, 244, 254-265, 275, 295, 300, 309-312, 319, 322, 327-328

Concept (conceptualisation) xvii-xviii, 2, 20, 32, 85, 104, 116-119, 149-150, 174, 257, 260, 279, 290, 309, 327

Concept formation xiii, 116-119, 149-150

Concrete noun 173, 215-217, 220, 225, 228, 244

Conditional 25-26, 42, 329

Consequence xviii, 106, 116, 148-149, 281-282, 286, 288, 295

Consumption (verbs of) 6-7, 91-92, 111, 149

Context (contextual) xiii, xv, 5, 7, 10, 18, 20, 24, 27, 33, 36, 44, 46, 59, 71, 76, 81, 84, 89, 93, 95, 97, 103, 111, 129, 137-138, 140, 142-143, 146, 167-168, 173-174, 192, 196-198, 203, 205-206, 209, 233-235, 245, 250-251, 256, 267-268, 271, 275, 280-281, 283, 289-290, 292, 314, 317, 320, 322-325, 332

Count (countable) 23, 28, 43, 58, 70-73, 81, 112, 216-217, 220, 261

Covert (expression) xviii, 42, 45, 105-106, 117, 128, 154, 171-172, 197

Creation (verbs of) 58, 91-92, 111, 149

Culmination 281-282

Current situation 97, 222, 291-292, 294, 315

Da-construction 48
De-adjectival 26-27
Default (meaning/interpretation) 42, 59, 82, 130, 218, 232
Definite (various meanings) 2, 17, 26-27, 32, 34-35, 42, 45, 56, 59-60, 64-65, 69-71, 74-75, 84-88, 95, 97, 105, 124-126, 132, 134, 138, 156, 159, 167, 189, 193-197, 202, 207, 215, 217, 219-220, 225, 255, 257, 289, 292, 300, 312, 322
Definite repetition 45
Definiteness (definite article) 56, 59-60, 65, 69-71, 74-75, 84-88, 95, 97, 105, 125-126, 132, 138, 156, 159, 189, 195-197, 207, 215, 219, 225, 257, 292, 300, 312, 322
Delimited (delimitedness) 257, 261, 284, 322
Delimitative 37, 282
Demonstrative 60, 65, 87-89, 123, 128
Determination (nominal) 26, 157
Determiner xxi, 28, 43, 52-53, Chapter 4, 95, 97, 105, 123-124, 127, 178, 188, 191, 196, 202, 217, 222, 226, 322, 326
Diagrammatic representations of situations and participants 132-135, 137, 140-143, 145-146, 154-155, 158, 160, 170-171, 175-177, 212, 300-306
Direct object 21, 65, 80-81, 91-92, 111, 195, 202, 230-231, 257, 261, 283, 311
Discourse xix, 16, 28, 52, 59, 81, 89, 93, 97, 105-106, 125, 146, 168, 184, 197, 209, 224, 238, 279-280, 285, 311, 317-320, 322, 324-325
Dual aspectual nature/potential 21-22, 202-204; see also *Push*-verbs
Duration 20, 27, 137, 163-166, 183, 283
Durative (Verkuyl's term) 47, 215, 233, 254, 264-265, 283, 324

Dutch 29, 39, 53, 55, 60, 69, 205, 227, 264-265, 271, 276
Dynamic (dynamicity) 282, 311
Elimination of boundedness 168-173, 176, 180, 214
Endpoint 7, 19-20, 42, 141-142, 176, 178, 183, 187, 194-195, 199, 201, 242, 245-246, 280-282, 285-286, 289-301, 304-305, 317
Episode 118, Chapter 13, 317-319, 325
Event xviii, xxi, 6, 10, 16, 20, 23-26, 40, 44-46, 79-80, 91-93, 95-96, 101-103, 106, 109-113, 120, 131, 148, 159, 165, 182, 187, 192, 200, 206, 208-209, 249, 255, 257, 261, 263, 274, 279, 281, 284, 286-287, 290, 293-298, 306, 312-313, 321, 323
Existential reading 96
Extension (time extension) 41, 67, Chapter 5, 144-148, 155, 199-200
External argument 66, 238, 255
Face value 101, 194, 197
Figure/ground distinction 118
Finnish 5, 157, 260
Formal markedness xiv-xv, xix, 6, 17, 19, 27-28, 44, 61, 65, 127, 132, 154, 156, 172, 180, 300, 326
For-time (adverbial, rule, test) 101, 110, 114, 137, 164, 183, 195, 203-206, 215, 236, Chapter 11, 265-271, 276-277, 282-290, 293-295, 298, 302-306
French 26, 31, 35, 185
Futurate 25-26, 42, 148, 329
Future (tense, time) 1, 4, 25, 46, 166-167, 243, 264, 273, 330-331
Generalised concept 116-119
Generic (genericity) 70-77, 84-85, 96, 110, 116, 292, 311, 325
Germanic (languages) xx, 3-5, 13-14, 47, 69, 89, 158, 263
Goal 19, 21-22, 31, 34, 284, 316
Gradual patient 91-92

Grammar xiii-xv, xx-xxi, 1-2, 16-17, 20 24-26, 33, 44, 56, 62, 69, 72, 76, 84, 115, 128, 133, 151, 157, 163, 166-167, 182, 190, 198, 209, 227, 243, 247-248, 257-258, 260, 310, 322, 327
Greek 17, 19
Ground see Figure/ground distinction
Groundedness (Cooper's term) 114
Habitual (habit) 6-7, 17, 36, 41, 46, 97, 124, 140-141, 186, 245-246, 266, 270-272, 289, 291-292, 294, 315-316, 324, 330
Have a look pattern 48, 207, 211-215, 283-286
Idiomatic 18, 236-237
Imperfect 6, 14, 16-17, 27, 29, 46, 48-52, 78, 143, 159, 165, 186, 191, 198, 243, 245, 253, 259, 266, 271-272, 275-276, 298-299, 303, 329-330
Inanimate (non-animate) 6, 27, 99, 116, 138, 149, 199, 220, 310
Inchoative 21, 139, 251, 292
Incremental theme 91-93
Indefinite (various meanings) 4, 11-12, 16, 23, 27-28, 36-37, 45-46, 59-61, 64-65, 69-71, 75, 77, 81, 85-88, 93, 96-97, 105, 115, 124-126, 129-137, 141-142, 146, 156, 159, 165, 183, 187, 213, 215, 218-219, 222-225, 229, 242, 245-246, 252, 264, 273, 299, 319-321, 330, 332
Indefiniteness (indefinite article) 59-60, 65, 69-71, 75, 87-88, 97, 105, 125-126, 132, 156, 159, 213, 215, 218-219, 222-225
Indirect object 65, 230-231, 238, 262, 283-284, 321
Individual xvii, 50, 72, 89, 100-120, 171-174, 178, 229, 263, 267-268, 272-273, 287
Infinitive 4, 44, 46, 48, 107, 165, 186, 188, 190-191, 193
Inner aspect (Verkuyl's term) 236, 265

Instrumental adverbial 260-262
Internal argument 66, 91, 238, 257
Interrupted accomplishment 289, 296
Interval 34-35, 57, 62-63, 66, 77, 91, 94, 98, 110, 154, 164-165, 169, 179, 194, 199, 220, 229-230, 250, 288, 292
In-time (adverbial, rule, test) 82, 114, 195, 235-236, 241, 247-258, 261, 265, 268, 270, 272, 277, 306
Intransitive (intransitivity) 22-23, 43, 193-194, 203-204, 283
Inverse relationship of markers of boundedness 156
Iterativity 59, 129, 131, 134-137, 142, 147, 242, 246, 251-252, 270-271, 276, 305, 315
Kind (Carlson's term) 89, 100-101, 110, 119, 172
Knowledge of the world xiii, xix, 79, 81-82, 111, 136, 174, 225-226, 255, 284, 291-293, 298, Chapter 14, 327
Leakage (Verkuyl's term) 231-232, 324
Located individual (Cooper's term) 105, 110, 113, 263
Locative 173, 260
Manner adverbial 27, 260-262, 318
Mapping xvii, 91-92, 118, 121, Chapter 6, 158-161, 169-172, 175-178, 187, 189, 193, 198, 207, 209, 212, 217, 224-225, 233-234, 244, 265, 274-275, 285, 294, 298-306, 321
Marked (markedness) xx, 6, 10, 19, 27-28, 35, 38, 41, 46, 48, 50, 52, 56-57, 61, 78, 82, 93, 105, 110, 125, 132-133, 137, 139, 144-145, 154-160, 169, 171-172, 175, 180, 209, 212, 242, 250, 300, 305, 310, 326
Marker xiii, xvi, 6, 14, 22, 26, 28, 50, 65, Chapter 4, 93, 120, 124, Chapter 7, 166-169, 185-202, 222, 263, 292, 314, 320
Mass (noun) 43, 71, 110, 255-257, 287, 309

INDEX OF TERMS

Material (physical) object see Object
Maxims (Grice's) of communication 316-317, 320
Measuring-out 58, 91-97, 112, 255, 257, 261
Memory xiii, 108, 117-120, 134, 150
Moment xv, 8, 19, 35, 45-47, 97-98, 109, 113, 117, 132, 138-139, 147, 164-167, 291-292
Momentary 26, 40, 183, 199, 217, 279, 282, 296
Multiplication 81, 133-135
Negative (negation, negatitvity) 65, 234, 262, Chapter 12, 331
Nested aspects (Lindstedt's term) 45, 246, 253
Neutral (context, etc.) 27, 36, 46, 58, 163, 184, 193, 256, 291, 293, 324
Non-bounded (non-boundedness) xv-xvi, xix-xxi, 2-4, 10, 16, 22-28, 32-35, 40-47, 50, 59-66, Chapter 4, 94-100, 106-114, 118-120, 124-142, 145-146, 149-151, 153, 157, 164, 169-176, 182-183, 188-191, 195-199, 202, 204, 207, 212-231, 234-235, 238, 242-256, 266-171, 274, 276, 279, 281, 283-293, 296-305, 311, 315, 317, 320-324, 329-330
Non-completed (non-completion, non-completedness) xiv-xv, xix, xxi, 1-6, 10, 16, 42, 46, 93, 98, 127-128, 163, 242, 244, 330
Non-count (non-countable) 23, 28, 43, 58, 70-73, 78, 216-217, 220
Non-delimited (Tenny's term) 93
Non-durative (Verkuyl's term) 260
Non-generic 70, 72-77, 85, 96, 138, 312
Non-grammatical (ungrammatical) 15, 20, 25, 28, 37, 73-74, 167, 221, 231, 248-249, 251, 253-256, 260-261, 264-265, 279, 287, 306
Non-inchoative 140, 250
Non-perfect xiv, 1, 6, 17, 19, 157, 193

Non-progressive xiv, 1, 4, 18, 40-42, 44, 46, 157, 169, 176, 193, 218, 245, 257, 306
Non-quantified (unquantified) 28, 57-58, 88, 94, 197, 221, 231, 235, 262
Non-repetition (non-repetitive) 8, 10, 36, 45, 242, 245
Non-specific (non-specificity) 75, 325
Non-stative 42, 104, 110-111, 207, 216, 256
Non-terminated (non-termination) 159, 245, 270, 282-283
"Normal" reading/interpretation 25, 36, 126, 133, 136, 138, 142-147, 156, 183-184, 194, 214, 229, 248, 252, 254-255, 261, 274, 279, 284, 290, 301, 313, 315-316, 321-322, 324, 326
Object (concrete/abstract) 6, 8-9, 50, 58, 63-67, 70, 77-81, 85, 88, Chapter 5, Chapter 6, 155, 172, 174, 184, 187-189, 200, 208, 218, 244, 268, 273-274, 287, 311
Object (syntactic) 5-10, 19-22, 26-29, 31, 37, 42-43, 47-53, 56-66, 74-81, 84, 88-89, Chapter 5, Chapter 6, 153-156, 159-161, 169-180, Chapter 9, 212, 216, 219, 224-234, 237-238, 244, 247, 257, 261-262, 274-275, 282-284, 291-292, 299-302, 305, 310-312, 321-325
Omission of determiner 83, 219, 322
"Ordinary speaker" xviii, xx, 13, 72, 89, 96, 105-107, 115, 120-121, 143, 148, 151, 154-155, 165, 182, 187, 217-218, 225, 229, 235, 274, 302
Outer aspect (Verkuyl's term) 236
Overt (expression) xiii, xvi, xviii-xx, 37, 52, 105, 107, 127, 133-134, 137, 143, 171, 187, 194, 228, 234, 274-275, 300, 320
Pair (aspectual) 11, 13, 17, 20, 35, 185
Participant xviii, xxi, 7, 10, Chapter 5, Chapter 6, 153-154, 159-160, 172-

180, 200, 229, 231, 239, 244, 263, 266-277, 290, 298-303, 305
Past (tense, time) 2-6, 24-28, 45-46, 49, 52, 58, 80-83, 93, 97-98, 126-127, 130, 159, 164-176, 193, 242-243, 251, 258, 264, 266, 271-273, 290-294, 300, 305, 325, 329-331
Patient 6, 91-92, 124, 189, 275
Perception 90, 104, 111-113, 117-119, 132, 150, 163, 189-190
Perceptual entity 124, 126, 149
Perfect xiv, 1, 4, 18, 44, 46, 157, 163, 165-167, 273, 295, 330-331
Period xv, 17, 19, 23, 31-35, 45-46, 63, 77, 93, 138-139, 144, 147, 164, 167, 183-184, 195, 219, 250, 283, 291-292
Physical (material) object see Object
Place (adverbial of) 113, Chapter 11
Plus-principle (Verkuyl's term) 228, 230-235
Pofective (Galton's term) 282-286, 295
Point (in time/space) 17, 20, 23, 111, 148, 165, 167, 169-170, 174, 179, 194-197, 199, 201, 208, 229, 250, 258, 279-282, 291, 295-296
Possessive 60-61, 65, 86-89, 123, 127
Pragmatic (factor, import etc.) xiv, xviii-xix, 21, 26, 44-45, 52, 79, 103, 105-111, 116, 119, 146, 148, 159, 174, 203, 215, 218, 224, 231, 242-243, 251, 255-257, 262, 282-293, 296-298, 304, Chapter 14, 327
Present (tense, time) 6, 25-26, 33, 36-37, 41-42, 46, 165, 167, 190-191, 264, 273, 295, 329-330
Primary aspectual reading (of a sentence) 59, 82, 137, 142, 153, 233-234, 268, 311, 314, 317, 319, 326
Process xxi, 8, 16, 20, 23-24, 36, 51, 112, 136, 139, 159-160, 190, 218, 270, 281-282, 286-287, 295-297, 305-307

Progressive xiii-xv, xvii, xix-xx, 1-3, 5, 7-8, 17-19, 23-24, 31, 33, 36-37, 40-42, 46, 49, 73, 93, 98, 115, 127, 137-141, 146, 150, 157, Chapter 8, 209, 217-218, 250, 266, 272, 282, 291, 293, 296-301, 304, 306, 310, 315, 320
Pronoun 27, 60-61, 65, 85-89, 123, 128, 310, 325
Proper name 60-61, 65, 85-89, 118, 126, 128, 139, 144, 178, 231, 235, 244
Prototypical (prototype) xxi, 25, 38, 41, 46-48, 52, 59, 91-92, 124, 129, 137, 146, 164-165, 169, 178, 184, 196-198, 204, 207, 226, 233-235, 243, 252, 266-272, 298, 304, 314, 317, 323, 330
Push-verb (Verkuyl's term) 111, 205, 280
Quantified 57-58, 88, 92, 105, 123-129, 138, 144, 179, 197, 202, 204, 221, 244, 262, 275-276
Quantifier xxi, 26, 28, 43, 52-53, 60-61, 65, 76, 88-89, 97, 105, 123-124, 127, 178, 191, 202, 222, 226, 322, 326
Recurring picture (recurrence) 124-126, 131, 134-135, 142-143, 268, 321
Redistribution of temporal parameters 130; see also Mapping
Repetition, repetitive, repeated (action, etc.) 6-11, 13, 16-19, 22, 25, 36-37, 45-46, 75, 93, 115, 124-127, 130, 134-136, 141-143, 155, 165, 219, 242, 245-246, 253, 256, 264, 292, 299, 303, 320-321, 329, 332
Result (of action, etc.) 31, 79, 183, 187, 242-243, 253, 279-282, 286-289, 296-297, 304, 311, 317, 330
Romance languages 5, 69, 89, 159
Russian xviii, 1-3, 19-21, 24, 35, 39-45, 51-52, 93, 127, 155-161, 169-171,

207, 237, 247, 259-260, 263-265, 282
Schema (aspectual/situational) xv, xxi, 31-40, 45, 56-58, 61, 64-65, 76-81, 98, 125-128, 133, 183, 197, 261, 281-286
Secondary aspectual reading (of a sentence) 82, 142, 185, 268, 276, 303, 317-319, 322-323, 326
Semelfactive 40-42, 282, 295-297, 306-307
Serialisation (series) 11-12, 16, 124, 131, 134-143, 243, 270, 274-275, 285, 321, 330-332
Simple Tense (Past, Present) 2-6, 24-27, 36-37, 41-49, 58, 93, 98, 127, 130, 164-165, 168-172, 175-179, 193 218, 242-243, 258, 266, 272-273, 290-293, 300, 305, 325
Slavic (languages) xiv-xx, 1-5, 10-21, 26-29, 35-55, 69, 80, 89, 93, 112, 127-129, 133, 137, 150-153, 159, 169, 172, 182, 185-186, 227, 236-238, 243, 251, 263-265, 290, 297, 332
Slice (temporal) Chapter 5, Chapter 6, 153-154
Spatio-temporal (approach, parameters, etc.) 92, 96, 101-104, 110-116, 263
Specific (specificity) 43, 76, 138 237, 325
Specified quantity (Verkuyl's term) 56-71, 76-78, 88, 94, 126, 133, 154, 230, 265
Stage xvii, 89, 100-120, 125-126, 138, 141-142, 146-149, 171-178, 208, 229, 267-268, 272-274, 303
State (stative, stativity) xviii, xxi, 5, 16, 19-24, 32-53, 60, 64, 99, 101, 104, 110-114, 120, 138-141, 144-150, 160, 167, 176-179, 181-184, 189-190, 199-203, 206-212, 216-219, 222-223, 226, 231, 249, 256-257, 263, 265, 270, 277, Chapter 13, 309, 311
Subject 5, 7, 9-10, 22, 27, 29, 31-32, 45, 47, 49-53, 56-66, 72, 74-89, Chapter 5, Chapter 6, 153-156, 159-161, 169-180, 187-191, 196-200, 207, 212, 216, 224, 226, 228-238, 244, 253-257, 261-263, 266-268, 271, 275-276, 282, 285, 287, 289-291, 299-302, 305, 309-314, 320-323,
'Television representation' 99-100, 113, 117-120, 146, 159
Telic (telicity) xx-xxi, 19-25, 34, 47, 60-61, 88, 111, 123, 127, 129, 132, 144-145, 150, 153, 185-208, 213, 222-226, 230, 250, 258-259, 290-291, 323
Temporal adverbial 7, 9, 21-22, 27-28, 31, 62, 82, 113-115, 124, 130-131, 137-140, 164, 167, 183, 195, 202-206, 215, Chapter 11, 265, 268, 270, 277, 282-295, 298-306, 309, 318-321, 330
Terminated (process, etc.)/termination 5, 7, 34, 159, 182-183, 242-245, 253, 270, 279-296, 317, 330
Terminative (Verkuyl's term) 47, 265, 290
To-place adverbial 250-251
Transitive (transitivity) 22-23, 37, 43, 203-206, 332
Ungrammatical see Non-grammatical
Ungroundedness (Cooper's term) 114
Universal reading 96
Unquantified see Non-quantified
Unspecified quantity (Verkuyl's term) 56-66, 71, 76-78, 81, 94-97, 124, 230
Viewpoint (Smith's term) 40-45, 290
Violation of pragmatic principles 316-326
Zero article (zero determiner) 42, 52, 56, 69-72, 75, 88, 113, 157, 215, 222, 225, 244, 247, 326

INDEX OF AUTHORS

Allen 26, 168, 244, 247
Allwood 312-320, 324-325
Andersson 173
Atanassova et al 11-12
Bach 23, 225, 296
Bache 215, 285
Bartsch xvii, 1, 18, 23, 115, 166, 215, 263, 296
Binnick xvi, xix, 1, 4, 17-18, 24, 105, 115, 165-166, 168-169, 284, 288
Brinton 1, 4, 24, 218
Bulygina 47, 51
Bybee xv-xvi, 166-167
Bybee et al xv-xvi, 23, 57-58, 166, 169, 218
Caenepeel xiii, 16, 296
Carlson G. xvii, 89, 100-101, 104-105, 110, 119-120, 147, 171-172, 174, 178, 208, 287
Carlson G. and Tanenhaus 119
Carlson L. 55, 172
Cavedon and Glasbey 76
Chung and Timberlake 296, 311
Comrie xiii, xv, 167, 169
Cooper xvii, 92, 100, 103-105, 110-112, 114-115, 179, 263
Dahl xv-xvi, 24, 50, 157, 166-167, 218
Danchev 16, 24, 26-28, 166, 184, 202, 256
Danchev and Alexieva 21, 184
Declerck 311-312
Derzhanski 108
Dowty xvii, 55, 82, 92, 179, 189, 199, 252, 254, 271, 275, 327
Dušková 4, 24
Enç 101
Fenn 166

Filip 115, 174
Fillmore 207
Fodor, Fodor and Garret 119
Forsyth 24
Friedrich 55, 227
Galton 179, 213, 225, 263, 282-286, 288, 294-295
Garey 22, 26, 31, 247
Geis 113
Glasbey xiii, 16, 27, 58, 76, 91, 92, 139, 275, 318-319
Goldschmidt and Woisetschlaeger 179
Grice 316, 317, 320, 324
Harlig 78, 82, 148, 312
Hatav 1, 18, 166
Heinämäki xvii, 55, 173, 202, 241, 327
Heller 14-15
Hinrichs xvii, xxi, 92, 100-106, 110-115, 127, 148, 179, 208, 252, 296
Hirtle 40, 218
Hoepelman 39-40, 148
Hopper and Thompson 58
Hornby 111-112, 163, 169, 174, 181-182, 190, 193, 196, 199, 203-204, 209, 220
Issatschenko 1, 52
Ivanova 21, 31
Jackendoff 95, 118
Jakobson 172
James 247
Jespersen 6, 18, 163
Joos 23-24
Kabakčiev ix-x, xvi, 14, 17, 52, 55, 100-101, 112, 114, 131, 151, 156-159, 169, 172, 180, 185, 215, 218, 222, 225, 227, 230, 237-238, 253, 262, 298-301, 303, 311, 320, 327

Kenny 22, 31
Kintsch 119
Klein 2, 45
Koenig 179
Koffka 118
Krifka xvii, 85, 91-92, 110-112, 114-115, 131, 179, 225
Langacker xvii, 41, 71, 104, 106, 174, 215, 218, 288
Larson and Segal 287
Lascarides 179
Leech 23
Leinonen 20, 118
Lindstedt 3, 5, 45, 218, 246, 253, 327, 332
Live 211-212
Lloyd 199
Lyons 215
Markkanen 5, 55, 218, 327
McCoard 166
Mellor 1, 3, 18, 39-40, 44, 166, 284, 288
Miller 207, 216
Miller and Johnson-Laird 118, 311
Mincoff 212
Mittwoch xvii, 247-248, 254, 257
Moens xiii, 24, 27, 184, 246, 256, 281-282, 296, 310
Mourelatos 31, 55
Musan 101, 105, 138, 178
Norreklit 119
Olsson 211-212
Palmer 24, 169, 205-206, 280
Parsons 148, 287
Partee 272
Psaltou-Joycey 166
Pustejovsky 287
Quine 100
Quirk et al xvii, 1, 18, 92, 163-166, 250, 257
Rankova et al 13
Reichenbach 165
Ridjanović 28-29, 58, 247
Russian Grammar 20, 264

Ryle 22, 31
Sapir 6, 18
Saurer 1
Scheffer 164, 168-169, 174
Schopf 55, 168
Seliverstova 47, 51
Shi 79, 82, 191, 232-233, 241
Slabakova 230
Smith xvii, 3, 24, 39-45, 92, 147, 218, 254, 282, 287, 290, 294-295
Smith and Medin 116, 134
Stephanides-Diósy 75
Taylor 179, 287
Tedeschi and Zaenen 327
Tenny xvii, 58, 71, 81, 91-93, 104, 112, 189, 191, 195, 228, 238, 254-257, 260-262, 280, 283, 309
Tobin xiii, xvii, 1, 18, 23
Vendler xvi-xviii, 22, Chapter 2, 56, 60, 64, 79, 163, 183, 190, 199, 218, 222, 226, 229, 231, 245, 247, 253, 257, 279, 281-283, 286-287, 295-296, 303, 318
Verkuyl xiii, xv-xviii, 29, 40, 47, 53, Chapter 3, 69-70, 76-82, 84, 88-90, 92, 94, 98-100, 110-111, 123, 125-128, 133, 135, 153-154, 183, 197, 205-206, 208, 227-239, 246-247, 254-255, 260-262, 264-268, 271, 275-276, 280, 284, 309-310, 314, 320, 324-325, 327
Vinogradov 19
Vlach 100-101, 179
Voroncova 19, 21, 31, 208
Wallace 118
Zandvoort 4, 18
Zucchi 215
Zydatiß 55, 327

Studies in Linguistics and Philosophy

1. H. Hiż (ed.): *Questions.* 1978   ISBN 90-277-0813-4; Pb: 90-277-1035-X
2. W. S. Cooper: *Foundations of Logico-Linguistics.* A Unified Theory of Information, Language, and Logic. 1978   ISBN 90-277-0864-9; Pb: 90-277-0876-2
3. A. Margalit (ed.): *Meaning and Use.* 1979   ISBN 90-277-0888-6
4. F. Guenthner and S.J. Schmidt (eds.): *Formal Semantics and Pragmatics for Natural Languages.* 1979   ISBN 90-277-0778-2; Pb: 90-277-0930-0
5. E. Saarinen (ed.): *Game-Theoretical Semantics.* Essays on Semantics by Hintikka, Carlson, Peacocke, Rantala, and Saarinen. 1979   ISBN 90-277-0918-1
6. F.J. Pelletier (ed.): *Mass Terms: Some Philosophical Problems.* 1979   ISBN 90-277-0931-9
7. D. R. Dowty: *Word Meaning and Montague Grammar.* The Semantics of Verbs and Times in Generative Semantics and in Montague's PTQ. 1979 ISBN 90-277-1008-2; Pb: 90-277-1009-0
8. A. F. Freed: *The Semantics of English Aspectual Complementation.* 1979   ISBN 90-277-1010-4; Pb: 90-277-1011-2
9. J. McCloskey: *Transformational Syntax and Model Theoretic Semantics.* A Case Study in Modern Irish. 1979   ISBN 90-277-1025-2; Pb: 90-277-1026-0
10. J. R. Searle, F. Kiefer and M. Bierwisch (eds.): *Speech Act Theory and Pragmatics.* 1980   ISBN 90-277-1043-0; Pb: 90-277-1045-7
11. D. R. Dowty, R. E. Wall and S. Peters: *Introduction to Montague Semantics.* 1981; 5th printing 1987   ISBN 90-277-1141-0; Pb: 90-277-1142-9
12. F. Heny (ed.): *Ambiguities in Intensional Contexts.* 1981   ISBN 90-277-1167-4; Pb: 90-277-1168-2
13. W. Klein and W. Levelt (eds.): *Crossing the Boundaries in Linguistics.* Studies Presented to Manfred Bierwisch. 1981   ISBN 90-277-1259-X
14. Z. S. Harris: *Papers on Syntax.* Edited by H. Hiż. 1981   ISBN 90-277-1266-0; Pb: 90-277-1267-0
15. P. Jacobson and G. K. Pullum (eds.): *The Nature of Syntactic Representation.* 1982   ISBN 90-277-1289-1; Pb: 90-277-1290-5
16. S. Peters and E. Saarinen (eds.): *Processes, Beliefs, and Questions.* Essays on Formal Semantics of Natural Language and Natural Language Processing. 1982   ISBN 90-277-1314-6
17. L. Carlson: *Dialogue Games.* An Approach to Discourse Analysis. 1983; 2nd printing 1985   ISBN 90-277-1455-X; Pb: 90-277-1951-9
18. L. Vaina and J. Hintikka (eds.): *Cognitive Constraints on Communication.* Representation and Processes. 1984; 2nd printing 1985   ISBN 90-277-1456-8; Pb: 90-277-1949-7
19. F. Heny and B. Richards (eds.): *Linguistic Categories: Auxiliaries and Related Puzzles.* Volume I: Categories. 1983   ISBN 90-277-1478-9
20. F. Heny and B. Richards (eds.): *Linguistic Categories: Auxiliaries and Related Puzzles.* Volume II: The Scope, Order, and Distribution of English Auxiliary Verbs. 1983 ISBN 90-277-1479-7
21. R. Cooper: *Quantification and Syntactic Theory.* 1983   ISBN 90-277-1484-3
22. J. Hintikka (in collaboration with J. Kulas): *The Game of Language.* Studies in Game-Theoretical Semantics and Its Applications. 1983; 2nd printing 1985   ISBN 90-277-1687-0; Pb: 90-277-1950-0
23. E. L. Keenan and L. M. Faltz: *Boolean Semantics for Natural Language.* 1985   ISBN 90-277-1768-0; Pb: 90-277-1842-3
24. V. Raskin: *Semantic Mechanisms of Humor.* 1985   ISBN 90-277-1821-0; Pb: 90-277-1891-4

Volumes 1–26 formerly published under the Series Title: Synthese Language Library.

Studies in Linguistics and Philosophy

25. G. T. Stump: *The Semantic Variability of Absolute Constructions.* 1985
    ISBN 90-277-1895-4; Pb: 90-277-1896-2
26. J. Hintikka and J. Kulas: *Anaphora and Definite Descriptions.* Two Applications of Game-Theoretical Semantics. 1985 ISBN 90-277-2055-X; Pb: 90-277-2056-8
27. E. Engdahl: *Constituent Questions.* The Syntax and Semantics of Questions with Special Reference to Swedish. 1986 ISBN 90-277-1954-3; Pb: 90-277-1955-1
28. M. J. Cresswell: *Adverbial Modification.* Interval Semantics and Its Rivals. 1985
    ISBN 90-277-2059-2; Pb: 90-277-2060-6
29. J. van Benthem: *Essays in Logical Semantics* 1986 ISBN 90-277-2091-6; Pb: 90-277-2092-4
30. B. H. Partee, A. ter Meulen and R. E. Wall: *Mathematical Methods in Linguistics.* 1990; Corrected second printing of the first edition 1993 ISBN 90-277-2244-7; Pb: 90-277-2245-5
31. P. Gärdenfors (ed.): *Generalized Quantifiers.* Linguistic and Logical Approaches. 1987
    ISBN 1-55608-017-4
32. R. T. Oehrle, E. Bach and D. Wheeler (eds.): *Categorial Grammars and Natural Language Structures.* 1988 ISBN 1-55608-030-1; Pb: 1-55608-031-X
33. W. J. Savitch, E. Bach, W. Marsh and G. Safran-Naveh (eds.): *The Formal Complexity of Natural Language.* 1987 ISBN 1-55608-046-8; Pb: 1-55608-047-6
34. J. E. Fenstad, P.-K. Halvorsen, T. Langholm and J. van Benthem: *Situations, Language and Logic.* 1987 ISBN 1-55608-048-4; Pb: 1-55608-049-2
35. U. Reyle and C. Rohrer (eds.): *Natural Language Parsing and Linguistic Theories.* 1988
    ISBN 1-55608-055-7; Pb: 1-55608-056-5
36. M. J. Cresswell: *Semantical Essays.* Possible Worlds and Their Rivals. 1988
    ISBN 1-55608-061-1
37. T. Nishigauchi: *Quantification in the Theory of Grammar.* 1990
    ISBN 0-7923-0643-0; Pb: 0-7923-0644-9
38. G. Chierchia, B.H. Partee and R. Turner (eds.): *Properties, Types and Meaning.* Volume I: Foundational Issues. 1989 ISBN 1-55608-067-0; Pb: 1-55608-068-9
39. G. Chierchia, B.H. Partee and R. Turner (eds.): *Properties, Types and Meaning.* Volume II: Semantic Issues. 1989 ISBN 1-55608-069-7; Pb: 1-55608-070-0
    Set ISBN (Vol. I + II) 1-55608-088-3; Pb: 1-55608-089-1
40. C.T.J. Huang and R. May (eds.): *Logical Structure and Linguistic Structure.* Cross-Linguistic Perspectives. 1991 ISBN 0-7923-0914-6; Pb: 0-7923-1636-3
41. M.J. Cresswell: *Entities and Indices.* 1990 ISBN 0-7923-0966-9; Pb: 0-7923-0967-7
42. H. Kamp and U. Reyle: *From Discourse to Logic.* Introduction to Modeltheoretic Semantics of Natural Language, Formal Logic and Discourse Representation Theory. 1993
    ISBN 0-7923-2403-X; Student edition: 0-7923-1028-4
43. C.S. Smith: *The Parameter of Aspect.* (Second Edition). 1997
    ISBN 0-7923-4657-2; Pb 0-7923-4659-9
44. R.C. Berwick (ed.): *Principle-Based Parsing.* Computation and Psycholinguistics. 1991
    ISBN 0-7923-1173-6; Pb: 0-7923-1637-1
45. F. Landman: *Structures for Semantics.* 1991 ISBN 0-7923-1239-2; Pb: 0-7923-1240-6
46. M. Siderits: *Indian Philosophy of Language.* 1991 ISBN 0-7923-1262-7
47. C. Jones: *Purpose Clauses.* 1991 ISBN 0-7923-1400-X
48. R.K. Larson, S. Iatridou, U. Lahiri and J. Higginbotham (eds.): *Control and Grammar.* 1992
    ISBN 0-7923-1692-4
49. J. Pustejovsky (ed.): *Semantics and the Lexicon.* 1993
    ISBN 0-7923-1963-X; Pb: 0-7923-2386-6

Studies in Linguistics and Philosophy

50. N. Asher: *Reference to Abstract Objects in Discourse.* 1993 ISBN 0-7923-2242-8
51. A. Zucchi: *The Language of Propositions and Events.* Issues in the Syntax and the Semantics of Nominalization. 1993 ISBN 0-7923-2437-4
52. C.L. Tenny: *Aspectual Roles and the Syntax-Semantics Interface.* 1994
ISBN 0-7923-2863-9; Pb: 0-7923-2907-4
53. W.G. Lycan: *Modality and Meaning.* 1994 ISBN 0-7923-3006-4; Pb: 0-7923-3007-2
54. E. Bach, E. Jelinek, A. Kratzer and B.H. Partee (eds.): *Quantification in Natural Languages.* 1995 ISBN Vol. I: 0-7923-3128-1; Vol. II: 0-7923-3351-9; set: 0-7923-3352-7; Student edition: 0-7923-3129-X
55. P. Lasersohn: *Plurality, Conjunction and Events.* 1995 ISBN 0-7923-3238-5
56. M. Pinkal: *Logic and Lexicon.* The Semantics of the Indefinite. 1995 ISBN 0-7923-3387-X
57. P. Øhrstrøm and P.F.V. Hasle: *Temporal Logic.* From Ancient Ideas to Artificial Intelligence. 1995 ISBN 0-7923-3586-4
58. T. Ogihara: *Tense, Attitudes, and Scope.* 1996 ISBN 0-7923-3801-4
59. I. Comorovski: *Interrogative Phrases and the Syntax-Semantics Interface.* 1996
ISBN 0-7923-3804-9
60. M.J. Cresswell: *Semantic Indexicality.* 1996 ISBN 0-7923-3914-2
61. R. Schwarzschild: *Pluralities.* 1996 ISBN 0-7923-4007-8
62. V. Dayal: *Locality in WH Quantification.* Questions and Relative Clauses in Hindi. 1996
ISBN 0-7923-4099-X
63. P. Merlo: *Parsing with Principles and Classes of Information.* 1996 ISBN 0-7923-4103-1
64. J. Ross: *The Semantics of Media.* 1997 ISBN 0-7923-4389-1
65. A. Szabolcsi (ed.): *Ways of Scope Taking.* 1997 ISBN 0-7923-4446-4; Pb: 0-7923-4451-0
66. P.L. Peterson: *Fact Proposition Event.* 1997 ISBN 0-7923-4568-1
67. G. Păun: *Marcus Contextual Grammars.* 1997 ISBN 0-7923-4783-8
68. T. Gunji and K. Hasida (eds.): *Topics in Constraint-Based Grammar of Japanese.* 1998
ISBN 0-7923-4836-2
69. F. Hamm and E. Hinrichs (eds.): *Plurality and Quantification.* 1998 ISBN 0-7923-4841-9
70. S. Rothstein (ed.): *Events and Grammar.* 1998 ISBN 0-7923-4940-7
71. E. Hajičová, B.H. Partee and P. Sgall: *Topic-Focus Articulation, Tripartite Structures, and Semantic Content.* 1998 ISBN 0-7923-5289-0
72. K. von Heusinger and U. Egli (Eds.): *Reference and Anaphoric Relations.* 1999
ISBN 0-7923-6070-2
73. H. Bunt and R. Muskens (eds.): *Computing Meaning.* Volume 1. 2000
ISBN 0-7923-6108-3
74. S. Rothstein (ed.): *Predicates and their Subjects.* 2000 ISBN 0-7923-6409-0
75. K. Kabakčiev: *Aspect in English.* A "Common-Sense" View of the Interplay between Verbal and Nominal Referents. 2000 ISBN 0-7923-6538-0

Further information about our publications on *Linguistics* is available on request.

Kluwer Academic Publishers – Dordrecht / Boston / London